Professional SAS® Programming Shortcuts

Over 1,000 Ways to Improve Your SAS Programs

Rick Aster

BREAKFAST

Also by Rick Aster:
PROFESSIONAL SAS PROGRAMMING LOGIC
PROFESSIONAL SAS PROGRAMMER'S POCKET REFERENCE

AIX, IBM, OS/2, OS/390, and RS/6000 are registered trademarks and System/370 is a
trademark of IBM.
Intel is a registered trademark of Intel Corporation.
Mac is a registered trademark of Apple Computer, Inc.
Microsoft is a registered trademark of Microsoft Corporation.
SAS, SAS/ACCESS, SAS/AF, SAS/CONNECT, SAS/GRAPH, SAS/SHARE, and
SAS/STAT are registered trademarks of SAS Institute Inc.
Solaris is a trademark of Sun Microsystems, Inc.

Any updates to this book will be posted at the author's web site at
http://www.globalstatements.com

Nothing happens until something moves.

— Albert Einstein

ISBN 9-781891-957116   1-891957-11-2

2nd Edition

Printing 9 8 7 6 5 4 3 2 1

Contents

4

6

Lists

Introduction

If SAS is in a league of its own when it comes to working with data, then think of this book as a playbook for that league — a book with page after page of things you can do and details of the ways you might do them. I have tried to list the foundational tasks you might want to do as you work with data in SAS, especially those that are not immediately obvious, then show the best ways I have found to accomplish them.

This book does not include an introduction to SAS, but if you have been doing any work at all in SAS, then you will be ready to try many of the techniques and tips you will find throughout the book. You can look for new things to do in SAS, better ways to do things you do already, and ways to approach new things you need to do. I do not attempt to cover SAS syntax or features in a thorough or systematic way, but to provide models and starting points to which you may add other options, routines, and statements to fit your particular requirements. To do this easily, you may want other books that focus on the SAS environment and SAS syntax, such as another book of mine, *Professional SAS Programmer's Pocket Reference*.

My subject here is the range of applications I call "working with data," including such tasks as analyzing, reporting, summarizing, validating, acquiring, combining, transforming, and managing data. These tasks form the building blocks of SAS applications large and small; they are not complete in themselves, but combine with others to form complete applications.

This is a book about the details of SAS programming. It is divided into thousands of small segments, each dealing with one specific piece of the SAS programming puzzle. The segments are grouped by subject into 88 chapters. To look for a specific answer, start by finding a chapter in the table of contents. Look through the chapter for ideas and answers.

This second edition differs from the first primarily because of new features in SAS and changes in computer technology. More than a few of the techniques I included previously are, thankfully, no longer necessary because SAS 9 has added functions or options to carry them out. Of course, the new features of SAS 9 also make new kinds of processing possible. The greatest changes took place in text processing, with the many new functions simplifying a myriad of tasks that involve character data.

The speed of computers has doubled, and SAS 9 provides a substantial speed boost over the already impressive performance of previous SAS versions. Efficiency techniques that seemed like a good idea a few short years ago now seem overly complicated even for most large-scale SAS projects. Accordingly, this edition leans more toward the simple, direct way to do things, and I trust this new focus makes the book easier to use.

Look for these symbols to help you find the various kinds of information that appear in this book:

- A prehistoric symbol, the spiral literally means "way," a road to walk or a method to follow. In this book, a spiral marks a way of doing something: a technique, demonstration, algorithm, code model, etc.
- When a circus poster tells you the reasons why you can't miss the big show, the pointed finger says "this is it." In this book, it might not be jugglers, acrobats, or lions, but it's something that deserves a moment in the spotlight: a tip, idea, interesting fact, suggestion, etc.
- In the last century, the diamond became the standard symbol for "caution" on everything from road signs to oxygen canisters. Here, diamonds highlight critical details, common mistakes, limitations, risks, etc.

Actual text for a SAS program appears in this CODE FONT. *Italic code* is not actual program text, but describes terms to substitute to form a program. Text that comes back from the computer, such as messages, reports, and text data, appears in this `computer font`.

1

The Log

If you're looking for a connecting thread that ties together all your work in SAS, you don't need to look any further than the log. The log is a sequential account of the events of a SAS session, and it is where diagnostic messages are written. Whenever you want to know what happened in a SAS session, the log is the place to start.

Running a SAS Program

 The actions required to run a SAS program depend on whether you are running in batch mode or in the interactive environment. In addition, many of the details depend on the operating system environment of the computer. Therefore, this is only a general description of the process.

To run a SAS program in batch mode, use an operating system command that identifies the SAS application and the SAS program file. The details depend on the operating system and on the way SAS was installed on the computer. These are examples of forms that the command might take for the program file myprogram.sas:

```
sas myprogram
sas82 myprogram.sas
sas -sysin myprogram.sas
sas -sysin "myprogram.sas"
"C:\sas82\sas.exe" -sysin "C:\Projects\Main\myprogram.sas"
sas82 options('sysin="myprogram.sas"')
```

As the SAS supervisor runs the program, it creates a log file. The location of the log file might be:

- a file indicated in the LOG= system option
- a file associated with the symbolic name LOG or SASLOG
- a file name similar to the program file name, but with the extension LOG

To run a SAS program in the interactive environment, start by opening the program file in the Editor or Program Editor window. It is also possible to create a new program file in these windows. Then submit the program for execution by entering the SUBMIT command or with the associated menu item, function key, or toolbar button. SAS runs the program until the end of the submitted statements is reached. It writes a log that you can find in the Log window. If you want to save the log, use the FILE command or the Save As menu item in the Log window.

A SAS program might also generate print output in the standard print file. In batch mode, this might be associated with the PRINT option or the symbolic name PRINT or SASLIST, or it might be a file name with the LST extension. In interactive mode, look for it in the Output window or the Results window.

Messages and Debugging

The log contains messages that describe the execution of the program. One of the most important uses of these messages is to find and correct errors in the program. With the log, SAS debugging is easy to do.

These are examples of the kinds of messages you find in a SAS log:

- Program lines with line numbers added.

```
15   PROC OPTIONS GROUP=ERRORHANDLING;
16   RUN;
```

- Notes that describe the actions and results of steps and global statements.

```
NOTE: There were 1 observations read from
      the data set WORK.VISIT.
NOTE: The data set WORK.EXT has 1
      observations and 3 variables.

NOTE: Libref MAIN has been deassigned.
```

- Notes that measure the system resources, especially time, used by steps.

```
NOTE: DATA statement used:
      real time            0.04 seconds
```

- Reasons why actions could not be completed.

```
WARNING: Variable SPILL not found in data
         set WORK.DRAW.

WARNING: Data set WORK.X was not replaced
         because of NOREPLACE option.
```

- Error messages indicating incorrect syntax or an incorrect reference. If a specific token

RUNNING INTERACTIVELY

These tips may be helpful in running programs in the interactive environment:

- If you edit a program and intend to save it and run it, save it first, then submit it.
- You can run programs in pieces, but you need a complete step before you can run. Steps you submit must end in a RUN statement to tell the SAS supervisor that the end of the step has been reached. (There are exceptions to this, especially for the SQL procedure.) If you submit a step and the SAS supervisor does not start to execute it, you might need to submit a RUN statement.
- If you submit part of a step, then decide you want to cancel it, submit a RUN CANCEL statement:

  RUN CANCEL;

- If SAS is copying everything you submit to the log, but is not running anything, it is because the SAS supervisor is in a special interpretive state — that is, it is inside something like a quoted string, macro definition, or comment, where characters do not mean what they usually mean. To get back to a normal interaction with the SAS supervisor, all you need to do is submit the right terminator. One or more of the following lines will terminate just about anything in SAS:

  ````
  ....
  *))%*';*"))*/;
  %MEND;
  RUN CANCEL;
  ````

These lines won't cause any further harm, so you can submit them without knowing what the specific problem is.

is incorrect, it may be underlined with a code number. Look for details of the error in a subsequent message.

```
63       INPUT 25 DISTANCE F8.;
         --
         22
ERROR 22-322: Syntax error, expecting one of the following: a name,
              #, +, @.

96       B = 4*(A + 1;
                   -
                   79
ERROR 79-322: Expecting a ).
```

- Notes that describe unusual or unexpected occurrences in the execution of the program.

```
NOTE: Variable X is uninitialized.
NOTE: Missing values were generated as a result of performing an
      operation on missing values.
      Each place is given by: (Number of times) at (Line):(Column).
      1 at 183:8
```

- A list of all variables and values for an observation in a data step in which an error condition occurred. Actions on incorrect data, such as dividing by 0 or providing an invalid argument to a function, result in error conditions. The list of variables and values might show you what is incorrect about the data.

```
ERROR: Array subscript out of range at line 223 column 10.
DISTANCE=141 PREV=5518 NEXT=. N=48 I=49 LOC=. _ERROR_=1 _N_=1
NOTE: The SAS System stopped processing this step because of errors.
```

- Input text data lines in which a data error occurred. These lines are written with a ruler to make it easier to find the relevant fields.

```
NOTE: Invalid data for X2 in line 232 6-8.
RULE:      ----+----1----+----2----+----3----+----4----+----5----+--
232             14 XXX   17  18    0
X1=14 X2=. X3=17 X4=18 X5=0 _ERROR_=1 _N_=5
```

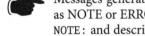

Messages generated from the SAS System's message catalogs start with a word such as NOTE or ERROR to indicate the general nature of the message. A note starts with NOTE: and describes the results of running the program. A warning message has the prefix WARNING: and indicates a situation in which the program's actions might not be what the programmer intended. An error message with the ERROR: prefix can indicate any of various kinds of errors that prevent the program from being executed the way it is written.

If you see a message with the FATAL: prefix, it indicates a fatal error, a kind of error that the SAS error-handling routines didn't know what to do with. In version 6, these errors occurred when a SELECT block had statements in an incorrect sequence. In more recent SAS versions, fatal errors are very infrequent, but they can occur, for example, when expressions have unbalanced parentheses.

LOG COLORS

When you look at the log in the Log window, NOTE, WARNING, and ERROR message lines are color-coded to make them easy to find.

A SAS program can write log lines that begin with these same words, followed by either a colon or hyphen, and these lines are also displayed in color in the Log window. The text NOTE-, WARNING-, or ERROR- is not displayed, but it provides the color for the line. To see this effect, submit the program lines below in an interactive SAS session.

```
OPTIONS NOSOURCE;
%PUT NOTE: This line is blue.;
%PUT NOTE- This line is blue.;
%PUT WARNING: This line is green.;
%PUT WARNING- This line is green.;
%PUT ERROR: This line is red.;
%PUT ERROR- This line is red.;
OPTIONS SOURCE;
```

```
NOTE: This line is blue.
      This line is blue.
WARNING: This line is green.
         This line is green.
ERROR: This line is red.
       This line is red.
```

 If you are using a text editor or the Log window to search a log for error messages, use the text search command to search for the text "ERROR:". In SAS, use the command:

```
find 'ERROR:'
```

 If the log indicates errors, use the messages to locate the errors in the program. Correct the program, save it, and run it again.

◆ The debugging process for a SAS program involves running the program repeatedly, making corrections until no errors remain. Therefore, whenever possible, write a SAS program so that it generates the same results if it is run repeatedly. For example, do not have a SAS program delete or change the input files it uses.

☞ In batch mode, after SAS encounters a significant error, it switches to syntax check mode. It continues to process the program statements, but it does not execute them. This can help you find additional syntax errors, but it can also lead to error messages that occur only because of syntax check mode. If an error message in syntax check mode does not seem to point to an error in the program, it is reasonable to hope that there is no error. When the log contains a sequence of error messages, focus mainly on the first error.

 Messages might indicate something to fix in a program even if the program appears to be running correctly. If messages refer to these conditions, look carefully to see if the program is incorrect or could be improved:

- automatic conversion from one data type to another
- missing values generated from an operation on missing values
- incorrect arguments for functions or CALL routines
- INPUT or PUT statement that goes past the end of a line
- invalid data for an informat
- division by 0
- apparent macro language reference
- END statement missing
- no observations in a SAS dataset (this could be the correct result, but check carefully)
- variable does not exist
- variable that is not initialized (this could indicate a misspelled name)

- array that has the same name as a function

Several system options determine which messages appear in the log. Most of these options are on/off options that determine the presence or absence of a specific kind of message.

- NOTES: notes.
- SOURCE: program lines from the primary program file.
- SOURCE2: program lines from secondary program files.
- ECHOAUTO: program lines from the autoexec program file.
- MPRINT: program lines generated by macros.
- SYMBOLGEN: text generated by macro variables.
- MLOGIC: additional notes about macro execution logic.
- OPLIST, VERBOSE, ECHO=, NEWS=: additional information from the startup process.
- STIMER, FULLSTIMER: notes about the use of system resources in each step.
- PRINTMSGLIST, MSGLEVEL=, ERRORS=: determine the level of detail in some messages.

System options that affect print output generally, such as the LINESIZE= and PAGESIZE= options, also affect the log.

OF COURSE I MEANT . . .

SAS automatically corrects some misspelled words. These are examples (see if you can guess which keywords were misspelled):

- PROOC, PORC, PROF
- DAT, DARA, DAYA, DAYTA, DATO
- CARBS, CATDS
- RUIN, RTUN, RUNN
- DOG
- GOO TON
- OTPIONS, POTIONS, OPINIONS

If SAS corrects your spelling, it writes a message that says what word you wrote and what word it used instead, such as:

```
257  OTPIONS OBS=1000;
     -------
     14
WARNING 14-169: Assuming the symbol
OPTIONS was misspelled as OTPIONS.
```

Read the message to make sure the interpretation is what you intended. Even if it is, fix the program if there is any chance you will use it again in the future. It would be risky to rely on SAS to continue to correct your misspelled keywords.

Two global statements provide spacing in the log. To skip a few lines in the log, use a SKIP statement, such as:

SKIP 5;

The number in the statement is the number of blank lines added to the log.
   To advance to a new page in the log, use the PAGE statement:

PAGE;

If a program is running incorrectly and the reason for the logical error is not immediately obvious, you can use regular SAS features to create additional diagnostic information to study.
   These are some of the features you might use often in debugging:

- PROC PRINT to display the data of a SAS dataset
- PROC CONTENTS to describe the structure of a SAS dataset, including the attributes of its variables
- PROC FREQ for a frequency table showing all the values of a variable in a SAS dataset
- The %PUT statement to write a message or the values of macro variables in the log

In a data step, use the PUT statement to add information to the log. (Use a FILE LOG statement before the PUT statement if necessary.) The most useful keyword to use in the PUT statement is _ALL_. This statement writes all variables and their values:

PUT _ALL_;

Use this statement to write a selected list of variables:

PUT (*variable list*) (=);

Add a slash to the format list to write each variable on a separate line:

PUT (*variable list*) (=/);

The PUTLOG statement is a version of the PUT statement that automatically directs text to the log, but it is meant for messages rather than debugging. The PUTLOG statement is not much help in debugging because it does not support variable lists.

If a program is taking too long to run while you are debugging it, reduce the amount of data the program reads to make it run faster. There are several ways you can do this. One approach is to use a test input data file that has a small fraction of the usual volume of data. Another is to use the OBS= system option. This option limits the number of input records or observations that any one data step statement or proc step will process.

Use the OPTIONS statement to set the OBS= option to a low number, for example:

OPTIONS OBS=1000;

SAS is flexible enough to let you test some SAS steps even when the input data they use is not available or is incomplete. For this kind of testing, use these system options:

NODSNFERR NOVNFERR DKRICOND=WARNING DKROCOND=WARNING

These options allow the SAS steps to continue running when the SAS datasets or variables they require do not exist. This approach to testing has its limits; a data type conflict or other error may prevent the program from running beyond the point where the error occurs, and if the test does run, it may fail to reveal some errors that the program contains. Still, if complete test data is not yet available, this kind of testing may let you get started at finding the errors in your code.

■ 2

Program Files

SAS programs, like programs in most programming languages, are stored as ordinary text files.

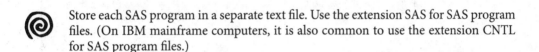

Store each SAS program in a separate text file. Use the extension SAS for SAS program files. (On IBM mainframe computers, it is also common to use the extension CNTL for SAS program files.)

The primary program file of a SAS session is the place where the SAS supervisor looks for program lines to execute. In batch mode, the primary program file is the main SAS program identified in the SYSIN= option. In interactive mode, the "primary program file" encompasses all the program lines that are submitted directly to the SAS supervisor, usually with the SUBMIT command.

SAS statements can execute during the SAS session's startup sequence. The autoexec file, if there is one, executes first. After that, any statements in the INITSTMT= system option execute. The primary program file starts next.

Use the %INCLUDE statement to execute a secondary SAS program as part of a SAS program. In the %INCLUDE statement, write the physical file name in quotes or the fileref of the secondary program file. This is an example of a %INCLUDE statement:

```
%INCLUDE "myprogram.sas";
```

The statements of the secondary program file, myprogram.sas, are executed at this point in the program. Then execution resumes with the statement that follows the %INCLUDE statement.

The %INCLUDE statement can include the S2= and SOURCE2 options, which are described below. Write the options at the end of the statement with a slash before them, for example:

```
%INCLUDE "myprogram.sas" / SOURCE2;
```

A few system options affect the way SAS program lines are treated. The most important is the S= option, which limits the length of the program line. For example, with the option S=80, any characters beyond 80 in a line in the primary program file are ignored. This option can be useful if a program file contains line numbers or other

10 Ways to Execute SAS Program Lines

The SAS supervisor executes SAS program lines from an execution queue that it maintains . . . but there are quite a few ways for program lines to find their way into the execution queue. These are some common ways program lines can be executed.

 Primary program file. The SYSIN= system option identifies the primary program file when SAS runs in batch mode. SAS executes all the SAS statements in the file. The SAS session ends when the SAS supervisor reaches the end of the file.

 Autoexec file. When the SAS session starts up, the SAS supervisor executes the autoexec file if it can find one. The autoexec file might be identified in the AUTOEXEC= system option, or it might be a file called `autoexec.sas` in the SAS System's default directory.

 INITSTMT= system option. Also at startup, the SAS supervisor executes the SAS statements in the INITSTMT= system option. This option can contain a SAS statement or sequence of statements to execute at startup.

SUBMIT command. In an interactive session, the Submit menu item, command, toolbar button, or function key submits the contents of the Editor or Program Editor window for execution. Another command, the SUBTOP command, submits the first line or the first few lines from the window.

 Secondary program file. Submitted SAS program lines can contain the %INCLUDE statement, which includes a secondary program file at that point in the execution queue.

Macro language reference. If a submitted SAS program line contains a reference to a macro, macro variable, or other macro object, the macro processor resolves the object. Usually, the object generates text for the SAS supervisor to execute, which can be a statement, several statements, or just part of a statement.

EXECUTE routine. A data step can call the EXECUTE routine with a string argument. The text of the argument is executed as soon as the data step is over.

GSUBMIT command. The GSUBMIT command submits a text string for execution. The text string is a quoted string in the command. With this command, it is possible to use a function key to submit a specific SAS statement in an interactive session.

SUBMIT block. SCL programs work behind the scenes in AF applications and elsewhere in the SAS environment. An SCL program can submit SAS statements for execution. The SAS statements are written between SUBMIT and ENDSUBMIT statements in the SCL program.

Remote session. With SAS/CONNECT, a SAS session can control another session, called a remote session, on another computer. The RSUBMIT statement or command submits statements to the remote session for execution.

spurious characters beyond a certain point in each line. The S= option affects only the primary program file.

Use the S2= option, which works the same way, for secondary program files. The S2= option also can be written in the %INCLUDE statement.

The CAPS system option affects data values in program lines. With this option on, the SAS supervisor converts all data values to capital letters.

The SOURCE system option determines whether SAS program lines are written in the log along with the log notes and other messages that appear in the log. Usually, it is helpful to have program lines in the log; having the program lines makes it easier to understand notes and error messages. The SOURCE option is on by default; turn it off to remove the program lines from the log.

The SOURCE option affects only the primary program file. Use the SOURCE2 option for secondary program files. This option is off by default. Turn it on to write secondary program lines in the log. The SOURCE2 option can also be written in the %INCLUDE statement for a specific secondary program file.

It is possible to store a SAS program in a SAS catalog. Usually, a SAS program should be a separate text file, but there are occasions when it is more convenient to store a SAS program as a catalog entry. Make the program a SOURCE entry. This is the preferred approach when a program is generated by a SAS program and used as a secondary program file later in the same SAS program as described in chapter 65, "Generating Program Statements." Also, if a SAS program is an integral part of a SAS/AF application, you might elect to store the SAS program in the same catalog where other components of the application are found.

The ENDSAS statement causes the end of the SAS session. Statements located after the ENDSAS statement do not execute. In general, the use of the ENDSAS statement to mark the end of a program is not recommended. Instead, let the end of the program file be the end of the program.

The ENDSAS statement can be a special concern in these situations.

- In a secondary program file, an ENDSAS statement ends not just the secondary program file, but the entire SAS session. Any subsequent statements in the primary program file do not execute.
- If there is an ENDSAS statement in an autoexec file, the primary program file never executes.
- If you submit an ENDSAS statement in the interactive environment, it closes the interactive environment. If you see the SAS session close abruptly after you submit a program, this is the likely reason why.

If an ENDSAS statement contains an additional term, it is being used to end a SAS process, not the SAS session. See the next chapter, "Startup," for details.

■ 3

Startup

When you start a SAS session, you use system options to tell the SAS supervisor what kinds of things the SAS session will do, what direction the session will be going in. The SAS supervisor follows a predictable sequence in finding the system options that it uses at startup. These options might direct it to start an interactive session, to run a program, or to do any of various other things. There are several other actions involved in starting a SAS session, and some of these can also be affected by system options.

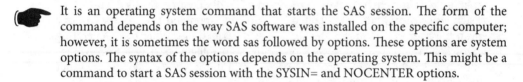 It is an operating system command that starts the SAS session. The form of the command depends on the way SAS software was installed on the specific computer; however, it is sometimes the word sas followed by options. These options are system options. The syntax of the options depends on the operating system. This might be a command to start a SAS session with the SYSIN= and NOCENTER options.

```
sas -sysin myprogram.sas -nocenter
```

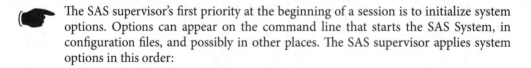 The SAS supervisor's first priority at the beginning of a session is to initialize system options. Options can appear on the command line that starts the SAS System, in configuration files, and possibly in other places. The SAS supervisor applies system options in this order:

- System default values
- Configuration files and environment variables
- The operating system command line

The last appearance of a particular option determines the value of the option at initialization. For example, options get system default values only if there are no settings for those options anywhere else in the startup process. Options set on the operating system command line override options set anywhere else at startup; however, these too might be overridden by options set during the session.

After the SAS supervisor initializes the system options, it takes these other actions:

- Initializes the WORK library and other necessary libraries
- Initializes the log and writes news text, if any, in the log
- Initializes the standard print file (depending on the PRINTINIT option)
- Executes the autoexec file, if any, followed by the statements of the INITSTMT= option, if any

You can use system options to affect the way these processes work.

- To prevent the initialization of the WORK library, start up with the NOWORKINIT option.
- The NEWS= option provides the physical file name of a text file that contains the news text. The NONEWS option skips the news text.
- The AUTOEXEC= option identifies the autoexec file. There is a default location for an autoexec file, with the file name `autoexec.sas`, but the details of this vary by operating system. The NOAUTOEXEC option skips the autoexec file, even if one is present.
- The INITSTMT= option can be used to add actions at the beginning of the SAS session, after the autoexec file is processed. The value of the option is a text string containing one or more SAS statements.

After this set of actions is complete, the SAS supervisor is ready for the main part of the session. In batch mode, this means running the main SAS program. In interactive mode, the SAS supervisor opens programming windows and other windows for the user to use.

Often, the autoexec file is part of the management of a project that consists of many different programs. The autoexec file for a project often contains these statements:

- LIBNAME statements to define librefs for the SAS data libraries used in the project.
- FILENAME statements to define filerefs for text data files.
- TITLE statements to define title lines.
- %LET statements to create global macro variables.
- %INCLUDE statements to execute other programs within the startup process.

Several system options generate startup log messages. Use these options to get more information about how a session starts up.

- The ECHOAUTO option shows the autoexec file in the log.
- The VERBOSE option describes system options set at startup.
- The OPLIST option lists system options set in the operating system command line.
- Use the ECHO= option with a text string to write a text message in the log at startup. You might use this option to write a log message to identify the configuration file that was used.

To pass parameters from the operating system command line to the SAS program, use the SYSPARM= system option. This option creates a parameter string, a text string that can contain any information you need to provide to the program. Inside the program, the SYSPARM macro variable contains the parameter string. Use a data step or macro programming to retrieve the parameter values from the SYSPARM macro variable. See chapters 61, "Macro Variables," 64, "Program Parameters," and 25, "Parsing," for related information.

Batch and Interactive Modes

Batch and interactive modes create two very different kinds of SAS sessions with different capabilitles. Batch mode is best when you know exactly what you want SAS to do, for example, in a production system. It is also the way to do things if you get frustrated with the slow pace of a multiuser computer's user interaction. Interactive mode gives you access to the entire SAS windowing environment. You can look at files, run SAS programs and interactive applications, view results, and read online help. An interactive session lets you do any combination of actions that come to mind.

 Use these system options for batch mode:

- *SYSIN=*. At startup, the SYSIN= system option is what tells SAS to run in batch mode. The SYSIN= option provides the physical file name of the primary program file. The session executes this program and ends as soon as the program ends.

SPECIAL MODES FOR SPECIAL PURPOSES

In addition to the standard batch and interactive modes, there are other modes that are associated with specific actions or special purposes.

- A SAS session can be a server, responding to requests from other SAS sessions or other programs. With the OBJECTSERVER option, a SAS session is a DCOM/CORBA server. A SAS session can also be a SAS/SHARE server, providing simultaneous access to SAS libraries for multiple users. There are various add-on components that allow SAS to function as a web server.
- SAS/CONNECT creates a remote session, a SAS session on another computer under the control of the SAS/SHARE statements and procedures on the first computer.
- The INITCMD= option executes an interactive application instead of opening the usual windows of a SAS session. The SAS session terminates automatically when the interactive application ends. This allows the user to go directly to the interactive application without having to see the details of the SAS interactive environment.

The value of the INITCMD= option is a string that contains a display manager command, a command that could execute in a display manager window, such as the Program Editor window. The command must open a window or execute an interactive application, such as an AF application, that displays a window. The SAS session terminates automatically when the application ends.

The INITCMD= option can contain multiple commands, separated by semicolons. The first command executes an interactive application; other commands can open other windows or take other actions.

- Interactive line mode is a user interface style optimized for use on an impact printer terminal. It is not available in all environments.
- With the SETINIT option, a SAS session can run a program to update the SAS licensing information. This is the only way SAS can run if its licensing information has expired.

- *LOG=*. In batch mode, the SAS session writes the log as a print file. You can read the log after the session ends. Use the LOG= option to provide the physical file name for the log file. If you omit the LOG= option, the session creates a file name based on the file name of the program file, with the extension `log`.
- *PRINT=*. If the SAS session creates a standard print file, you can read or print that too after the session ends. The PRINT= option identifies the standard print file. If you omit the PRINT= option, the session creates a file name based on the file name of the program file, with the extension `lst` or `LIST`.

To start an interactive-mode session, use the DMS, EXPLORER, or DMSEXP option at startup. These three system options differ only in what windows are open at the beginning of the session: the programming windows, Explorer window, or both.

An interactive SAS session uses a graphical user interface except on IBM mainframe systems, where only a text-mode user interface style is available.

SAS Processes

With SAS processes, a single SAS session can do more than one thing at a time. SAS processes are asynchronous, not synchronized with each other; each executes its own sequence of actions and runs at its own speed. A SAS process usually executes a SAS program.

The idea of SAS processes is to allow multiple programs to run independently of one another in the same SAS session. By dividing the actions of a program among several SAS processes, you can sometimes make more efficient use of a multiprocessing computer. A SAS process can also let you run a SAS program while simultaneously working in the interactive environment. That is, you can start a program, then take other actions without waiting for the program to finish.

Before you start using SAS processes, consider these cautions:

- You must make sure that SAS processes do not interfere with each other. Conflicts are most likely to happen when two SAS processes attempt to access the same file at the same time.
- Each SAS process uses additional memory.
- It is hard to predict how SAS processes will affect performance. If improved performance is your goal, be prepared to try several alternatives and scrutinize the results.

Write a STARTSAS statement with system options to start a SAS process. Include the SYSIN= system option to identify the SAS program to run and any other system options that are necessary. Write options the same way they appear in the OPTIONS statement. This is an example of a STARTSAS statement:

STARTSAS SYSIN="myprocess.sas" LOG="myprocess.log";

If you have a large number of options, you might find it easier to list them in a configuration file. Use the CONFIG= option in the STARTSAS statement to identify the configuration file.

To run an interactive application in a SAS process, use the INITCMD= option instead of the SYSIN= option. (The INITCMD= option is described in "Special Modes for Special Purposes" earlier in this chapter.)

A process ID identifies each SAS process, and a SAS process might also have a name. Obtain the process ID from the automatic macro variable SYSSTARTID as soon as you start a SAS process. Use a %LET statement to assign the ID to another macro variable so that you can refer to it later. Write a statement such as this immediately after the STARTSAS statement:

%LET MYPROCESSID = &SYSSTARTID;

If you need the process name, obtain it from the automatic macro variable SYSSTARTNAME. These macro variables contain the most recently started process, so you must get their values before you start another SAS process.

A SAS process can use the results of another SAS process, but it should wait for the other SAS process to end first. Use the WAITSAS statement to suspend execution until another SAS process is complete. Write the process ID in the WAITSAS statement, usually in the form of a macro variable, for example:

WAITSAS &MYPROCESSID;

List multiple process IDs in the WAITSAS statement to wait until all the processes have ended. The WAITSAS statement has no effect if the processes are already complete or if the process IDs are incorrect. Write the WAITSAS statement before a step or statement that cannot start processing until another SAS process has finished its processing.

It is possible for one SAS process to cancel another SAS process. Write the process ID in the ENDSAS statement, for example:

ENDSAS &MYPROCESSID;

As with the WAITSAS statement, this statement has no effect if the other SAS process has already ended.

You can list multiple process IDs in an ENDSAS statement. To end the SAS session and cancel all SAS processes that are still running, use this statement:

ENDSAS ALL;

■ 4
System Options

System options make it possible to control many of the details of the way the SAS System operates. For example, you can control the size of the page in the log file and the level of detail of log messages. With other system options, you can control the way missing values are displayed and the way the SAS supervisor searches for formats. There are several hundred system options.

There are various terms that are used in describing system options. To avoid confusion over terminology, these are the meanings of some of the terms:

- *SAS system option:* another term for system option. This term is used when it is important to distinguish between the SAS environment and other environments that might contain options.
- *SAS option:* also means system option. This term appears in log messages.
- *Initialization option, startup option:* can be set only at the beginning of a SAS session or process.
- *Session option:* can be changed at any time in a SAS session.
- *Command line option:* an option in an operating system command, which could be a SAS system option written as part of the operating system command that launches the SAS application.
- *Configuration option:* a system option set at startup in a configuration file.
- *Host option:* is implemented for a specific operating system.
- *Portable option:* is available in all the operating systems of a SAS release.
- *Options subsystem:* the SAS component that keeps track of system options.
- *Keyword option:* a Boolean option that can be given a value by indicating just the option name or the option name with the prefix NO.
- *Keyword-value option:* an option that must be written with the name and a value.

Each system option represents an aspect of the SAS environment that you can control. These are the essential properties of each system option:

- *Name.* The name is a word that identifies the option in any statement, window, or report.
- *Value.* An option always has a value. In this respect, it is similar to a variable.
- *Set of possible values.* Every option is restricted to a particular set or range of values. For example, the OBS= option accepts whole numbers and MAX as

values; the value of the COMPRESS= option must be a single word. Boolean options accept values of 0 and 1 only. If you attempt to set an option to an incorrect value, SAS generates an error message.

- *Default.* If you take no action to set an option, it has a default value that SAS provides at startup.
- *Changeability.* Some options can be changed at any time during a SAS session, but others can be set only at specific times. Also, some options change automatically to reflect changes in the SAS environment.

In addition, a system option might have these properties:

- *Alias.* An alias is an alternate name that identifies the option. For example, AE is an alias for AUTOEXEC; instead of writing AUTOEXEC, you can write its alias AE.
- *Option group.* An option group is a set of options that can be displayed separately in the OPTIONS procedure and the System Options window. There are about 20 option groups. For example, the EXTFILES option group includes system options that control the way SAS programs access text and print files. It is possible for an option to belong to more than one option group.

To understand what system options can and cannot do, these are the key points to consider:

- System options are defined by the SAS System. A SAS program cannot create system options. It can only use the system options that already exist.
- A system option always has a value. The SAS supervisor sets every system option at startup.
- System option values tend to stay the same. It takes specific actions to change the value of a system option.
- The scope of system options is the SAS process. Ordinarily, a system option has the same value everywhere in a SAS session. The only way a system option can have different values at the same time at different places in a SAS session is if you start a separate SAS process.

Setting System Options

There are various ways to set system options, and each one has its own way of indicating the options and their values.

System options use SAS option syntax in SAS statements, but other syntax styles elsewhere. For example, if you write system options in the operating system command when you start a SAS session, you must use operating system command syntax. The option settings mean the same thing even though they are written in different ways.

To set options in the OPTIONS statement, write the option name or alias, an equals sign, and the value. For example, this statement sets the LINESIZE=, PAGESIZE=, and CENTER options:

```
OPTIONS LINESIZE=75 PAGESIZE=64 CENTER=0;
```

An OPTIONS statement can set any number of system options. For Boolean options, you can write the option name by itself to set a value of 1, or on. Write the option name with the prefix NO to set a value of 0, or off. This statement turns the option CLEANUP on and turns the option FMTERR off:

OPTIONS CLEANUP NOFMTERR;

It is also possible to write an equals sign and a value of 1 or 0 for a Boolean option, as shown in the previous example for the CENTER option.

 The OPTIONS statement is a global statement; it changes system options between steps. For clarity, write the OPTIONS statement between steps. Add a RUN statement before it if necessary.

 If the same option appears more than once in an OPTIONS statement, the statement sets the option each time it appears. The final value for the option is the value that appears last in the statement.

For options that take numeric values, you can use the special values MIN and MAX to indicate the lowest and highest allowable values. For example, this statement sets the value of the PAGENO= option to 1, which is the lowest valid value:

OPTIONS PAGENO=MIN;

 If you set system options incorrectly in a SAS statement, log messages describe the errors, as shown in this example.

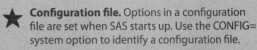

9 Ways to Set System Options

A system option can get its value in any of these ways.

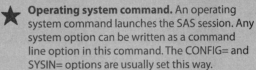 **Configuration file.** Options in a configuration file are set when SAS starts up. Use the CONFIG= system option to identify a configuration file.

Operating system command. An operating system command launches the SAS session. Any system option can be written as a command line option in this command. The CONFIG= and SYSIN= options are usually set this way.

OPTIONS statement. An OPTIONS statement can change session options anywhere in a SAS program or at any point during a SAS session. Session options are written as statement options in the OPTIONS statement.

STARTSAS statement. The STARTSAS statement starts a new SAS process. Options in the statement set system options for the SAS process.

System Options window. In an interactive SAS session, this window shows most system options and allows you to change the values of session options. It displays options in option groups so you can see related options together.

AF applications. SCL programs can use the OPTSETC and OPTSETN functions to change session options. Often, AF applications change options when they initialize and change them back when they terminate. Creating AF applications requires SAS/AF.

Defaults. At the start of the SAS session, the SAS supervisor gives default values to all system options that are not specifically set in the configuration file or command line.

Environment variable. Some operating systems let you create environment variables, text objects managed by the operating system that applications can access by name. When a SAS session starts up, the SAS supervisor checks a specific environment variable for system options.

Automatic changes. Several system options change automatically to reflect changes in the SAS environment. For example, the value of the PAGENO= system option is the page number of the next page of print output. For every page, the page number changes, and the value of the system option changes.

OPTIONS LS=63 OOPS=0;

```
ERROR 18-12: Option value for SAS option LINESIZE must be between 64 and
             256.

ERROR 13-12: Unrecognized SAS option name, OOPS.
```

In most operating systems, system options in the operating system command line and configuration file follow syntax conventions derived from Unix. Precede each option name with a hyphen. Write a space (not an equals sign) between the option name and the value. This operating system command line starts a SAS session with the same system option settings shown in the two earlier examples:

```
sas -linesize 75 -pagesize 64 -nocenter -cleanup -nofmterr
```

This example assumes that sas is the command to start a SAS session. The actual command depends on the way SAS software is installed on the specific computer.

In z/OS, options are written following the option syntax conventions of TSO and JCL, which are more similar to SAS option syntax. In JCL, you can write a string of options in the OPTIONS= option in the EXEC statement that calls the SAS cataloged procedure.

In most operating systems, the option syntax in a configuration file is almost the same as in the operating system command line. However, in a configuration file, you can write each option on a separate line, and you can include delimited comments, as shown in this example.

```
/* An example of system options in a configuration file */

/* Line size and page size */
-linesize 75
-pagesize 64

/* Left-align output */
-center 0

/* Free memory continuously */
-cleanup

/* When a format cannot be found, use a default format */
-nofmterr
```

System options do not carry over from one SAS session to the next. If you want to have the same system options every time you work on a particular project, write the options in the configuration file or autoexec file that you use in the project or repeat them in each program file.

Obtaining Values of System Options

This is a summary of the ways you can determine the value of system options:

- *Procedure.* The OPTIONS procedure lists system options in the log.
- *System Options window.* Use this window to display option groups in an interactive session.
- *Data step.* Use the GETOPTION function to get the text of the value of a specific system option.
- *Macro programming.* Use the %SYSFUNC macro function to call the GETOPTION function.
- *AF applications.* Use the OPTGETC and OPTGETN functions to obtain the values of system options in an SCL program. Creating AF applications requires SAS/AF.

The OPTIONS procedure shows system options with values and very short descriptions. To list all system options, write the PROC OPTIONS statement without options:

```
PROC OPTIONS;
RUN;
```

The procedure writes in the log two alphabetical lists containing all the system options. This is an excerpt of the output:

```
Portable Options:
...
 NOBATCH          Do not use the batch set of default values for SAS
                  system options
 BINDING=DEFAULT  Controls the binding edge for duplexed output
...
Host Options:

 ALTLOG=          Specifies the destination for a copy of the SAS log
 ALTPRINT=        Specifies the destination for a copy of the SAS
                  procedure output file
...
```

Use these options in the PROC OPTIONS statement:

- *OPTION=.* Sometimes you want to see the value of just one system option. Write the OPTION= option with the option name or alias, for example, OPTION=PS.
- *GROUP=.* To list an option group, use the GROUP= option with the name of the option group.
- *VALUE.* The VALUE option provides additional information about system options, such as how the options were set. This example shows output for the VALUE option:

```
PROC OPTIONS OPTION=PRINTMSGLIST VALUE;
RUN;
```

Top 10 System Options

Among the hundreds of system options, the ten most popular account for close to half of all system option use. These ten options also illustrate the variations in styles of usage among system options.

 SYSIN. When you start a batch-mode SAS session (or SAS process) the SYSIN= option identifies the SAS program file to run. The value of the option is the file name. This is an example of the SYSIN option in an operating system command line:

```
sas -sysin myprogram.sas
```

Or, this SAS statement starts a SAS process:

```
STARTSAS SYSIN="myprogram.sas";
```

The SYSIN= option is a startup option; it cannot change after a SAS session or process has started.

 CONFIG. The CONFIG= option also provides a file name, or possibly a list of files. It is an initialization option; it can only be set at the start of the SAS session. Most initialization options are set in the configuration file, but since the CONFIG= option identifies the configuration file, it is usually set in the operating system command line.

 AUTOEXEC. Another startup option, the AUTOEXEC= option identifies an autoexec file, an initialization program that executes at the beginning of the SAS session. The autoexec file typically includes global statements such as LIBNAME and TITLE statements. This line in a configuration file might identify the autoexec file:

```
-autoexec "myinit.sas"
```

To tell the SAS supervisor not to execute an autoexec file, even though one is present, you can use the option with the NO prefix, for example:

```
-noautoexec
```

 LINESIZE. The LINESIZE= system option sets the number of characters per line in print output files, including the log and standard print files. It is a session option; its value can be changed at any point. The LINESIZE= option can also be identified by its alias, LS. For example, this statement sets the LINESIZE option to 75:

```
OPTIONS LS=75;
```

The values for the LINESIZE= option are limited to the range from 64 to 256.

 PAGESIZE. Similarly, the PAGESIZE= system option controls the number of lines on a page. Its alias is PS. Valid values go from 15 to 32767.

 CENTER. Title lines and procedure output can be centered or left-aligned, according to the CENTER option. It is a Boolean option; turn it on or off with the word CENTER or NOCENTER, for example:

```
OPTIONS CENTER;
```

The alias for the CENTER option is CENTRE.

 PAGENO. The PAGENO= option is the page number for the next page of print output the SAS program writes. SAS automatically updates the value when it writes a page of output. To reset the page number to 1, use this statement:

```
OPTIONS PAGENO=1;
```

The value for the PAGENO= option can only be a positive integer value. The alias for the PAGENO= option is the abbreviation PAGNO.

 YEARCUTOFF. The YEARCUTOFF= option controls the meaning of two-digit years. The value of the option is the earliest year that a two-digit year could indicate. For example, YEARCUTOFF=1942 means two-digit years fall in the range from 1942 to 2041.

Valid values cover the years from 1582 to 19900.

 OBS. The OBS= option limits the number of observations or records that a data step statement or proc step reads from an input file. For example, with the option OBS=1, it stops after reading only 1 observation or record. The value can be a whole number or the word MAX. The word MAX represents the idea of using all available observations or records, but it actually indicates a large positive integer, such as 2147483647.

 COMPRESS. When new SAS data files are created, the compression routine they use comes from the COMPRESS= option. Only YES, NO, or the name of an installed compression routine is a correct value for this option. The compression routines in SAS 8–9 are CHAR and BINARY. YES is an alias for CHAR. NO indicates not to use compression. COMPRESS= is also a dataset option you can use when you create a specific SAS data file. The COMPRESS= system option provides a default for the COMPRESS= dataset option.

```
Option Value Information For SAS Option PRINTMSGLIST
    Option Value: PRINTMSGLIST
    Option Scope: Default
    How option value set:  Shipped Default
```

- *SHORT.* The SHORT option lists the options and values without descriptions. This is useful if you want to get text that you can use directly in an OPTIONS statement.
- *HOST.* With the HOST option the OPTIONS procedure lists host options.
- *PORTABLE.* With the PORTABLE or NOHOST option the procedure lists portable options.

 Use the GETOPTION function to get the value of a system option in a data step. Provide the option name or alias in a character value as the one argument of the function. The function returns the text of the option value. The example below demonstrates how you can assign the option value text to a variable.

```
DATA _NULL_;
  OPTIONTEXT_LS = GETOPTION('LS');
  OPTIONTEXT_ENGINE = GETOPTION('ENGINE');
  OPTIONTEXT_PRINTINIT = GETOPTION('PRINTINIT');
  PUT (_ALL_) (=/);
RUN;
```

```
OPTIONTEXT_LS=75
OPTIONTEXT_ENGINE=V8
OPTIONTEXT_PRINTINIT=NOPRINTINIT
```

For an option that has a numeric value, the function converts the numeric value to text. For a Boolean option, the function returns the option name, with the prefix NO if the option is off. In the example above, the option PRINTINIT has a Boolean value of 0, so the GETOPTION function returns the value NOPRINTINIT.

 To get the numeric value of an option, use the INPUT function and F informat to convert the return value of the GETOPTION function to a number. For example, the expression INPUT(GETOPTION('LS'), F12.) obtains the numeric value of the LINESIZE= option, using the alias LS for the option.

 To get the Boolean value of a Boolean option, use the = operator to test whether the option text from the GETOPTION function is the same as the option name. This example obtains the Boolean value of the CENTER option and uses the result to position a heading.

```
CENTER = GETOPTION('CENTER') = 'CENTER';
IF CENTER THEN PUT HEADERTEXT $F75. -C;
ELSE PUT HEADERTEXT $F75. -L;
```

The alignment option -C centers the value of HEADERTEXT in the field if the system option CENTER is on. If the option is off, the alignment option -L in the other PUT statement left-aligns the value.

To use a system option value in a statement or a macro expression, use the %SYSFUNC macro function to call the GETOPTION function. This example uses a macro expression to set the page size as half the line size.

OPTIONS PAGESIZE=%EVAL(%SYSFUNC(GETOPTION(LINESIZE))/2);

For example, if the value of the LINESIZE= option is 75, this statement resolves as:

OPTIONS PAGESIZE=37;

To write a log message that contains one or more system option values, use the %SYSFUNC macro function with the GETOPTION function in a %PUT statement. This example obtains the international date format language from the DFLANG= option and writes it in the log.

%PUT The international date format language is %SYSFUNC(GETOPTION(DFLANG)).;

```
The international date format language is ENGLISH.
```

In some kinds of utility programs that use system options, it is important to reset the options to the values they had at the beginning of the program. For example, if the program changes the value of the MISSING= option, it might change the option back to its previous setting at the end of the program. When a utility program is used as part of a larger program, this approach keeps the utility program from affecting other unrelated parts of the program in which it is used.

Start by creating a macro variable with the value of the system option at the beginning of the program. Refer to this macro variable in an OPTIONS statement at the end of the program to reset the option. Using the MISSING= option as an example, these are the statements involved:

```
* Note previous value of system option. ;
%LET RESET_MISSING = %SYSFUNC(GETOPTION(MISSING));

* Set system option for use in program. ;
OPTIONS MISSING=' ';

*
  Other statements in program
  . . .
*;

* Reset system option to previous value. ;
OPTIONS MISSING="&RESET_MISSING";
```

5
Libraries

Libraries contain SAS files. SAS does not access SAS files directly; instead, it accesses them as members of a library. The two-level name of a SAS file consists of a libref and a member name. For example, WORK.SASMACR is the libref WORK and the member name SASMACR. The libref is a reference to the library that contains the SAS file. Use a LIBNAME statement to define a libref and associate it with a specific library.

To define a libref, write the libref and physical file name of the library in a LIBNAME statement. This example defines the libref MAIN.

LIBNAME MAIN '/projects/main';

In most file systems, a library is a path or directory. Write the path or directory name as the physical file name in the LIBNAME statement. In the z/OS file system, a library is stored as a single physical file. Write the dataset name of this file in the LIBNAME statement. The library, a *bound* library, contains its own file system to keep track of the SAS files it contains.

Routines called engines connect the SAS supervisor to the specific file types that it treats as SAS files. A library engine is associated with each library you use in a SAS session. When you define a new or empty library, the SAS supervisor automatically uses the default BASE engine for it, which is the best engine for most purposes. When you define a library that already exists, the SAS supervisor uses the engine that created the library or its members. If you need to use a different engine with a library, write the engine after the libref in the LIBNAME statement.

The most frequent reason to use a different engine is for compatibility with an older version of SAS. This example defines the LEGACY fileref using the V6 engine.

LIBNAME LEGACY V6 '/projects/trend/history';

To see the definition of a libref, write a LIBNAME statement with the libref and the option LIST. The statement writes a log note that describes the definition of the libref. This example lists the definition of the BIG library.

LIBNAME BIG LIST;

To list all defined librefs, use this statement:

LIBNAME _ALL_ LIST;

To clear a libref, write a LIBNAME statement with the libref and the CLEAR option. This example clears the LOCATION libref.

LIBNAME LOCATION CLEAR;

Several librefs are defined automatically when the SAS session starts up. These librefs identify libraries that have specific purposes in the SAS environment.

- WORK is a place for storing temporary files, files that will be used only in the current SAS session.
- SASUSER stores files associated with a specific user, including the user profile.
- SASHELP contains the AF applications that are part of the SAS System. It may also contain samples of data and programs.

These librefs are created automatically. Do not use LIBNAME statements with these librefs.

It is possible to associate a libref with a combination of libraries. This way of combining libraries is called a concatenation. To define a libref with multiple libraries, first define each separate library. Then define the concatenation with a different libref and the list of librefs in parentheses.

For example, to define the libref COMBINE as the concatenation of the libraries MAIN and CORP, use this statement:

LIBNAME COMBINE (MAIN CORP);

When you ask for a member of the COMBINE library, the SAS supervisor looks first in the MAIN library for the member. If it does not find the member there, it looks in the CORP library.

If you create a new member in a library concatenation, the SAS supervisor places the member in the first library. In this example, if you create COMBINE.SUBJECT, it is stored as MAIN.SUBJECT because MAIN is the first library in the concatenation.

You can use the syntax for library concatenation to substitute one libref for another. This is especially useful when you want to test a program in the WORK library, even though the program normally uses SAS files stored in another library. For example, with the MAIN library defined this way:

LIBNAME MAIN (WORK);

a reference to a file such as MAIN.CLEANUP becomes an indirect way to access the member of the WORK library, WORK.CLEANUP. This approach can provide a quick way to test a program in the WORK library without having to create a separate test library and without putting the live data of a permanent library at risk.

Just as you concatenate libraries, you can concatenate catalogs. Write a CATNAME statement with a catref and a list of catalogs. The catref is a two-level name that you use as a catalog name for the catalog concatenation. Usually, you should use the WORK libref as the first level of the catref. A catref has the same form as a SAS file name, but it is not actually a SAS file. This is an example of a catref definition:

CATNAME WORK.APPL (MAIN.APPL MAIN.KEYS WORK.NEW);

With this catref definition, you can refer to entries in the listed catalogs as if they were entries in the WORK.APPL catalog. For example, if you request the entry WORK.APPL.RESET.SCL, the SAS supervisor looks for RESET.SCL in MAIN.APPL. If it does not find it there, it goes on to look in MAIN.KEYS, then WORK.NEW.

If you create a new entry in a catref, the SAS supervisor stores it in the first of the concatenated catalogs.

Libraries and SAS files are structured differently in different environments to reflect the way the computer hardware and operating system work with data values. When you create a library in one environment, there are limitations on the way you can access it in another environment. However, using a feature called Cross-Environment Data Access (CEDA), you can access most libraries from other environments using an ordinary LIBNAME statement. The bound libraries used in the z/OS file system cannot be accessed as CEDA libraries, and there are other restrictions and limitations on the use of CEDA libraries. See chapter 72, "Porting Files and Data," for details.

With additional SAS products, a SAS session can access libraries through another SAS session that runs at the same time.

- A shared library is managed by a SAS/SHARE server to allow multiple users to access the library and its members simultaneously. SAS/SHARE software is required to operate a SAS/SHARE server and to access the shared libraries.
- A remote library is a library of a remote session. The remote session is another SAS session, usually on another computer, under the control of a SAS session. SAS/CONNECT is required on both computers to start a remote session. This feature of SAS/CONNECT is called Remote Library Services (RLS).

Shared and remote libraries use additional options in the LIBNAME statement. The SERVER= option is required to identify the SAS session that owns the library. For a shared library, the value of the SERVER= option is the server ID of the SAS/SHARE server. For a remote library, it is the session ID of the remote session.

■ 6

Dataset Options

Dataset options are options for SAS datasets. They modify the way a SAS dataset is stored, read, or written. When a dataset option is used on an input SAS dataset, it affects the way data is read from the SAS dataset, but it does not change the SAS dataset itself. On an output SAS dataset, it does change the SAS dataset itself. It might affect the way the SAS dataset is organized, the data it contains, or its header information.

The syntax of dataset options is the same regardless of where or how you use them. Write dataset options in parentheses after the name of the SAS dataset. If a SAS dataset has multiple dataset options, write the list of options separated by spaces. For each option, write the option name, an equals sign, and a value. This is an example of a SAS dataset with two dataset options, KEEP= and COMPRESS=.

WORK.PRIOR (KEEP=ID LEVEL SIZE COMPRESS=CHAR)

The value of the KEEP= option is the variable list ID LEVEL SIZE. Several dataset options have lists as values. Whenever you see a single word in a list of dataset options, such as LEVEL in this example, read it as part of a list that is the value of an option.

A few dataset options — WHERE=, INDEX=, and RENAME= — take values that can contain equals signs. The values of these options must be enclosed in parentheses, for example:

WORK.JOURNAL (RENAME=(OLD1=NEW1 OLD2=NEW2))

Dataset options are valid in proc steps and in the DATA, SET, MERGE, MODIFY, and UPDATE statements of the data step. They are allowed in SQL statements. They can be used in the arguments to some functions and in some interactive applications where users provide SAS dataset names.

 The most commonly used dataset options select a subset of data. These options read selected observations and variables from a SAS dataset or store selected observations and variables when writing to a SAS dataset.

 Use the KEEP= option with a list of variables to select the variables to use. Alternatively, use the DROP= option with a list of variables to leave out.

To change the names of variables, use the RENAME= option. With this option, a variable can be stored with a different name than it has in the program where it is used. The value of the RENAME= option is a list of variable name changes in parentheses. Write each name change with the old name, an equals sign, and the new name.

This example changes the name of the variable NMX to NAME:

RENAME=(NMX=NAME)

Use the WHERE= option to select observations based on a rule or condition. The value of the option is a condition enclosed in parentheses, for example:

WHERE=(AGE > 14)

If a WHERE= option is used on an input SAS dataset, only the observations that meet the condition are available to the program. If a WHERE= option is used on an output SAS dataset, only observations that meet the condition are stored in the output SAS dataset.

A WHERE condition can only use variables that are available in the SAS dataset.

If you use the WHERE= option when updating a SAS dataset, the WHERE condition applies to observations on input. The WHEREUP= option determines whether the WHERE condition is also applied to output observations. With the option WHEREUP=YES, observations are not added or updated if the new values do not meet the condition. Use the option WHEREUP=NO to allow observations to be changed so that they no longer meet the WHERE condition.

Use the OBS= and FIRSTOBS= dataset options to select observations from an input SAS dataset based on observation numbers. The FIRSTOBS= option is the lowest observation number that is used. The OBS= option is the highest observation number. For example, the SET statement below reads observations 11 through 20 from the SAS dataset WORK.AVERAGE.

SET WORK.AVERAGE (FIRSTOBS=11 OBS=20);

These rules apply when you use combinations of dataset options:

- The KEEP= and DROP= options cannot be used together.
- If you use the KEEP= and RENAME= options at the same time, use the old variable names in the KEEP= option.
- Always use the variable name that is stored in the SAS dataset when you use the WHERE= option. This rule also applies to the INDEX= option, which defines an index for a new SAS data file.
- If you use the WHERE= option at the same time as the FIRSTOBS= or OBS= option, the WHERE= option is applied first. Only the observations that remain after considering the WHERE= option are counted toward the FIRSTOBS= or OBS= option.

- If the value of the FIRSTOBS= option is greater than the value of the OBS= option, no observations are read from the SAS dataset. This is also the case if the FIRSTOBS= option has a value that is greater than the number of observations in the SAS dataset.

 These dataset options add descriptive information to a SAS dataset:

- The LABEL= option adds a dataset label to a SAS dataset. The dataset label can describe the contents of the SAS dataset.
- The TYPE= option identifies a SAS dataset as containing a specific type of data. This option is used by some statistics procedures.
- The value of the SORTEDBY= option is a sort order clause that indicates how the SAS dataset is sorted. Use _NULL_ as the value of the option to indicate that the SAS dataset is not sorted.

Dataset options can be used for a new SAS dataset to prevent it from replacing an existing SAS dataset. The REPLACE=NO option prevents a SAS dataset from replacing an existing SAS dataset of the same name. The REPEMPTY=NO option prevents a SAS dataset that has no observations from replacing an existing SAS dataset of the same name.

Several dataset options are associated with system options of the same name. The system option applies whenever the dataset option is not used. This is true for the FIRSTOBS, OBS, COMPRESS, REUSE, and REPLACE options.

The DLDMGACTION= dataset option indicates the action for the SAS supervisor to take if it discovers that the SAS dataset is damaged. System crashes and other software failures can damage SAS datasets that are open at the time. The most useful value for this option is REPAIR, which tells the SAS supervisor to repair the SAS dataset if it can. If repairing the SAS dataset is not appropriate, use FAIL as the value. The SAS supervisor generates an error condition. Other available values are ABORT and PROMPT. DLDMGACTION= is also a system option.

The DKRICOND= and DKROCOND= system options determine how to handle variable name errors in dataset options. The DKRICOND= system option affects errors in DROP=, KEEP=, and RENAME= dataset options for input SAS datasets, especially errors in which the dataset option refers to a variable that is not found in the SAS dataset. The DKROCOND= system option relates to the same dataset options for output SAS datasets. For either option, use the value ERROR to generate an error condition, WARNING or WARN to generate a warning message, or NOWARNING or NOWARN to ignore the incorrect variable reference.

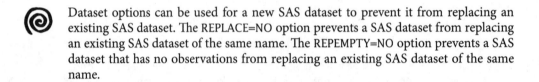

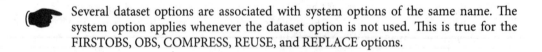

These are other common uses for dataset options:

- To create indexes for SAS data files. See the next chapter, "Indexes."
- To compress a new SAS data file. See chapter 71, "Compression."
- To create generation datasets and audit files.
- To identify the SAS dataset that provided an observation in a data step. The IN= option is used for this purpose; this dataset option has no effect outside of the data step. See chapter 51, "Combining Data."
- To set the control level for a SAS dataset that might be used in two places at the same time. Use the CNTLLEV= option for this. See chapter 87, "Client-Server Design."

Password Options

When a SAS file is password-protected, a program or user has to provide the password to access the file. The password options are used as dataset options for SAS datasets and with same syntax for other SAS files. However, passwords cannot be used for catalogs. Use the same option to create a password for a new SAS file or to access that file subsequently. There are three levels of password protection for different kinds of access to the file. Each has its own option.

 READ= A read-level password protects the contents of the file from being read without a password. For a SAS dataset, using a read-level password protects the data values in the SAS dataset.

 WRITE= A write-level password protects the contents of the file from being changed. If there is a write-level password but no read-level password, a user without a password can read the file, but cannot change it. In a SAS dataset, the write-level password is required for actions that change values in existing observations or that add or delete observations. A user with a write-level password can use that password to read and write data in the file.

 ALTER= An alter-level password protects the file from changes in its structure. In a SAS dataset, the alter-level password is required to change attributes of variables. It is also required if you replace the SAS dataset with a new SAS dataset. With the alter-level password, it is possible to reset or change any of the passwords.

 PW= The PW= option can be a substitute for any or all of the other password options. When you create passwords, use the PW= option to create the same password for all three password levels. When you access the file, use the PW= option to supply any password.

These other dataset options can be used with passwords of SAS datasets.

 ENCRYPT=YES This option adds file encryption to a SAS data file. This adds another level of protection to the data and makes it difficult for a file-utility program to read any of the data in the file.

 PWREQ= The PWREQ= option determines the response if a password is not provided in a program that runs in an interactive session. With PWREQ=YES, the SAS supervisor displays a requestor window in which the user can enter the password. With PWREQ=NO, the password must be written in the program, and if it is not, the file cannot be accessed.

7

Indexes

Add indexes to a SAS data file to make it easier to retrieve data based on key values. With the right index:

- WHERE clauses find observations faster.
- A SAS data file can be read with a BY statement in an order different from the order in which it is stored.
- A SET or MODIFY statement can use the KEY= option to read a specific observation. (This technique is described in chapter 53, "Table Lookup From SAS Data Files.")

An index of one key variable is a simple index. An index of two or more key variables is a composite index. There are a few differences in syntax between simple and composite indexes, the most important of which has to do with the name of the index. The name of a simple index is the name of the key variable. The name of a composite index cannot be the same as any variable name.

What key variables do you need in an index?

- If you are using an index to locate observations, include the variables necessary to identify the observation. If an observation has a unique identifying code, make an index that uses only that code variable.
- If you are using an index to read the observations in sorted order, use all variables from the sort order in the index key, in the same order.
- If your objective is to speed up processing of a WHERE clause, include the more distinctive variables of the WHERE clause in the index key. For a WHERE clause that uses only one variable, make an index on that variable. If a WHERE clause uses several variables, you may not want to include all the variables in the index. Usually, you should not include variables that are merely measurements or classifications in a composite index. However, it is not always easy to predict what index will work best for a WHERE clause, so you might try several indexes to see which is fastest for a particular WHERE clause and a particular set of data.

Use the INDEX= dataset option to create indexes at the same time that you create the SAS data file. The option can define one index or several of them. Either way, write parentheses around the value of the option:

INDEX=(*index definition*)
INDEX=(*index definition* . . .)

For a simple index, with just one key variable, the index definition is just the variable name (which is also the index name). For example INDEX=(HOME) creates an index on the variable HOME. For a composite index, the index definition is the index name, an equals sign, and in parentheses, the list of key variables. For example, INDEX=(STOF= (STATE OFFICE)) creates an index on the variables STATE and OFFICE. The example below, creates the SAS data file WORK.EQUIP and two indexes, LOC and UNIT.

```
DATA WORK.EQUIP (INDEX=(LOC UNIT=(MFR SERIAL)));
   INFILE EQUIP DLM=',';
   LENGTH MFR $ 8 SERIAL $ 16 DESCR $ 40 LOC $ 8;
   INPUT MFR SERIAL DESCR LOC;
RUN;
```

To create indexes for an existing SAS data file, use the DATASETS procedure. Use these statements:

```
PROC DATASETS LIBRARY=library NOLIST;
   MODIFY member;
   INDEX CREATE index definition . . . ;
RUN;
```

The syntax of an index definition in the INDEX CREATE statement is the same as in the INDEX= option. The example below adds the simple index ARTIST to the SAS dataset MUSIC.CAT.

```
PROC DATASETS LIBRARY=MUSIC NOLIST;
   MODIFY CAT;
   INDEX CREATE ARTIST;
RUN;
```

After an index is defined, SAS automatically uses the index when appropriate. The index is used when you read a SAS dataset with a BY statement whose sort order clause matches the key variables of the index. An index is also used when the SAS supervisor estimates that the index will speed up processing of a WHERE clause.

Two dataset options, IDXWHERE= and IDXNAME=, can be used to tune the use of indexes when processing a WHERE clause.

By default, the SAS supervisor estimates the speed of processing the WHERE clause with or without an index. It uses an index if it estimates that it will be faster. If there are multiple indexes, it selects the index that it estimates will be fastest. Use the IDXWHERE=NO dataset option to prevent the SAS supervisor from considering an index for a specific WHERE clause. Use the IDXWHERE=YES dataset option to tell the

SAS supervisor to use the best available index, even if it estimates that the index will slow down processing.

If there are multiple indexes that the SAS supervisor could use for a WHERE clause, you can use the IDXNAME= dataset option to name one specific index to use.

Use these options to speed up processing if your tests show that one index is fastest for a particular WHERE clause.

It takes a small amount of time to maintain an index whenever you make changes in a SAS data file that has indexes. If you are making extensive changes, it can be faster to delete all indexes beforehand and rebuild them afterward.

Similarly, indexes use a small amount of storage space. If you will not be using a SAS dataset for a long time, consider deleting the indexes and rebuilding them when you are ready to use the SAS dataset again.

SAS cannot maintain indexes when you make some kinds of changes. An index is automatically deleted if you sort the SAS dataset in place or remove a key variable. All indexes are also deleted if you delete or replace a SAS dataset.

Use the INDEX DELETE statement in the DATASETS procedure to delete an index. Use these statements:

```
PROC DATASETS LIBRARY=library NOLIST;
  MODIFY member;
  INDEX DELETE name . . . ;
RUN;
```

There are also SQL statements for creating and deleting indexes. These statements create indexes:

```
CREATE INDEX PRODUCT ON MAIN.CAT (PRODUCT);
CREATE INDEX EVENT ON WORK.UNIVERSE (TIME, PLACE);
```

This statement deletes an index:

```
DROP INDEX EVENT FROM WORK.UNIVERSE;
```

Execute SQL statements after a PROC SQL statement; see chapter 42 for details.

■ 8

Actions on SAS Datasets

Usually, in a SAS program, you work with a SAS dataset one observation at a time. Sometimes, though, it makes sense to think of working with the SAS dataset as a whole. This is especially the case in database-style applications, which are likely to keep SAS datasets for an extended period of time and use them both interactively and in SAS programs.

Creating

A SAS dataset can be created in a data step or a proc step. By default, a data step creates a SAS dataset that contains all the variables of the data step, with just a few kinds of variables excluded. The data step writes one observation to the output SAS dataset each time it reads input data; a data step that does not read input data writes just one observation. Proc steps also create SAS datasets; the procedure determines what observations and variables it creates.

Usually, a SAS dataset is created together with the data that it contains. However, it is also possible to create an empty SAS dataset. The idea is that you will add data to the SAS dataset in a later process. There are several ways to create an empty SAS dataset.

 To create a new, empty SAS data file in a data step, write a LENGTH statement to define the variables. If necessary, use other statements, such as LABEL and FORMAT statements, to define other attributes of the variables. This example creates a SAS data file CORP.MEMBER with two variables, NAME and DOB, and no observations.

```
DATA CORP.MEMBER;
  LENGTH NAME $ 28 DOB 4;
  FORMAT DOB DATE9.;
  INFORMAT DOB DATE9.;
  STOP;
RUN;
```

```
NOTE: Variable NAME is uninitialized.
NOTE: Variable DOB is uninitialized.
NOTE: The data set CORP.MEMBER has 0 observations and 2 variables.
```

To create a new, empty SAS data file with the same variables and attributes as an existing SAS dataset, use a data step with a SET statement and a STOP statement. This data step creates a new SAS data file CORP.NX based on CORP.MEMBER.

```
DATA CORP.NX;
  SET CORP.MEMBER;
  STOP;
RUN;
```

Alternatively, use the OBS=0 dataset option in the SET statement. With the OBS=0 dataset option, the STOP statement is not necessary.

To create a SAS data file that has the variables of several existing SAS datasets, list those SAS datasets in the SET statement of a data step, followed by a STOP statement. The new SAS data file contains every variable that is in any of the SAS datasets listed.

Use the KEEP= or DROP= dataset option to create a new SAS dataset that contains only some of the variables of an existing SAS dataset.

Describing

The CONTENTS procedure creates a report that shows the details of the form of a SAS dataset. Identify the SAS dataset in the PROC CONTENTS statement:

```
PROC CONTENTS DATA=SAS dataset;
RUN;
```

The information that is available about the SAS dataset depends on the environment and engine. The general information about the SAS dataset is followed by a table of all the attributes of the variables. It lists variables in alphabetical order.

Use the OUT= option to create a SAS dataset of most of this information. The output SAS dataset contains one observation for each variable.

Changing

There are many ways to change the data contained in a SAS data file, including these:

- Use a data step with a SET statement to replace the SAS data file.
- Use a data step with a MODIFY statement to modify the SAS data file in place.
- Edit the SAS data file interactively in the Viewtable application, the FSEDIT or FSVIEW procedure, or an AF entry that uses an extended table to allow editing of the SAS data file.
- Add a set of observations from another SAS dataset with the APPEND procedure, as described later in this chapter.
- Add, delete, or change observations with SQL statements.
- Use the SORT procedure to change the order of observations.

Use the CHANGE statement of the DATASETS procedure to change the name of a SAS dataset or other SAS file. The DATASETS procedure requires you to provide the libref and member name separately. Indicate the libref in the LIBRARY= option in the PROC DATASETS statement. Indicate member names in the specific action statements of the procedure. In the CHANGE statement, write the old name, an equals sign, and the new name for the member. This example changes the name of WORK.OFFICE to WORK.PLACE:

```
PROC DATASETS LIBRARY=WORK NOLIST;
  CHANGE OFFICE=PLACE;
RUN;
```

```
NOTE: Changing the name WORK.OFFICE to WORK.PLACE (memtype=DATA).
```

Ordinarily, the PROC DATASETS statement writes a member list in the log. Use the NOLIST option whenever you will not be using the member list.

To swap the names of two SAS files, use the EXCHANGE statement in the DATASETS procedure. This example changes the name of WORK.SPACE to WORK.PLACE and changes the name of WORK.PLACE to WORK.SPACE:

```
PROC DATASETS LIBRARY=WORK NOLIST;
  EXCHANGE SPACE=PLACE;
RUN;
```

```
NOTE: Exchanging the names WORK.SPACE and WORK.PLACE (memtype=DATA).
```

The AGE statement of the DATASETS procedure renames a sequence of SAS files and deletes a SAS file in a single action. Each member listed in the AGE statement has its name changed to the next name in the list. The last member in the list is deleted. This example deletes BE.BEFORE, changes the name of BE.NOW to BE.BEFORE, and changes the name of BE.NEXT to BE.NOW.

```
PROC DATASETS LIBRARY=BE NOLIST;
  AGE NEXT NOW BEFORE;
RUN;
```

```
NOTE: Deleting BE.BEFORE (memtype=DATA).
NOTE: Aging the name BE.NOW to BE.BEFORE (memtype=DATA).
NOTE: Aging the name BE.NEXT to BE.NOW (memtype=DATA).
```

To change the dataset label or dataset type of a SAS dataset, use the MODIFY statement of the DATASETS procedure. In the MODIFY statement, write the member name, followed by dataset options: the LABEL= option or the TYPE= option, respectively. This example changes the dataset label of CORP.NEWS to "The latest news stories."

```
PROC DATASETS LIBRARY=CORP NOLIST;
  MODIFY NEWS (LABEL='The latest news stories');
RUN;
```

To change the length of a variable in a SAS dataset, replace the SAS dataset with a new SAS dataset in which you set the length of the variable. Use a data step with a LENGTH statement followed by a SET statement. This example changes the length of the variable NAME in the SAS dataset CORP.MEMBER to 32.

```
DATA CORP.MEMBER;
  LENGTH NAME $ 32;
  SET CORP.MEMBER;
RUN;
```

 There is no direct way to change the type of a variable in a SAS dataset. Instead, it is necessary to replace the SAS dataset while creating a new variable of the new type and removing the old variable. See chapter 50, "Type Conversion," for details.

SQL TABLE ACTIONS

Most of the actions on SAS datasets can also be done using SQL table actions. Write SQL statements after a PROC SQL statement:

PROC SQL;

To create an empty SAS data file by defining variables, use the CREATE TABLE statement with column definitions (a list of them, in parentheses, separated by commas). A definition starts with the name, then the data type, which can be CHARACTER(*width*) or NUMERIC, or abbreviated as CHAR and NUM. SQL syntax allows several other data type names, but SAS implements all the SQL data types as either the numeric or character data type. The width argument for the character data type determines the length of the character variable.

The column attributes INFORMAT=, FORMAT=, and LABEL= can follow the data type to set other attributes of the variable. Unfortunately, the LENGTH= attribute is not recognized in this kind of CREATE TABLE statement, and there is no attribute that will set the length of a numeric variable.

This example creates the same SAS data file that was created in the earlier data step example, except that the numeric variable DOB has the default length of 8.

```
CREATE TABLE CORP.MEMBER
  (NAME CHARACTER(28),
  DOB NUMERIC INFORMAT=DATE9.
  FORMAT=DATE9.);
```

```
NOTE: Table CORP.MEMBER created, with 0
      rows and 2 columns.
```

To create an empty SAS data file with the same variables as an existing file, use a CREATE TABLE statement with a LIKE clause, as in this example.

CREATE TABLE CORP.NX LIKE CORP.MEMBER;

The DESCRIBE TABLE statement provides information about attributes of variables in the form of a CREATE TABLE statement:

```
PROC SQL;
DESCRIBE TABLE CORP.MEMBER;
```

```
NOTE: SQL table CORP.MEMBER was created like:

create table CORP.MEMBER( bufsize=4096 )
  (
   NAME char(28),
   DOB num format=DATE9. informat=DATE9.
  );
```

To copy a SAS dataset, use the CREATE TABLE statement with as AS SELECT * FROM clause:

CREATE TABLE *SAS dataset* AS SELECT * FROM *SAS dataset*;

Add an ORDER BY clause with a list of columns to create a sorted copy.

To delete SAS data files and SQL views, use the DROP TABLE and DROP VIEW statements. This example deletes one SAS data file.

DROP TABLE WORK.OBSOLETE;

To remove all observations from a SAS data file, use the DELETE FROM statement.

DELETE FROM *SAS dataset*;

To change the names and other attributes of variables in a SAS data file, use secondary statements after the MODIFY statement in the DATASETS procedure. Use the INFORMAT, FORMAT, LABEL, and RENAME statements. The code model below shows the use of these statements.

```
PROC DATASETS LIBRARY=libref NOLIST;
  MODIFY SAS dataset;
    INFORMAT variable . . . informat . . . ;
    FORMAT variable . . . format . . . ;
    LABEL variable='label' . . . ;
    RENAME old name=new name . . . ;
RUN;
```

Copying

There are several ways to copy a SAS dataset in a SAS program, each with its own advantages and disadvantages.

- The COPY procedure is the most direct way to copy a SAS file. It is the only way to copy indexes along with a SAS dataset. It cannot change the member name of a SAS dataset that it copies or copy SAS datasets within the same library.
- Using a data step to copy a SAS dataset has several advantages. It is the most efficient way to make multiple copies at the same time, and the data step makes it possible to make changes in the data. It can create a standard SAS data file, regardless of the form of the SAS dataset being copied.
- The CREATE TABLE statement of SQL offers another way to copy data while making changes, such as computing additional variables.
- The SORT procedure is the way to copy a SAS dataset if you want the copy to have a different sort order.
- The APPEND procedure provides an efficient way to add observations from one SAS dataset to another.

To copy all the SAS files of one library to another, use the COPY procedure. Use the IN= and OUT= options in the PROC COPY statement to identify the libraries. No other statements are required.

```
PROC COPY IN=libref OUT=libref;
RUN;
```

To restrict the actions of the COPY procedure to specific member types, write the MTYPE= option in the PROC COPY statement. To copy only SAS datasets, indicate the member types DATA and VIEW, as shown here:

```
PROC COPY IN=libref OUT=libref MTYPE=(DATA VIEW);
RUN;
```

To copy only selected members of a library, add the SELECT statement to the PROC COPY step. This example copies WORK.STATUS to MAIN.STATUS.

```
PROC COPY IN=WORK OUT=MAIN;
  SELECT STATUS;
RUN;
```

Alternatively, use the EXCLUDE statement to copy all members except specific ones you mention.

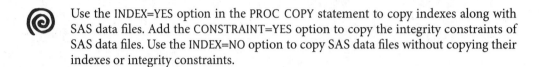

Use the INDEX=YES option in the PROC COPY statement to copy indexes along with SAS data files. Add the CONSTRAINT=YES option to copy the integrity constraints of SAS data files. Use the INDEX=NO option to copy SAS data files without copying their indexes or integrity constraints.

To copy a SAS file and change its name, first make the copy using the COPY procedure. Then use the CHANGE statement of the DATASETS procedure to change the name. This example copies WORK.STATUS to MAIN.STATE.

```
PROC COPY IN=WORK OUT=MAIN;
  SELECT STATUS;
RUN;
PROC DATASETS LIBRARY=MAIN NOLIST;
  CHANGE STATUS=STATE;
RUN;
```

```
NOTE: Copying WORK.STATUS to MAIN.STATUS (memtype=DATA).
NOTE: There were 141 observations read from the data set WORK.STATUS.
NOTE: The data set TEST.STATUS has 141 observations and 2 variables.

NOTE: Changing the name MAIN.STATUS to MAIN.STATE (memtype=DATA).
```

◆ The system options OBS= and FIRSTOBS= affect the COPY procedure. To copy all the observations of SAS data files, use the default values FIRSTOBS=1 OBS=MAX.

To copy a SAS dataset in a data step, use a SET statement, as shown in this code model.

```
DATA SAS dataset;
  SET SAS dataset;
RUN;
```

To make multiple copies, list several output SAS datasets in the DATA statement. To make changes in the data, add additional statements to the data step.

To copy observations from one SAS dataset to the end of another SAS dataset, use the APPEND procedure. This example copies the observations of ADD to the end of HERE.

```
PROC APPEND DATA=ADD OUT=HERE;
RUN;
```

The APPEND procedure works only if the two SAS datasets are reasonably similar to each other. Use the FORCE option in the PROC APPEND statement if the input SAS dataset has variables that are longer than those in the output SAS dataset or are not in the output SAS dataset. If the variable names do not match, use the RENAME= dataset option on the input SAS dataset to make them match.

To make a copy of a SAS dataset, use the APPEND procedure with an output SAS dataset that does not already exist. If necessary, you can delete the output SAS dataset beforehand with the DATASETS procedure, as shown in this example.

```
PROC DATASETS LIBRARY=WORK NOLIST NOWARN;
   DELETE TO (MTYPE=DATA);
RUN;
PROC APPEND DATA=WORK.FROM OUT=WORK.TO;
RUN;
```

To create a sorted copy of a SAS dataset, use the OUT= option in the SORT procedure. This example creates WORK.USSORT as a sorted copy of WORK.US.

```
PROC SORT DATA=WORK.US OUT=WORK.USSORT;
   BY KEY1 KEY2;
RUN;
```

For more information about sorting, see chapter 43, "Sorting."

Deleting

Use the DATASETS procedure to delete SAS datasets and other SAS files.

Before deleting a file, make sure that you no longer need the file and that you have correctly identified the file to delete.

To delete all the SAS files in a library, use the KILL option in the PROC DATASETS statement. This example deletes all SAS files in the WORK library.

```
PROC DATASETS LIBRARY=WORK NOLIST KILL;
RUN;
```

To delete specific SAS files from a library, list them in a DELETE statement. This example deletes the SAS data files WORK.TEMP and WORK.TEST.

```
PROC DATASETS LIBRARY=WORK MTYPE=DATA NOLIST NOWARN;
   DELETE TEMP TEST;
RUN;
```

Ordinarily, the DELETE statement writes a log note if the member to delete does not exist. Use the NOWARN option in the PROC DATASETS statement to suppress this log note.

The MTYPE= option can also be written in the DELETE statement, for example:

```
PROC DATASETS LIBRARY=WORK NOLIST NOWARN;
  DELETE TEMP TEST / MTYPE=DATA;
RUN;
```

Writing the option this way makes it possible to delete different member types in separate DELETE statements in the same step.

 To delete all but a few SAS files from a library, write a SAVE statement listing the members to keep. This example deletes everything from the WORK library except WORK.RESULT and WORK.FORMATS.

```
PROC DATASETS LIBRARY=WORK NOLIST NOWARN;
  SAVE RESULT FORMATS;
RUN;
```

 To delete all the observations from a SAS data file while keeping the variables, replace the SAS data file in a data step with a SET statement and a STOP statement, as shown in this code model.

```
DATA SAS dataset;
  SET SAS dataset;
  STOP;
RUN;
```

 A SAS dataset is automatically deleted when you replace it with a new SAS dataset of the same name. This deletion occurs as soon as the new SAS dataset is successfully written. To avoid accidentally deleting SAS datasets by replacing them, give each SAS dataset its own name.

 A SAS dataset can only replace another SAS dataset of the same kind. An error condition occurs if a new SAS dataset has the same name as a SAS dataset of a different kind. It is an error if you attempt to:

- replace a SAS data file with a view
- replace a view with a SAS data file
- replace a view with a different kind of view

To avoid the error, delete or rename the old SAS dataset before you create the new SAS dataset. Alternatively, use a new name for the new SAS dataset.

■ 9
Data Type and Length

Data type and length are the two attributes of a variable that control the way the variable holds data values.

SAS supports two data types. Every variable you create is one of these two types.

- The numeric data type organizes numeric values in the double-precision (8-byte floating-point) format that is native to the computer. Double precision provides a very accurate approximation of real numbers. The numeric data type also includes 27 distinct missing values.
- The character data type contains data values that are treated as a succession of characters. It can also contain any kind of data.

The length of a variable is the number of bytes it occupies when it is stored. Length has different implications for character and numeric variables. The length of a character variable determines how many characters or how much data the variable can contain. Character variables can have lengths from 1 to 32,768.

The length of a numeric variable determines how precise its values are when it is stored in a SAS dataset. The usual length of a numeric variable is 8, which provides the full accuracy of the double-precision format. A numeric variable can be as short as 3 bytes. In the IBM mainframe environment, a numeric variable can be as short as 2 bytes. The length has no direct effect on the way a variable is processed in a data step; in memory, numeric variables are always given the full 8 bytes.

The data type and length of a variable are determined when a variable is created, usually in a data step. Declaring the data type and length is not a strict requirement. It is often necessary to specifically indicate the length of a character variable. It is usually not necessary to declare a numeric variable.

 Use a LENGTH statement near the beginning of the data step to set the data types and lengths of variables. In the LENGTH statement, a $ indicates character variables. This is an example of a LENGTH statement:

    LENGTH NAME LOCATION $ 32 AGE 3;

This statement creates three variables. NAME and LOCATION are character variables with a length of 32. AGE is a numeric variable with a length of 3.

It is possible to change the length of a numeric variable in a subsequent LENGTH statement. When a character variable is created in a data step, its length is set and is not affected by any subsequent statement.

In a data step, if you read a character variable from a SAS dataset in a SET statement, the length of the variable in the SAS dataset determines its length in the data step.

If a data step reads the same character variable from more than one SAS dataset, it takes the variable's length from the first SAS dataset.

If you want the length in the data step to be something different, you can set a different length in a LENGTH statement. This works only if the LENGTH statement comes before the SET statement.

When you create variables as array elements, declare their type and length in the ARRAY statement. In this example, the terms $ 1 define the array's elements, RATING1-RATING10, as character variables with a length of 1.

```
ARRAY RATING{10} $ 1;
```

Many other data step statements can determine the data type of a variable and the length of a character variable. Variables are often defined by their appearance in the assignment, INPUT, and DO statements. The RETAIN statement can determine the data type of a variable and the length of a character variable if it provides an initial value for the variable.

In general, use the numeric data type for these kinds of variables:

- Values that are used in arithmetic.
- Variables for which statistics are computed.
- A variable that defines an axis of a graph.
- A measurement of the time of day (a SAS time value) or of elapsed time.
- A measurement of the date (a SAS date value).
- A measurement of the date and time of day (a SAS datetime value).
- A measurement of the day of the week (use Sunday=1, . . ., Saturday=7).
- Any other measurement of time.
- Logical (true and false) values (use Boolean values, 1 for true and 0 for false), especially if the variable is used in a regression or other statistical model.

Use the character data type for character strings, serial numbers and other identifying codes, flags, binary data objects, and any other kind of value not mentioned above for the numeric data type.

Make a character variable long enough to hold the longest character string that it may contain. For example, suppose a variable could contain these values:

RED   BLACK   ORANGE   YELLOW   WHITE   GRAY   GREEN

Set its length to 6, the length of the longest value. Consider giving the variable a longer length if you might subsequently want it to contain longer values.

 Truncation occurs when a character variable is not long enough to contain the values that are assigned to it. For example, suppose you expected a character variable to contain the values listed above, but you find instead that it contains these values:

RED   BLA   ORA   YEL   WHI   GRA   GRE

This is the effect of truncation. The values are only three characters long because that is the length of the variable. Revise the program to give the variable a sufficient length.

 In business data, names are usually truncated to a slight extent. Last names, for example, could theoretically be any length, but it is usually sufficient to give them a length of 16. So few last names are longer than 16 characters that there is little chance that confusion will result from shortening them to 16 characters. Limiting the length of a character variable in this way can save storage space and execution time.

      For the greatest efficiency, use a length that is a multiple of 8 when you truncate a variable this way.

 If a character variable has only a few different values, you can save storage space by using discrete binary encoding (chapter 30). This allows the variable to be stored with a length of 1, regardless of the lengths of the character strings it represents.

 Usually, use the default length of 8 for numeric variables.

 When it is important to save storage space, you can reduce the lengths of some numeric variables. Many variables contain small integer values. These variables can be shortened without losing any information. You can use a length of 3 for a variable that has integer values up to 8,192, or a length of 4 for a variable with integer values up to 2,097,152. A length of 4 is sufficient for SAS date values and for SAS time values that do not contain fractions of seconds.

 Other numeric variables can be shortened if precision is not a priority. A numeric variable with a length of 3 is still accurate to within a fraction of a percent.

 When fractional values (numeric values that are not exact integers) are stored with a length less than 8, their values may be altered by truncation. The truncation can result in comparisons that work incorrectly, as this program demonstrates:

```
DATA COMPARE;
  LENGTH X8 8 X6 6;
  RETAIN X8 X6 0.1;
RUN;
DATA _NULL_;
```

```
    SET COMPARE;
    PUT X8= X6=;
    IF X8 = X6 THEN PUT 'Equal';
    ELSE PUT 'Unequal';
RUN;
```

```
X8=0.1  X6=0.1
Unequal
```

Because of the truncation, the values of the two variables are slightly different. In this example, the difference is not large enough to be seen when the values are printed, but the comparison still indicates the difference.

 You can use the TRUNC function to duplicate the effects of truncating a numeric value. Use this function in comparisons with truncated variables, for example:

```
DATA COMPARE;
    LENGTH X8 8 X6 6;
    RETAIN X8 X6 0.1;
RUN;
DATA _NULL_;
    SET COMPARE;
    PUT X8= X6=;
    IF TRUNC(X8, 6) = X6 THEN PUT 'Equal';
    ELSE PUT 'Unequal';
RUN;
```

```
X8=0.1  X6=0.1
Equal
```

The second argument of the TRUNC function is the length to truncate to. The variable X6 has been truncated to 6 bytes, so the value of X8 can be made equal to it by truncating it to a length of 6 using the TRUNC function.

This process still works even if the truncated values are different enough to show a difference, as this example demonstrates.

```
DATA COMPARE;
    LENGTH X8 8 X4 4;
    RETAIN X8 X4 0.1;
RUN;
DATA _NULL_;
    SET COMPARE;
    PUT X8= X4=;
    IF TRUNC(X8, 4) = X4 THEN PUT 'Equal';
    ELSE PUT 'Unequal';
RUN;
```

```
X8=0.1  X4=0.0999999642
Equal
```

You can see that the values are different, but as in the previous example, the difference is only due to truncation. As a result, the truncated comparison finds the values to be equal.

■ 10

Text Data Files

Text data files are important in SAS because they are the standard for exchanging data between applications. They are used in everything from data center applications to spreadsheet programs, and the SAS language has features to read and write almost any kind of text data file.

Use data steps to access text files. Use an INFILE statement to identify an input text file and INPUT statements to read it. For an output text file, use a FILE statement to identify the file and PUT statements to write data to it.

Filerefs

A fileref is a one-word name for a text file. After you define a fileref, you can use the fileref in SAS statements and commands to refer to the file. Filerefs are also called file shortcuts.

An advantage of filerefs is that they work the same way in any operating system, even though different operating systems use very different file systems. SAS programs that use filerefs to refer to files can run in any operating system that SAS supports.

 Use a FILENAME statement to define a fileref for a text data file. In the FILENAME statement, write the fileref and a character constant that contains the physical file name. This is an example of a FILENAME statement:

FILENAME NEW "newtextdata.txt";

This statement defines the fileref NEW.

Alternatively, in some operating systems, you can use operating system commands to define filerefs.

 To concatenate several files that you plan to read in a data step, list the physical file names in parentheses in the FILENAME statement. This is an example:

FILENAME ALLDATA ("somedata.txt" "moredata.txt");

Filerefs are not just for text files. You can also assign filerefs to binary files and directories.

The filerefs CARDS, DATALINES, LOG, and PRINT have special meanings. DATALINES refers to data lines in a program file that a data step reads as input text data. CARDS is another name for DATALINES. LOG is the log file. PRINT is the standard print file. These filerefs are defined automatically. Do not write FILENAME statements to define them.

You can test the syntax of a program before you receive the text data file that the program starts from. Use the DUMMY device in place of the physical file name when you define the fileref, as shown in this example:

FILENAME X DUMMY;

When you read from this fileref, the SAS supervisor treats it the same as an empty file, and you get this log message:

NOTE: 0 records were read from the infile X.

If you write to a fileref defined with the DUMMY device, the SAS supervisor discards the output records without storing them anywhere.

To associate a fileref with a catalog entry that contains text, use the CATALOG device name after the device in the FILENAME statement and write the full four-level catalog name (in quotes) in place of the physical file name. This is an example:

FILENAME LINES CATALOG "WORK.TEMP.LINES.SOURCE";

You can define a fileref for a CATAMS, SOURCE, LOG, or OUTPUT entry and read it or write it with a data step.

To determine the definition of a fileref, write a FILENAME statement with the LIST option, for example:

FILENAME NEW LIST;

The statement writes a log message that identifies the physical file name associated with the fileref. To list information about all defined filerefs, use this statement:

FILENAME _ALL_ LIST;

To clear a fileref, write a FILENAME statement with the CLEAR option, for example:

FILENAME NEW CLEAR;

The statement removes the fileref definition.

Input Text Data

Use a data step to obtain data from a text data file. Write an INFILE statement to identify the input file and one or more INPUT statements to read the fields of the input records and create variables from them.

Both the INFILE and INPUT statements have far too many features to mention here. The INFILE statement has options for correctly interpreting various kinds of files. The INPUT statement uses many different kinds of terms for moving to points in the file and interpreting fields.

Write an INPUT statement to read one record from the input file. The automatic loop of the data step repeats the actions of the data step until the entire file is read.

To read a fixed-field text record, one in which fields are located at fixed positions in the record, use the formatted form of the INPUT statement. Write an informat after each variable name. Use the width of the field as the width argument of the informat.

To skip characters in the record, use the + pointer control. After the +, write an integer value that indicates the number of character positions to skip over. For example, use the pointer control +4 to skip 4 character positions.

This is an example of records from a fixed-field text data file:

```
A  1water
A  2high fructose corn syrup
A  3apple juice concentrate
```

In this record layout, the first character is a code that can be disregarded; the next three characters are a number that indicates a rank; and the next 40 characters are a character value, a name. The record can be read with this INPUT statement:

```
INPUT
  +1
  RANK F3.
  NAME $CHAR40.
  ;
```

The INPUT statement creates the variables RANK and NAME.

Usually, use the TRUNCOVER option in the INFILE statement for this kind of record. With the TRUNCOVER option in the INFILE statement, the INPUT statement can use short fields at the end of the record.

This could be a complete data step to read the file:

```
DATA WORK.COMPONENT;
  INFILE NEW TRUNCOVER;
  INPUT
    +1
    RANK F3.
    NAME $CHAR40.
    ;
RUN;
```

Top 5 Informats

Informats convert input text to data values. These are some of the most useful informats.

 $CHAR. This informat creates a character value with the exact text of the field.

 $F. The $F informat, also written as $, is useful for text values. It removes leading spaces and converts a period to a blank value.

 F. The standard numeric informat, also called F, reads standard numerals and scientific notation.

 COMMA. The COMMA informat reads numeric fields that might contain commas, dollar signs, and similar punctuation.

 $UPCASE. This informat converts text to uppercase letters.

DATA LINES

An input text data file can be placed in the program file. Write a DATALINES (or CARDS) statement at the end of the data step in place of the RUN statement. Place data lines after the DATALINES statement. After the data lines, write a line that contains a semicolon to mark the end of the data lines.

Use DATALINES (or CARDS) as the fileref in the INFILE statement. DATALINES is the default input fileref in a data step, so you usually can omit the INFILE statement.

```
DATA WORK.FITNESS;
    LENGTH LASTNAME $ 20 FIRSTNAME
      $ 16 SITUPS PUSHUPS CLIMBHT 8;
    INPUT LASTNAME FIRSTNAME SITUPS
      PUSHUPS CLIMBHT;
DATALINES;
HATTER HEATHER 40 12 12
MASTERS KRIS 28 9 12
NICELY MARTY 41 9 12
;
```

This example shows list input with the default delimiter, which is a space.

If it is possible that the data lines could contain semicolons, use a DATALINES4 statement instead of the DATALINES statement. Write a line of four semicolons after the data lines. This code model shows the use of the DATALINES4 statement:

```
DATALINES4;
data lines (may contain semicolons)
;;;;
```

 Alternatively, a fixed-field record can be read using the @ pointer control to indicate the column position of the beginning of each field. With this approach, the + pointer control is not necessary. The INPUT statement of the example above could be rewritten:

```
INPUT
    @2 RANK F3.
    @5 NAME $CHAR40.
    ;
```

 To read a delimited file, use the DLM= option in the INFILE statement to identify the delimiter character. Also use the DSD option if the file can contain quoted strings, as are found, for example, in a CSV file. The DSD option also makes it possible for fields to be empty. Declare the data types and lengths of the variables in a LENGTH statement, then read them using the list input style of the INPUT statement. In the INPUT statement, list the variable names in order. For details, see chapter 12, "Delimited Files."

The example below reads four fields from a CSV file, a comma-delimited file that can contain quoted strings.

```
DATA WORK.PARTS;
    LENGTH MODEL $ 8 PART $ 7
      DESCRIPTION $ 18 LOC 8;
    INFILE WR TRUNCOVER DLM=',' DSD;
    INPUT MODEL PART DESCRIPTION LOC;
RUN;
```

Output Text Data

Use a data step to write an output text data file. Identify the output file in the FILE statement and create the output record in the PUT statement.

If the purpose of a data step is to write an output text file, use the special name _NULL_ in place of a SAS dataset name in the DATA statement. The name _NULL_ tells the data step not to create an output SAS dataset.

 Write the fileref of the output text file in a FILE statement. There are options that can be used in the FILE statement, but they are usually not needed for text data files.

This example uses the file associated with the fileref RESULT as the output text file. The fileref would have been defined in an earlier FILENAME statement.

```
FILE RESULT;
```

Write a PUT statement to create an output record. In most cases, the PUT statement can be written with the same terms as an INPUT statement. You can also write character constants in a PUT statement to write constant fields.

The example below writes the same kind of fixed-field records that were read in an earlier example. It uses data from the SAS dataset WORK.COMP.

```
DATA _NULL_;
  SET WORK.COMP;
  FILE RESULT;
  PUT
    'A'
    RANK F3.
    NAME $CHAR40.
  ;
RUN;
```

The PUT statement above could also be written in this style:

```
PUT
  @1 'A'
  @2 RANK F3.
  @5 NAME $CHAR40.
  ;
```

You can use PUT or PUTLOG statements to write log messages. The PUTLOG statement's output is automatically directed to the log. Use the fileref LOG in the FILE statement to direct the output of the PUT statement to the log. LOG is the default output fileref in a data step, so the FILE statement is not always necessary.

A data step can create multiple output text data files. Write a FILE statement and a PUT statement for each file.

When there are multiple output text files, it is important to know that the FILE statement is an executable statement. This means you can use control flow statements, such as IF-THEN statements, to control FILE statements. A PUT statement writes to the file selected in the most recently executed FILE statement in the same observation.

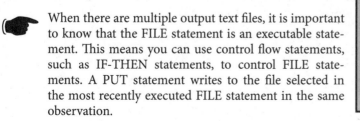

Top 5 Formats

Formats convert data values to output text to display or write in a text file. These are some of the most useful formats.

★ **$CHAR or $F.** Like the $CHAR informat, these formats keep a character value unchanged. But like all character formats, they can change the length of the value with a shorter or longer width argument.

★ **BEST.** The BEST format writes a number with as much precision as possible in the width of the field.

★ **F.** The standard numeric format, F, writes numbers in standard notation. Use the F format to specify the number of decimal places to write.

★ **COMMA.** This format writes numbers with commas between every three digits.

★ **DOLLAR.** This format writes numbers with commas and dollar signs.

■ 11

Data Fields

 To read and write most kinds of data fields that you are likely to encounter in text data files, use the informats and formats that are provided in base SAS software. This chapter describes how to work with a few other field types.

Scientific Notation

Scientific notation writes a number in two parts: a small mantissa is multiplied by an power of 10 indicated by the exponent part of the value. In computer data, scientific notation is most often written with an E between the mantissa and the exponent. For example, in 2.5E4, the mantissa is 2.5, and the exponent is 4. The number this indicates is 2.5×10^4, or 250,000.

Scientific notation may be written in various ways. Informats such as F and E read the forms of scientific notation generated by most computer software, and the E and BEST formats write scientific notation in two different ways. To read and write any other kind of scientific notation, handle the mantissa and exponent separately.

 To read a form of scientific notation that cannot be read with the F or E informats, read the mantissa and exponent as separate fields and compute the resulting value. The example below reads scientific notation written as shown here, with a 12-character mantissa and a signed 3-digit exponent.

```
4.0504893782+003
-1.000000000+000
6.1068455917-025
```

This code fragment reads the mantissa and exponent with the F informat and computes the value in the subsequent assignment statement.

```
INPUT MANTISSA F12. EXPONENT F4.;
VALUE = MANTISSA*10**EXPONENT;
PUT VALUE;
```

```
4050.4893782
-1
6.106846E-25
```

To write scientific notation as components:

1. Calculate the exponent.
2. Calculate the mantissa.
3. Write the mantissa and exponent along with any constant parts of the field.

The way the exponent is calculated depends on the rules used for the mantissa. Most scientific notation uses a mantissa of at least 1, but less than 10. The exponent can then be calculated with these statements.

```
IF VALUE THEN EXPONENT = FLOOR(LOG10(ABS(VALUE)));
ELSE EXPONENT = 0;
```

Another common form of scientific notation uses a fractional mantissa. The mantissa is less than 1, but not less than .1. This requires an exponent that is 1 greater than the value calculated above. The exponent can be calculated with these statements.

```
IF VALUE THEN EXPONENT = FLOOR(LOG10(ABS(VALUE))) + 1;
ELSE EXPONENT = 0;
```

Engineering notation is a form of scientific notation that uses a mantissa between 1 and 1000 and an exponent that is a multiple of 3. These statements calculate the exponent for engineering notation.

```
IF VALUE THEN EXPONENT = 3*FLOOR(LOG10(ABS(VALUE))/3);
ELSE EXPONENT = 0;
```

After the exponent is calculated, calculate the mantissa by dividing the value by that power of 10, as shown here.

```
MANTISSA = VALUE/10**EXPONENT;
```

The example below writes scientific notation in 10 characters, using two or (if necessary) three digits for the exponent, writing a lowercase e before the exponent, and using the remaining character positions for the mantissa and sign. The positioning of the written parts of the value depend on whether the mantissa or exponent has a negative sign.

```
DATA _NULL_;
  DO VALUE = 123456789, -.0000123456789, .123456789;
    IF VALUE THEN EXPONENT = FLOOR(LOG10(ABS(VALUE)));
    ELSE EXPONENT = 0;
    MANTISSA = VALUE/10**EXPONENT;
    IF 0 <= EXPONENT <= 99 THEN DO;
      IF MANTISSA >= 0 THEN PUT MANTISSA F7.5 'e' EXPONENT Z2.;
      ELSE PUT MANTISSA F7.4 'e' EXPONENT Z2.;
      END;
    ELSE IF EXPONENT >= -99 THEN DO;
      IF MANTISSA >= 0 THEN PUT MANTISSA F6.4 'e' EXPONENT Z3.;
      ELSE PUT MANTISSA F6.3 'e' EXPONENT Z3.;
      END;
```

```
        ELSE DO;
          IF MANTISSA >= 0 THEN PUT MANTISSA F5.3 'e' EXPONENT Z4.;
          ELSE PUT MANTISSA F5.2 'e' EXPONENT Z4.;
          END;
       END;
RUN;
```

```
1.23457e08
-1.235e-05
1.2346e-01
```

Signed Numerals

 Numeric informats read fields that contain + or − signs only if the sign comes immediately before the first digit (or the initial decimal point) of the numeral. If the sign is written in any other way, the field cannot be read with ordinary numeric informats, and it must be read in another way.

If a sign is found in the first position of a field with the possibility of spaces between the sign and the first digit, and the numeral is otherwise right-aligned in the field, read the field with the BZ informat.

Another approach does not require a field to be right-aligned. Read the field as a character value, remove all spaces with the COMPRESS function, then read the resulting value with the F informat. That logic is demonstrated in this example.

```
DATA _NULL_;
  INFILE DATALINES;
  INPUT FIELD $CHAR6.;
  FIELD  = COMPRESS(FIELD);
  VALUE = INPUT(FIELD, F6.);
  PUT VALUE;
DATALINES;
+     1
-   200
;
```

```
1
-200
```

If the sign is in a fixed position in the field, you can read the sign as a separate field and negate the value if the sign is a negative sign.

```
DATA _NULL_;
  INFILE DATALINES;
  INPUT SIGN $CHAR1. VALUE F5.;
  IF SIGN = '-' THEN VALUE = -VALUE;
  PUT VALUE;
DATALINES;
```

```
+     1
-   200
;
```

```
1
-200
```

Use a similar approach for signs that are written in a fixed position after the numeral.

In some fields, a negative sign is written as the last character of a right-aligned field. Read these fields as a character value, then check for the presence of the negative sign and read the numeric value accordingly, as shown in this example.

```
DATA _NULL_;
   INFILE DATALINES;
   INPUT FIELD $CHAR8.;
   IF SUBSTR(FIELD, 8) = '-' THEN VALUE = -INPUT(FIELD, F7.);
   ELSE VALUE = INPUT(FIELD, F8.);
   PUT VALUE;
DATALINES;
        0
      24-
    5.00-
;
```

```
0
-24
-5
```

To write a numeric field with a separate sign, write the absolute value and sign as separate variables. The example below writes a positive or negative sign separately at the beginning of the field.

```
DATA _NULL_;
   DO VALUE = -2 TO 2;
      SELECT (SIGN(VALUE));
         WHEN (-1) SIGN = '-';
         WHEN (1) SIGN = '+';
         OTHERWISE SIGN = ' ';
         END;
      IF SIGN(VALUE) = -1 THEN ABS = -VALUE;
      ELSE ABS = VALUE;
      PUT SIGN $CHAR1. ABS F7.3;
      END;
RUN;
```

```
-     2.000
-     1.000
      0.000
+     1.000
+     2.000
```

Use the PUT function to create a numeral in a character variable. You can then change the character variable in any way that is necessary before you write the numeral to an output file.

To write a positive sign immediately before the first digit of a numeric field, combine the positive sign and the numeral with the concatenation operator, as shown in this example:

```
DATA _NULL_;
  DO VALUE = -2 TO 2;
    IF VALUE > 0 THEN  FIELD = '+' || LEFT(PUT(VALUE, F6.));
    ELSE FIELD = LEFT(PUT(VALUE, F7.));
    PUT FIELD $CHAR7. -R;
    END;
RUN;
```

```
        -2
        -1
         0
        +1
        +2
```

In this example, the -R format modifier right-aligns the field. The actual value of the variable FIELD is left-aligned, but the alignment in the value does not matter when a format modifier is used to align the output field.

Implied Decimal Points

An implied decimal point is a decimal point that is not specifically written in a data field. For example, the field 2500 can represent the number 25 if there is an implied decimal point after the second digit.

Use a decimal argument with the F informat to read a field with an implied decimal point. This example reads a field that has two decimal places, but no written decimal point.

```
DATA _NULL_;
  INFILE DATALINES;
  INPUT VALUE F6.2;
  PUT VALUE;
DATALINES;
   314
  6400
;
```

```
3.14
64.00
```

To write a field with a specific number of decimal places without writing a decimal point, multiply the value by that power of 10 before writing it. Write it using the Z format with no decimal argument. The Z format is similar to the standard numeric format F, but it writes leading zeroes, which are often needed when a field uses an implied decimal point. This example writes a field with two implied decimal places.

```
DATA _NULL_;
  DO VALUE = .25, 1, 16;
    XVALUE = VALUE*100;
    PUT XVALUE Z6.;
    END;
RUN;
```

```
000025
000100
001600
```

Measured Strings

A file might contain a variable-length string as a field, with an earlier field indicating the length of the field. In a binary file, this might be a block of data, with an indication of the size of the block. Use the $VARYING informat to read and the $VARYING format to write variable-length fields. Be sure that the character variable involved is long enough to contain the largest length possible for the field.

The $VARYING informat and format work only in the INPUT and PUT statements, respectively, and they require a length variable as an additional argument to the informat or format. In input, the length variable should usually be the value that was read from the earlier field. In some cases, the length variable is not that value itself, but is calculated from it.

The example below is based on the kind of data records shown here. The second field in the record indicates the length of the third field.

```
FILE 4File1025
EDIT 4Edit1026
FRMT 6Format1027
LABL 5Label1028
TOOL 5Tools1029
WNDO 6Window1030
```

In this example, the $VARYING informat is used to read the variable-length field in the records shown above.

```
INPUT
  ABBR $CHAR4.
  NAMELEN F2.
  NAME $VARYING32. NAMELEN
  NUMBER F4.
  ;
```

The second time NAMELEN appears in the statement, it is as a length argument to the $VARYING informat.

The $VARYING format works in much the same way in the PUT statement. The length of the field must be available in a numeric variable that you write after the $VARYING format as the length argument.

Variable Number of Fields

In the same way that the length of a field can vary, the number of occurrences of a certain field in a record can vary. Use a DO loop to read the field the indicated number of times.

In this example, the first field in a record is a shipment ID. The second field is the number of packages in the shipment, and the subsequent fields are the package IDs for each of the packages. The DO loop reads up to 26 package IDs as elements of the array PKG. If there are more packages IDs, it does not read the additional fields, but it moves the pointer so that the fields that follow can be read correctly.

```
ARRAY PKG{26} $ 14;
. . .
INPUT SHIPMENT $CHAR11. PKGCOUNT 4. @;
DO I = 1 TO PKGCOUNT;
  IF I < DIM(PKG) THEN INPUT PKG{I} $CHAR14. @;
  ELSE INPUT +14 @;
  END;
INPUT WEIGHT 4. DATE YYMMDD6.;
```

In some cases, it might make more sense to create a separate output observation for each repetition of a field. This approach is especially likely when it is not just one field, but a set of related fields being repeated. Read the fields as individual variables rather than array elements, and use an OUTPUT statement inside the DO loop where the fields are read.

Continuation Character

Some text data files are written with a continuation character. When this character, often a hyphen, appears at the end of a line, it indicates that the data continues on the next line. This is an example of a record written this way:

```
Names: New Jersey, Delaware, Maryland, Virginia, North Carolina, South -
Carolina, Georgia, Florida
```

To read this kind of file, check the last nonblank character of each line for a continuation character. Combine records by copying them into a buffer variable until you find a line that does not end with the continuation character, as shown here:

```
INDEX = 1;
DO UNTIL (SUBSTR(BUFFER, INDEX, 1) NE '-');
  INPUT RECORD $F80.;
  IF INDEX <= VLENGTH(BUFFER) THEN SUBSTR(BUFFER, INDEX) = RECORD;
  INDEX = LENGTH(BUFFER);
  END;
```

This creates a single character variable BUFFER that contains the combined record. Be sure to declare this buffer variable with a sufficient length.

Typically, you will then need to divide the buffer variable into a series of text items. Chapter 25, "Parsing," shows how this may be done. To save storage space, do not store the variables BUFFER, INDEX, and RECORD in the output SAS dataset.

12

Delimited Files

A delimited file is a text data file that uses a designated character, a delimiter, to separate fields. Delimited files are often chosen as a compact way to store data because each field uses only as many characters as it needs in each record. The two most common delimiters are the comma and the tab character.

The tab is a control character specifically designated to separate fields. A file that uses the tab as a delimiter is a tab-delimited file. It is natural to use the tab as a delimiter; the tab is invisible, so no data value would contain a tab. Invisibility can also be a disadvantage. Tab-delimited data is harder to view and edit. When a visible delimiter is needed, the usual choice is the comma. The most common type of comma-delimited file is a comma separated values (CSV) file. Most database and spreadsheet programs import and export both tab-delimited and CSV files.

Another common delimiter is the space character. Space-delimited files can be used when it is not possible for a data value to contain a space.

Most examples in this chapter use comma-delimited data so that you can see the delimiter. The techniques for delimited data are essentially the same regardless of what character is chosen as the delimiter. This is an example of comma-delimited data:

```
1,George Washington,1789,1797
2,John Adams,1797,1801
3,Thomas Jefferson,1801,1809
4,James Madison,1809,1817
5,James Monroe,1817,1825
6,John Quincy Adams,1825,1829
7,Andrew Jackson,1829,1837
8,Martin Van Buren,1837,1841
9,William Henry Harrison,1841,1841
```

Use data step programming to read or write a delimited file.

Write the tab character as a character hexadecimal constant. In the ASCII character set, the tab character is:

'09'X

The EBCDIC tab character is:

'05'X

To read a delimited file, use the DLM= option in the INFILE statement. In the INPUT statement, use list input or the : (colon) informat modifier.

In the INFILE statement, the DELIMITER= or DLM= option identifies the delimiter character or characters. The value of the option is a character constant or variable. For a tab-delimited file on an ASCII computer, use this option:

DLM='09'X

For a comma-delimited file, use this option:

DLM=','

To read a CSV file, also use the DSD option. With the DSD option, fields can be enclosed in double quotes, and these fields can contain the delimiter character. The delimiter character inside the quotes is not a delimiter, and the quotes are not part of the value of the field.

The DSD option also means that each delimiter character is a separate delimiter. That is, if there are two consecutive delimiter characters, it means that there is a field between them, but the field is a null field, one that contains no characters. Without the DSD option, consecutive delimiter characters are considered to be a single delimiter, as is often the case in space-delimited files. Therefore, use the DSD option with any input delimited file that might contain null fields.

In the INPUT statement, write the variables in the order in which they appear in the file. Write the variable name by itself (a technique called list input) or write the variable name, a colon, and an informat. Either way, the INPUT statement looks for the delimiter to mark the end of the field.

This is an example of INFILE and INPUT statements to read the comma-delimited data records shown above.

```
DATA PRES;
  INFILE LIST DLM=',' DSD;
  INPUT NUMBER NAME : $F32. STARTYEAR ENDYEAR;
RUN;
```

This example could also be written this way:

```
DATA PRES;
  LENGTH NUMBER 8 NAME $ 32 STARTYEAR ENDYEAR 8;
  INFILE LIST DLM=',' DSD;
  INPUT NUMBER NAME STARTYEAR ENDYEAR;
RUN;
```

If you define all the variables in order in a LENGTH statement, you can use the _ALL_ abbreviated variable list in the INPUT statement, as shown below. This way, you do not have to repeat the same list of variables in the INPUT statement, because the special name _ALL_ stands for the complete list of variables.

```
DATA PRES;
  LENGTH NUMBER 8 NAME $ 32 STARTYEAR ENDYEAR 8;
  INFILE LIST DLM=',' DSD;
  INPUT (_ALL_) (:);
RUN;
```

In the simplest cases you can write a delimited file in nearly the same way you read it. Use the DLM= option in the FILE statement. Write the fields using list output.

This example writes records like the records that are read in the example above.

```
DATA _NULL_;
  SET PRES;
  FILE OUT DLM=',';
  PUT NUMBER NAME STARTYEAR ENDYEAR;
RUN;
```

This approach works only if none of the variables contain the delimiter character and it is okay to remove leading and trailing spaces.

 Use the DSD option in the FILE statement whenever you write a CSV file. With the DSD option the PUT statement writes double quotes around any field that contains the delimiter character. This makes a valid CSV file even if some data values contain commas. The FILE statement might be:

```
FILE OUT DSD DLM=',';
```

This is an example of CSV data with some fields quoted because they contain commas:

```
1,"Washington, George",1789,1797
2,"Adams, John",1797,1801
```

Without the DSD option, the data would be written without the quote characters, and Washington and George would appear to be separate fields.

 If leading and trailing spaces are an essential part of character values that you write to a delimited file, then it may be necessary to keep track of the lengths of the values in the data step and write them using the $VARYING format. See chapter 26, "Variable-Length Strings," for details.

If it is only the leading spaces that are significant, and trailing spaces do not matter, or if you need to write the full fixed length of the variable for any other reason, write the variable using the $CHAR format and do not use the : modifier. Write the delimiter after the variable as a character constant. This way, you write the full length of the variable including any leading and trailing spaces. The example below writes three character variables with ASCII tab characters between them.

```
PUT STATE $CHAR. '09'X CITY $CHAR. '09'X LOCATION $CHAR.;
```

REMOVING DELIMITERS FROM CHARACTER DATA

In an ordinary delimited file, a data value cannot contain the delimiter character. You might need to check every character variable and remove the delimiter character wherever you find it.

First, define an array using the abbreviated variable list _CHARACTER_. The array includes all character variables defined in the data step. Write this statement after the statements that define the variables.

```
ARRAY CHAR{*} _CHARACTER_;
```

Then, the following statements remove all commas from character variables in the data step.

```
DO I = 1 TO DIM(CHAR);
  CHAR{I} = COMPRESS(CHAR{I}, ',');
  END;
```

Similarly, the statements below find ASCII tab characters in character variables and convert them to spaces.

```
DO I = 1 TO DIM(CHAR);
  CHAR{I} = TRANSLATE(CHAR{I}, ' ', '09'X);
  END;
```

EXPORTING WITH VARIABLE LABELS

When you export data to a spreadsheet, you may want to include a header record that contains the labels of the variables. The program below creates this kind of file. It writes a tab-delimited file of all the variables in a SAS dataset, with a header record containing the labels of the variables. To use this program, substitute the actual name of the input SAS dataset and the fileref of the output text file.

```
DATA _NULL_;
  LENGTH TYPE $ 1 FMT $ 32;
  * Labels, character values, and fields are limited to these maximum lengths.;
  LENGTH LABEL $ 40 CVAL FIELD $ 256;
  * Output text file.;
  FILE OUT DLM='09'X LRECL=8192;  * ASCII '09'X EBCDIC '05'X ;
  * Input SAS dataset.;
  DSID = OPEN('WORK.MYDATA');
  * Write labels of variables.;
  NVARS = ATTRN(DSID, 'NVARS');
  IF _N_ = 1 THEN DO N = 1 TO NVARS;
    LABEL = VARLABEL(DSID, N);
    IF LABEL = '' THEN LABEL = VARNAME(DSID, N);
    PUT LABEL @;
    END;
  PUT ;
  * Read and write data.;
  NOBS = ATTRN(DSID, 'NLOBS');
  DO I = 1 TO NOBS;
    RC = FETCH(DSID);
    IF RC THEN LEAVE;
    DO N = 1 TO NVARS;
      TYPE = VARTYPE(DSID, N);
      FMT = VARFMT(DSID, N);
      LEN = VARLEN(DSID, N);
      SELECT (TYPE);
        WHEN('C') DO;
          IF FMT = '' THEN FMT =
            '$CHAR' || TRIM(LEFT(PUT(LEN, F5.))) || '.';
          CVAL = GETVARC(DSID, N);
          FIELD = PUTC(CVAL, FMT);
          END;
        WHEN('N') DO;
          IF FMT = '' THEN FMT = 'BEST12.';
          NVAL = GETVARN(DSID, N);
          FIELD = PUTN(NVAL, FMT);
          END;
        END;
      PUT FIELD @;
      END;
    PUT ;
    END;
  RC = CLOSE(DSID);
  STOP;
RUN;
```

On an EBCDIC system, change the DLM= option to DLM='05'X, the EBCDIC tab character.

This program uses low-level I/O routines to determine the number of variables in the input SAS dataset and their labels and values. Because it works this way, it can work with any input SAS dataset, regardless of what variables it contains.

■ 13
Hierarchical Files

A hierarchy is a top-down arrangement of objects. It arranges objects into levels. Each object is associated with one object in the next higher level. Each person in a military hierarchy, for example, reports to just one superior officer. In taxonomy, each species of plants or animals belongs to a genus, each genus belongs to a family, each family belongs to an order, and so on.

A hierarchical file is a hierarchy in a text data file. There are different kinds of records for each level of the hierarchy. It is the order of records that indicates the association of one record at one level of the hierarchy to another record at the next higher level of the hierarchy.

Using the taxonomy example, each order record is followed by the records for the families that the order contains, each family record is followed by the records for the genuses in the family, and each genus record is followed by the records for the species in the genus. To find out what genus and family a species belongs to, you can find the species record in the file, then find the genus and family records that precede it.

As in any text data file that has multiple record types, there is a code in the record that indicates the type of the record. Usually, each record type has a different record layout, so you need to read the record type before you read the rest of the record.

SAS data is strictly table-oriented; that is, each file contains just one kind of record. However, this does not mean it is difficult to work with a hierarchical file in a SAS program. The data step logic required to read or write a hierarchical file follows a simple pattern.

This is an example of a hierarchical file of taxonomy data:

```
O Arales
F Acoraceae
G Acorus                    sweet flag
S Acorus americanus         sweet flag
S Acorus calamus            sweet flag
F Araceae
G Arisaema
S Arisaema dracontium       dragonroot
S Arisaema triphyllum       jack-in-the-pulpit
S Arisaema atrorubens
S Arisaema triphyllum
G Calla
S Calla palustris           wild calla
G Peltandra
```

```
S Peltandra virginica      tuckahoe
G Symplocarpus
S Symplocarpus foetidus    skunk cabbage
F Lemnaceae
G Lemna                     duckweed
S Lemna aequinoctialis     lesser duckweed
S Lemna minor              common duckweed
S Lemna obscura            purple duckweed
S Lemna perpusilla         least duckweed
S Lemna trisulca           forked duckweed
S Lemna turionifera        perennial duckweed
S Lemna polyrrhiza         giant duckweed
G Wolffia                   water-meal
S Wolffia borealis         Northern water-meal
S Wolffia brasiliensis     Brazilian water-meal
S Wolffia columbiana       common water-meal
O Asterales
F Asteraceae
G Achillea                  yarrow
S Achillea millefolium     common yarrow
S Achillea ptarmica        sneezeweed
G Ambrosia                  ragweed
S Ambrosia artemisiifolia  common ragweed
S Ambrosia psilostachya    western ragweed
S Ambrosia tomentosa       bur ragweed
S Ambrosia trifida         giant ragweed
...
```

In this file, the codes O, F, G, and S identify records for orders, families, genuses, and species. Each record contains a scientific name and, in some, a common name.

Input

To read a hierarchical file and create a SAS dataset from it, read the record type code and process each record type separately in a SELECT block. When you read a record at one level, set the values of all lower-level variables to missing. Use a global RETAIN statement so that variables are not otherwise set to missing.

Write an output observation for only the lowest level of the hierarchy. Alternatively, create a separate SAS dataset for each level of the hierarchy.

This program reads the file shown above to create the SAS dataset TAX.MAGNOL.

```
DATA TAX.MAGNOL (DROP=RECORDTYPE);
  RETAIN;
  LENGTH ORDER FAMILY $ 24
     GENUS GENUSC SPECIES SPECIESC $ 32;
  INFILE MAGNOLIO TRUNCOVER;
  INPUT @1 RECORDTYPE $CHAR1. @;
  SELECT (RECORDTYPE);
    WHEN ('O') DO;
      INPUT @3 ORDER $CHAR24.;
      FAMILY = '';
      GENUS = ''; GENUSC = '';
      SPECIES = ''; SPECIESC = '';
      END;
    WHEN ('F') DO;
      INPUT @3 FAMILY $CHAR24.;
```

```
      GENUS = ''; GENUSC = '';
      SPECIES = ''; SPECIESC = '';
      END;
    WHEN ('G') DO;
      INPUT @3 GENUS $CHAR24. @28 GENUSC $CHAR24.;
      SPECIES = ''; SPECIESC = '';
      END;
    WHEN ('S') DO;
      INPUT @3 SPECIES $CHAR24. @28 SPECIESC $CHAR24.;
      OUTPUT;
      END;
    OTHERWISE ;
    END;
RUN;
```

The excerpt below shows the form of the resulting SAS dataset (with the variable GENUSC omitted and some values truncated). Although organized in table form, the SAS dataset contains the same data values as the original hierarchy.

Obs	ORDER	FAMILY	GENUS	SPECIES	SPECIESC
1	Arales	Acoraceae	Acorus	Acorus americanus	sweet flag
2	Arales	Acoraceae	Acorus	Acorus calamus	sweet flag
3	Arales	Araceae	Arisaema	Arisaema dracontium	dragonroot
4	Arales	Araceae	Arisaema	Arisaema triphyllum	jack-in-the-pulpit
5	Arales	Araceae	Arisaema	Arisaema atrorubens	
6	Arales	Araceae	Arisaema	Arisaema triphyllum	
7	Arales	Araceae	Calla	Calla palustris	wild calla
8	Arales	Araceae	Peltandra	Peltandra virginica	tuckahoe
9	Arales	Araceae	Symplocarpus	Symplocarpus foetidu	skunk cabbage
10	Arales	Lemnaceae	Lemna	Lemna aequinoctialis	lesser duckweed
11	Arales	Lemnaceae	Lemna	Lemna minor	common duckweed
12	Arales	Lemnaceae	Lemna	Lemna obscura	purple duckweed
13	Arales	Lemnaceae	Lemna	Lemna perpusilla	least duckweed
14	Arales	Lemnaceae	Lemna	Lemna trisulca	forked duckweed
15	Arales	Lemnaceae	Lemna	Lemna turionifera	perennial duckweed
16	Arales	Lemnaceae	Lemna	Lemna polyrrhiza	giant duckweed
17	Arales	Lemnaceae	Wolffia	Wolffia borealis	Northern water-mea
18	Arales	Lemnaceae	Wolffia	Wolffia brasiliensis	Brazilian water-me
19	Arales	Lemnaceae	Wolffia	Wolffia columbiana	common water-meal
20	Asteral	Asteraceae	Achillea	Achillea millefolium	common yarrow
21	Asteral	Asteraceae	Achillea	Achillea ptarmica	sneezeweed
22	Asteral	Asteraceae	Ambrosia	Ambrosia artemisiifo	common ragweed
23	Asteral	Asteraceae	Ambrosia	Ambrosia psilostachy	western ragweed
24	Asteral	Asteraceae	Ambrosia	Ambrosia tomentosa	bur ragweed
25	Asteral	Asteraceae	Ambrosia	Ambrosia trifida	giant ragweed

Another approach is to create a separate SAS dataset for each level of the hierarchy. The program below revises the previous example to create SAS datasets at the family, genus, and species levels. The changes are in the DATA and OUTPUT statements.

```
DATA
  TAX.FAMILY (KEEP=ORDER FAMILY)
  TAX.GENUS (KEEP=FAMILY GENUS GENUSC)
  TAX.SPECIES (KEEP=GENUS SPECIES SPECIESC)
  ;
```

```
   RETAIN;
   LENGTH ORDER FAMILY $ 24
      GENUS GENUSC SPECIES SPECIESC $ 32;
   INFILE MAGNOLIO TRUNCOVER;
   INPUT @1 RECORDTYPE $CHAR1. @;
   SELECT (RECORDTYPE);
      WHEN ('O') DO;
         INPUT @3 ORDER $CHAR24.;
         FAMILY = '';
         GENUS = ''; GENUSC = '';
         SPECIES = ''; SPECIESC = '';
         END;
      WHEN ('F') DO;
         INPUT @3 FAMILY $CHAR24.;
         GENUS = ''; GENUSC = '';
         SPECIES = ''; SPECIESC = '';
         OUTPUT TAX.FAMILY;
         END;
      WHEN ('G') DO;
         INPUT @3 GENUS $CHAR24. @28 GENUSC $CHAR24.;
         SPECIES = ''; SPECIESC = '';
         OUTPUT TAX.GENUS;
         END;
      WHEN ('S') DO;
         INPUT @3 SPECIES $CHAR24. @28 SPECIESC $CHAR24.;
         OUTPUT TAX.SPECIES;
         END;
      OTHERWISE ;
      END;
   RUN;
```

The SAS dataset at each level must contain the identifying variable of the next higher level so that the hierarchical connections are maintained. This is an excerpt of the output SAS dataset TAX.FAMILY:

Obs	ORDER	FAMILY
1	Arales	Acoraceae
2	Arales	Araceae
3	Arales	Lemnaceae
4	Asterales	Asteraceae

The output below is an excerpt of the output SAS dataset TAX.GENUS. The values of the variable FAMILY are the same values that are found in TAX.FAMILY.

Obs	FAMILY	GENUS	GENUSC
1	Acoraceae	Acorus	sweet flag
2	Araceae	Arisaema	
3	Araceae	Calla	
4	Araceae	Peltandra	
5	Araceae	Symplocarpus	
6	Lemnaceae	Lemna	duckweed
7	Lemnaceae	Wolffia	water-meal
8	Asteraceae	Achillea	yarrow
9	Asteraceae	Ambrosia	ragweed

Similarly, in the output SAS dataset TAX.SPECIES, below, the values of the variable GENUS are the same as those found above in TAX.GENUS.

Obs	GENUS	SPECIES	SPECIESC
1	Acorus	Acorus americanus	sweet flag
2	Acorus	Acorus calamus	sweet flag
3	Arisaema	Arisaema dracontium	dragonroot
4	Arisaema	Arisaema triphyllum	jack-in-the-pulpit
5	Arisaema	Arisaema atrorubens	
6	Arisaema	Arisaema triphyllum	
7	Calla	Calla palustris	wild calla
8	Peltandra	Peltandra virginica	tuckahoe
9	Symplocarpus	Symplocarpus foetidus	skunk cabbage
10	Lemna	Lemna aequinoctialis	lesser duckweed
11	Lemna	Lemna minor	common duckweed
12	Lemna	Lemna obscura	purple duckweed
13	Lemna	Lemna perpusilla	least duckweed
14	Lemna	Lemna trisulca	forked duckweed
15	Lemna	Lemna turionifera	perennial duckweed
16	Lemna	Lemna polyrrhiza	giant duckweed
17	Wolffia	Wolffia borealis	Northern water-meal
18	Wolffia	Wolffia brasiliensis	Brazilian water-meal
19	Wolffia	Wolffia columbiana	common water-meal
20	Achillea	Achillea millefolium	common yarrow
21	Achillea	Achillea ptarmica	sneezeweed
22	Ambrosia	Ambrosia artemisiifolia	common ragweed
23	Ambrosia	Ambrosia psilostachya	western ragweed
24	Ambrosia	Ambrosia tomentosa	bur ragweed
25	Ambrosia	Ambrosia trifida	giant ragweed

Output

If a SAS dataset contains grouped data in sorted order, you can write it as a hierarchical file in a data step. Use a BY statement to identify the key variables that form the levels of the hierarchy. Write the higher-level records only on the first observation of a BY group.

This example creates a hierarchical file with the same format as the file that was read in the previous example. It gets its data from the SAS dataset TAX.FERN, which has the same structure as TAX.MAGNOL. The program first sorts the SAS dataset, then uses a data step to create the text data file.

```
PROC SORT DATA=TAX.FERN OUT=WORK.FERNS;
  BY ORDER FAMILY GENUS SPECIES;
RUN;
DATA _NULL_;
  SET WORK.FERNS;
  BY ORDER FAMILY GENUS SPECIES;
  FILE FERN;
  IF FIRST.ORDER THEN PUT @1 'O' @3 ORDER $F24.;
  IF FIRST.FAMILY THEN PUT @1 'F' @3 FAMILY $F24.;
  IF FIRST.GENUS THEN PUT @1 'G' @3 GENUS $F24. @28 GENUSC $F24.;
  PUT @1 'S' @3 SPECIES $F24. @28 SPECIESC $F24.;
  OUTPUT;
RUN;
```

■ 14

Binary Files

In SAS programming, binary data files are treated as a special kind of text file. Binary files are not text files, but you can access them using the same statements: FILENAME, INFILE, INPUT, FILE, and PUT.

A binary file is usually accessed in one of the following ways:

- *As a byte stream.* When a file is considered as a byte stream, each byte in the file is considered in order. The file is a sequence of bytes.
- *As a word stream.* The difference between a byte stream and a word stream is that the basic unit of data in a word stream is larger than a byte. Usually, it is 2, 4, or 8 bytes.
- *As fixed-length records.* If a binary file is organized as fixed-length records, you can treat it the same as a text file. The only difference is that it contains binary fields.
- *With direct access.* Use this technique to access parts of a binary file that are located at specific byte addresses.

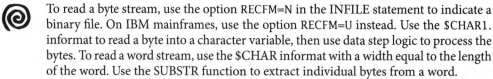

To read a byte stream, use the option RECFM=N in the INFILE statement to indicate a binary file. On IBM mainframes, use the option RECFM=U instead. Use the $CHAR1. informat to read a byte into a character variable, then use data step logic to process the bytes. To read a word stream, use the $CHAR informat with a width equal to the length of the word. Use the SUBSTR function to extract individual bytes from a word.

The only pointer control you are likely to use in a byte stream or word stream is the + pointer control. Use it to skip ahead in the file, or use it with a negative value (in parentheses) to back up in order to reread a section of the file.

To write a byte stream, write the RECFM=N (or U) option in the FILE statement. Use the $CHAR1. or S370FPIB1. format to write each byte. To write a word stream, use the $CHAR format with a width equal to the length of the word. Usually, do not use any pointer controls when writing a byte stream or word stream.

To read or write fixed-length records, use the RECFM=F option in the INFILE or FILE statement. Use the LRECL= option to set the record length. Work with binary fields using binary informats or formats.

To use direct access techniques with a binary file, use the RECFM=N (or U) option in the INFILE or FILE statement. Use the column pointer control @ to move to a specific byte address in the file. Think of this as treating the entire file as a single record. With the RECFM=N (or U) option, you cannot use line pointer controls.

 If the bytes of a field could contain any binary value, then the field is considered a binary field. Use binary fields only in binary files and files with fixed record lengths. In ordinary text files, some of the binary values that could occur in a binary field would be seen as control characters, and that could lead a program that reads the file to identify its records incorrectly.

 Do not use the $F (or $) informat with a binary field. This informat moves leading spaces to the end of the value, which can be good for text data, but is bad for binary data.

 Use the $CHAR informat to read the binary value of a field into a character variable. Make the character variable the same length as the width of the field. Use the $CHAR format to write the binary value of a character variable as a binary field.

These ideas may help you work with character variables that contain binary data:

- To compare the binary value of a character variable to a binary constant value, write the constant value as a character hexadecimal constant. For example, 255 in hexadecimal is FF, so to test whether the value of the character variable BYTE is a binary 255, write the condition (BYTE = 'FF'X).
- Use the SUBSTR function to isolate a specific byte or segment of a value. For example, the expression (SUBSTR(IPB, 2, 1) = 'FF'X) tests whether the second byte of IPB is 255.
- To convert a binary value of a character variable to a form that is easier to examine and manipulate, use the $HEX or $BINARY formats. The $HEX format converts each byte to two hexadecimal characters, which is especially useful if you want to examine four-bit parts of the value. This example converts the value of BYTE to hexadecimal in order to test the second hexadecimal digit:

  IF SUBSTR(PUT(BYTE, $HEX2.), 2, 1) = 'C' THEN . . .

- Use the $BINARY format to convert each bit of the binary value to a separate character, a 0 or 1 character. This lets you examine the specific bits of a binary value.
- A field in which a byte is divided into its individual bits can be treated as a bitfield. See chapter 31, "Bitfields," for details.
- If you store a character variable containing binary data in a SAS dataset, setting the transcode attribute of the variable to NO prevents SAS from incorrectly treating the values as text in some circumstances, such as moving the data to another computing environment. Set this attribute in the ATTRIB statement, for example:

  ATTRIB BYTE TRANSCODE=NO;

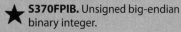

Binary Integer Informats and Formats

For each of the six kinds of binary integer fields, there is an informat and format. The informat and corresponding format use the same name.

★ **S370FPIB.** Unsigned big-endian binary integer.

★ **S370FIB.** Signed big-endian binary integer.

★ **PIBR.** Unsigned little-endian binary integer.

★ **IBR.** Signed little-endian binary integer.

★ **PIB.** Unsigned native binary integer.

★ **IB.** Signed native binary integer.

 These are situations in which you would not use the $CHAR informat and format with a binary field:

- If the bytes are in the opposite order from what you would expect, use the $REVERJ informat and format to reverse the order of the bytes.
- If a binary field varies in length, use the $VARYING informat to read it and the $VARYING format to write it.
- The null character is used to fill any empty spaces in most binary files. Write a null character as the constant value '00'X in the PUT statement. Use a repetition factor to write a sequence of null characters, for example, 32*'00'X. If the number of bytes of filler is not a constant, but can be determined in the logic of the data step, use a DO loop to write the null bytes.

 To read integer values from binary fields, use any of the SAS binary integer informats. Use a format of the same name to write the field.

Binary integer fields are defined based on these properties:

- *Sign bit.* A signed integer field has a sign bit as its most significant bit. If there is a 1 in this bit, a constant value (128 for a one-byte field) is subtracted to produce a negative number. As a result, the field can contain negative, zero, or positive values. An unsigned field does not have a sign bit. It can contain only 0 and positive values.
- *Byte order.* The bytes of a field can be in mathematical order or in the reverse order. A big-endian field starts with the most significant byte of the value. A little-endian field has its bytes reversed to start with the least significant byte. A native field is big-endian or little-endian, depending on which is most natural in the environment where it is running. Byte order is not an issue for fields that are only one byte in length.
- *Length.* Use the width argument of informat or format to set the length of the field. The length can be 1 to 8 bytes for any integer informat or format.

 To read the numeric value of a byte or other binary field, use the S370FPIB informat. For a one-byte field, the result of the informat is a whole number from 0 to 255. For a two-byte field, it is a whole number from 0 to 32,767. Use the corresponding format to write a numeric value as a binary field.

For example, a 16-bit stereo audio block contains a sequence of four-byte samples. Each sample contains two two-byte unsigned integer values, one for the left channel and one for the right channel of the stereo signal. The DO loop below reads the data of an audio block and writes an observation for each sample.

```
DO C = 1 TO BLOCKSIZE/4;
  INPUT (LEFT RIGHT) (S370FPIB2.);
  OUTPUT;
  END;
```

 With a width of 1, the PIB informat and format are the same as the S370FPIB informat and format.

 One's complement integer values, once common but now rare, use the sign bit to indicate the negative of the value contained in the rest of the field. To interpret the value of a one's complement field, start by using the $CHAR informat and $BINARY format to convert the value to a string of 0s and 1s.

The example below shows the actions needed to interpret a two-byte big-endian one's complement field.

```
INPUT FIELD $CHAR2.;
BITS = PUT(FIELD, $BINARY16.);
VALUE = INPUT(SUBSTR(BITS, 2, 15), BINARY15.);
IF BITS =: '1' THEN VALUE = -VALUE;
```

 When it is necessary to write a binary value as text data, the easiest way to write it uses two hexadecimal digits for each byte of the binary value. This is called a binhex representation of data. It makes it possible to send binary data through e-mail or in other places that handle text characters correctly, but cannot be relied upon to handle other kinds of data accurately.

Use the $HEX format to write binhex data and the $HEX informat to read binhex data. If a byte value is in a numeric variable, write it with the HEX2. format and read it with the HEX2. informat.

Floating-Point Informats and Formats

Floating-point fields can contain both integers and fractional numbers. Use these floating-point informats and formats for any of these common types of floating-point fields.

 RB. Native double precision.

 FLOAT. Native single precision.

 IEEE. IEEE (the kind used by most computers).

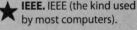 **S370FRB.** IBM mainframe.

15

Value Formats

Formats convert data values to text for displaying or printing. Value formats are formats that you can create to convert specific data values or ranges of values to specific text labels.

Use the VALUE statement of the FORMAT procedure to create a value format. The VALUE statement includes these terms:

- a format name
- format options
- ranges, sets of data values
- labels, text values that the format produces for specific ranges

A format works with values of one specific data type, either numeric or character. The data type is indicated in the name of a value format, and the data values that are indicated in the ranges of the format are values of that data type. The labels of a value format are always character values because the purpose of a format is to produce text to display or print.

Consider these limitations when you select a name for a value format:

- The name of a character format must begin with a dollar sign ($). This indicates the data type of the format.
- Shorter names are easier to use. The total length of the name, including the dollar sign in the name of a character format, cannot be more than 32 characters.
- The first character of the name of a numeric format must be a letter or underscore. In the name of a character format, the second character must be a letter or underscore.
- The last character of a format name cannot be a digit.
- All formats should have distinct names. Do not use the name of a SAS format for any format you create. Do not reuse the name of any other format that might be used in the same project.

Format options for value formats include the MIN=, MAX=, and DEFAULT= options, which set the minimum, maximum, and default width of the format. Another option, the FUZZ= option, can be used for numeric value formats. This option extends values and intervals by a small amount to cover values that almost match a value or interval. For example, with the option FUZZ=.01, values that are within .01 of a value in a range are considered to fall within the range. Write format options in parentheses after the format name.

 A range can be:

- a single value, such as 0.
- an interval, such as 2-99.
- a comma-separated list of single values and intervals, such as 0, 1, 2-99.
- the special keyword OTHER, which includes all values that do not fall into any other range.

When writing intervals, use a less-than sign (<) before or after the hyphen to exclude an endpoint from the interval. For example, the interval 0<-<1 includes all values between 0 and 1, but it does not include 0 or 1. You can use the special keywords LOW and HIGH as interval endpoints. LOW is the lowest possible value; HIGH is the highest possible value. For example, the interval 99<-HIGH includes all values greater than 99.

After each range, write an equals sign and a label. Write the label as a character constant.

The example below creates the value format LVR, which formats numeric values as `True` and `False`, according to the way SAS treats logical values.

```
PROC FORMAT;
VALUE LVR
   ._-.Z, 0 = 'False'
   LOW-<0, 0<-HIGH = 'True'
   ;
RUN;
```

 After you define a value format, use it the same way you would use any format. Value formats can be used in the PUT statement, the PUT function, the FORMAT statement, and window definitions. The example below demonstrates the use of the LVR format.

```
VALUE = 5;
PUT VALUE LVR.;
```

True

 If you use a value format as the format attribute of a variable in a SAS dataset that you store permanently, make sure the value format is available whenever the SAS dataset might be used. The value format should usually be stored in a format catalog. See chapter 18, "Format Catalogs and Control Datasets," for details.

Use value formats to display the full text of values that are stored as short codes. Consider, for example, a variable in which a value of E really means Eastern Conference and a value of W means Western Conference. You can write that text using the format $CFN defined in these statements.

```
PROC FORMAT;
VALUE $CFN
  'E' = 'Eastern Conference'
  'W' = 'Western Conference'
;
RUN;
```

Define value formats with intervals as ranges to group numeric values into ranges for reporting or analysis. This example defines the format XRANGE to group scores from 0 to 100 into three ranges, Low, Medium, and High.

```
PROC FORMAT;
VALUE XRANGE
  0-71 = 'Low'
  72-85 = 'Medium'
  86-100 = 'High'
;
RUN;
```

Use a format such as this one as the format of a class variable or categorical variable in a proc step to make the variable form only a few groups of observations.

Sometimes report mockups are created with X's in place of the digits of the numbers in the report. With the report mockup, you can show the layout of the report without showing the actual numeric data. To create a value format for this purpose, define intervals based on the number of digits in the value. This step creates the format XXX that displays X's in place of digits.

```
PROC FORMAT;
PICTURE XXX
  LOW--1E4 = '-XXXXX'
  -1E4<--1000 = ' -XXXX'
  -1000<--100 = ' -XXX'
  -100<--10 = ' -XX'
  -10<-<0 = ' -X'
  0-<10 = ' X'
  10-<100 = ' XX'
  100-<1000 = ' XXX'
  1000-<1E4 = ' XXXX'
  1E4-<1E5 = ' XXXXX'
  1E5-HIGH = 'XXXXXX'
;
RUN;
```

The XXX format displays numbers as sequences of X's, as shown here:

```
Minimum      Mean    Maximum

   -XX       XXXXX     XXXXX
   XXX       XXXX      XXXXX
     X        XXX       XXXX
     X       XXXX       XXXX
```

As defined here, the XXX format indicates a maximum of 6 digits. For more digits, add more ranges to the format definition.

 If you create a value format for interactive editing of a SAS dataset, you also need a corresponding value informat. See the next chapter, "Value Informats," for details.

---

5 Useful Value Formats

These statements define value formats you might be able to use immediately.

 YN. The YN format writes Boolean values, 1 and 0, as the words Yes and No. Use this format with a width of 1 to write the letters Y and N.

VALUE YN (MIN=1) 1 = 'Yes' 0 = 'No' OTHER = ' ';

 ORD. This format writes ordinal words for the numbers 1–4.

VALUE ORD 1 = 'first' 2 = 'second' 3 = 'third' 4 = 'fourth';

 ILLIONS. Use this format to write a general indication of the magnitude of large numbers.

VALUE ILLIONS
    1000 -< 1E6 = 'thousands'
    1E6 -< 1E9 = 'millions'
    1E9 - HIGH = 'billions';

 BE. The BE format and similar formats can be useful when writing sentences, to make the number of the verb agree with a numeric value.

VALUE BE -1 - 1 = 'is' OTHER = 'are';

 STARS. This format provides extra visibility for standard missing values.

VALUE STARS . = '***********' OTHER = (|BEST12.|);

■ 16

Value Informats

Informats convert input text to data values. Value informats convert specific input text values to specific text labels. They work much the same way as value formats, which are described in the previous chapter, "Value Formats."

Use the INVALUE statement of the FORMAT procedure to create a value informat. The INVALUE statement includes these terms:

- an informat name
- format options for the informat
- ranges, sets of input text or numeric values
- labels, data values that the informat produces for specific ranges

An informat produces either numeric or character values. The data type is indicated in the informat name; names of character informats begin with a dollar sign ($).

Names for value informats must follow all the rules that apply to names of value formats. In addition, the name of a value informat cannot be more than 31 characters in length. If you create a value format and a value informat for use with the same values and the same fields, give them the same name.

Two format options are useful for most value informats.

- The UPCASE option converts input text values to uppercase letters before the informat puts them into ranges. This allows you to read input values without distinguishing between uppercase and lowercase letters.
- The JUST option removes leading spaces before putting input text values into ranges. This allows you to read input values without considering how the values are justified or aligned within the field.

The MIN=, MAX=, DEFAULT=, and FUZZ= format options work the same as for value formats. The FUZZ= option can be used for numeric value informats that use numeric ranges.

The kind of values that can be used in ranges and labels depend on the data type of the value informat.

For a character informat, all range and label values are character values. Range values are the input text values; label values are the resulting data values.

For a numeric informat, range values can be either character or numeric values. Character range values are the input text values. Numeric range values are the numeric values that result from interpreting the input text as numbers using the standard numeric informat. The label values for a numeric informat are the numeric values that the informat generates.

As with value formats, a range can be a single value, an interval, a comma-separated list of values and intervals, or OTHER. Write the range, an equals sign, and the corresponding label.

The example below creates the value informat LVR, which interprets the words True and False and several other words as the Boolean values 1 and 0.

```
PROC FORMAT;
INVALUE LVR (UPCASE JUST)
  'FALSE', 'NO', 'F', 'N', '0', '-' = 0
  'TRUE', 'YES', 'T', 'Y', '1', '+' = 1
  ;
RUN;
```

 Use a value informat in the INPUT statement, the INPUT function, the INFORMAT statement, or anywhere else an informat is used.

 A value informat can use two special label values.

- _ERROR_ tells the informat to treat values in the range as invalid data. The informat generates a data error when those values are found.
- _SAME_ tells the informat to interpret the input text values as standard data. In a character informat, this means that the values are unchanged, except for the effects of the UPCASE and JUST options. For a numeric informat, it means that the values are interpreted as ordinary numeric data if possible. Values that cannot be interpreted as numeric data result in an error condition.

This example creates the informat NZ, which treats a value of 0 as invalid data, but accepts all other numeric values as input.

```
PROC FORMAT;
INVALUE NZ (UPCASE JUST MIN=1 MAX=32)
  0 = _ERROR_
  OTHER = _SAME_
  ;
RUN;
```

 To read Roman numerals, use a value informat such as the ROMAN informat that this example creates.

```
PROC FORMAT;
INVALUE ROMAN (UPCASE JUST MIN=1 MAX=32)
  ' ' = 0 'I' = 1 'II' = 2 'III' = 3 'IV' = 4 'V' = 5
  'VI' = 6 'VII' = 7 'VIII' = 8 'IX' = 9 'X' = 10
  'XI' = 11 'XII' = 12 'XIII' = 13 'XIV' = 14 'XV' = 15
  'XVI' = 16 'XVII' = 17 'XVIII' = 18 'XIX' = 19 'XX' = 20
  'XXI' = 21 'XXII' = 22 'XXIII' = 23 'XXIV' = 24 'XXV' = 25
  'XXVI'= 26 'XXVII'= 27 'XXVIII'= 28 'XXIX' = 29 'XXX' = 30
  ;
RUN;
```

A more complete Roman numeral informat can be found in chapter 18, "Format Catalogs and Control Datasets."

5 Useful Value Informats

These are statements to define five value informats you might have an immediate use for.

 YN. This value informat reads the letters Y and N as the Boolean values 1 and 0.

```
INVALUE YN (UPCASE JUST)
  'N' = 0
  'Y' = 1
  OTHER = .;
```

 MZERO. This informat converts standard missing values to zeros.

```
INVALUE MZERO (JUST)
  '.', ' ' = 0
  OTHER = _SAME_;
```

 HDT. If you read "a.m." and "p.m." as a separate field, you can use this informat, which reads the two halves of the day as SAS time values.

```
INVALUE HDT (UPCASE JUST)
  'A.M.', 'AM' = 0
  'P.M.', 'PM' = 43200;
```

 AZ. Sometimes letters are used like numbers to form a sequence. This informat converts letters to the corresponding numbers.

```
INVALUE AZ (UPCASE JUST MIN=1)
  'A' = 1 'B' = 2 'C' = 3 'D' = 4 'E' = 5 'F' = 6 'G' = 7 'H' = 8
  'I' = 9 'J' = 10 'K' = 11 'L' = 12 'M' = 13 'N' = 14 'O' = 15
  'P' = 16 'Q' = 17 'R' = 18 'S' = 19 'T' = 20 'U' = 21 'V' = 22
  'W' = 23 'X' = 24 'Y' = 25 'Z' = 26 'AA' = 27 'BB' = 28
  'CC' = 29 'DD' = 30 'EE' = 31 'FF' = 32 'GG' = 33
  'HH' = 34 'II' = 35 'JJ' = 36 'KK' = 37 'LL' = 38
  'MM' = 39 'NN' = 40 'OO' = 41 'PP' = 42 'QQ' = 43
  'RR' = 44 'SS' = 45 'TT' = 46 'UU' = 47 'VV' = 48
  'WW' = 49 'XX' = 50 'YY' = 51 'ZZ' = 52;
```

 GP. The GP informat converts letter grades to numeric grade points — a necesssary step if you want to compute a grade point average, or g.p.a.

```
INVALUE GP (UPCASE JUST)
  'A' = 4 'B' = 3 'C' = 2 'D' = 1 'F' = 0
  OTHER = .;
```

■ 17
Picture Formats for Numbers

Unlike a value format, which formats a range of values as a specific text label, a picture format associates a range with a picture, a text string that uses parts of the numeric value in the text it generates. Picture formats work only with numeric values. The more common kind of picture format is designed to add punctuation to numbers.

Digits that appear in the picture are used as digit selectors, which represent character positions at which a routine called the picture processor will substitute the characters of the value being formatted. For example, if the picture '00,001.11' is used to format the value 1,250, the resulting text might be 1,250.00. However, various details of the way the picture processor works can be modified by picture options.

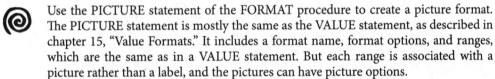

Use the PICTURE statement of the FORMAT procedure to create a picture format. The PICTURE statement is mostly the same as the VALUE statement, as described in chapter 15, "Value Formats." It includes a format name, format options, and ranges, which are the same as in a VALUE statement. But each range is associated with a picture rather than a label, and the pictures can have picture options.

Picture formats use the MIN=, MAX=, DEFAULT=, and FUZZ= options, which are the same as for numeric value formats. Another format option, ROUND, tells the picture processor to round the value that is being formatted instead of truncating it.

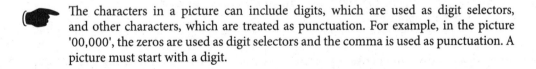

The characters in a picture can include digits, which are used as digit selectors, and other characters, which are treated as punctuation. For example, in the picture '00,000', the zeros are used as digit selectors and the comma is used as punctuation. A picture must start with a digit.

If you want a picture to write leading zeros, use digit selectors other than zero. You can write all the digit selectors as ones, for example. To have a picture not write leading zeros, use zero digit selectors at the beginning of the picture for digit positions that should not include leading zeros.

The table at right shows examples of pictures that write numbers without leading zeros, along with formatted values these pictures might generate.

'001'	'001.11'	'00,001'
0	0.01	0
1	1.00	123
12	123.45	1,234
123		12,345

If a picture contains only zero digit selectors, then it writes a zero value as a completely blank field, as shown in the center column in the table at right. Also, as with any punctuation symbol, a decimal point in a picture does not print unless there is a digit printed before it. With zero digit selectors, numbers print without the decimal points they need, as you see in the center column in the table. To format fractional numbers correctly, write a nonzero digit selector before the decimal point, as shown in the right column in the table.

Value	'000.00'	'001.11'
0		0.00
.01	1	0.01
.12	12	0.12
1	1.00	1.00
12345	123.45	123.45

Picture options affect the way the picture processor substitutes the digits of the numeral for the digit selectors in the picture.

- The MULTIPLIER= or MULT= option indicates a multiplier, a factor to apply to the value before converting it to a numeral. The default multiplier is a factor of 10 that adjusts for the decimal point in the picture. Specifically, the default multiplier is 10 raised to the power of the number of digit selectors after the first period in the picture. For example, for the picture '001.11', the default multiplier is 10 to the power 2, or 100. To select a different multiplier, use the MULTIPLIER= picture option.
- The PREFIX= picture option indicates a character constant of one or two characters which is used as a prefix. The prefix is substituted for the last one or two fill positions. Fill positions are the character positions of zero digit selectors at the beginning of the picture that are not used for digits, along with any punctuation positions before the first digit. To use a prefix, you must use zero digit selectors at the beginning of the picture in order to create fill positions, and the numeral must be small enough to allow fill positions for the prefix.
- The FILL= picture option indicates a character that is used for any other fill positions. The default fill character is a space.
- To include a text label in a picture format, write a picture that does not include any digits, or use the NOEDIT picture option. The picture process does not process the text label; it works the same way as in a value format.

Write picture options in parentheses after the picture. The example below shows the use of picture options.

To write a negative number in a picture format, use a hyphen (a minus sign) as a prefix. The example below creates the format PCTC, which writes values from -1 to 1 as percents from -100% to +100%. It writes 0 as the text label Unch. The table shows examples of the way the PCTC format writes values.

```
PROC FORMAT;
PICTURE PCTC (ROUND)
   -1-<0 = '0001%' (MULTIPLIER=100 PREFIX='-')
   0 = 'Unch.'
   0<-1 = '0001%' (MULTIPLIER=100 PREFIX='+')
   ;
RUN;
```

-1	-100%
-.7995	-80%
-.001	-0%
0	Unch.
.001	+0%
.1	+10%

The number of digits in the numeral the picture processor creates is based on the number of digit selectors the picture contains. If the value is too large to fit in that many digits, the picture processor uses the least significant digits of the value. For example, if the value 12345 is applied to the picture '111', the formatted value is 345. To avoid having partial values appear, set the range for a picture so that it only includes values that will be formatted correctly. For example, the range for a three-digit picture might be 0-999.

A picture format can be used simply to add descriptive text to a numeral. The format defined here is designed to print numbers from 1 to 100, adding text to values of 10 or below to tag them as "Low."

```
PROC FORMAT;
PICTURE LOW
  1-10 = '001 (Low)'
  OTHER = '001      '
  ;
RUN;
```

This is an example of a column of output that might be produced by this format:

```
48
51
 5 (Low)
 7 (Low)
```

The descriptive text can sometimes make a table of numbers easier to read or make it easier for the reader to find the important details in the table.

A more robust way to add this kind of descriptive text to a report is to format the number with the standard numeric format and add the text as a separate field using a value format.

To write numbers that begin with decimal points, use the PREFIX= option to write the decimal point. Use the MULTIPLIER= option to create the decimal places. Use only nonzero digit selectors. Allow one digit selector for the decimal point. The example below writes values with five decimal places, so there are six digit selectors.

```
PROC FORMAT;
PICTURE DECIMAL 0-<1 = '111111' (MULTIPLIER=100000 PREFIX='.');
RUN;
```

The DECIMAL format writes fields such as these:

```
.00000
.00011
.25000
```

■ 18

Format Catalogs and Control Datasets

A format or informat created in the FORMAT procedure is stored as a catalog entry. A catalog that contains formats and informats is a format catalog. It is also possible to store a format or informat, or several of them, in a SAS dataset, called a control dataset. This makes it possible to edit a format or informat or to convert existing data to a format or informat.

Format Catalogs

When the FORMAT procedure creates a format or informat, it stores it in a format catalog. You can use options to store the new entries in a specific catalog and to tell the SAS supervisor where to look for formats and informats.

 By default, the FORMAT procedure stores the formats and informats it creates in the catalog WORK.FORMATS. Use the LIBRARY= option in the PROC FORMAT statement to store formats and informats in another catalog.

The value of the LIBRARY= option can be either a libref or a catalog. If you specify only a libref, the procedure stores the formats and informats in a catalog named FORMATS in that library.

For example, to store formats in the catalog MAIN.FORMATS, use this statement:

PROC FORMAT LIBRARY=MAIN;

When you create formats and informats for use only in the current SAS session, store them in the default WORK library.

 If you create one permanent format catalog, a catalog of formats and informats that you store between sessions, make it the LIBRARY.FORMATS catalog. That is, store the catalog in a library that you associate with the LIBRARY libref, and give the catalog the entry name FORMATS. Use this PROC FORMAT statement:

PROC FORMAT LIBRARY=LIBRARY;

There are four entry types for stored formats and informats.

- FORMAT is the entry type of a numeric format. This includes both value formats and picture formats. The name of the format is the entry name.
- FORMATC is the entry type of a character value format. The name of the format, with the dollar sign removed, is the entry name.
- INFMT is the entry type of a numeric value informat. The name of the informat is the entry name.
- INFMTC is the entry type of a character value informat. The name of the informat, with the dollar sign removed, is the entry name.

For example, a value format called $XER is stored with the entry name XER and the entry type FORMATC.

The SAS supervisor first looks for a format or informat within the SAS System's own set of routines. This means that you cannot create a format or informat to override a SAS format or informat. If you were to create a format that had the same name as a SAS format, SAS would never find it.

When a SAS program uses a format or informat name that does not belong to a SAS format or informat, the SAS supervisor looks for the format or informat first in the catalog WORK.FORMATS. If it does not find it there, it then looks in the catalog LIBRARY.FORMATS.

You can change the format search sequence with the FMTSEARCH= system option. In this option, write a list (in parentheses) of format catalogs. Include WORK.FORMATS and LIBRARY.FORMATS in the list; if you leave them out, the SAS supervisor still searches these two catalogs first and second.

This is an example of an OPTIONS statement to set the FMTSEARCH= option.

OPTIONS FMTSEARCH=(WORK.FORMATS MAIN.FORMATS LIBRARY.FORMATS);

The SAS supervisor searches these three catalogs in order.

If you list a libref in the FMTSEARCH= option, the libref stands for the FORMATS catalog contained in that library. Thus, the statement above could also be written

OPTIONS FMTSEARCH=(WORK MAIN LIBRARY);

If the FMTSEARCH= option refers to a libref that is not defined or a catalog that does not exist, it is not an error. The SAS supervisor merely skips over that catalog in the list. If the LIBRARY libref is not defined, the SAS supervisor does not look for formats and informats in the LIBRARY.FORMATS catalog.

Use the FMTERR option to control the SAS supervisor's response if it cannot find the format or informat it is looking for. With this option on, the SAS supervisor creates an error condition and does not execute the step. With this option off, the SAS supervisor uses a default format or informat in place of the missing format or informat.

If you create a format for use as the format attribute of a variable in a SAS dataset, make sure the format is available whenever you access the SAS dataset. If you store the SAS dataset between SAS sessions, also store the format.

An error can occur if you attempt to display or print a SAS dataset that depends on a format that the SAS supervisor cannot find. To avoid this error, do one of the following:

- If the format is stored in a format catalog, add the format catalog to the FMTSEARCH= option so that the SAS supervisor can find the format.
- If you can find the source code for the format, that is, the PROC FORMAT step that defines the format, execute this code to define the format before you access the SAS dataset.
- Use the MODIFY and FORMAT statements of the DATASETS procedure to change the format attribute so that it uses a format that is available.
- Turn off the FMTERR system option so that the SAS supervisor can use a default format in place of the missing format.

If you are editing a SAS dataset, these considerations also apply to informats used in informat attributes of variables.

Use the CONTENTS statement of the CATALOG procedure to list the entries of a format catalog. The step below lists all the entries of the catalog MAIN.FORMATS.

```
PROC CATALOG CAT=MAIN.FORMATS;
  CONTENTS;
RUN;
```

In the resulting table, look at the name and entry type columns to identify the formats and informats. FORMAT and FORMATC entries are formats; INFMT and INFMTC entries are informats.

To delete a format or informat, delete its catalog entry. The example below deletes the formats XMP and $IF from the catalog WORK.FORMATS.

```
PROC CATALOG CAT=WORK.FORMATS;
  DELETE XMP.FORMAT IF.FORMATC;
RUN;
```

To print the format and informat definitions of a format catalog, use the FMTLIB option of the PROC FORMAT statement. Use the LIBRARY= option to identify the format catalog. The procedure writes the complete definition of each format and informat in table form.

To print the routines in the catalog WORK.FORMATS, use this step:

```
PROC FORMAT LIBRARY=WORK FMTLIB;
RUN;
```

If the catalog WORK.FORMATS contains the LVR and $CFN formats, as defined in chapter 15, "Value Formats," this is the print output the step above generates:

```
        FORMAT NAME: LVR     LENGTH:    5   NUMBER OF VALUES:    4
    MIN LENGTH:   1  MAX LENGTH:  40  DEFAULT LENGTH   5  FUZZ: STD

    START            END              LABEL  (VER. 8.2      16JAN2002:13:44:31)

                         ._              .Z False
    LOW                                  0<True
                    0                    0 False
                    0<HIGH               True



        FORMAT NAME: $CFN     LENGTH:   18   NUMBER OF VALUES:    2
    MIN LENGTH:   1  MAX LENGTH:  40  DEFAULT LENGTH  18  FUZZ:          0

    START            END              LABEL  (VER. 8.2      16JAN2002:14:04:09)

    E                E                Eastern Conference
    W                W                Western Conference
```

In the output, the symbol < after a value indicates that the value is not included in the interval.

To print each routine on a separate page, add the PAGE option to the PROC FORMAT statement.

To print selected routines, write a SELECT statement. In the SELECT statement, identify formats using the format name, which for character informats includes the dollar sign. Identify informats with the informat name preceded by an at-sign.

The example below demonstrates the use of the SELECT statement.

```
PROC FORMAT LIBRARY=WORK FMTLIB PAGE;
  SELECT YN $XSP @YN @$YTER;
RUN;
```

This step prints the details of the informats YN and $XSP and the informats YN and $YTER. With the PAGE option, it prints each routine on a separate page.

An alternative to the SELECT statement is the EXCLUDE statement. In the EXCLUDE statement, list routines to skip over or leave out when you process a format catalog.

Control Datasets

A control dataset is a SAS dataset that contains the information necessary to define a format or informat or any combination of formats and informats. The FORMAT procedure can create a control dataset from a format catalog. It can also create formats and informats from control datasets.

To create a control dataset from a stored format or informat, write a PROC FORMAT statement with the LIBRARY= option to select the format catalog and the

CNTLOUT= option to identify the control dataset. Write a SELECT statement to select the format or informat. For an informat, write an at-sign before the informat name in the SELECT statement.

This example creates a control dataset from the format $X in the catalog MAIN.FORMATS.

```
PROC FORMAT LIBRARY=MAIN CNTLOUT=WORK.X;
  SELECT $X;
RUN;
```

 Variables in the control dataset correspond to the values and options that define a format or informat. A control dataset can contain these variables:

- TYPE, a one-letter code indicating the type of the routine. The code is N for a numeric value format, C for a character value format, I for a numeric value informat, J for a character value informat, or P for a picture format. This variable can be omitted for a numeric value format.
- FMTNAME, the name of the routine.
- The numeric option variables DEFAULT, MIN, MAX, FUZZ, and MULT, corresponding to the options of the same names.
- START and END, values that define a range interval. Only START is required.
- SEXCL and EEXCL, codes that exclude the start and end value, respectively, form the interval. A code value Y excludes the value. A code value N includes the value as part of the interval.
- HLO, a variable that contains codes related to the range. Each code is a single letter, and the variable can contain a combination of these codes. The code letters are listed below.
- LABEL, the label associated with the range. For a picture format, this variable contains the picture.
- Eight more variables that indicate options of picture formats: MULT, NOEDIT, PREFIX, FILL, DATATYPE, LANGUAGE, DECSEP, and DIG3SEP.

Other than the numeric option variables, the variables of a control dataset are ordinarily character variables. For a numeric value format or informat, the variables START, END, and LABEL may contain numerals that represent numeric values.

The code letters that the HLO variable can contain include these:

- H, L, and O indicate the special ranges HIGH, LOW, and OTHER, respectively.
- U and J indicate the informat options UPCASE and JUST, respectively.
- I, for a numeric value informat, indicates that the range values are numeric values.
- F indicates that the label is a format or informat.

 After you create a control dataset, you can print it to show the definition of the format or informat.

To modify the definition of the format or informat:

1. Create a control dataset, as described above.
2. Edit the control dataset interactively, or use a program to change the control dataset.
3. Create a new format or informat from the control dataset, as described below.

If you edit a format or informat regularly, store the control dataset permanently. This saves you from having to do step 1 of this list.

You can create a control dataset from existing data using any kind of SAS program that creates a SAS dataset. If you create a control dataset from existing data, you must at least include the FMTNAME, START, and LABEL variables.

If the variables in the control dataset do not have the correct variable names, use the RENAME= dataset option to rename them.

To define a format or informat from a control dataset, write a PROC FORMAT step with the CNTLIN= option to identify the control dataset. The FORMAT procedure reads the data from the control dataset and creates the format or informat that it indicates.

By default, as always, the FORMAT procedure stores the format or informat as an entry in the WORK.FORMATS catalog. Use the LIBRARY= option to store the entry in a different format catalog.

This example creates a format or informat from the data in the control dataset WORK.CNTL1 and stores the resulting entry in the catalog MAIN.FORMATS.

```
PROC FORMAT CNTLIN=WORK.CNTL1 LIBRARY=MAIN;
RUN;
```

You cannot tell from the PROC FORMAT step what format or informat is being defined. That information can be found inside the control dataset itself and in the log notes that the procedure generates. If appropriate, write comments with the PROC FORMAT step to identify the formats and informats that the step creates.

Usually, it only takes a data step to create a control dataset from the data in a SAS dataset. Write a RETAIN statement to create the FMTNAME and TYPE variables, along with any other variables that are the same for every observation in the control dataset. Create variables such as START and LABEL by renaming existing variables or by assigning values in assignment statements.

It is just as easy to create a control dataset from a text data file. Use an INPUT statement to create variables directly from input fields, and use assignment and RETAIN statements to create the other required variables for the control dataset.

If necessary, add an observation for the special range OTHER. For this observation, assign blank values to the START and END variables, and assign the value "O" (for OTHER) to the variable HLO. If the label for the OTHER range is a reference to another format or informat, assign the value OF to the variable HLO.

For efficiency, the control dataset can be a data step view, indicated by the VIEW= option in the DATA statement. This is shown in the examples that follow.

If a SAS dataset contains observations that define intervals and associated values or labels, you can convert this data to a value format. The example below starts from the SAS dataset shown here, which provides names for temperature ranges.

```
LOW_F      HIGH_F    NAME

-500         32      Freezing
  32         40      Cold
  40         71      Cool
  71         84      Warm
  84        159      Hot
```

The program below converts the data above to a control dataset, then creates the value format TFR, in the format catalog LIBRARY.FORMATS.

```
DATA WORK.CNTL1 / VIEW=WORK.CNTL1;
  SET MAIN.TEMPS (RENAME=(LOW_F=START HIGH_F=END NAME=LABEL));
  RETAIN FMTNAME 'TFR' EEXCL 'Y' TYPE 'N';
RUN;
PROC FORMAT CNTLIN=WORK.CNTL1 LIBRARY=LIBRARY;
RUN;
```

```
NOTE: Format TFR has been written to LIBRARY.FORMATS.
```

If a format or informat forms ranges with single values rather than intervals of values, the END variable can be omitted from the control dataset. Use the START variable to indicate the value.

Some SAS formats do not have corresponding informats, but you may be able to create a control dataset for an informat from the format. This is the solution you need if you want to read Roman numerals. The short program below creates a ROMAN informat from the ROMAN format that is part of base SAS.

```
DATA WORK.CNTL1 / VIEW=WORK.CNTL1;
  RETAIN TYPE 'I' FMTNAME 'ROMAN' HLO 'UJ';
  DO LABEL = 1 TO 9999;
    START = PUT(LABEL, ROMAN21.);
    OUTPUT;
    END;
RUN;
PROC FORMAT CNTLIN=WORK.CNTL1;
RUN;
```

```
NOTE: DATA STEP view saved on file WORK.CNTL1.
NOTE: A stored DATA STEP view cannot run under a different operating
      system.

NOTE: Informat ROMAN has been output.

NOTE: There were 9999 observations read from the data set WORK.CNTL1.
```

The value 'UJ' for the variable HLO represents the UPCASE and JUST informat options. These options allow the ROMAN informat to disregard leading spaces and to read Roman numerals written in lowercase letters.

The following program demonstrates the use of the ROMAN informat.

Program	Input	Output
DATA _NULL_;	X	10
INFILE I;	XI	11
INPUT X ROMAN21.;	L	50
PUTLOG X;	C	100
RUN;	D	500
	MMI	2001
	MMMMMM	6000

In a similar way, formats and informats can be derived indirectly from existing formats or functions. The two examples below create formats and informats that you might have an immediate use for. They convert between the names and numbers of the days of the week and the months of the year.

This first program creates a format and an informat named WDN for the names of the days of the week. It uses the year 2005 as its base because that year happens to start on a Saturday. The program creates the SAS dataset WORK.WDN and uses this same SAS dataset as the control dataset for both the format and the informat.

```
DATA WORK.WDN;
  RETAIN TYPE1 'I' TYPE2 'N' FMTNAME 'WDN' HLO 'UJ';
  DO WEEKDAY = 1 TO 7;
    NAME = UPCASE(LEFT(PUT('01JAN2005'D + WEEKDAY, DOWNAME9.)));
    OUTPUT;
    END;
RUN;
PROC FORMAT CNTLIN=WORK.WDN (KEEP=TYPE1 FMTNAME NAME WEEKDAY
  RENAME=(TYPE1=TYPE NAME=START WEEKDAY=LABEL));
RUN;
PROC FORMAT CNTLIN=WORK.WDN (KEEP=TYPE2 FMTNAME NAME WEEKDAY HLO
  RENAME=(TYPE2=TYPE WEEKDAY=START NAME=LABEL));
RUN;
```

The text value, the variable NAME, becomes the START variable for the informat and the LABEL variable for the format. Conversely, the data variable WEEKDAY is the LABEL variable for the informat and the START variable for the format.

The second program creates a format and an informat named MX for the names of the months. The informat reads both the complete month names and their three-letter abbreviations. This program uses the year 1960, but it could use any year.

```
DATA WORK.MXFORMAT;
  RETAIN TYPE 'N' FMTNAME 'MX';
  DO MONTH = 1 TO 12;
    NAME = UPCASE(LEFT(PUT(MDY(MONTH, 1, 1960), MONNAME9.)));
    OUTPUT;
    END;
RUN;
PROC FORMAT CNTLIN=WORK.MXFORMAT
  (RENAME=(MONTH=START NAME=LABEL));
RUN;
```

```
DATA WORK.MXINFMT;
  RETAIN TYPE 'I' FMTNAME 'MX' HLO 'UJ';
  DO MONTH = 1 TO 12;
    NAME = UPCASE(LEFT(PUT(MDY(MONTH, 1, 1960), MONNAME9.)));
    OUTPUT;
    IF LENGTH(NAME) > 3 THEN DO;
      NAME = SUBSTR(NAME, 1, 3);
      OUTPUT;
      END;
    END;
RUN;
PROC FORMAT CNTLIN=WORK.MXINFMT
  (RENAME=(NAME=START MONTH=LABEL));
RUN;
```

Both the WDN and MX formats write names in uppercase letters. This is the result of the UPCASE function calls in the data steps that create the control datasets.

One reason to use a format in place of a function for table lookup is to eliminate the error conditions that a function generates when its argument is invalid. The program below creates a format from the ZIPSTATE function. Like the function, the $ZIPST format places ZIP codes in U.S. states. Unlike the function, the format does not create an error condition when a ZIP code is not found.

```
* This step generates invalid argument messages. ;
DATA WORK.CNTLZIP;
  LENGTH START $ 5 LABEL $ 2;
  RETAIN TYPE 'C' FMTNAME '$ZIPST';
  DO I = 00000 TO 99999;
    START = PUT(I, Z5.);
    LABEL = ZIPSTATE(START);
    IF LABEL NE '' THEN OUTPUT;
    END;
  START = '';
  LABEL = '';
  HLO = 'O';
  OUTPUT;
  _ERROR_ = 0;
RUN;
PROC FORMAT CNTLIN=WORK.CNTLZIP;
RUN;
```

Just as a format catalog can contain multiple routines, it is possible for a control dataset to contain the data of multiple routines. When the FORMAT procedure creates a control dataset, it contains the entire data of a format catalog unless you select specific routines with the SELECT statement.

If a control dataset in the CNTLIN= option contains data for multiple routines, it must be sorted so that all the observations for each routine are consecutive. For example, sort the control dataset by TYPE and FMTNAME. The FORMAT procedure can create any number of routines from a single control dataset. Usually, it is easier to create a separate control dataset for each routine, but there are also situations in which it is more convenient to create just one control dataset that includes several routines.

■ 19

Time

Time is as confusing as it is simple. Time data values are simple numeric measurements based on well-known units. In spite of this, it is easy to get confused about the way time is measured. Why is this? In part, it is because the three ways to measure time are so similar that there is no need to differentiate them in casual conversation. When working with data, however, the same casual approach to time measurement can lead to error. Whenever you are working with time data values, it is important to know which of these kinds of measurements it is:

- a time interval, usually a designated part of the calendar, such as 2003 or January 2004;
- a point in time, such as January 26, 2004 at 6:00 a.m.;
- a duration, or elapsed time, such as 2 hours, 24 minutes.

SAS includes specific support for values that represent points in time. There are functions, informats, formats, and constants that allow you to work with these values. These same routines can also be used for values that represent time intervals, provided that you are clear on how you are using them. In addition, because points in time and durations are measured in nearly the same way, some of these same features can be used for durations.

 Therefore, when you see a time measurement, you cannot necessarily tell from its context or appearance that it is one kind of measurement or another. Look to information about the source and meaning of the data to find out what kind of time measurement it is.

SAS specifically supports three linear ways of measuring time. A SAS datetime value and a SAS date value measure points in time as time elapsed since the beginning of 1960. SAS datetime values measure time in seconds since 1960. SAS date values measure time in days since 1960. Either kind of value can be used equally well to measure a point in time; however, SAS includes specific support for representing dates and other parts of the calendar using SAS date values and for representing the date and time of day using SAS datetime values.

The only difference between a SAS date value and a SAS datetime value that represent the same point in time is the unit of measure. The SAS datetime value is 86,400 times as great as the SAS date value. The factor 86,400 is the number of seconds in a day.

While in theory a SAS date value represents a point in time, in practice it is almost always an integer value and represents a time interval, such as a day or month. Consider the SAS date 16071. It is not necessarily just the moment that marks the beginning of January 1, 2004; it usually means that entire day. Or, it could mean the month of January 2004 or the year of 2004. In general, the SAS date value for any time interval is the value for the beginning of the time interval.

The third kind of special time measurement in SAS is a SAS time value, which measures the time of day in seconds since midnight. The time of day is written in hours, minutes, and seconds. Elapsed time is written in the same way, so the routines for SAS time values are also useful for elapsed time.

The purpose of most of the time routines in SAS is to convert among SAS datetime values, SAS date values, SAS time values, and the various elements of the calendar and clock that are used for points in time, such as the year, month, day, hour, minute, and second. For example, the DATEPART function extracts a SAS date value from a SAS datetime value; the MONTH function or format extracts the month from a SAS date value. See chapter 36, "Time Conversions," for specifics.

These noteworthy limitations apply to time data:

- Pope Gregory XIII adopted the current standard calendar, the Gregorian calendar, on Friday, October 15, 1582. SAS accepts dates back to January 1 of that year and creates an error condition for years before 1582.
- In the previous century, many programs were written to use 2-digit years with the assumption that all years fell in the 1900s. Programs had to be revised to accept years before 1900 or beyond 1999 — the infamous "Year 2000" problem.
- Many systems still record dates using 2-digit years. This kind of data can only represent distinct dates within a 100-year period. In SAS, the YEARCUTOFF= system option sets the interval for two-digit years. The value of the option is the beginning year of the 100-year period to which SAS applies 2-digit years. For example, with the option YEARCUTOFF=1976, a year value of 75 is 2075, but a year value of 76 is 1976. If data values include two-digit years, set the value of the YEARCUTOFF= system option before the oldest year in the data, but less than 100 years before the newest year in the data. For example, if data values include years from 1987 to 2014, written in two digits, the two-digit years will be interpreted correctly if you set the value of YEARCUTOFF= anywhere between 1915 and 1987.
- Most systems record and display dates with 4-digit years. These systems are unable to handle years beyond 9999. This is the "4-Digit Year" problem.
- The double-precision numbers used in SAS can count days only up to about 20000, or about 18,000 years in the future. This affects both SAS date values and SAS datetime values. This is the "Year 20000" problem. SAS routines may not process years beyond 20000.

SAS counts days of the week starting with Sunday. The program below demonstrates the numbers and names of days of the week. It prints the days of the week as both names and numbers, using the DOWNAME and WEEKDAY formats, for seven consecutive SAS date values.

Program	Output	
```DATA _NULL_;```	Sunday	1
``` DO DATE = 15549 TO 15555;```	Monday	2
``` PUTLOG DATE DOWNAME9. -L +3 DATE WEEKDAY1.;```	Tuesday	3
``` END;```	Wednesday	4
```RUN;```	Thursday	5
	Friday	6
	Saturday	7

 Associate a format with any variable that contains a SAS date value, SAS time value, or SAS datetime value. With an appropriate format, the values display in a meaningful form. With the default format, they would display as simple numbers. Among the many formats available, these are common choices for showing the complete value:

- DATE9. for a SAS date value
- DATETIME18. for a SAS datetime value
- TIME8. for a SAS time value

If you create the variable in a data step, write a FORMAT statement in the data step to associate the format with the variable.

 To write a SAS date value in a program, write a SAS date constant. Write the day number, three-letter month abbreviation, and year, quoted and followed by the letter D. These are examples of SAS date constants:

```
'1JAN2001'D
"01mar2001"d
```

Write a SAS time value in a program as a SAS time constant, with the hour and minute or hour, minute, and second separated by colons. Use the 24-hour clock or write AM or PM at the end. Enclose the value in a quoted string followed by the letter T. These are examples of SAS time constants:

```
'00:00'T
'15:15:00't
'23:59:59.9999'T
"5:00 PM"T
```

 A SAS datetime constant is like a combination of a SAS date constant and a SAS time constant. Write the date and the time of day with a space or colon between them. Enclose the value in a quoted string followed by the letters DT. This is an example of a SAS datetime constant:

```
'15AUG1977 09:31'DT
```

A measurement of elapsed time, or duration, can also be written as a SAS time constant, even though it is not, strictly speaking, a SAS time value.

If you write a constant value in minutes and seconds, remember to include 0 hours as the first part of the constant. For example, write 4 minutes, 59 seconds as:

'0:04:59'T

If a duration is greater than 24 hours, write the SAS time constant with more than 24 hours. This SAS time constant represents 168 hours, or a week of elapsed time:

'168:00'T

A time differential (or offset) can be either positive or negative. Write a negative sign at the beginning of a SAS time constant to indicate a negative time differential. This is negative 5 hours:

'-05:00'T

Alternatively, write the negative sign before the SAS time constant:

-'05:00'T

Function calls provide the current time from the computer system's clock. The DATETIME, DATE, and TIME functions return SAS datetime, SAS date, and SAS time values, respectively. These functions do not use arguments.

This statement obtains the current date as a SAS date value and assigns it to a variable:

DATE = DATE();

TIME CONFUSION

If you handle time measurements incorrectly in a SAS program, you can get meaningless results. These are signs of time confusion that you might find, along with the likely causes.

- Values before 5 a.m.: a SAS date value was formatted as a SAS time value.
- Values on January 1, 1960 before 5 a.m.: a SAS date value was formatted as a SAS datetime value.
- All values fall on January 1, 1960: a SAS time value was used as a SAS datetime value.
- Values between years 1960 and 2196, centering around 2078: a SAS time value was formatted as a SAS date value.
- Years you never heard of: a SAS datetime value was formatted as a SAS date value, or computations incorrectly combined SAS date values and SAS datetime values.
- Seven-digit hour numbers: a SAS datetime value was mistaken for a SAS time value:
- Years in the wrong century: two-digit years were interpreted with the YEARCUTOFF= system option set incorrectly
- Values at approximately half-hour intervals: the MONTH time interval code was used with a SAS datetime value.

This statement obtains the current time of day as a SAS time value:

TIME = TIME();

This statement obtains the current point in time as a SAS datetime value:

DATETIME = DATETIME();

To determine the current year, month, day, or day of the week, start with the DATE function and use functions to extract the specific calendar parts from it, as shown here:

YEAR = YEAR(DATE());
MONTH = MONTH(DATE());
DAY = DAY(DATE());
WEEKDAY = WEEKDAY(DATE());

Use macro variables to determine the time at which the SAS session started. There are several automatic macro variables that format that point in time in a few different ways.

- SYSDATE9 is the date as formatted by the DATE9. format, with the day number, three-letter month abbreviation, and year, such as 05MAY2004.
- SYSDATE is the same, but with a two-digit year. It contains the date as formatted by the DATE7. format.
- SYSTIME is the time of day, with the hour, minute, and second, separated by colons, such as 14:42:31. It uses the 24-hour clock.
- SYSDAY is the name of the day of the week.

These macro variables can form constants that you can use in a SAS program. This is the start of the SAS session as a SAS date constant:

"&SYSDATE9"D

A SAS time constant:

"&SYSTIME"T

A SAS datetime constant:

"&SYSDATE9 &SYSTIME"DT

Use the macro variables to determine the date or time of day when you need a value that will remain the same for the entire execution of a SAS program. Use the function calls if you need to account for the time that elapses between events or steps in a program. Use the DATETIME function to record the time of a user action in an interactive application.

■ 20

Informats and Formats for Time

Time measurements are single numeric values, but they are almost always written in parts, such as year, month, and day or hours and minutes. These parts are time elements defined by the calendar or clock, and time is counted using various combinations of these calendar and clock elements. To make things more complicated, there are multiple ways of writing the same calendar or clock element. For example, 02, Feb, and February all refer to the same month. To handle these and other issues, there are a great number of informats and even more formats for reading and writing time fields.

 To select the informat for reading a field that contains a time measurement:

1. Identify the combination of calendar and clock elements found in the field, including the specific form of each element. For example, a field that contains the value 03/21/99 has the month number, the day, and the two-digit year.
2. Look for a SAS informat that reads that combination of elements. In the example of 03/21/99, the informat MMDDYY is available.
3. If there is no suitable informat, use separate informats for each element of the field. Then use functions to combine the elements; see chapter 36, "Time Conversions," for details of this.
4. If there is no informat to read an element the way it is written, create a value informat for that element. For example, to read month names as a separate field, create a value informat that converts the names to the numbers 1 to 12. See chapter 16, "Value Informats," for details.

 To select the format for writing a time measurement:

1. Identify the combination of calendar and clock elements to write.
2. Look for a SAS format that writes that combination of elements. Formats write different combinations of elements with different width arguments, so determine the necessary width argument.
3. If specific punctuation is required and punctuation variations are available for the format, select the punctuation variation of the format.
4. If there is no suitable format, create a picture format. See chapter 22, "Picture

Formats for Time." Alternatively, write each element using a separate format. If necessary, create value formats.

5. If the variable does not have the kind of value that a selected format requires, create another variable and convert the measurement to the right kind of value. For example, it is usually necessary to convert SAS datetime values to SAS date values to write them as dates. See chapter 36, "Time Conversions," for details.

These are examples of informats for SAS date values:

- DATE reads fields like 02MAY2004
- MMDDYY reads fields like 05/02/2004
- MONYY reads fields like MAY2004
- YYMMDD reads fields like 2004-05-02

The informats that read sequences of numbers as SAS date values are flexible enough to read most patterns of punctuation that you are likely to find in a date field. The main restriction is that there can be only one character used as a delimiter. This delimiter can be the space character, but spaces cannot be combined with any other delimiter in the same field.

These are examples of fields the MMDDYY informat reads successfully:

```
10=9=2005
6\02\23
11/25/2/8
10 9 2005
6/2/23
11.25.2.215
6/2/23/11
```

The delimiter can be just about any character. It is permissible to have an additional number at the end of the field; this number is assumed to represent hours, and it does not become part of the SAS date value.

These are examples of fields that the MMDDYY informat cannot read (although in version 6, which was more forgiving about punctuation, it could read any of these):

```
 6/ 2/23
6. 2.23
6 02/23
6\02/23
6/2/23 A
6/2/23A
6/2/23/A
6/2/23/
```

The informat rejects these text values and generates a data error because of the combination of delimiters, an extra delimiter at the end of the field, or spurious non-numeric characters in the field.

Use the TIME informat to read SAS time values. The TIME informat reads fields such as these:

```
9:11 am
5:00:00 PM
23:14:49
```

Like date informats, the TIME informat is not strict about punctuation. Also, it can read fields written in the 24-hour clock or with AM or PM, which can be shortened to A or P. These are a few more examples of acceptable fields for the TIME informat:

```
9:11 a
4:44 p
4.44.00pm
```

The TIME informat does not accept fields in which the abbreviations *a.m.* or *p.m.* are written with periods. This is an example of a field the TIME informat cannot read:

```
9:11 a.m.
```

Use the DATETIME informat to read SAS datetime values. The DATETIME informat reads fields such as these:

```
02MAY04:9:11 am
02MAY2004:5:00:00 PM
02MAY2004:23:14:49
02MAY2004 23:14:49
```

The YEARCUTOFF= system option affects the way informats interpret 2-digit years. Set the YEARCUTOFF= option so that all 2-digit years fall into a 100-year span beginning with the value of the option. For example, if years range from 1979 to 2049, the option YEARCUTOFF=1950 interprets the 2-digit year numbers (from 79 to 49) correctly. The option YEARCUTOFF=1979 would also work.

To handle invalid data that might appear in an input field, especially a date field, read the field with the ?? error control. Also read the same field again using the $CHAR informat to obtain its text value, or using several informats to read the elements of the field separately. If the field results in a missing value, check the parts or text of the field and adjust the value accordingly.

Consider a field that usually contains a year, month, and day, such as:

```
1999-03-21
```

Suppose that sometimes, the month and day elements are blank, but the year is still valid, such as:

```
1999-  -
```

These statements read the field and use the year to form a value if the month and day are not present or do not form a valid date.

INPUT @1 DATE ?? YYMMDD10. @1 YEAR ?? F4.;
IF DATE = . AND YEAR > 1582 THEN DATE = MDY(1, 1, YEAR);

Use a similar approach to adjust for other anomalies that could occur in a date field.

The ?? error control before an informat prevents the error condition that otherwise occurs when the informat encounters invalid data.

These are examples of formats for SAS date values:

- DATE writes fields like 02MAY2004 or 02MAY04
- MONYY writes fields like MAY2004 or MAY04
- MONNAME writes fields like Aug or August
- WORDDATE writes fields like August 15, 2018
- MMDDYY writes fields like 05/02, 05/02/04, or 05/02/2004
- YYMMDD writes fields like 2004-05-02
- MONTH, WEEKDAY, DAY, and YEAR write individual calendar elements as numbers

With smaller widths, formats may write fewer calendar elements or shorten the elements they write. For example, with a width of 4, the MMDDYY format writes only the month number and day number of a date, with no punctuation, such as 0502.

Formats that write a succession of calendar elements as numbers have punctuation variations. This includes the DDMMYY, MMDDYY, MMYY, YYMM, YYMMDD, YYQ, and YYQR formats. Indicate a punctuation symbol by adding a one-letter suffix to the format name. For example, the YYMMP format (YYMM with the P suffix) writes the year and month with a period for punctuation, such as 2004.11.

The punctuation suffixes are:

- B for a space (blank)
- C for a colon
- D for a hyphen (dash)
- N for no punctuation character
- P for a period (dot)
- S for a slash

Formats for SAS time values include TIME, TIMEAMPM, HOUR, and HHMM. Write time durations with the TIME, HOUR, HHMM, MMSS, and F formats. Formats for SAS datetime values are DATETIME, DATEAMPM, TIMEAMPM, TOD, DTDATE, DTYEAR, DTYYQC, DTMONYY, and DTWKDATX.

International date formats and informats exist to handle date fields written in other languages from Finnish to Afrikaans. See the next chapter, "International Data Formats," for details.

■ 21

International Date Formats

International date formats write dates in various European languages. The formats, and a few corresponding informats, use the names and punctuation of specific languages and national styles.

 International date formats are based on regular SAS formats that write dates using names of months and of days of the week. They are the equivalents of these formats:

DATE DATETIME DDMMYY DOWNAME
MONNAME MONYY WEEKDATX WEEKDAY WORDDATX

International date informats are equivalent to these informats:

DATE DATETIME MONYY

 The name of an international date format is constructed as a combination of three parts: a three-letter language prefix, the root DF, and a suffix that indicates the equivalent format.

These are examples of the date format languages and their prefixes:

Language	Prefix	Language	Prefix	Language	Prefix
Norwegian	NOR	Finnish	FIN	Russian	RUS
Danish	DAN	Swedish	SVE	Czech	CSY
Dutch	NLD	German	DEU	Swiss_German	DES
English	ENG	French	FRA	Swiss_French	FRS
Portuguese	PTG	Spanish	ESP	Italian	ITA

These are the suffixes for the equivalent formats:

Format	Suffix	Format	Suffix	Format	Suffix
DATE	DE	DOWNAME	DWN	WEEKDATX	WKX
DATETIME	DT	MONNAME	MN	WEEKDAY	DN
DDMMYY	DD	MONYY	MY	WORDDATX	WDX

Combine a prefix and a suffix with the DF root to form the format name. For example, to form the Swedish equivalent of the MONYY format, combine SVE for Swedish, DF, and MY for MONYY. The resulting name is SVEDFMY. The example below uses this format to write months in Swedish.

```
DATA _NULL;
  DO MONTH = 1 TO 12;
    DATE = MDY(MONTH, 1, 2001);
    PUTLOG DATE SVEDFMY. +3 @;
    END;
RUN;
```

```
jan01   feb01   mar01   apr01   maj01   jun01   jul01   aug01
sep01   okt01   nov01   dec01
```

The widths required by international date formats are sometimes larger than the widths of the equivalent English-language formats. It depends on the words and abbreviations that are used in the language that the format writes.

Instead of using a prefix of a specific language, you can use the EUR prefix and set the language in the DFLANG= system option. The value of this option is a language name such as those listed above with the language prefixes. Use this approach to make it possible for different people to use the same program to write different languages.

The example below uses the DFLANG= system option to write a date in three different languages.

```
OPTIONS DFLANG=Dutch;
DATA _NULL;
  DATE = '25DEC2001'D;
  PUTLOG DATE EURDFDE.;
RUN;
OPTIONS DFLANG=Norwegian;
DATA _NULL;
  DATE = '25DEC2001'D;
  PUTLOG DATE EURDFDE.;
RUN;
OPTIONS DFLANG=Czech;
DATA _NULL;
  DATE = '25DEC2001'D;
  PUTLOG DATE EURDFDE.;
RUN;
```

```
25dec01

25des01

25prosinec01
```

■ 22

Picture Formats for Time

Picture formats are not limited to formatting ordinary numerals. They can also format SAS date values, SAS time values, and SAS datetime values using any combination of the calendar and clock elements in the value and any other text. In this kind of picture format, a picture contains picture directives, which are escape sequences that indicate a specific calendar or clock element.

 Define a picture format in the PICTURE statement of the FORMAT procedure. The PICTURE statement is essentially the same as the VALUE statement. The difference is that it contains pictures in place of labels. See chapters 15, "Value Formats," and 17, "Picture Formats for Numbers," for more about the syntax of statements in the FORMAT procedure.

Each picture is followed by picture options in parentheses. The DATATYPE= option is required for a picture that formats a SAS date value, SAS time value, or SAS datetime value. Use the value DATE, TIME, or DATETIME for this option to indicate the kind of value that the picture will format.

Usually, a picture format for a time measurement can be defined with just one picture. Use this picture with the special range OTHER. When OTHER is the only range for a format, it includes all values. That is, the format uses the same picture for any value it formats.

The following example creates a format DTMX that writes a SAS datetime value with the month name abbreviation, a plus sign, and the day of the month.

```
PROC FORMAT;
PICTURE DTMX OTHER='%b+%d ' (DATATYPE=DATETIME);
RUN;
```

In this program:

- DTMX is the name of the format.
- '%b+%d ' is the picture for the special range OTHER.
- In the picture, %b and %d are picture directives, which stand for the specific calendar and clock elements that the format writes.
- The other characters in the picture are literal text characters. The format uses these characters, unchanged, as part of the text field it writes.

- DATATYPE=DATETIME is a format option. It indicates that the calendar or clock elements in the picture are taken from a SAS datetime value.

 Picture directives consist of a percent sign and a single letter that indicates a specific calendar or clock element. In some cases, there can be a 0 between the percent sign and the letter to indicate the use of leading zeros. These are selected picture directives:

- The year: %Y
- The 2-digit year: %0y
- The month number: %m or %0m
- The month name: %B or %b
- The day: %d or %0d
- The day of the week: %A, %a, or %w
- The hour, minute, and second: %0H, %0M, and %0S

Use the directive %% to write a percent sign in a picture.

 Use single quotes to enclose a picture that contains picture directives. This ensures that the macro processor does not mistake the picture directives for macro calls.

 It is usually necessary to write a picture with trailing spaces. Make the picture at least as long as the formatted value that the picture processor will produce when it substitutes calendar and clock elements for the picture directives. Otherwise, the formatted value may be truncated.

 Use the DATATYPE= picture option to indicate what kind of value provides the calendar and clock elements for the picture. Use the option DATATYPE=DATETIME for a SAS datetime value, DATATYPE=DATE for a SAS date value, or DATATYPE=TIME for a SAS time value. Write the picture option in parentheses after the picture.

The program below creates the format YBDH to write SAS date values.

```
PROC FORMAT;
PICTURE YBDH OTHER = '%Y-%b-%d   ' (DATATYPE=DATE);
RUN;
```

This format writes the year, month abbreviation, and day with hyphens between them. The program below demonstrates the use of the format.

```
DATA _NULL_;
  DO DATE = '31JUL2002'D TO '01JAN2003'D BY 14;
    PUTLOG DATE YBDH. +1 @;
    END;
RUN;
```

```
2002-JUL-31 2002-AUG-14 2002-AUG-28 2002-SEP-11 2002-SEP-25 2002-OCT-9
2002-OCT-23 2002-NOV-6  2002-NOV-20 2002-DEC-4  2002-DEC-18 2003-JAN-1
```

With a picture format, it is possible to write dates using one-digit values for the month and day, as in the date 8/7/2002. This is something you cannot do with formats such as MMDDYY, which always uses two digits for the month and day. The step below defines the formats MDYYYY, which writes date fields such as 8/7/2002, and MDYY, which is the same except that it writes two-digit years, such as 8/7/02.

```
PROC FORMAT;
PICTURE MDYYYY OTHER = '%m/%d/%Y ' (DATATYPE=DATE);
PICTURE MDYY OTHER = '%m/%d/%0y' (DATATYPE=DATE);
RUN;
```

One use of picture formats is to write SAS datetime values directly as dates. The formats in the example below write the same kinds of date fields that several familiar SAS formats write, but they format SAS datetime values rather than SAS date values.

```
PROC FORMAT;
PICTURE SMMDDYY OTHER = '%0m/%0d/%0y' (DATATYPE=DATETIME);
PICTURE SYYMMDDP OTHER = '%0y.%0m.%0d' (DATATYPE=DATETIME);
PICTURE SWORD OTHER = '%B %d, %Y     ' (DATATYPE=DATETIME);
PICTURE SWEEK OTHER = '%A, %B %d, %Y          ' (DATATYPE=DATETIME);
PICTURE SMONNAME OTHER = '%B     ' (DATATYPE=DATETIME);
PICTURE SYEAR OTHER = '%Y  ' (DATATYPE=DATETIME);
RUN;
```

Picture formats can write fields in many other languages. The DFLANG= system option determines what language the format writes. To set the language of a format to one specific language, use the LANGUAGE= picture option with one of the language names of international date formats. See the previous chapter, "International Date Formats," for details of international date format languages and the DFLANG= system option.

This example demonstrates an Italian-language date format.

```
PROC FORMAT;
PICTURE IYBDH OTHER = '%Y-%b-%d   ' (DATATYPE=DATE LANGUAGE=ITALIAN);
RUN;
DATA _NULL_;
  DO DATE = '31JUL2002'D TO '01JAN2003'D BY 14;
    PUTLOG DATE IYBDH. +1 @;
    END;
RUN;
```

```
2002-Lug-31 2002-Ago-14 2002-Ago-28 2002-Set-11 2002-Set-25 2002-Ott-9
2002-Ott-23 2002-Nov-6  2002-Nov-20 2002-Dic-4  2002-Dic-18 2003-Gen-1
```

■ 23

Validation

The objective of validation is valid data, having each value in the data makes sense. The focus of the process of validation, though, is on the potentially invalid values, those that can be shown to be incorrect. The program might change an invalid value or exclude the observation that contains it.

Informats and Error Controls

When data comes from a text file or from text entered by a user, validation starts with informats. If an informat reads input text that it cannot convert to a value, it generates an error condition.

 In an interactive application, when a user enters a value that the informat cannot interpret, the application displays an error message and highlights the incorrect value. The user can immediately replace the rejected value with a corrected value.

In the Viewtable application, if you enter a value that the informat cannot interpret, the application highlights the invalid value and displays this error message:

ERROR: Invalid data was entered. Please specify another value.

You can then enter a different value to correct the error.

 When a data step reads an input text file, you can control whether an invalid field generates an error condition or not. When an informat finds invalid text, it reports an error condition to the INPUT statement. The INPUT statement then generates an error condition and log messages; however, you can use an error control to change the way the INPUT statement responds.

The example below uses the standard numeric informat, F, to read this input text, which is not a valid numeric value:

(a)

The statement that reads this field is:

INPUT RATE F8.;

The informat cannot interpret the field, so the data step writes a sequence of log messages such as:

```
NOTE: Invalid data for RATE in line 17 1-8.
RULE:       ----+----1----+----2----+----3----+----4----+----5----+
17              (a)
RATE=. _ERROR_=1 _N_=1
```

The informat does not return a value, so the INPUT statement provides a missing value for the variable. With the error condition, the INPUT statement sets the value of the automatic variable _ERROR_ to 1. As a result of this, the data step writes the input record and a list of all data step variables and their values in the log, as shown above.

To suppress the error condition that result from invalid data, write the error control ?? before the informat. If the INPUT statement is

INPUT RATE ?? F8.;

then there is no error condition. The variable RATE still gets a missing value, but the INPUT statement does not set _ERROR_ to 1 or generate any log messages.

Use the error control whenever an input field can properly contain incorrect text. When you suppress the error condition and log messages, the program runs faster and it is easier to see actual errors in the log.

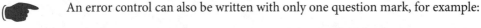 An error control can also be written with only one question mark, for example:

INPUT RATE ? F8.;

With this error control, the INPUT statement generates an error condition for an invalid value, but there is no specific log message. This is useful if you want to use data step logic to check for an invalid value. Test the automatic variable _ERROR_ for a value of 1, indicating an error condition. If _ERROR_ is 1, use additional statements to identify the invalid value and respond accordingly. After you correct the invalid value, set _ERROR_ to 0 to remove the error condition.

Error controls work the same way in the INPUT function. The INPUT function interprets a text argument using an informat. If the text is not valid for the informat, it results in an error condition and log messages, as shown in this example.

```
TEXT = ' (a) ';
RATE = INPUT(TEXT, F8.);
PUT RATE=;
```

```
NOTE: Invalid argument to function INPUT at line 31 column 8.
RATE=.
TEXT=(a) RATE=. _ERROR_=1 _N_=1
NOTE: Mathematical operations could not be performed at the following places.
      The results of the operations have been set to missing values.
      Each place is given by: (Number of times) at (Line):(Column).
      1 at 31:8
```

With the error control, the invalid text only generates a missing value:

```
TEXT = ' (a) ';
RATE = INPUT(TEXT, ?? F8.);
PUT RATE=;
```

RATE=.

 If a numeric field sometimes contains single letters as codes, read the letter codes as special missing values. See chapter 33, "Missing Values," for details.

 To change the way specific values are interpreted in a field, create a value informat. Use a value informat for any of these situations:

- The input field contains meaningful code values that the informat treats as invalid data. For example, a field contains the text FREE and that text actually indicates a value of 0.
- Specific values should be treated as code values instead of ordinary values. For example, an input field of –1 does not actually mean a value of –1, but means a missing value.
- A range of values is not valid in the field and should be treated as an error. For example, if a field indicates an age value, values less than 0 are incorrect.
- A blank field means something other than a missing value. In some data, for example, a blank field actually means a quantity of 1.

Use the INVALUE statement of the FORMAT procedure to create a value informat. In the INVALUE statement, associate each specific input text value or range of values with instructions for interpreting it. The instructions can be a specific data value or _ERROR_ for an error condition. Associate the special range OTHER, which includes all values not otherwise listed, with either the keyword _SAME_ or a specific informat. For the full details of the INVALUE statement, see chapter 16, "Value Informats."

This example creates an informat, NNZ, that converts negative values to zero.

```
PROC FORMAT;
INVALUE NNZ
  LOW-<0 = 0
  OTHER = _SAME_;
RUN;
```

This example treats negative values as errors in the informat NNX.

```
PROC FORMAT;
INVALUE NNX
  LOW-<0 = _ERROR_
  OTHER = _SAME_;
RUN;
```

This example treats N/A and UNK. as two distinct special missing values and uses the COMMA informat to interpret all other values.

```
PROC FORMAT;
INVALUE NU (UPCASE JUST)
  'N/A' = .A
  'UNK.' = .K
  OTHER = (|COMMA12.|);
RUN;
```

Validation Logic

If informats do not provide all the validation you need, write validation logic in a data step. Write IF-THEN statements and similar control flow statements to identify invalid values and control the program's response.

Write an IF-THEN statement with an assignment statement as its action to correct an invalid value. For example, if negative and missing values are invalid for the variable ITEMCT and should be converted to 0 values, this statement does the conversion:

IF ITEMCT < 0 THEN ITEMCT = 0;

To check a dependency between variables, use an IF-THEN statement with a condition that includes the variables involved. This statement checks a dependency between the variables ITEMCT and WEIGHT.

IF ITEMCT = 0 AND WEIGHT NE 0 THEN WEIGHT = 0;

To delete invalid observations, write an IF-THEN statement that has a DELETE statement as its action, or write a subsetting IF statement. The example below deletes observations that have a negative value for TEMP.

IF .Z < TEMP < 0 THEN DELETE;

   To leave out invalid observations when there is no data step, write a condition in a WHERE statement or dataset option.

In many applications, invalid observations cannot simply be discarded. Rejected observations, called exceptions, are collected for a subsequent reporting. Write an OUTPUT statement to store an exception in a separate SAS dataset, then a DELETE statement to remove itfrom any further processing.

   The example below reads an input text file to create the SAS dataset WORK.ADD. It also creates two SAS datasets of exceptions. Observations that have blank ID values are directed to WORK.X1; those that do not have a positive value for AMOUNT are stored in WORK.X2. Valid observations are saved in the primary output SAS dataset, WORK.ADD.

```
DATA WORK.ADD
   WORK.X1 (KEEP=XID AMOUNT NAME)
   WORK.X2 (KEEP=XID AMOUNT ID NAME)
   ;
   INFILE ADD TRUNCOVER;
   INPUT XID $CHAR6. AMOUNT F7. ID $CHAR8. NAME $CHAR14.;

   IF ID = " THEN OUTPUT WORK.X1;
   IF AMOUNT <= 0 THEN OUTPUT WORK.X2;
   IF AMOUNT <= 0 OR ID = " THEN DELETE;

   OUTPUT WORK.ADD;
RUN;
```

Another kind of validation involves checking to see whether a value belongs to a list of acceptable values. For example, you might need to determine whether a code value belongs to a set of defined code values or whether an account number belongs to an open account.

Conversely, you might need to check that a value is not on a list; usually, this is to make sure that the identifier for a new object is not the same as an identifier for an object that already exists.

In either case, it is a table lookup problem; see chapter 52, "Table Lookup," for a review of the ways table lookup can be implemented.

 If character values look exactly the same, but SAS says they don't match, it could be because one of the values contains control characters that look like spaces when the value is displayed. Show the values with the $HEX format to unmask the control characters. If you find that a character variable contains control characters that should be spaces, use the TRANSLATE function to convert them to spaces. See a description of the TRANSLATE function in the next chapter, "Strings."

 If a variable is meant to be a unique identifier, validating it involves making sure that each value is unique — that each observation has a unique value. If duplicate observations are found, the program might write log notes, create a report of the duplicates, arbitrarily select one to use, or select one according to a rule.

Start by sorting by the identifier to group duplicate observations together. Then, in a data step, use the automatic FIRST. and LAST. variables to identify the duplicates.

For example, to identify duplicates of the variable ID in the SAS dataset WORK.ALL, first sort WORK.ALL by ID, as shown here:

```
PROC SORT DATA=WORK.ALL;
   BY ID;
RUN;
```

Then this data step writes log notes of any duplicate observations:

```
DATA _NULL_;
   SET WORK.ALL;
   BY ID;
   IF NOT (FIRST.ID AND LAST.ID) THEN PUTLOG 'DUPLICATE ' _ALL_;
RUN;
```

To create an exception report, create a SAS dataset and substitute an OUTPUT statement for the PUT statement. Print the resulting SAS dataset.

 To arbitrarily select one observation when there are duplicates, use the NODUPKEY option of the SORT procedure. Use the OUT= option to name the new SAS dataset that is free of duplicates, WORK.UNIQUE in this example:

```
PROC SORT DATA=WORK.ALL NODUPKEY OUT=WORK.UNIQUE;
   BY ID;
RUN;
```

A log note tells how many duplicate observations were eliminated, for example:

```
NOTE: 2 observations with duplicate key values were deleted.
```

 It is possible to save the duplicate observations in a SAS dataset. Name this second SAS dataset in the DUPOUT= option in the PROC SORT statement.

 To use a rule to select one observation among duplicates, sort the data so that the selected observation appears first or last. Then use a subsetting IF statement with the FIRST. or LAST. variable, such as:

IF FIRST.ID;

The example below resolves duplicates by selecting the most recent observation, which it identifies according to the highest value of the variable DATE. The sorting process puts the observations for each ID value in order of DATE, so that the last one can be selected.

```
PROC SORT DATA=WORK.ALL;
  BY ID DATE;
RUN;
DATA WORK.ALL;
  SET WORK.ALL;
  BY ID;
  IF LAST.ID;
RUN;
```

Integrity Constraints

An integrity constraint attaches a rule of data integrity to a SAS dataset. The rule prevents data from being added or changed in the SAS dataset in a way that would violate the rule. Integrity constraints are useful when a SAS dataset is updated or edited. When a program updates the SAS dataset or a user edits it, the integrity constraint prevents specific kinds of changes to the data and generates an error condition if such changes are attempted. Use statements of the DATASETS procedure to create and manage integrity constraints.

 Of the various kinds of integrity rules, the CHECK rule is the simplest. Use this kind of rule to check the values of variables in a SAS dataset. A CHECK rule is written with the word CHECK followed by a WHERE= option in parentheses.

This is a code model for creating an integrity constraint with a CHECK rule:

```
PROC DATASETS LIBRARY=libref NOLIST;
  MODIFY member;
    IC CREATE name=CHECK(WHERE=(condition));
```

Identify the SAS dataset by writing the libref in the PROC DATASETS statement and the member name in the MODIFY statement. Supply the name and the condition for the integrity constraint in the IC CREATE statement.

The step below creates two integrity constraints with CHECK rules. These integrity constraints belong to the SAS dataset WORK.NEWHIRE and check values of the variables DOB and HIREDATE.

```
PROC DATASETS LIBRARY=CORP NOLIST;
  MODIFY NEWHIRE;
    IC CREATE BORN=CHECK(WHERE=(DOB < DATE()));
    IC CREATE EST_HIRE=CHECK(WHERE=(HIREDATE >= '01JAN1989'D));
RUN;
```

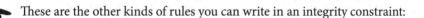

```
NOTE: Integrity constraint BORN defined.
NOTE: Integrity constraint EST_HIRE defined.
```

If a changed value or added observation would violate the integrity constraint, the observation is not added or changed. There is a message that describes the actions of the integrity constraint. In a data step, a violation of an integrity constraint results in a message such as this one:

```
NOTE: There were 0 rejected updates, 1 rejected adds, and 0 rejected
      deletes.
```

It also sets the automatic variable _ERROR_ to 1 to indicate an error condition, and this results in log messages that describe the data of the observation.

In a PROC APPEND step, a violation results in warning messages such as this one:

```
WARNING: Add/Update failed for data set CORP.NEWHIRE because data value(s)
         do not comply with integrity constraint BORN. (Occurred 1 times.)
```

There is a separate message for each integrity constraint that rejected an observation. The messages count the number of observations that are affected. Each observation is counted only once even if it violates multiple integrity constraints. As soon as a violation is found in an observation, processing stops for that observation and any other integrity constraints are not checked.

☞ These are the other kinds of rules you can write in an integrity constraint:

- A NOT NULL rule forces a variable to have a nonmissing value. For example, with the rule NOT NULL(ID), the variable ID cannot have a missing value.
- With a UNIQUE rule, each observation must have a different value for a variable or a different combination of values for a list of variables. For example, with the rule UNIQUE(GROUP PID), each observation must have a unique combination of values for the variables GROUP and PID. If you try to add an observation that has the same values of GROUP and PID as an existing observation, it results in an error condition.
- A PRIMARY KEY rule creates the same limitation as a UNIQUE rule, and it also make it possible for the primary key it creates to be used in another SAS dataset's FOREIGN KEY rule. A SAS dataset can have only one primary key.
- With a FOREIGN KEY rule, the values of variables must match the values in the primary key of another SAS dataset.

Use any combination of integrity constraints in a SAS dataset. Give each integrity constraint a distinct name.

These are examples of statements to define integrity constraints with NOT NULL and UNIQUE rules:

```
IC CREATE ISID=NOT NULL(ID);
IC CREATE UNIQUEID=UNIQUE(ID);
```

Use the CONTENTS procedure to list the integrity constraints of a SAS dataset. See chapter 8, "Actions on SAS Datasets," for details.

Some kinds of integrity constraints require indexes, and they create the indexes they need if the indexes do not exist already. When the CONTENTS procedure lists the indexes, it indicates which ones are used by integrity constraints. If an integrity constraint uses an index, you cannot delete the index unless you delete the integrity constraint first.

To delete an integrity constraint, list it in the IC DELETE statement of the DATASETS procedure. The example below deletes two integrity constraints of CORP.NEWHIRE.

```
PROC DATASETS LIBRARY=CORP NOLIST;
  MODIFY NEWHIRE;
    IC DELETE BORN EST_HIRE;
RUN;
```

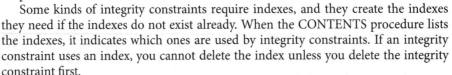

You can add descriptive text to an integrity constraint's violation message. Add the MESSAGE= option to the IC CREATE statement. This example creates two integrity constraints with message text.

```
PROC DATASETS LIBRARY=CORP NOLIST;
  MODIFY NEWHIRE;
    IC CREATE BORN=CHECK(WHERE=(DOB < DATE()))
      MESSAGE='Birth date must be before today.';
    IC CREATE EST_HIRE=CHECK(WHERE=(HIREDATE >= '01JAN1989'D))
      MESSAGE='Hire date is missing or is too early.';
RUN;
```

The message text of the integrity constraint is used as the first part of the message when a violation occurs. These are examples of log messages from a PROC APPEND step:

```
WARNING: Birth date must be before today. Add/Update failed for data set
         CORP.NEWHIRE because data value(s) do not comply with integrity
         constraint BORN. (Occurred 1 times.)
WARNING: Hire date is missing or is too early. Add/Update failed for data
         set CORP.NEWHIRE because data value(s) do not comply with
         integrity constraint EST_HIRE. (Occurred 1 times.)
```

Add the MSGTYPE=USER option to the IC CREATE statement to have the custom message text appear without the standard message.

■ 24

Strings

Most character values are meant to be seen as a succession of characters. This kind of character value is a *string*. Strings can be measured, tested, and transformed using expressions based on functions and operators.

Examples throughout this chapter are based on variables, such as STRING, but this does not mean the expression can be formed only with a variable; any string value can be used in place of STRING. Some examples involving functions use constant values as arguments to illustrate particular effects; the functions would more commonly be formed with variables or expressions based on variables as the arguments. Expressions based on operators are shown enclosed in parentheses. Leave out these parentheses if you use the expression shown as an entire expression, but be sure to keep them if you use the expression as the operand of another operator to form a larger expression.

Measuring and Testing Strings

Use function calls and expressions based on functions to determine most qualities and conditions of string values.

 The most frequent question about a string variable is whether it has a particular value. That is, does the variable match a specific known value? Use the = operator to compare the string to a constant. This WHERE statement, for example, selects observations in which the value of the variable STATE matches the constant value TN:

WHERE STATE = 'TN';

Comparisons ignore trailing spaces, so it does not matter whether the constant or the string has the value 'TN' or 'TN '. The values are compared only up to the last nonblank character, so any spaces added at the end of the value are not considered.

 These are other ways to make character comparisons:

- To compare a value to a list of constant values, use the IN operator:
  (STATE IN ('TN', 'IL', 'MO'))
- To compare a value to a succession of values, use a SELECT block.
- To check for a value that does not match, use the NE or NOTIN operators:
  (STATE NE 'TN') or (STATE NOTIN ('TN', 'IL', 'MO'))

- To compare two string values only up to the length of the shorter value, use the =: operator. The expression 'AX' =: 'AXLE' is true because only the first two characters are compared. Similarly, use the IN:, NE:, and NOTIN: operators to compare with truncation.

The COMPARE function compares two string values in a different way. COMPARE(STRING1, STRING2) returns 0 if STRING1 and STRING2 are equal. If they are different, it returns a positive or negative integer that indicates both the position of the first nonmatching character in the strings and which string is greater.

ABS(COMPARE(STRING1, STRING2)) is the position of the first character that differs. The value returned by the COMPARE function is positive if the first string is greater, negative if the second string is greater.

For example, COMPARE('candle', 'card') is -3, because the strings differ in character position 3, and the second string is greater.

You can write modifier codes in an optional third argument. One useful modifier code is I, which ignores case when comparing letters. For example, COMPARE('cel', 'Cal') is 2. The first letters match when case is ignored, but the second letters do not match. Another modifier code, L, skips leading spaces.

Functions provide information about the length of a string. The string is the only argument to these functions.

- LENGTHN or LENGTH returns the length of the string, not counting trailing spaces. For example, LENGTHN('Thursday') is 8. The value returned by the LENGTH function is always at least 1.
- LENGTHC counts the number of characters in the string; this is the length of the string, counting trailing spaces. For example, LENGTHC('X') is 1, but LENGTHC('X ') is 2.
- LENGTHM or VLENGTH returns the memory length. This is the maximum length that the expression can produce. Use VLENGTH only with a variable; it returns the length of the variable. The VLENGTH, LENGTHC, and LENGTHM functions all return the same result when a variable is used as the argument.

There are several ways to check for a blank string. A string is blank or null if it is equal to a blank or null string. Use the expression (STRING = '') to test whether STRING is blank. A blank value is considered a missing value, so you can also use the MISSING function to test for a blank value. If MISSING(STRING) is 1, then STRING is blank. The length functions can also be useful. The LENGTHN function returns 0 for a blank value; if LENGTHN(STRING) is greater than zero, then STRING has a nonblank value.

Use the LENGTHC function to specifically check for a null string. This function returns 0 for a null string. In SAS, character variables do not have null values; they are always padded with trailing spaces to their full length. Several functions, however, can return null strings.

Other functions measure strings in relation to sets of characters. Use one of the ANY functions to determine whether a string contains one of a class of characters. For example, use ANYLOWER(STRING) to find out whether STRING contains any lowercase letters. The function returns 0 if the string does not contain any characters that belong to the class. If the string does contain one of the characters, the function returns the location of the first such character it finds. For example, ANYLOWER('Cal') returns 2.

These are a few of the character classes:

- ALPHA, UPPER, LOWER: letters, uppercase letters, and lowercase letters
- DIGIT: digits
- ALNUM: alphanumeric characters — letters and digits
- GRAPH: visible characters
- WHITE: whitespace characters such as spaces and tabs
- PUNCT: punctuation characters

Form the function name by combining ANY with the name of the character class: ANYALPHA, ANYUPPER, etc. To check for characters that do not belong to the character class, use a function from the NOT family. Form the function name from NOT and the name of the character class. For example, NOTDIGIT('011M5A') is 4 because the first character in 011M5A that is not a digit is in character position 4.

Use an optional second argument with the ANY and NOT functions to search for additional occurrences. The second argument tells where to start searching. For example, NOTDIGIT('011M5A', 5) is 6 because searching 011M5A starting in position 5 finds a character that is not a digit in character position 6. This search argument can be negative to count positions from the end of the string. The function still returns a positive value for a result; the return value counts character positions from the beginning of the string even if the search argument counts from the end of the string.

To search a string for a specific set of characters that you select, use the INDEXC and VERIFY functions. Write the set of characters as the second argument to the function. The INDEXC function returns the position of the first character in the string that matches a character in the set of characters. For example, INDEXC('AXIS', 'XY') is 2. The X in AXIS is the first X or Y to be found in the value. The INDEXC function returns 0 if none of the characters are found in the string.

To search for a single specific character, write a single character as the second argument for INDEXC. For example, INDEXC(EMAIL, '@') finds the at-sign in the variable EMAIL.

Use the VERIFY function to find the first character that does not belong to the set you specify. The VERIFY function returns 0 if all the characters in the string belong to the set of characters. For example, VERIFY('0100010101', '01') is 0. Use the VERIFY function to verify a string value if only a specific set of characters is permitted in the value. If the function returns 0, the value is valid. If it returns a nonzero value, the string coutains a character other than the ones you expect.

If you need to find out how many characters match or do not match, use the COUNTC function. For example, if you want to make sure EMAIL has exactly one at-sign, use the condition (COUNTC(EMAIL, '@') = 1). Use the modifier code V in the third argument of the COUNTC function to count characters that do not match. For example, COUNTC(STRING, '0123456789', 'V') counts the number of characters in STRING that are not digits. The I modifier code, to ignore the case of letters, is also available.

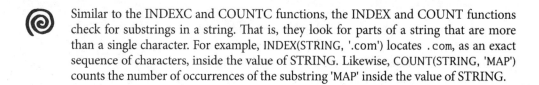

Functions that consider character sets are affected by spaces in the string value and in the character set value. Use the TRIMN and COMPRESS functions, found later in this chapter, to remove spaces from the arguments if necessary.

Similar to the INDEXC and COUNTC functions, the INDEX and COUNT functions check for substrings in a string. That is, they look for parts of a string that are more than a single character. For example, INDEX(STRING, '.com') locates .com, as an exact sequence of characters, inside the value of STRING. Likewise, COUNT(STRING, 'MAP') counts the number of occurrences of the substring 'MAP' inside the value of STRING.

The FINDC and FIND functions are similar to the INDEXC and INDEX functions, but can provide additional control over the search process. Optional arguments can indicate the starting point for the search, as in the ANY and NOT functions, and provide the I and V modifier codes, as in the COUNTC function.

You may need to count the number of leading and trailing spaces in a string. Count leading spaces by finding the first nonblank character with the VERIFY function. The number of leading spaces (for a nonblank string) is:

(VERIFY(STRING, ' ') - 1)

If the string is blank, this expression results in a value of -1.

The number of trailing spaces is computed as the difference between the visual length returned by the LENGTHN function and the character length returned by the LENGTHC function. This expression determines the number of trailing spaces:

(LENGTHC(STRING) - LENGTHN(STRING))

Functions that measure strings can also be used as tests of strings. For example, at the same time that the ANYDIGIT function tells you the position of a digit in a string, it also tells you that at least one digit character is present. If that is what you care about, the ANYDIGIT function returns a true value if at least one digit character is present, a false value if no digit characters are found.

String Transformations

Often, the objective in working with a string is to produce a new version of it that reflects a particular change. Most of the effects are transformations or translations applied to one entire string. Other effects involve extracting a part of the string or combining two or more strings.

Functions provide most of the simple string transformations you are likely to need. Use these functions when they provide the effect you are looking for.

- UPCASE converts letters to uppercase.
- LOWCASE converts letters to lowercase.

- PROPCASE converts the first letter of each word to uppercase and other letters to lowercase. This effect may be known as proper case or title case.
- LEFT left-aligns a string; it moves leading spaces to the end of the string.
- RIGHT right-aligns a string; it moves trailing spaces to the beginning of the string.
- TRIMN removes trailing spaces.
- TRIM also removes trailing spaces. However, for a completely blank string, it retains the first character of the string.
- STRIP removes leading and trailing spaces.
- REVERSE reverses the order of the characters.
- COMPRESS removes all spaces from a string.
- COMPBL converts each sequence of consecutive spaces to single spaces.

The program below demonstrates the use of several of these functions.

```
DATA _NULL_;
  LENGTH STRING UPCASE LOWCASE PROPCASE REVERSE COMPRESS $ 16;
  STRING = 'New York';
  UPCASE = UPCASE(STRING);
  LOWCASE = LOWCASE(STRING);
  PROPCASE = PROPCASE(STRING);
  REVERSE = REVERSE(STRING);
  COMPRESS = COMPRESS(STRING);
  PUT (_ALL_) (=);
RUN;
```

```
STRING=New York UPCASE=NEW YORK LOWCASE=new york PROPCASE=New York
REVERSE=kroY weN COMPRESS=NewYork
```

The named output style used here does not write leading and trailing spaces. The REVERSE function returns leading spaces and other functions return trailing spaces that are not shown above.

 The TRANSLATE function performs any specific character substitutions you select. Write the characters to search for as the third argument of the function and the corresponding replacement characters as the second argument. (Be careful of the order of arguments with this function!) This example changes all vowel letters in a string to asterisks:

TRANSLATE(STRING, '**********', 'AaEeIiOoUu') .

 The TRANWRD function replaces a specific substring, or sequence of characters, with another substring. Write the substring to search for as the second argument and the replacement substring as the third argument. For example, the expression TRANWRD(STRING, '99', '1999') changes all occurrences of 99 to 1999.

 The COMPRESS function with a second argument removes selected characters from a string. For example, COMPRESS('43-A-80', 'AB -') is 4380.

This example removes all semicolons, hyphens, and commas from a string:

COMPRESS(STRING, ';-,')

Be careful not to include a space in the character set argument of the COMPRESS function if you do not want to remove all the spaces from a string. If a variable is used as the character set argument, it may be necessary to use the COMPRESS function to remove the spaces from it, as: COMPRESS(STRING, COMPRESS(CHARS)).

To remove all characters *other than* the selected characters, apply the COMPRESS function twice to the string. For example, COMPRESS(STRING, COMPRESS(STRING, '0123456789')) keeps the digits in STRING and removes all other characters.

To remove all occurrences of a character sequence from a string, call the TRANWRD function with a null string as the third argument.

Compare a string to a transformation of it to test whether the string already has the quality of the transformation. For example, (STRING = LEFT(STRING)) tests whether a string is left-justified; (STRING = UPCASE(STRING)) tests whether all letters in a string are uppercase letters.

Similarly, use measurements of transformations of strings to make measurements that have exclusions. For example, LENGTHN(COMPRESS(STRING)) counts the number of nonblank characters in STRING.

These functions convert to and from specific encodings:

- QUOTE converts a character value to a quoted string. DEQUOTE interprets a quoted string to obtain the character value it represents.
- HTMLENCODE and HTMLDECODE convert values to and from HTML (web page) encoding.
- URLENCODE and URLDECODE convert values to and from URL (network address) encoding.
- NLITERAL converts a string to a SAS name literal.

Use the TRIMN or TRIM function with arguments of the encoding functions to avoid encoding trailing spaces in the result. The following example demonstrates the difference this can make.

```
LENGTH NAME $ 24 QUOTE1 QUOTE2 $ 32;
NAME = 'Rumi';
QUOTE1 = QUOTE(NAME);
QUOTE2 = QUOTE(TRIMN(NAME));
PUT (NAME QUOTE1 QUOTE1) (=/)
```

```
NAME=Rumi
QUOTE1="Rumi                 "
QUOTE2="Rumi"
```

The encoded version of a string can be somewhat longer than the original value, so set variable lengths accordingly.

Substrings and Concatenations

Use the SUBSTRN, SUBSTR, and SUBPAD functions to extract parts of strings. For each of these functions, the first argument is the string, the second argument is the starting character position of the substring, and the optional third argument is the length of the substring. For example, SUBSTRN('EASTERN', 3, 2) is ST, a substring of length 2 beginning at character position 3 in the string EASTERN. The SUBSTR and SUBPAD functions return the same result for these arguments.

The functions differ in the way they react when the arguments are inconsistent. The SUBSTRN function returns a null string if the starting position and length are incorrect or do not select any part of the string; the SUBSTR function generates an error condition when that happens and may ignore the inconsistent arguments. If you use a length argument with the SUBPAD function, it always returns a result of that exact length, padding with trailing spaces when necessary.

These are examples of substring expressions:

- SUBSTRN(STRING, 1, 1) extracts the first character of a string.
  SUBSTRN(STRING, 2) extracts the rest of the characters.
- SUBSTRN(STRING, LENGTHC(STRING)) extracts the last character of a string.
- SUBSTRN(STRING, LENGTHC(STRING)/4, LENGTHC(STRING)/2) extracts the middle part of a string.
- SUBPAD(STRING, 1, 5) changes the length of a string to 5 characters or extracts the first 5 characters of a string.
- SUBSTRN(STRING, N + 1) extracts characters beginning with character position N, or shifts the string value N characters to the left.
- SUBSTRN(STRING, ANYDIGIT(STRING), 1) extracts the first digit from a string, if the string contains a digit.

Use the LENGTH statement to set lengths for variables that you create using the substring functions.

Use substring functions to test parts of a string separately. For example, the expression (SUBSTRN(ZIP, 1, 5) = '90125') checks for a specific value in the first five characters of ZIP, ignoring the other characters that the variable contains.

The expression below tests whether a string contains valid characters to form a SAS word or name. It uses the NOTFIRST function to verify that the first character is a letter or underscore, as is required for a SAS word. It uses the NOTNAME function to verify that the remaining characters, trailing spaces excluded, are letters, underscores, and digits.

NOT (NOTFIRST(SUBSTRN(NAME, 1, 1)) OR NOTNAME(TRIMN(SUBSTRN(NAME, 2))))

SUBSTR is also a pseudo-variable. Assign a value to it in order to replace specific characters of a character variable. This example changes the first character of CODE to an asterisk:

SUBSTR(CODE, 1, 1) = '*';

Use SUBSTR on both sides of the assignment to apply a conversion to part of a character variable. This statement converts all letters in SENTENCE, except the first character, to lowercase letters:

SUBSTR(SENTENCE, 2) = LOWCASE(SUBSTR(SENTENCE, 2));

Use the REPEAT function to generate a string as a repeating pattern. The first argument is the pattern to repeat. It can be a single character or a sequence of characters. The second argument is a number that determines how many times the pattern is repeated. This shows two examples of the use of the REPEAT function:

```
LENGTH REPEAT1 REPEAT2 $ 80;
REPEAT1 = REPEAT('*', 4);
REPEAT2 = REPEAT('END ', 9);
PUT REPEAT1 / REPEAT2;
```

```
*****
END END END END END END END END END END
```

The REPEAT function returns the pattern repeated one more time than the value of the argument. In the first example above, the repetition argument is 4, so the resulting value contains five occurrences of the character.

Use a LENGTH statement to set the length of the variable to which you assign the result of the REPEAT function.

If the pattern argument is a variable and could contain trailing spaces that you would not want in the result, apply the TRIM function to the argument, for example, REPEAT(TRIM(PATTERN), 131). If you do not know the length of the pattern, but you want to use it to fill a certain length, simply repeat the pattern a large number of times and allow the result to be truncated when it is assigned to a variable.

Combine strings using the concatenation operator || and the concatenation functions CAT, CATS, CATT, and CATX.

The concatenation operator and the CAT function concatenate strings. For example, '440' || 'A' or CAT('440', 'A') is 440A.

The concatenation functions can have any number of arguments, and the arguments can be any combination of character and numeric values. The functions convert numeric arguments to text numerals without any spaces before or after. For example, CAT('2', 4, -2.2, 'EX') returns 24-2.2EX.

If you assign the result of a concatenation function to a variable, the variable must be long enough to contain the resulting string. If the variable is not long enough, the function generates an error condition and returns a blank value.

The CATS function removes leading and trailing spaces from strings before concatenating. This is usually what you want when you are combining parts of words or codes. For example, CATS('frog', 's') forms *frogs* as the plural of *frog*.

The CATT function removes trailing spaces, but keeps leading spaces. To help you remember these functions and their effects, the S in CATS stands for the STRIP function; the T in CATT stands for the TRIMN function. CAT, of course, is short for *concatenate*.

The CATX function removes leading and trailing spaces and places a delimiter between them. Use this function to form a sentence, list, or other readable text that uses a delimiter. Write the delimiter as the first argument. These are examples:

- CATX(' ', 'I am', N, 'years old.') forms a sentence such as
  `I am 7 years old.`
- CATX(', ', CITY, STATE) combines two names with a comma and space between to form a string such as `Poughkeepsie, NY`.
- CATX(', ', OF N1-N5) writes numbers as a list, such as `1, 2, 3, 4, 5`.
- CATX('-', START, END) forms text indicating a range, such as `1992-2005`.

More complex results can be obtained by combinations of string techniques.

To center text in a character variable, determine how many spaces can be added before and after the text and place half of them before the text. This is easiest to do using several statements, as shown here:

```
LENGTH TEXT CENTER $ 24;
TEXT = LEFT(TEXT);
SPACECT = LENGTHC(CENTER) - LENGTHN(TEXT);
SUBSTR(CENTER, 1 + 0 MAX FLOOR(SPACECT/2)) = TEXT;
```

When a title is too long to display, it may be shortened by leaving out characters from the the end or the middle, substituting three periods to represent an ellipsis. The statements below shorten the value of TEXT, if necessary, to place it in the shorter variable TITLE. These statements shorten by removing characters from the end:

```
TITLE = LEFT(TEXT);
IF LENGTH(LEFT(TEXT)) > VLENGTH(TITLE) THEN
   SUBSTR(TITLE, VLENGTH(TITLE) - 2) = '...';
```

These statements shorten by removing characters from the middle:

```
TITLE = LEFT(TEXT);
IF LENGTH(LEFT(TEXT)) > VLENGTH(TITLE) THEN DO;
   SUBSTR(TITLE, FLOOR(VLENGTH(TITLE)/2), 3) = '...';
   SUBSTR(TITLE, FLOOR(VLENGTH(TITLE)/2) + 3) =
     SUBSTR(TEXT, LENGTH(TEXT) - CEIL(VLENGTH(TITLE)/2) - 3));
   END;
```

These other approaches are available for specialized string processing:

- The SAS System includes routines to implement two versions of the regular expression language (PRX and RX). These sublanguages can perform many kinds of string measurements and transformations.
- The SCAN and SCANQ functions extract words, tokens, or other logical units from strings. See the next chapter, "Parsing," for details.
- Virtually any string programming task can be accomplished by considering the string one character at a time in a loop. This is described in chapter 40, "Character Loops."
- To process text in a meaningful way, consider it as a set of words, as shown in chapters 81, "Text Processing," and 82, "Text Analysis."

■ 25

Parsing

Parsing is any process of dividing text into its meaningful units. Whenever language is written as text, parsing breaks it into the words, symbols, tags, and other elements in the text. Text data files are parsed to separate the data elements. When codes are made up of components, parsing might be used to extract the parts of the code.

You can often see at a glance the different parts of a text value. For example, even if you are not familiar with chemical notation, it is no problem to pick out the parts of a simple chemical symbol such as H2O, NaHCO3, or CaCl2; the part for each chemical element begins with a capital letter. But writing a program that can find this kind of distinction is not nearly as simple as seeing the distinction yourself.

If you are merely dividing records from an input text file into fields, do that kind of parsing in an INPUT statement. See chapter 12, "Delimited Files."

Parsing is easiest when a specific character, a delimiter, separates data elements. Use the SCAN function to divide the text at the delimiters. The SCAN function's arguments are the string value, the part number to extract, and the delimiter characters.

An e-mail address, for example, consists of a user ID and a domain name, with an at-sign between them. The program below demonstrates how to parse an e-mail address to isolate the user ID and domain name.

```
DATA _NULL_;
  EMAIL = 'pro@globalstatements.com';
  USERID = SCAN(EMAIL, 1, '@');
  DOMAIN = SCAN(EMAIL, 2, '@');
  PUT (_ALL_) (=);
RUN;
```

```
EMAIL=pro@globalstatements.com USERID=pro DOMAIN=globalstatements.com
```

Values returned by the SCAN function can require further processing. Consider names written with the last name first, such as:

```
Wiedlin, Jane
Carlisle, Belinda
```

The comma is the delimiter that separates the last name from the first name, but there is also a space after the comma. Use the LEFT function to remove this space from the first name.

```
LASTNAME = SCAN(NAME, 1, ',');
FIRSTNAME = LEFT(SCAN(NAME, 2, ','));
```

If NAME is `Wiedlin, Jane`, LASTNAME is `Wiedlin` and FIRSTNAME is `Jane`.

The SCAN function uses a default set of delimiters if you omit the third argument. This set of delimiters can be used for many kinds of parsing. For example, it does a respectable job of finding the words in English text.

The example below extracts the words in a sentence and computes some simple word length statistics. The program uses a DO loop, calling the SCAN function repeatedly until it finds all the words of the sentence. The SCAN function returns a blank value when there are no more words to find.

```
DATA _NULL_;
  SENTENCE = 'I think, therefore I am.';
  DO I = 1 TO 80;
    WORD = SCAN(SENTENCE, I);
    IF WORD = '' THEN LEAVE;
    L = LENGTH(WORD);
    IF L < MIN OR MIN < 1 THEN MIN = L;
    IF L > MAX THEN MAX = L;
    SUM + L;
    N = I;
    END;
  MEAN = SUM/N;
  PUT (N SUM MIN MEAN MAX) (=);
RUN;
```

```
N=5 SUM=18 MIN=1 MEAN=3.6 MAX=9
```

Use the SCANQ function instead of the SCAN function if tokens might contain quoted strings. The SCANQ function disregards delimiters that occur within a quoted string. Use the DEQUOTE function, as needed, to interpret the quoted strings.

To parse CSV records, use statements such as:

```
FIELD = SCANQ(LINE, N, ',');
IF COUNTC(FIELD, '"') >= 2 THEN
  FIELD = DEQUOTE(FIELD);
```

PARSING BY SUBSTRINGS

Not all parsing is as simple as finding delimiters. The characters that identify the beginnings or ends of elements could be part of the elements. A different approach is required, using character-search functions to find the next token and the SUBSTRN function to break the string at that point.

Consider the problem of separating the elements in a simple chemical symbol. To do this, you need to break the character string at every capital letter, as demonstrated here:

```
DATA _NULL_;
  COMPOUND = 'NaHCO3';
  REM = COMPOUND;
  ARRAY EL{16} $ 6;
  DO I = 1 TO DIM(EL) WHILE (REM NE '');
    LEN = ANYUPPER(REM, 2) - 1;
    IF LEN = 0 THEN LEN = LENGTH(REM);
    EL{I} = SUBSTRN(REM, 1, LEN);
    REM = SUBSTRN(REM, LEN + 1);
    PUT EL{I};
    END;
RUN;
```

```
Na
H
C
O3
```

As this program executes, the variable REM contains the remaining unparsed characters of the chemical symbol. As the program finds each element, it adds it to the EL array and removes it from REM. Finally, it writes the element as an output line.

The variable LEN is the length of the element, the number of characters it contains. It is calculated based on the ANYUPPER function, which looks for the next capital letter in REM. The subsequent assignment statements use this length with the SUBSTRN function to get the element from REM.

When there are no more capital letters, the entire value of REM is used as the last element, REM becomes blank, and the WHILE condition in the DO statement stops the loop.

The SCAN and SCANQ functions count two or more consecutive delimiter characters as as a single delimiter, so this approach may not work for records that contain empty fields.

Some kinds of data files and parameter files are arranged with one value or parameter on each line, preceded by a text label or name. In reading parameter lines of this kind, parsing is necessary to separate the label from the value. Sometimes a colon follows the label, as shown in these data lines:

```
ISBN: 9-781891-957116
TITLE: Professional SAS Programming Shortcuts
AUTHOR: Rick Aster
```

Use the SCAN function, indicating the specific delimiter, to extract the label and value and the LEFT function to remove any leading spaces from the value. In this example, the data line is the variable LINE, and the label and value are extracted as the variables LABEL and VALUE.

```
LENGTH LINE $ 80 LABEL $ 32 VALUE $ 72;
. . .
LABEL = SCAN(LINE, 1, ':');
VALUE = LEFT(SCAN(LINE, 2, ':'));
```

In another common structure for this kind of file, the label is enclosed in brackets at the beginning of the line, for example:

```
[ISBN]1-891957-06-6
```

Use brackets as the delimiters when parsing this kind of data line, as shown here.

```
LABEL = SCAN(LINE, 1, '[]');
VALUE = LEFT(SCAN(LINE, 2, '[]'));
```

It is sometimes necessary to apply two levels of parsing. This is necessary, for example, when a parameter line of the kind described above contains a list of values separated by commas, as in this example:

```
[COLORS]Yellow, Black, White, Tan
```

After extracting the list of values from the line, parse it using the list delimiter to extract the individual values. This is shown here, as the text in LIST is parsed and assigned to elements of the array LISTITEM.

```
LABEL = SCAN(LINE, 1, '[]');
VALUE = LEFT(SCAN(LINE, 2, '[]'));
DO I = 1 TO DIM(LISTITEM);
   LISTITEM{I} = LEFT(SCAN(VALUE, I, ','));
   IF LISTITEM{I} = '' THEN LEAVE;
   END;
```

■ 26

Variable-Length Strings

The value of a SAS character variable can only be the length of the variable. If a shorter value is assigned to the variable, it is automatically extended to the length of the variable by adding spaces to the end. In most character data, trailing spaces are of no consequence. On those rare occasions when the trailing spaces in a character string are important, you need to take specific actions to keep track of them.

Terminated Strings

The easiest way to mark the length of a string is to use a special character as a terminator, a delimiter placed immediately after the last character of the string. The character that is most commonly used for this is the null character; this is the standard in the C programming language. The null character ('00'X) would not be a part of any normal character string, so it is a natural character to use as a delimiter.

There are surprisingly few compromises in using null-terminated strings in the SAS environment. The null characters tend to display and print the same as blanks. The values compare and sort correctly. The coding required to create and use them is simpler than you might imagine and is based on familiar character functions and operators.

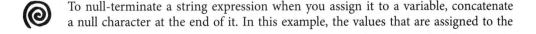 When you declare a variable that you will use for terminated strings, make the variable long enough to hold the string, plus one extra byte for the terminator. If you can do this, it makes the programming much simpler.

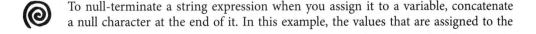 If you can determine the intended length of a string that is already contained in a variable, it is easy to turn it into a null-terminated string. Use the SUBSTR pseudo-variable to change the next character to a null. In this code model, the string variable is STRING, and the length is a numeric variable LEN.

SUBSTR(STRING, LEN + 1) = '00'X;

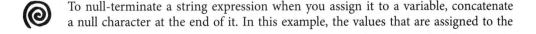 To null-terminate a string expression when you assign it to a variable, concatenate a null character at the end of it. In this example, the values that are assigned to the

variable RTEXT are null-terminated.

IF RCP = . THEN RTEXT = 'Not yet ' || '00'X;
ELSE RTEXT = PUT(RCP, TIME8.) || '00'X;

To determine the length of a null-terminated string, use the INDEXC function to find the terminator, then subtract 1.

LEN = INDEXC(STRING, '00'X) - 1;

The above technique works only if you are sure the string contains a null terminator. If it might not, add a second statement to handle that possibility.

LEN = INDEXC(STRING, '00'X) - 1;
IF LEN < 0 THEN LEN = VLENGTH(STRING);

The VLENGTH function returns the length of the variable.

To extract the string value from a null-terminated string so that you can use it in an expression, use the SCAN function with a null character as the delimiter.

SCAN(STRING, 1, '00'X)

An alternative way to extract the string value is with the SUBSTR function.

SUBSTR(STRING, 1, INDEXC(STRING, '00'X) - 1)

To compare a null-terminated string to a regular string, remove the terminator from the terminated string. This IF-THEN statement tests the value of STRING to see if it is the word *Today*.

IF SCAN(STRING, 1, '00'X) = 'Today' THEN . . .

To write a null-terminated string in an output text file, use the $VARYING format in the PUT statement. The $VARYING format requires a length variable, which must follow the format in the PUT statement. The value of the length variable determines how many characters the format writes.

LEN = INDEXC(STRING, '00'X) - 1;
PUT STRING $VARYING. LEN @;

To concatenate null-terminated strings, remove the terminator from all strings in the concatenation except the last one. This example concatenates two null-terminated strings, STRING1 and STRING2.

(SCAN(STRING, 1, '00'X) || STRING2)

Another way to combine null-terminated strings is by using the SUBSTR pseudo-variable to add characters to the end of a null-terminated string variable. Use the location of the null terminator in the variable as the starting point for the SUBSTR pseudo-variable. This example adds the value of the null-terminated string variable ADD to the end of the null-terminated string variable STRING.

```
STRING = 'Fleet Center, July 31' || '00'X;
ADD = ' (SOLD OUT)' || '00'X;
SUBSTR(STRING, INDEXC(STRING, '00'X)) = ADD;
PUT STRING=;
```

```
STRING=Fleet Center, July 31 (SOLD OUT)
```

In the output line, you can see that the null-terminated string looks the same as a regular string value.

Sometimes it is better to use a visible character as a terminator. This makes it possible to see directly how the terminator is working, and this can let you track down logical errors faster. However, the terminator cannot be any character that could be included in a data value.

Measured Strings

You can use terminated strings only if you know what characters might appear in the data values. If any character could appear, you can still implement a variable-length string by maintaining a separate measurement of the length of the string.

Whenever you assign a value to a measured string variable, assign a value to the length variable at the same time.

To extract the value from a measured string, use the SUBSTR function with the length variable as the length argument. In this example, MSG is the string variable, and MSGLEN is the length variable.

```
SUBSTR(MSG, 1, MSGLEN)
```

Use this extracted value for any string comparisons.

To concatenate two measured strings, concatenate their extracted values and sum their lengths. This example concatenates the values of PART1 and PART2 to form a value for MSG. The respective length variables are PART1LEN, PART2LEN, and MSGLEN.

```
MSG = SUBSTR(PART1, 1, PART1LEN) || SUBSTR(PART2, 1, PART2LEN);
MSGLEN = PART1LEN + PART2LEN;
```

Pascal Strings

A string value and the measurement of its length can be combined in a single variable by placing the length as a binary integer in the first byte of a character value and placing the characters of the string starting in the second byte. I call this kind of value a Pascal string because it is the way strings are structured in the Pascal programming language. Strings of this kind appear in many binary data files.

The largest binary integer value that one byte can hold is 255, so Pascal strings are limited to strings no longer than this length. To allow this maximum length, declare a Pascal string as a character variable of length 256:

LENGTH PS $ 256;

To create a Pascal string, concatenate the binary form of the length with the string value. Use the PIB1. (or S370FPIB1.) format to convert the numeric integer length value to a binary value. In this example, TEXT is the text of the character string, and LEN is its length. These values are combined to form PS, a Pascal string.

PS = PUT(LEN, PIB1.) || TEXT;

To make any practical use of a Pascal string, you need to extract its string value with the SUBSTR function. This expression extracts the string value of the Pascal string PS.

SUBSTR(PS, 2, INPUT(PS, PIB1.))

The INPUT function reads only the first byte of the Pascal string because the width argument of the informat is 1.

To convert a Pascal string to a null-terminated string, remove the length byte and add the null terminator, as shown in this expression.

(SUBSTR(PS, 2, INPUT(PS, PIB1.)) || '00'X)

Do the reverse to convert a null-terminated string to a Pascal string, as shown in this expression.

(PUT(INDEXC(STRING, '00'X) - 1, PIB1.) || SCAN(STRING, 1, '00'X))

27
Foreign Data Types

Only two data types, numeric and character, are native to SAS, but a character variable can contain any binary value. This makes it possible to work with data types that are foreign to SAS. Foreign data types are more difficult to work with than the native SAS data types, but you might use them when you access the data of another environment or for the special advantages they offer for some applications.

A binary integer is the most compact form for an integer value. As a signed integer, a byte can contain values from –128 to 127. As an unsigned integer, it can contain values from 0 to 255. When the values of a variable fall into one of these ranges and compactness is the top priority, you can use a one-byte variable to contain the value. This is the idea of the char data type of the C programming language. There are also occasions for using integer values of two bytes or more for integer values that may go beyond the range of a one-byte integer.

Declare a one-byte integer variable as a character variable with a length of 1. Associate the $HEX or $BINARY informat and format with the variable to make it possible to display and edit the binary values.

Use the PUT function and the S370FPIB format to convert a numeric value to a binary unsigned integer value. This example assigns the value of the numeric variable N to the unsigned binary integer variable BYTE.

```
LENGTH BYTE $ 1;
INFORMAT BYTE $HEX2.;
FORMAT BYTE $HEX2.;
N = 100;
BYTE = PUT(N, S370FPIB1.);
```

Use the INPUT function and the S370FPIB informat to obtain the numeric value of a binary unsigned integer variable. This expression gets the value of the unsigned binary integer variable BYTE.

```
INPUT(BYTE, S370FPIB1.)
```

It is necessary to obtain the numeric value of a binary integer variable before you can use the value for any purpose other than assignment, sorting, or comparison.

Unsigned integer variables can be sorted and compared the same way as ordinary numeric variables.

Use the S370FIB format and informat for a binary signed integer value. Signed integer values cannot be sorted or compared numerically.

Change the length of the variable and the width of the informat and format to create a binary integer of 2 to 8 bytes. Consider this approach for data items only when compactness is paramount. A 2-byte unsigned integer can hold values from 0 to 65,535.

A SAS date value converted to a 2-byte binary unsigned integer can hold dates from 1960 to 2138. This kind of variable can still be sorted and compared, and it takes only half as much storage space as a 4-byte numeric variable.

A union is a variable that may contain multiple kinds of values, but only one at a time. If two variables cannot both have values at the same time, it is possible to combine them into one variable. Programmers do this to save space, especially when working with very large files.

Use unions when a SAS dataset contains different kinds of observations that have different variables. For example, a SAS dataset that contains both pending and completed transactions might contain the date and time of completed transactions and the status of pending transactions.

If the elements of a union are of different data types, you can store them in the same variable only after you convert them both to the same data type, usually character. Define a character variable for a union with a length long enough to hold any of the elements of the union. Make sure there is a way to know which element of the union is present at any particular time. Only look for the element that is there.

A structure is a variable that is divided into multiple values. A character variable can contain more than one value this way. C and many other programming languages support the use of structures, and you might have to deal with structures in SAS if you work with data created in these languages. Structures have other possible advantages in SAS; they can sometimes arrange data more compactly, and they can simplify programming of SELECT blocks and arrays.

To design a structure, decide how many characters or bytes to use for each element and how the data of each element is organized. This is the same way that a record layout for a fixed-length record in a data file is designed.

As an example, a structure for grades might contain a letter grade in byte 1 and a numerical score as an unsigned binary integer in byte 2. The total length of the structure is 2 bytes.

Define a structure as a character variable with a length that is the sum of the lengths of the elements. This example uses a LENGTH statement to define the grade structure.

```
LENGTH GRADE $ 2;
```

Use the SUBSTR pseudo-variable to assign values to an element of a structure. This example assigns a letter grade, A, and a numerical grade, 94, to the grade structure.

```
SUBSTR(GRADE, 1, 1) = 'A';
SUBSTR(GRADE, 2, 1) = PUT(94, S370FPIB1.);
```

Use the SUBSTR function with the same arguments to obtain the value of an element of a structure.

To print the value of the first element of a structure, print the structure variable with a format width that is sufficient for only that element.

Another way to assemble a structure is to concatenate its elements. With this approach, a structure can be a single expression, such as ('A' || PUT(94, S370FPIB1.)). A structure expression might be used in a comparison SELECT block when the actions to take depend on multiple variables. Concatenate the variables in the SELECT statement and the constant values in the WHEN statements. This example shows how this might work for actions that depend on both state and year.

```
SELECT(STATE || PUT(YEAR, Z4.));
   WHEN ('AL2001') . . .
   WHEN ('AL2002') . . .
   . . .
   WHEN ('AK2001') . . .
   . . .
```

When a program uses several closely related arrays, the data can sometimes be easier to work with if it is arranged as an array of structures.

Consider a questionnaire that asks about 25 areas of interest, such as outdoor activities, music, computers, movies, books, and so on. The questionnaire asks the same 12 questions about each subject area: their level of interest, how often they are involved in activities, whether they belong to a club or organization, and so on. The answers would typically be arranged as one array for each question, perhaps defined as:

```
ARRAY INTE{12};
ARRAY FREQ{12};
ARRAY CLUB{12} $ 1;
. . .
```

However, the data might be easier to handle as a single array of structures, with the answers to the 12 questions being elements of each structure in the array.

```
ARRAY ACT{12} $ 31;
```

When a format is used for table lookup, the key value or the lookup value can be a structure. This is a complicated approach, but makes it possible to use a format to do a lookup based on two or more key values. When a table lookup format generates a structure as its result, this is faster and sometimes simpler than using two separate table lookup formats for two related variables.

If two structures are the same type, use an assignment statement to assign the entire value of one structure to the other.

Like a structure, a pseudo-array contains multiple data elements. However, the elements of a pseudo-array all have the same form. Most often, the elements of a pseudo-array are single characters; however, they could be any data type. A pseudo-array is used like an array, but is defined as only one variable.

Design a pseudo-array by determining the number of elements and the length of each element. Multiply these numbers and use the product as the length of the pseudo-array. Declare a pseudo-array as a character variable. For example, if STATUS is a pseudo-array with 12 elements, each a single character, define it as shown here.

LENGTH STATUS $ 12;

Use the SUBSTR pseudo-variable to assign a value to an element of a pseudo-array. Set the second argument of the SUBSTR pseudo-variable to select a specific element of the pseudo-array. This example assigns a value to the 5th element of STATUS.

SUBSTR(STATUS, 5, 1) = 'X';

Use the SUBSTR function in the same way to obtain the value of an element of a pseudo-array.

If the element length is greater than 1, calculate the starting position of element *i* using the formula

$$(i - 1)*length + 1$$

The following macro can be used to implement references to the elements of a pseudo-array.

```
%MACRO PSAY(NAME, INDEX, LENGTH);
SUBSTR(&NAME, %EVAL((&INDEX - 1)*&LENGTH + 1), &LENGTH)
%MEND;
```

The parameters of the PSAY macro are the variable name, element number, and element length. If RANGE is a pseudo-array with 6-byte elements, then %PSAY(RANGE, 5, 6) is a reference to its 5th element.

Pseudo-arrays are commonly used for table lookup. This is an especially efficient technique when the lookup values are single characters.

The letters of the alphabet provide a familiar example of table lookup. This pseudo-array ALPHABET can be used to translate between the letters of the alphabet and the corresponding numbers:

RETAIN ALPHABET 'ABCDEFGHIJKLMNOPQRSTUVWXYZ';
To find the letter that corresponds to a specific number, use an expression such as:

SUBSTRN(ALPHABET, N, 1)

To find the number of a letter of the alphabet, use this kind of expression:

FINDC(ALPHABET, LETTER)

A character value might also represent a set of characters without implying any sequence. That is, the order of the characters in the value does not matter because the program only considers whether specific characters are present or not. For example, this is the way the character set arguments for functions such as FINDC, COUNTC, and COMPRESS are used. In addition, these functions can be used to process a character set variable.

To determine whether a character set variable contains a specific character, use the FINDC (or INDEXC) function with the character as first argument and the character set as the second. For example FINDC('U', CHARS) returns 1 if CHARS contains the letter U, 0 if it does not.

Usually, sets of characters do not contain the space character. When you use the set of characters in an expression, use the TRIMN (or COMPRESS) function to remove any trailing spaces from the set. That is, if the variable CHARS contains a set of characters, use the expression TRIMN(CHARS) to refer to it.

To add a character to a set of characters, concatenate it. This statement adds the + character to the set of characters in the variable CHARS.

```
CHARS = CATS(CHARS, '+');
```

Use the COMPRESS function to remove a character from a set. This statement removes the # character from CHARS.

```
CHARS = COMPRESS(CHARS, '#');
```

Most of the time, the order of characters in a set does not matter, and duplicate characters make no difference. However, if you want to compare two variables that contain sets of characters, you must first standardize their values by sorting the characters and eliminating the duplicates.

The simplest technique for sorting a set of characters is the bubble sort. This example sorts the value of the variable CHARS, ignoring any trailing spaces that the variable might contain.

```
LENGTH SWAPCHAR $ 1;
N = LENGTH(CHARS);
* Bubble sort: swap characters until all characters are in order. ;
DO UNTIL (COUNT = 0);
  COUNT = 0;
  DO C = 2 TO N;
    IF SUBSTR(CHARS, C, 1) >=SUBSTR(CHARS, C - 1, 1) THEN CONTINUE;
    COUNT + 1;
    SWAPCHAR = SUBSTR(CHARS, C - 1, 1);
    SUBSTR(CHARS, C - 1, 1) = SUBSTR(CHARS, C, 1);
    SUBSTR(CHARS, C, 1) = SWAPCHAR;
    END;
  END;
```

After you sort a set of characters, remove duplicates. Check consecutive characters; if they match, remove one of them. The statements here remove duplicate characters from the character variable CHARS.

```
DO C = 2 TO VLENGTH(CHARS);
  IF C > LENGTH(CHARS) THEN LEAVE;
  DO WHILE (SUBSTR(CHARS, C - 1, 1) = SUBSTR(CHARS, C, 1));
    IF C + 1 > VLENGTH(CHARS) THEN SUBSTR(CHARS, C) = ' ';
    ELSE SUBSTR(CHARS, C) = SUBSTR(CHARS, C + 1);
    IF C > LENGTH(CHARS) THEN LEAVE;
    END;
  END;
```

■ 28

Codes

A code is a symbol or value that identifies or stands for something. Codes are often called numbers, but they are not numbers in the usual sense; they do not indicate a quantity or measurement. They are not used in arithmetic, and they often contain letters or symbols that are not used for writing numbers. The table at left shows examples of some familiar kinds of codes.

In addition to the codes that you find in the data you work with, you might also create codes for use in a specific program or variable, or for the exchange of information between one program and another. When databases are designed, it is usually necessary to create unique identifying codes for the people, events, and other items that are represented in the database.

FAMILIAR CODES

License plate number	PZ 0000
Social security number	123-45-6789
Telephone number	1-800-555-1212
Universal Product Code	7-68068-26001-8
ZIP code	19301-0176
Size	XL

 Usually, codes should be character variables. However, it is possible for some codes that are written as numbers or digits to be implemented as numeric variables, and some programmers use numeric variables for codes whenever they can. When you have to decide the data type for a code variable, consider these points.

- Character variables can contain codes of any length (up to 32,768 characters).
- Numeric variables can contain codes that consist only of digits. However, a numeric variable cannot accurately contain a value longer than 15 digits.
- Many people think of codes as "numbers."
- When codes are character variables, it ensures that the code variables will not accidentally be analyzed or summarized as numeric values.
- Leading zeros are optional in writing some kinds of codes, such as account numbers. The code values are sometimes written with leading zeros and sometimes written without leading zeros. If the code values are short enough, it might be easier to handle this kind of code as a numeric variable. If you make this kind of code a character variable, you may need to fill in leading zeros when you read a value from an input file or other source.
- If code values vary in length and have leading zeros, you must use a character variable for the code.

- Many code values are displayed with punctuation that is not actually part of the data. The values can be stored more compactly without the punctuation. The program must translate between the stored form, without punctuation, and the visual form, with punctuation. This translation is easier to do with character variables.

Code I/O and Conversions

 Use the $CHAR or $F informat and format to read and write standard character code values.

 Use the Z format to write numeric code values with leading zeros.

 If a code field in a file uses a packed decimal format or another condensed form of a digit string, it takes two statements to create a character code variable from it. First use the appropriate numeric informat to read the field, then use the PUT function with the Z format to convert the numeric value to the character code value. This example reads a three-byte packed decimal field that contains a five-digit ZIP code.

```
DATA ZIP (DROP=ZIP_NUMBER);
. . .
   INPUT @1 ZIP_NUMBER PD3.;
   ZIP = PUT(ZIP_NUMBER, Z5.);
. . .
```

As shown here, do not save the temporary numeric variable (ZIP_NUMBER in this example) in the resulting SAS dataset.

 A code that consists of a fixed number of characters, all digits, is a digit string. Usually, a digit string should be stored in character form. If the variable is used mainly for display, comparing, grouping, and sorting, or if efficiency is important, a digit string may be stored in packed hexadecimal form (sometimes called "binary coded decimal"). This approach reduces the size of the code variable by half.
To work with a digit string in packed hexadecimal form:

- Declare the variable as a character variable with a length that is half the number of digits. If the code has an odd number of digits
- Use the $HEX informat and format to read and write the code values. Use the INFORMAT and FORMAT statements to permanently associate the informat and format with the variable.
- To compare a packed hexadecimal variable to a constant, write the constant value as a character hexadecimal constant, for example, IF SKU = '1485'X . . .
- If the code has an odd number of digits, the packed hexadecimal value has an extra 0 at the end. Write this extra zero in any constant values.

The following example demonstrates these points using the variable ZIP for a five-digit ZIP code. The sixth digit in ZIP will always be 0.

Program	Input	Output

DATA PLACES;
  LENGTH ZIP $ 3;
  INFORMAT ZIP $HEX5.;
  FORMAT ZIP $HEX5.;
  INFILE IN;
  INPUT ZIP $HEX5.;
  IF ZIP = '193010'X THEN PUTLOG ZIP=;
RUN;
	08623
	10001
	19301
	33337
	40201
		ZIP=19301

Some codes are stored without punctuation, but are displayed with a specific pattern of punctuation. For example, a database usually stores only the digits of a telephone number, but when a telephone number is displayed, you may want to show it with punctuation added to make it easier to read.

Use the COMPRESS function to remove punctuation from a code. This example removes common punctuation characters from telephone numbers.

```
DATA _NULL_;
  PHONE1 = '800-555-1212';
  PHONE2 = COMPRESS(PHONE1, '()-+ .,/');
  PUTLOG PHONE1= PHONE2=;
RUN;
```

PHONE1=800-555-1212 PHONE2=8005551212

To add punctuation at fixed positions in a code, use the SUBSTR pseudo-variable for each part of the code. This example shows hyphens added to a telephone number.

```
DATA _NULL_;
  LENGTH PHONE $ 10 PPHONE $ 12;
  PHONE = '8005551212';
  SUBSTR(PPHONE, 1, 3) = SUBSTR(PHONE, 1, 3);
  SUBSTR(PPHONE, 4, 1) = '-';
  SUBSTR(PPHONE, 5, 3) = SUBSTR(PHONE, 4, 3);
  SUBSTR(PPHONE, 8, 1) = '-';
  SUBSTR(PPHONE, 9, 4) = SUBSTR(PHONE, 7, 4);
  PUTLOG PHONE= PPHONE=;
RUN;
```

PHONE=8005551212 PPHONE=800-555-1212

If a code is anything other a regular character value, convert it to a text characters and use the text form as the starting point for adding punctuation.

Some codes are constructed as combinations of other codes. Use functions to assemble these codes and to extract the component code values from them.

Use the SUBSTR function to extract a part of a code based on character positions. This example extracts the area code from the first three digits of a telephone number.

```
DATA _NULL_;
  LENGTH PHONE $ 10 AREACODE $ 3;
  PHONE = '8005551212';
```

```
   AREACODE = SUBSTR(PHONE, 1, 3);
   PUTLOG PHONE= AREACODE=;
RUN;
```

```
PHONE=8005551212  AREACODE=800
```

Use the SCAN function to extract a part of a code based on punctuation. Chapter 23, "Parsing," describes the use of this function.

Use the CATS function to assemble a code with punctuation if the parts may vary in length. If the variables IP1-IP4 contain the IP address numbers 111, 22, 34, and 5, the expression CATS('.', OF IP1-IP4) combines them to form the value 111.22.34.5, the visual form of the IP address.

Use the INPUT function with an informat or the PUT function with a format to convert a code between numeric, character, and packed hexadecimal forms.

- Use the standard numeric (F) informat to convert a digit string to a numeric value.
- Use the Z format to convert a numeric code value to a character code value with leading zeros.
- Use the $HEX informat to convert a character code value to a packed hexadecimal code value. Use the $HEX format for the opposite conversion.
- Use the $PK format to convert a numeric code value to a packed hexadecimal code value. Use the $PK informat for the opposite conversion.

Sometimes when a code is expanded, the values are converted by adding a prefix, usually zeros, before the existing code values. If account numbers are expanded from 8 to 10 characters, the account number 22031579 might become 0022031579.

This example concatenates the prefix 00 and an 8-digit code to generate a 10-digit code.

```
DATA _NULL_;
   LENGTH CODE8 $ 8 CODE10 $ 10;
   CODE8 = '22031579';
   SUBSTR(CODE10, 1, 2) = '00';
   SUBSTR(CODE10, 3, 8) = CODE8;
   PUTLOG CODE10=;
RUN;
```

```
CODE10=0022031579
```

Use the SUBSTR function to do the reverse conversion, removing leading zeros to convert a code back to the older, shorter form. Make sure, though, that the digits you remove are the expected prefix value. If they are not, you cannot do the conversion.

This example extracts an 8-digit code from a 10-digit code by removing two leading zeros. It generates an error message if the first two digits of the 10-digit code are not zeros.

```
DATA _NULL_;
```

```
LENGTH CODE8 $ 8 CODE10 $ 10;
CODE10 = '0022031579';
IF CODE10 =: '00' THEN CODE8 = SUBSTR(CODE10, 3, 8);
ELSE DO;
  CODE8 = 'EEEEEEEE';
  PUTLOG 'Data error: ' CODE10 'is not a valid 8-digit code. (' _N_= +(-1) ')';
  END;
RUN;
```

 It is sometimes necessary to replace one code with another. For example, when two databases are combined, the ID codes of one database may have to be converted to the ID codes of the other database. Replacing one code with another is a process called recoding, and this can be done with any table lookup technique. See chapter 52, "Table Lookup," for details.

Serial Numbers and Check Digits

The codes that identify individual appliances, musical instruments, and other manufactured items may be called serial numbers regardless of how they are generated. However, in the most literal meaning of serial number, it is a code generated as a consecutive counting number. That is, each new serial number is generated by adding 1 to the numeric value of the previous one. This is the simplest way to create unique identifying codes, and these kinds of codes are used often. For example, serial numbers are printed on tags and stickers that are attached to physical items, and on blank documents, such as checks. Computer programs also generate serial numbers to identify various kinds of items, such as events and transactions.

 Use a control dataset, a separate permanent SAS dataset with a single observation, to keep track of the components of the serial number generation process. Store the last serial number that was assigned, the next one that is available, or both. It is usually easiest to store these numbers in numeric variables, even when the generated serial numbers are character values. A control dataset for generating serial numbers might look like this:

```
PROC PRINT DATA=MAIN.ESERIAL WIDTH=FULL;
RUN;
```

Obs	LAST_SERIAL	NEXT_SERIAL
1	1000	1001

Use the MODIFY statement with the POINT= option and the REPLACE statement to access and update the control dataset. Update the control dataset for every serial number you generate.

Use the PUT function and a format to convert the numeric value to a character code value. Use the PK format if the code variable is in packed hexadecimal format.

This program demonstrates the process of generating serial numbers as identifiers for data that is read from input text records.

```
DATA NEW.HIRE (KEEP=EMPL NAME HIREDATE SSN) MAIN.ESERIAL;
  LENGTH EMPL $ 4;
  INFORMAT EMPL $HEX8.;
  FORMAT EMPL $HEX8.;
  INFILE HIRE;
  INPUT NAME $40. HIREDATE YYMMDD10. SSN $11.;
  * Generate employee ID number. ;
  POINT = 1;
  MODIFY MAIN.ESERIAL POINT=POINT;
  EMPL = PUT(NEXT_SERIAL, PK4.);
  LAST_SERIAL = NEXT_SERIAL;
  NEXT_SERIAL = NEXT_SERIAL + 1;
  REPLACE MAIN.ESERIAL;
  OUTPUT NEW.HIRE;
RUN;
```

If the value of NEXT_SERIAL is 1001 before this step runs, and the step reads two input records, then it assigns them the serial numbers 00001001 and 00001002, and it changes the value of NEXT_SERIAL to 1003.

Do not store the variables of the serial number generation process, other then the generated serial number itself, in any output SAS dataset. In this step, the KEEP= option ensures that only the relevant variables are kept in NEW.HIRE.

However you generate serial numbers, the set of code values you generate is finite. That is, you could eventually generate the last serial number in the set. Handle this possibility in one of these ways:

- Determine how many serial numbers could eventually be needed, and make the code variable long enough to hold this many distinct serial numbers.
- Wrap around to start again at 0 or 1 after the last serial number is generated. This approach works well when serial numbers are used to identify items that are of interest only for a limited period of time. One way to do this is with the MOD function, for example:

```
NEXT_SERIAL = MOD(NEXT_SERIAL + 1, 1E8);
```

- Have the program write a warning message when it is approaching the end of the set of serial numbers. Reset or redesign the system at that point.

The double precision format of SAS numeric values can accurately generate serial numbers of up to 15 digits. If serial numbers must be longer than this, you will need a more elaborate technique to generate them.

Often, a code is constructed by concatenating a fixed character value with a serial number. This is the way serial numbers of most manufactured items are generated. For example, the prefix CMB102X could be combined with the number 00002458 to form the serial number CMB102X-00002458. Store the prefix in the control file along with the next available serial number.

This code fragment shows how this kind of serial number can be generated.

```
POINT = 1;
```

```
MODIFY MAIN.PSERIAL POINT=POINT;
SERIAL = PREFIX || '-' || PUT(NEXT_SERIAL, Z8.);
LAST_SERIAL = NEXT_SERIAL;
NEXT_SERIAL = NEXT_SERIAL + 1;
REPLACE MAIN.PSERIAL;
```

In this example, the variable PREFIX from the control dataset contains the fixed part of the serial number. This is concatenated with a hyphen and the numeric part of the serial number to form the complete serial number, which is assigned to the variable SERIAL.

 The systematic way serial numbers are generated makes them predictable, and this quality is sometimes a disadvantage. For security reasons, do not use serial numbers as account numbers or for any identifying codes that customers use to access sensitive information. Instead, use a more complicated algorithm that includes elements of randomness to make it difficult for anyone to guess what the code values might be.

 Many serial numbers and other numeric codes have an extra digit added to the end. This check digit is computed from the other digits of the code value. Using a check digit makes it possible to catch most errors that occur when code numbers are transcribed.

Compute a check digit based on the rule that defines the check digit for the specific kind of code. For this simplistic example, suppose that the code consists of a seven-digit serial number followed by a check digit, and the check digit is selected so that the sum of all the digits is a multiple of 10. The program calculates the appropriate check digit and adds it to the code value.

```
DATA _NULL_;
  CODE = '0123456 ';

  DIGITSUM = 0;
  DO I = 1 TO 7;
    DIGITSUM + INPUT(SUBSTR(CODE, I, 1), F1.);
    END;
  CHECK = 10 - MOD(DIGITSUM, 10);
  SUBSTR(CODE, 8, 1) = PUT(CHECK, F1.);

  PUT CODE=;
RUN;
```

```
CODE=01234569
```

The sum statement inside the DO loop extracts each digit in turn, converts it to a numeric value, and adds it to the digit sum. From this, the numeric value of the check digit is computed. The check digit value is converted to a character and added to the code value as its eighth digit.

Use the same rule to validate a code value that includes the check digit. Reject a code number if the check digit you compute does not match the check digit actually contained in the code.

29
Text Encryption

The purpose of encryption is to make data harder to read. It applies a specific process to convert data to a form that cannot be easily recognized.

Encryption can protect data from scrutiny only if key parts of the encryption process are kept secret. An encryption process written into a SAS program cannot provide that level of security because SAS programs are not any more secure than other text files. But by obscuring data to a degree, this level of encryption can make it possible for people to work with the data without learning its actual meaning. In a research project, for example, this would reduce the risk that researchers would apply any kind of unconscious bias as they analyze or manage the data.

Character Substitution

Character substitution is one of the oldest encryption techniques. It uses a set of characters, mapping each character in the set onto a different character. To encrypt text in this way, you might change A to X, B to M, C to A, and so on. To decrypt the text, you need to know the encryption mapping so that you can do the inverse mapping, changing X to A, M to B, and so on.

Consider the text POVT WGONWTD KOL OPPTNPACN. At a glance, this text is meaningless, but if you know the mapping involved, you can decipher the coded text to arrive at the actual message, TAKE CHANCES PAY ATTENTION.

To set up a character mapping, write a set of characters as a character string, then write the same set of characters in a completely different sequence as a second character string. It can be convenient to make these strings macro variables. This example uses a character set of only capital letters, but the same technique can apply to any set of characters.

```
%LET ALPHA = ABCDEFGHIJKLMNOPQRSTUVWXYZ;
%LET ORDER = OUWFTHQGASVIZNCKBEDPRXMJLY;
```

Use the TRANSLATE function with the two different sequences of the character set to encrypt a value.

```
TEXT = 'TAKE CHANCES PAY ATTENTION';
CODE = TRANSLATE(TEXT, "&ORDER", "&ALPHA");
PUTLOG CODE=;
```

```
CODE=POVT WGONWTD KOL OPPTNPACN
```

To decrypt a value, swap the two character set arguments in the function call.

```
CODE = 'POVT WGONWTD KOL OPPTNPACN';
TEXT = TRANSLATE(CODE, "&ALPHA", "&ORDER");
PUTLOG TEXT=;
```

```
TEXT=TAKE CHANCES PAY ATTENTION
```

Transposition

A transposition algorithm changes the order of characters according to a defined pattern. That is, when a value is encrypted, it still uses the same characters, but they appear in a different order. Transposition is especially useful for code numbers.

To set up a transposition mapping, determine the number of characters in the variable to encrypt. Write the counting numbers from 1 to this number, but arrange them in an arbitrary sequence. Make this sequence a macro variable. This example is designed to encrypt a 16-character code, so it uses the numbers from 1 to 16.

```
%LET RES = 13 11 5 15 3 10 2 6 8 9 14 7 4 16 12 1;
```

In a data step, define an array of temporary variables, initializing it with these values.

```
ARRAY SEQUENCE{16} _TEMPORARY_ (&RES);
```

Use the SUBSTR pseudo-variable and function in a DO loop for both encryption and decryption. To encrypt, set each character in the encrypted value to the character selected by the corresponding element.

```
DATA _NULL_;
  LENGTH PLAIN CRYPT $ 16;
  ARRAY SEQUENCE{16} _TEMPORARY_ (&RES);
  PLAIN = '6011000123456789';
  DO I = 1 TO 16;
    SUBSTR(CRYPT, I, 1) = SUBSTR(PLAIN, SEQUENCE{I}, 1);
    END;
PUTLOG CRYPT=;
RUN;
```

```
CRYPT=6408130012701956
```

Long sequences of digits look meaningless to most people, so the encrypted code shown here looks just as plausible as the original code.

To decrypt, reverse the terms of the assignment statement so that the DO loop is:

```
DO I = 1 TO 16;
  SUBSTR(DECRYPT, SEQUENCE{I}, 1) = SUBSTR(CRYPT, I, 1);
  END;
```

It is possible to use both character substitution and transposition on the same variable. When you use the two techniques together, it does not matter which one you apply first.

■ 30
Discrete Binary Encoding

Nearly all SAS data includes variables that define categories, or groups of observations, and variables that identify specific qualities of an observation. Categorical and qualitative variables are usually character variables. They could have any length and can make up a significant fraction of the size of a dataset. However, in most cases, it is possible to dramatically shorten these variables without losing any information. Many variables can be shortened to a length of 1 byte. This can significantly reduce the size of SAS datasets and increase the speed of programs, and it can do so without a great cost in the use of memory and without any elaborate programming techniques.

Variables are made shorter by substituting discrete binary codes for the text values of the variable. Discrete binary encoding is especially useful when:

- The variable is displayed as text of two characters or more.
- The values of the variable belong to a relatively fixed set. That is, you do not expect to encounter frequent new values for the variable.
- The variable has a limited number of distinct values — especially if the number is less than 256.
- There are thousands of observations, or there are many variables that use the same set of values.

Discrete binary encoding makes use of these SAS features:

- Value informats, which convert text values to binary values.
- Value formats, which convert the binary values back to text values for display.
- The control dataset feature of the FORMAT procedure, which allows formats and informats to be defined from values in a SAS dataset.
- The informat and format attributes of variables, which allow the value informats and value formats to be used automatically with a variable.
- The S370FPIB informat and format, which convert between a one-byte character value and the corresponding numeric integer value.

 Start by creating a sorted list of the text values that a variable takes on. You might already have this list as part of the definition of a database, file, or code. If not, you can obtain it by writing a program to make a list of the values.

This SQL example creates the SAS dataset (table) MAIN.REGION that includes all the distinct values of REGION that it finds in the SAS dataset MAIN.LOC.

```
CREATE TABLE MAIN.REGION AS
SELECT DISTINCT(REGION) FROM MAIN.LOC
ORDER BY REGION;
```

The ORDER BY clause puts the values in sorted order, an important detail. When you sort a binary code variable, its values come out in binary order. Sort the list of text values before you assign numbers to them to ensure that the binary sort order will match the order of the sorted text.

A series of sidebars in this chapter shows the four key components of discrete binary encoding. Sidebar 1, at left, shows an example of a numbered list of values.

From the list of text values, you can define the value informat and value format for the binary encoding. If there are only a few different values and you don't mind writing in hexadecimal, you can write INVALUE and VALUE statements to define the informat and format.

For the value informat, use the text values as ranges and the corresponding numbers, written as character hexadecimal constants, as labels. Give the informat an appropriate name (beginning with a dollar sign). Use the JUST informat option unless values could contain leading spaces. Usually, use the UPCASE informat option and write the text values in uppercase letters.

Include two special ranges. Start with a blank range with a 0 (null) label. This gives you a way to handle missing values. Conclude with the special range keyword OTHER, which handles unexpected input values. Use the label 'FF'X, the highest value of a byte, as a catch-all "other" value. Or, if an unexpected value should be treated as a data error, use the special label keyword _ERROR_.

For the value format, use the character hexadecimal form of the numbers as ranges. Use the text values as labels. Give the format the same name as the informat. Include a 0 range with a blank label. Also include the special range keyword OTHER and the label '[$HEX2.]' or '(|$HEX2.|)' — a reference to the $HEX format that allows any invalid values that occur to be seen.

Sidebar 2, at right, creates the informat $COUNTY and a format of the same name from the list in Sidebar 1.

1. VALUES

Start with a sorted list of values. This is a list of counties in Ireland.

```
 1   Carlow
 2   Cavan
 3   Clare
 4   Cork
 5   Donegal
 6   Galway
 7   Kerry
 8   Kilkenny
 9   Laois
10   Leitrim
11   Limerick
12   Longford
13   Mayo
14   Offaly
15   Roscommon
16   Sligo
17   Tipperary
18   Waterford
19   Westmeath
20   Wexford
```

2. FORMAT/ INFORMAT

Create a value informat and a value format.

```
PROC FORMAT
   LIBRARY=LIBRARY;
INVALUE $COUNTY
   (UPCASE JUST)
   ' ' = '00'X
   'CARLOW' = '01'X
   'CAVAN' = '02'X
   'CLARE' = '03'X
   'CORK' = '04'X
   'DONEGAL' = '05'X
   'GALWAY' = '06'X
   'KERRY' = '07'X
   'KILKENNY' = '08'X
   'LAOIS' = '09'X
   'LEITRIM' = '0A'X
   'LIMERICK' = '0B'X
   'LONGFORD' = '0C'X
   'MAYO' = '0D'X
   'OFFALY' = '0E'X
   'ROSCOMMON' ='0F'X
   'SLIGO' = '10'X
   'TIPPERARY' = '11'X
   'WATERFORD' = '12'X
   'WESTMEATH' = '13'X
   'WEXFORD' = '14'X
   OTHER = 'FF'X;
VALUE $COUNTY
   '00'X = ' '
   '01'X = 'Carlow'
   '02'X = 'Cavan'
   '03'X = 'Clare'
   '04'X = 'Cork'
   '05'X = 'Donegal'
   '06'X = 'Galway'
   '07'X = 'Kerry'
   '08'X = 'Kilkenny'
   '09'X = 'Laois'
   '0A'X = 'Leitrim'
   '0B'X = 'Limerick'
   '0C'X = 'Longford'
   '0D'X = 'Mayo'
   '0E'X = 'Offaly'
   '0F'X = 'Roscommon'
   '10'X = 'Sligo'
   '11'X = 'Tipperary'
   '12'X = 'Waterford'
   '13'X = 'Westmeath'
   '14'X = 'Wexford'
   OTHER = '[$HEX2.]';
RUN;
```

3. TRANSLATE

Use the value informat to convert the character data to binary data.

```
DATA LOC2 (DROP=COUNTYX);
   SET LOC1;
   LENGTH COUNTY $ 1;
   INFORMAT COUNTY $COUNTY.;
   FORMAT COUNTY $COUNTY.;
   COUNTY = INPUT(COUNTYX, $COUNTY.);
RUN;
```

Use the LIBRARY=LIBRARY option, as shown in the example, to store the resulting informat and format in the catalog LIBRARY.FORMATS. This makes them available for use in the future.

4. DISPLAY

Use the value format to display the binary values.

```
COUNTY = '0D'X;
FORMAT COUNTY $COUNTY.;
PUT COUNTY=;
```

```
COUNTY=Mayo
```

To troubleshoot, use the $HEX2. format.

```
COUNTY = '0D'X;
PUT 'County (hexadecimal): ' COUNTY $HEX2.
   / 'County (text): ' COUNTY $COUNTY.;
```

```
County (hexadecimal): 0D
County (text): Mayo
```

 Use the value informat to read or translate the values for the binary code variable. If the text values are already in a SAS dataset, create a new SAS dataset with the binary code values. Use the INPUT function with the value informat to translate the values.

After you create the binary variable, you can drop the text variable. This is shown in the example in Sidebar 3. Not saving the much longer text variable can save a considerable amount of storage space, in proportion to the length of the text.

 If you read text values from a text data file, use the value informat to read the variable.

 Set the informat and format attributes of the binary code variable to use the value informat and format. This makes it possible to display and edit the SAS dataset interactively, and it makes debugging easier.

 Use the value format whenever you display or write the binary code variable. The output of the value format is the same text that you expect to see for the variable.

If you need to troubleshoot a binary code variable or its value format, display the variable using the $HEX format.

TWO-BYTE BINARY CODES

A one-byte binary code variable is limited to 254 distinct values, plus a blank value and an error value. With a two-byte binary code variable, you can use up to 65,534 distinct values. To use a two-byte binary code variable:

- Declare the variable with a length of 2.
- Use four-digit character hexadecimal constants in INVALUE and VALUE statements.
- Use 'FFFF'X instead of 'FF'X as the error value in the value informat.
- Use a width argument of 2 with the S370FPIB format and informat.

Value informats and value formats that have very large numbers of ranges are less efficient and can be problematic. Taken to the extreme, they can cause programs to run slowly, run out of memory, or crash. For this reason, using a binary code variable with a length of more than 2 bytes is not recommended.

2(A). FORMAT/INFORMAT

Create the value informat and format automatically from a SAS dataset containing the values.

```
PROC SORT DATA=COUNTY NODUPKEY;
  BY COUNTY;
RUN;
* Create value informat $COUNTY *;
DATA CNTL1;
  LENGTH TYPE $ 1 FMTNAME $ 8
    START $ 10 LABEL $ 8 HLO $ 4;
  RETAIN TYPE 'J' FMTNAME '$COUNTY' HLO 'UJ ';
  SET COUNTY (KEEP=COUNTY
    RENAME=(COUNTY=START)) END=LAST;
  START = UPCASE(START);
  LABEL = PUT(_N_, S370FPIB1.);
  OUTPUT;
  IF LAST THEN DO;
    * Missing value. ;
    START = ' ';
    LABEL = '00'X;
    OUTPUT;
    * Invalid value. ;
    START = ' ';
    LABEL = 'FF'X;
    HLO = 'UJO ';
    OUTPUT;
    END;
RUN;
PROC FORMAT CNTLIN=CNTL1 LIBRARY=LIBRARY;
RUN;

* Create value format $COUNTY *;
DATA CNTL2;
  LENGTH TYPE $ 1 FMTNAME $ 8
    START $ 1 LABEL $ 10 HLO $ 1;
  RETAIN TYPE 'C' FMTNAME '$COUNTY';
  SET COUNTY (KEEP=COUNTY
    RENAME=(COUNTY=LABEL)) END=LAST;
  START = PUT(_N_, S370FPIB1.);
  OUTPUT;
  IF LAST THEN DO;
    * Missing value. ;
    START = '00'X;
    LABEL = ' ';
    OUTPUT;
    * Invalid value. ;
    START = ' ';
    LABEL = '(|$HEX2.|)';
    HLO = 'O';
    OUTPUT;
    END;
RUN;
PROC FORMAT CNTLIN=CNTL2 LIBRARY=LIBRARY;
RUN;
```

Change the SET, LENGTH, LABEL, and RETAIN statements to create a value informat and value format for a different variable.

Sidebar 4 demonstrates the display of the binary code variable created in the previous sidebar.

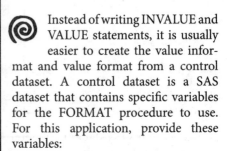 Instead of writing INVALUE and VALUE statements, it is usually easier to create the value informat and value format from a control dataset. A control dataset is a SAS dataset that contains specific variables for the FORMAT procedure to use. For this application, provide these variables:

- TYPE. A one-letter code: J for the informat, C for the format.
- FMTNAME. The name of the informat or format. Include the dollar sign at the beginning of the name.
- START. The range value.
- LABEL. The label value. For the OTHER range in the informat, use 'FF'X as the label, or use '_ERROR_' as the label to create an error condition.
- HLO. More one-letter codes: U and J for the UPCASE and JUST options for the informat, O for the special OTHER range.

■ 31
Bitfields

Bitfields make data values as compact as they can be. Ordinarily, the space a data value takes up is measured in bytes. A value uses one or, more often, several bytes. However, in a bitfield, each bit is a separate value; there are eight distinct values squeezed into each byte. The values are Boolean values, 1 or 0, representing true and false, or on and off.

Bitfields are difficult to access, so they are not a likely choice for quick programs or for values that are referred to especially often. Their compact size is an advantage, though, in situations that use a large number of Boolean values and in data files that must be optimized for efficiency.

Only a few things can be done directly with bitfields. For the most part, you have to expand a bitfield to a pseudo-array in order to use it. The pseudo-array that corresponds to a bitfield is a character string of 1s and 0s. The binary 1s and 0s of the bitfield become character 1s and 0s in the pseudo-array.

To see how bitfields are used, consider an attendance record for a course with 40 scheduled classes. For one student, the sequence of digits below might represent the student's attendance at the classes. Each 1 represents a class at which the student was present; each 0 represents a class at which the student was absent.

```
1111111101111111101000111111111111011111
```

This could be a character variable 40 bytes long. Or, for compactness, it can be converted to a bitfield, which contains the same data, but is only 5 bytes long. To calculate the length of a bitfield, divide the number of elements by 8 and round up the next whole integer.

 Use the $BINARY informat to convert a Boolean pseudo-array to a bitfield. In this example, ATN_STR is the pseudo-array, and ATN_BIT is the bitfield.

```
LENGTH ATN_STR $ 40 ATN_BIT $ 5;
. . .
ATN_BIT = INPUT(ATN_STR, $BINARY40.);
```

Use the $BINARY format to convert a bitfield to a pseudo-array.

```
ATN_STR = PUT(ATN_BIT, $BINARY40.);
```

To access the elements of a bitfield, convert the bitfield to a pseudo-array and use the SUBSTR function to access the characters of the pseudo-array.

This example sets the 31st element to 1 if either the 30th or 32nd element is 1.

```
ATN_STR = PUT(ATN_BIT, $BINARY40.);
IF SUBSTR(ATN_STR, 30, 1) = '1' OR SUBSTR(ATN_STR, 32, 1) = '1'
   THEN SUBSTR(ATN_STR, 31, 1) = '1';
ATN_BIT = INPUT(ATN_STR, $BINARY40.);
```

To count the 1s or 0s in a bitfield, convert it to a pseudo-array and use the COUNTC functions to count occurrences of the 0 or 1 character. This example counts the number of number of classes attended, according to the bitfield ATN_BIT:

```
ATN_COUNT = COUNTC(PUT(ATN_BIT, $BINARY40.), '1');
```

Use the $BINARY format as the format attribute of a bitfield so that the bitfield can be displayed in a meaningful way. The bitfield looks exactly like the pseudo-array, as demonstrated below. Use the $BINARY informat as the informat attribute to make it possible to edit the bitfield value. Use the number of elements in the bitfield as the width of the informat and format.

```
FORMAT ATN_BIT $BINARY40.;
INFORMAT ATN_BIT $BINARY40.;
PUT ATN_STR= / ATN_BIT=;
```

```
ATN_STR=1111111101111111101000111111111111011111
ATN_BIT=1111111101111111101000111111111111011111
```

BITFIELD CALENDAR

A calendar can be organized as a bitfield with an element for each day of the year. Perhaps each 1 is a day on which a business's offices are open, and each 0 a day on which the offices are closed. If the calendar for the current year is a bitfield called OPENDAY, this code fragment determines whether the offices are open today.

```
TODAY = DATE();
Y = YEAR(TODAY);
DAYOFYEAR = TODAY - MDY(1, 1, Y) + 1;
OPENNOW = INPUT(SUBSTR(PUT(OPENDAY,
   $BINARY366.), DAYOFYEAR, 1), F1.);
```

The DATE function returns today's date, and DAYOFYEAR is computed as the day of the year. This is the character index for extracting a character from the pseudo-array version of the calendar bitfield. The numeric value of this character is assigned to OPENNOW. OPENNOW is 1 if the calendar indicates that offices are open today.

Bit testing is a special feature of the = comparison operator that allows bits in a bitfield to be tested directly. Selected bits are compared to a bit mask, a special kind of constant used only for this purpose. To write a bit mask, write a 0 for each bit that should be 0, a 1 for each bit that should be 1, and a period for each bit that could be either 0 or 1. You can write spaces to make the bit mask easier to read. Enclose the bit mask in quotes and write the letter B after it. This is an example of a bit mask.

```
'0000.... 11......'B
```

This bit mask tests whether bits 1–4 of a bitfield are 0 and bits 9–10 are 1.

Use a bit mask only as the right operand of the equality comparison operator:

```
(BITFIELD = '0000.... 11......'B)
```

If the bits being tested in the bit mask match the corresponding bits in the bitfield, the result of the comparison is true. If any bit does not match, the result is false.

 A numeric value can also be used as a bitfield in SAS. The numeric value is truncated to form an integer value, then converted to a 32-bit integer format, which forms a bitfield with 32 bits.

This is much more complicated than using a character value as a bitfield, but there are reasons for using numeric bitfields. Many operating system codes are defined as numeric bitfields. When the SUMMARY procedure generates a numeric _TYPE_ variable, indicating the use of class variables, this variable is also a numeric bitfield.

Numeric bit testing is based on a 32-bit signed integer format. This is the same format that the S370FIB4. format produces from a numeric value. To look at a numeric bitfield as it is used in bit testing, apply the S370FIB4. format, then apply the $BINARY32. format to the result. This produces a Boolean pseudo-array. This statement converts the numeric bitfield NB to the Boolean pseudo-array SA:

SA = PUT(PUT(NB, S370FIB4.), $BINARY32.);

Display SA to see what NB looks like when you use it as a numeric bitfield.

In bit testing with a numeric bitfield, the bitfield is compared against a 32-bit mask. If you use a shorter bit mask, the bit mask is right-aligned against the bitfield. That is, the bit mask is compared to the least significant bits of the bitfield. It is the same as having a longer bit mask with periods at the beginning. For example, (_TYPE_ = '11001'B) is the same as (_TYPE_ = '........ ....11001'B).

BITWISE FUNCTIONS

The bitwise functions perform operations on the bits of numeric bitfields. The BAND, BOR, BXOR, and BNOT functions do the bitwise logical operations that their names suggest. (The XOR, or exclusive OR, operation tests for unequal bits.) A separate logical operation is done for each bit position. For example, a bitwise NOT operation on the bits 1011 results in the opposite bits 0100.

The bitwise functions are based on a 32-bit unsigned integer format, the same as that of the S370FPIB4. format. They require bitfield arguments between 0 and $2^{32} - 1$. Numeric values from 0 to $2^{31} - 1$ form the same bitfields in the bitwise functions as they form in numeric bit testing. To look at a numeric bitfield as it is used in the bitwise functions, display it with the BINARY32. format.

The BLSHIFT and BRSHIFT functions shift bits left and right, respectively, within a numeric bitfield, moving the bits to other positions. For example, shifting right by 7 bits moves the value of bit 1 to bit 8, the value of bit 2 to bit 9, and so on, filling in 0s for bits 1–7. The first argument is the numeric bitfield. The second argument is the shift distance, an integer value from 0 to 31. Numerically, bit shifting can be seen as multiplying or dividing by powers of 2. Shifting right 3 bit positions, for example, is the same as dividing by 2^3 (truncating to get the integer part of the result). Conversely, shifting left 3 bit positions is the same as multiplying by 2^3.

```
FORMAT BITFIELD SHIFTED BINARY32.;
BITFIELD = INPUT('00000001111111100000000010101010', BINARY32.);
SHIFTED = BRSHIFT(BITFIELD, 7);
PUT BITFIELD= / +1 SHIFTED=;
```

```
BITFIELD=00000001111111100000000010101010
 SHIFTED=00000000000000011111111000000001
```

32
Numeric Effects

You can write expressions to form numbers based on other numbers. Most of the time, you can form these expressions with operators, using them in a direct, obvious way. Other expressions require combinations of functions and operators.

Rounding

 In computing, most actions on numbers produce only approximate results. Precision in numeric computing is not absolute, but is measured in relative terms. SAS uses double-precision numbers, which represent a limited set of numbers. The exact details vary from one kind of computer to another, but on some computers, the next number higher than 1 is approximately 1.000000000000000222. If a mathematical operation results in a number between 1 and 1.000000000000000222, the computer provides one of these numbers or the other as an approximation of the actual mathematical result.

The program below measures the granularity of the double-precision format by computing large integer values. In this program, A is a power of 2, and B is computed by adding 1 to A. Up to a point, B is computed accurately, but beyond that point, it is not.

```
%PUT Environment: &SYSSCP;
DATA _NULL_;
  DO X = 45 TO 58;
    A = 2**X;
    B = 1 + A;
    PUT X 2. +2 A F20. +2 B F20.;
    END;
RUN;
```

The following output shows the results of this program for two different environments, Microsoft Windows and

```
Environment: WIN

45           35184372088832           35184372088833
46           70368744177664           70368744177665
47          140737488355328          140737488355329
48          281474976710656          281474976710657
49          562949953421312          562949953421313
50         1125899906842624         1125899906842625
51         2251799813685248         2251799813685249
52         4503599627370496         4503599627370497
53         9007199254740992         9007199254740992
54        18014398509481984        18014398509481984
55        36028797018963968        36028797018963968
56        72057594037927936        72057594037927936
57       144115188075855872       144115188075855872
58       288230376151711744       288230376151711744


Environment: OS

45           35184372088832           35184372088833
46           70368744177664           70368744177665
47          140737488355328          140737488355329
48          281474976710656          281474976710657
49          562949953421312          562949953421313
50         1125899906842624         1125899906842625
51         2251799813685248         2251799813685249
52         4503599627370496         4503599627370497
53         9007199254740992         9007199254740993
54        18014398509481984        18014398509481985
55        36028797018963968        36028797018963969
56        72057594037927936        72057594037927936
57       144115188075855872       144115188075855872
58       288230376151711744       288230376151711744
```

z/OS. In Microsoft Windows, as in most kinds of computers, the computation produces exact results when it computes $2^{52} + 1$, but the results are no longer exact for $2^{53} + 1$. Z/OS provides exact results until it computes $2^{56} + 1$.

The effects of rounding error in any single computation are small, but these small errors can be compounded to form much larger errors in some sequences of computations. Statisticians need to consider this effect when applying some kinds of statistical models.

 The most common situation that can create substantial rounding errors is when summing a large number of values of dramatically different magnitudes. To minimize rounding error in this situation, sort the set of values by magnitude and sum them in increasing order of magnitude. Or, at least, sum the values of small magnitude first, before the values of large magnitude.

More severe rounding errors can result when fractional numbers are stored in SAS datasets with lengths less than 8. See chapter 9, "Data Type and Length," for a discussion of this.

 Currency values should be exact decimal values, but adding, subtracting, and multiplying them can result in values that are not quite the same as the decimal values they represent. To eliminate a problem with this, apply the ROUND function to currency computations to round the result to an appropriate decimal value.

Suppose P is an amount of money in dollars and cents, and Y is computed as:

```
Y = 12*P;
```

Y could get values that are slightly different from the intended values. Write the computation of Y instead as:

```
Y = ROUND(12*P, .01);
```

Use the same technique for rounding if you use a formula to compute a price or charge and need to state the resulting value as an exact currency value.

Use the CEIL, FLOOR, INT, and ROUND functions to do various kinds of rounding. The expressions below are examples of common kinds of rounding. Any numeric expression could be used in place of the variable X in these expressions.

- Rounding a number to the nearest integer: ROUND(X)
- Rounding a number to the next higher integer: CEIL(X)
- Rounding a number to the next lower integer: FLOOR(X)
- Integer truncation: INT(X)
- Rounding a money value to the nearest cent: ROUND(X, .01)
- Rounding a money value to the next higher cent: (CEIL(X*100)*.01)
- Rounding a money value to the next lower cent: (FLOOR(X*100)*.01)
- Rounding to the nearest million: ROUND(X, 1000000)
- Rounding a data size to the next higher multiple of 1024 (1 K): (CEIL(X/1024)*1024)

Range Effects

It is often necessary to restrict values within ranges, and there are other effects that are related to ranges.

The expressions below demonstrate the use of the MAX and MIN operators to limit a value, X, to a range.

- Limiting a value to a maximum of 100 (capping X at 100): (X MIN 100)
- Limiting a value to a minimum of 0 (treating negative and missing values as 0): (X MAX 0)
- Limiting a value to the range from 0 to 1: (0 MAX X MIN 1)
- Limiting a value to the range from A to B (with A ≤ B): (A MAX X MIN B)

To obtain the fractional part of a number, use the INT function to obtain the integer part, and subtract this from the number:

(X - INT(X))

To obtain the cents of a money value, multiply the fractional part of the number by 100, then use the INT function to get a whole number.

INT(100*(X - INT(X)))

To obtain the magnitude of a number, use the ABS (absolute value) function.

ABS(X)

For example, the magnitude of either 2.5 or -2.5 is 2.5.

For the order of magnitude of a number (or the number of digits in the integer part of a value), apply the ABS, LOG10, and FLOOR functions, and add 1.

(FLOOR(LOG10(ABS(X))) + 1)

For example, this expression calculates the order of magnitude of 1000 or 5000 as 4.

Percents

A percent is a factor or rate multiplied by 100. For example, a factor of .114 may be expressed as 11.4 percent (typically written as 11.4%). To convert a factor to a percent, multiply by 100. To convert a percent to a factor, multiply by .01 or divide by 100.

An incremental change is usually reported as a percent change, which is the difference from 100 percent. For example, a change from 4 to 5 is described not as 125 percent, but as a 25 percent increase. The formula for computing the percent change between old and new values OLD and NEW is:

PERCENT_CHANGE = (NEW - OLD)/OLD*100;

Testing Numbers

Use the comparison operators for simple comparisons of numbers. More complicated expressions can be formed to test numbers in other ways. These are Boolean expressions; they result in a 1 for true or a 0 for false.

To test whether a number X is an integer, compare the number to the result of a rounding function, such as:

```
(X = FLOOR(X))
(X = CEIL(X))
(X = INT(X))
```

Use the MOD function to test whether a value is an exact multiple of a value. The expression (MOD(X, N) = 0) is true if X is a multiple of N. This can also be written as (NOT MOD(X, N)). An integer is an even value if it is a multiple of 2, as indicated by the expression (MOD(X, 2) = 0). An integer is an odd value if it is 1 more than an even value, indicated by the expression (MOD(X, 2) = 1).

To determine whether a value is positive, negative, zero, or missing, use comparison operators or the SIGN function. SIGN(X) returns 1 if X is positive, 0 if X is 0, –1 if X is negative, or a standard missing value if X is missing. Or, (X > 0) indicates a positive value, (X = 0) tests for 0, (.Z < X < 0) indicates a negative value, and (X <= .Z) indicates a missing value.

The MISSING function also tests for a missing value. MISSING(X) is 1 if X is missing, 0 if X is a number. This statement is the fastest way to convert missing values to 0 for the variable X:

IF MISSING(X) THEN X = 0;

To test whether two numbers are approximately equal, subtract them and test the magnitude of the difference. This expression tests whether X and Y are within .0005 of each other:

(ABS(X - Y) <= .0005)

■ 33
Missing Values

A missing value indicates the absence or unavailability of a value, especially a numeric value. A standard missing value is written as a period in input and output data and in SAS programs. Special missing values are other numeric values that are written in a SAS program as a period followed by a letter or underscore. For character variables, a blank value is considered a missing value.

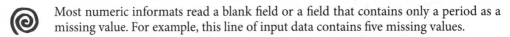

Most numeric informats read a blank field or a field that contains only a period as a missing value. For example, this line of input data contains five missing values.

```
    .       .       .       .       .      6    7    8    9    10    11
```

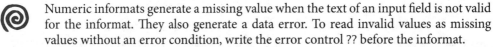

Numeric informats generate a missing value when the text of an input field is not valid for the informat. They also generate a data error. To read invalid values as missing values without an error condition, write the error control ?? before the informat.

For example, the INPUT statement below reads an input record to obtain a value for FOLIO. However, if the input field contains something other than valid numeric data, the informat generates a missing value for the variable FOLIO, and there is no error condition.

INPUT FOLIO ?? F12.;

Use the error control ? to generate an error condition with reduced log messages. Error controls work in the INPUT statement and in the INPUT function.

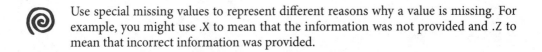

Use special missing values to represent different reasons why a value is missing. For example, you might use .X to mean that the information was not provided and .Z to mean that incorrect information was provided.

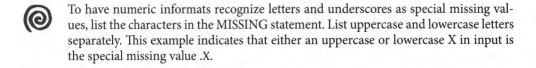

To have numeric informats recognize letters and underscores as special missing values, list the characters in the MISSING statement. List uppercase and lowercase letters separately. This example indicates that either an uppercase or lowercase X in input is the special missing value .X.

MISSING x X;

 To change the missing value that numeric informats generate for invalid data, use the INVALIDDATA= system option. The value of this option is not the missing value itself, but a one-character constant value that represents that missing value. For example, with the option set as shown here, numeric informats generate the special missing value .I for invalid data.

OPTIONS INVALIDDATA='I';

 To assign a missing value to a variable, use an assignment statement with a missing value constant, as in these examples.

REMAINDER = .;
COUNT = .N;

10 Ways to Generate Missing Values

Missing values are created throughout the SAS System whenever a value is unavailable. These are some of the ways missing values find their way into SAS data.

RTM. An automatic data step action called Reset to Missing (RTM) sets variables to missing values at the beginning of each iteration of the observation loop. In addition, most data step variables are initialized to missing at the beginning of the step.

Variable not in observation. When a statement combines data from multiple SAS datasets, some variables may not be available for some observations; these variables get missing values for those observations. It is similar when a proc step creates a SAS dataset and some variables are not used in some of the observations that are created.

Missing constant. You can write a missing value as a constant and assign it to a variable in an assignment statement or use it to initialize a variable or array element.

Propagation of missing values. If you use missing values in computations, the result may also be a missing value.

Illegal operands. Numbers that are not valid operands for an operator result in missing values and an error condition. Division by 0 is the most familiar example of this.

Illegal arguments. If a function is called with arguments that the function does not consider valid values, the function returns a missing value and generates an error condition.

Overflow. Extreme mathematical effects can result in numeric values too large for the computer to handle. SAS substitutes missing values.

Informat. Informats generate missing values when input text is blank or not valid for the informat. It is the same thing when automatic type conversion from a character value to a numeric value fails because the character value does not represent a numeric value.

Short input record. If an INPUT statement does not find values for all of its variables, it may provide missing values for the remaining values.

Attribute not available. Some I/O statement options create variables that provide attributes of an input file. An example of this is the NOBS= option in the SET statement. If the attribute is not available, the variable has a missing value. This is the case, for example, if you use the NOBS= option with a view or a tape-format SAS data file.

Some data files are written with numerals that represent missing values. For example, a value such as -9 might indicate a missing value. When you read these files, translate the missing-value code numerals to missing values. You can do this with an IF-THEN statement. For example, if -9 means a missing value for the variable PRICE, translate that value with this statement:

IF PRICE = -9 THEN PRICE = .;

Alternatively, you can use a value informat to do this kind of translation. Creating an informat is the easier approach if you are doing the same missing value translations for many variables. The informat MISN created in this example reads the values -9 and -99 as missing values.

```
PROC FORMAT;
INVALUE MISN
   -9, -99 = .
   OTHER = _SAME_
   ;
RUN;
```

In comparisons and sorting, the standard missing value and the 27 special missing are all distinct from each other, and they compare less than numbers. The sort order of numeric values, from smallest to largest, is:

._

.

.A - .Z
negative numbers
0
positive numbers

When missing values are used in mathematical expressions, the result of the expression is a standard missing value. This effect is known as propagation of missing values. The SAS supervisor writes log messages that indicate the specific places in the program where this occurs.

Most numeric functions return missing values if missing values are used as arguments. There are exceptions: statistic functions ignore missing arguments, and some financial functions require at least one missing argument.

Arithmetic operators, such as + and /, result in a missing value if any operand is a missing value. Other operators treat missing values differently. Comparison operators treat missing values the same as other values, as described above. This is also true of the MIN and MAX operators.

When missing values are used as conditions or with logical operators, they are considered false values, the same as 0.

To add missing values without generating missing values as a result, use the SUM function with 0 as one of its arguments, as shown in this example.

TOTAL = SUM(0, IS, OS);

Use the MISSING function to test for a missing value: For example, MISSING(X) tests whether the variable X has a missing value.

The fastest way to convert missing values to 0 is with an IF-THEN statement:

IF MISSING(X) THEN X = 0;

To substitute 0 for a missing value in an expression, use the COALESCE function. This function can have any number of arguments and returns the first nonmissing argument, so COALESCE(X, 0) returns X, or 0 if the value of X is missing.

To convert special missing values to standard missing values in an expression, use any arithmetic formula that leaves numbers unchanged. These are three examples.

(--X)
(X + 0)
(X*1)

Do not use the unary + operator for this purpose.

The MIN and MAX functions do not treat missing values the same way as the MIN and MAX operators. Like other statistic functions, the MIN and MAX functions ignore missing values used as arguments. The program below demonstrates this difference.

```
DATA _NULL_;
  A1 = . MIN 1;
  A2 = MIN(., 1);
  B1 = .C MIN .E;
  B2 = MIN(.C, .E);
  C1 = 64 MAX .;
  C2 = MAX(64, .);
  D1 = .E MAX .Y;
  D2 = MAX(.E, .Y);
  PUT (_ALL_) (= /);
RUN;
```

```
A1=.
A2=1
B1=C
B2=.
C1=64
C2=64
```

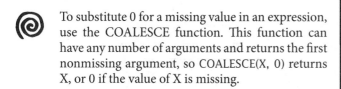

10 Uses for Special Missing Values

When you use special missing values, they mean what you mean them to mean. Use them to indicate any special or distinct reason why a value is not available or anything else that is convenient to record about a missing value. A special missing value could mean:

★ **Value not provided.** There was no response, no opinion, no report, an equipment outage, etc.

★ **Invalid value.** A validation rule rejected the value that was provided. You could use a separate special missing value for each validation rule.

★ **See explanation.** Refer to another variable or a separate note that explains why the value is missing.

★ **No estimate available.** The attempt to generate or estimate the value failed.

★ **Censored.** The summary data of a small group is not made available in order to protect the privacy of members of the group.

★ **Not yet known.** The value will not be known until a future event takes place.

★ **Canceled.** The event that would have provided the value did not take place.

★ **Too large.** The value is too large to measure. In the familiar cliché, the weight of an object is unknown because it broke the scale.

★ **Too small.** The value is too small to be of interest. It is below the threshold at which values start to be measured and recorded.

★ **Call for price.** Additional information or a business decision is required to determine the value, as when a catalog advises you to talk to its sales representatives to get the current price of an item.

```
D1=Y
D2=.
```

Missing values are not valid in some places in SAS statements. Do not use a missing value:

- as an array subscript
- as an index value in a DO statement
- as an observation number

A missing value here results in an error condition, and the step stops running immediately. If necessary, test variables before you use them in places such as these.

Formats write standard missing values as periods. They write special missing values as uppercase letters and underscores. These values are aligned with the decimal points in the output field.

To change the character that formats print for a standard missing value, indicate the character in the MISSING= system option. This example tells formats to write standard missing values as an asterisk.

OPTIONS MISSING='*';

To write blank fields for standard missing values, use a space character in the MISSING= system option, as shown here.

OPTIONS MISSING=' ';

To write missing values as words, or to change the way special missing values are written, use the FORMAT procedure to create a value format that writes the missing values as specific text labels. This example creates the format MXNA, which writes the special missing value .X as N/A.

```
PROC FORMAT;
VALUE MXNA
   .X = '      N/A'
   OTHER = (|BEST12.|)
   ;
RUN;
```

■ 34
Boolean Values

The comparison and logical operators produce Boolean values — logical values that use 1 for true and 0 for false. For example, the comparison 2 > 1 is true, so when this expression is evaluated, it results in a value of 1.

Boolean values are most often used as conditions. Use Boolean values and other logical values:

- In IF, DO, and WHEN statements to control what actions take place.
- In WHERE clauses to select observations.
- As operands for the logical operators AND, OR, and NOT.
- As arguments to the IFC and IFN functions to select a value within an expression.

Boolean variables are useful in statistical models. A linear regression model can use Boolean variables in the same way it uses other kinds of numeric variables. In this context, Boolean variables are sometimes called dummy variables.

If a Boolean variable is stored in a SAS dataset, save storage space by giving the variable the shortest length allowed for a numeric variable — either 2 or 3, depending on the operating system.

Several kinds of variables can indicate a condition or state.

- When a variable represents the simple presence or absence of a state, make it a Boolean variable.
- When a variable indicates two or more mutually exclusive states, make it a character code variable. See chapter 28, "Codes."
- If a set of data includes hundreds of Boolean variables and you need to store them compactly, consider making them a bitfield. See chapter 31, "Bitfields."

Boolean values are not the only logical values you can use in a SAS program. Any numeric value can be a logical value. Positive and negative values are interpreted as true; zero and missing values are false.

The cleanest way to convert a logical value to a strict Boolean value is by applying the NOT operator twice. If X is a logical value, the expression (NOT NOT (X)) produces the equivalent Boolean value.

Sometimes a numeric measure can be used by itself as a logical expression from a value. This is especially seen in dividing. If there is a chance that the denominator could be 0, it is best to test the denominator to avoid dividing by zero. The denominator variable itself can be the condition; it is a false logical value and division is impossible if the value is 0 or missing. This is an example of a simple division:

```
IF TIME THEN RATE = AMOUNT/TIME;
ELSE RATE = .;
```

There are multiple ways to write any logical expression. For example, the expressions (NOT A AND NOT B) and (NOT (A OR B)) are equivalent. Pick the one that seems to provide the best description of the condition as you think of it.

When Boolean values are used, some numeric operators and functions are equivalent to some logical operators.

- The MAX operator and function are equivalent to the OR operator.
- The MIN operator and function are equivalent to the AND operator.
- Comparison operators are equivalent to some compound logical expressions.

If you are not sure a logical expression produces the results you expect, write data step statements to test it. Use nested DO loops with false and true values for each logical component of the expression. The example at right tests an expression of two logical variables, A and B. The result is assigned to the variable X.

```
DO A = 0, 1;
  DO B = 0, 1;
    X = NOT A OR NOT B;
    PUT A= B= X=;
  END;
END;
_____

A=0  B=0  X=1
A=0  B=1  X=1
A=1  B=0  X=1
A=1  B=1  X=0
```

Assign values to a Boolean variable in any of these ways:

- Assign a constant value of 1 to the variable if the programming logic has determined that the state represented in the variable is present.
- Assign a constant value of 0 to the variable if the programming logic has determined that the state is absent.
- Assign a Boolean expression that defines the condition of the variable.

These are two examples of statements that might be used for a Boolean variable DOMESTIC that identifies items made in the United States.

```
IF SRCN = 'United States' THEN DOMESTIC = 1;
ELSE DOMESTIC = 0;

DOMESTIC = SRCN = 'United States';
```

Create a Boolean variable when the same condition is used several times. Assign the condition to a variable and use the variable in subsequent expressions.

This example creates and uses the Boolean variable WEEKDAY.

```
WEEKDAY = 2 <= DAYOFWEEK <= 6
IF (WEEKDAY AND NX < 1000) OR (NOT WEEKDAY AND CNX < 2500);
```

TRUTH TABLES

Truth tables can show you the simple way of writing a logical expression. A truth table shows the effect of a logical operation or expression. For each combination of Boolean values, it shows the result. If you not sure how to write a logical expression, writing a truth table can clarify the logic involved.

There are 16 possible truth tables for an operation on two Boolean values. The 16 different results are shown here for the values A and B, along with the corresponding logical expressions and alternate forms of the expressions. Table cells that represent results of 1 are shaded to make it easier to see the patterns of true and false values. Some of the truth tables are trivial, but are included for the sake of completeness.

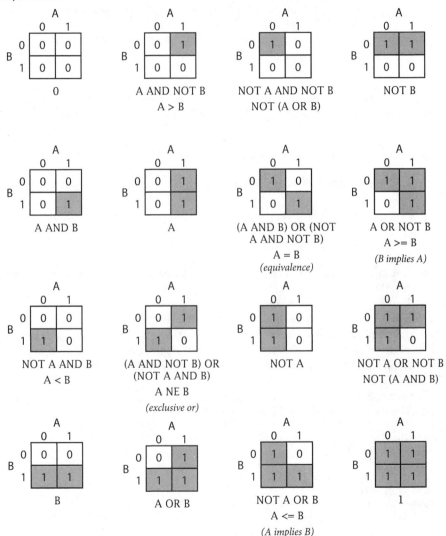

Truth tables for three or more Boolean values are not simple two-way tables, but can be drawn in a few different ways. The geometric shape of a truth table is not important as long as you can see the relationship of the logical values.

If you create Boolean variables only for use within a data step, do not store them in an output SAS dataset that the data step creates. Use the KEEP= or DROP= dataset option to exclude any unnecessary variables from the output SAS dataset.

The data step and statement options create Boolean variables such as these.

- The automatic variable _ERROR_ indicates the presence of certain kinds of data errors.
- When there is a BY statement, the FIRST. and LAST. automatic variables mark the first and last observations of BY groups.
- The IN= dataset option creates a Boolean variable that indicates the involvement of an input SAS dataset in an input observation.
- The END= statement option and various other options in the INFILE, FILE, SET, and other I/O statements create Boolean variables.

Count occurrences by adding Boolean values. For example, the question, "How many of the major food groups are included?" might be answered by a statement such as this:

NGROUP = (C1 > 0) + (C2 > 0) + (C3 > 0) + (C4 > 0) + (C5 > 0) + (C6 > 0);

The expression in this statement counts the positive values among the variables C1–C6.

In a proc step, use the SUM statistic with a Boolean variable to count occurrences.

Use logical values in the IFN function to select a value in an expression. With three arguments, the IFN function selects the second argument if the first argument is true, or the third argument if the second argument is false. For example, IFN(A > B, 5, 3) returns 5 if A is greater than B, or 3 otherwise. The IFN function is especially useful when computing a score by adding several terms, each of which depends on a condition. It allows a formula to be written in a single expression. This matches the way people think about formulas better than the alternative of adding terms in a series of IF-THEN statements.

This example computes a score by adding or subtracting 1, 2, or 3 points for each of several measurements that fall into specified ranges.

```
SCORE = IFN(PRICE < 1000, 0, -1)
   + IFN(DISTANCE < 50, 1, -1)
   + IFN(WEIGHT <= 20, 0, -2)
   + IFN(LENGTH < 48, 2, 0)
   + IFN(SN > 70, 3, 0)
   + IFN(SN > 80, 2, 0)
   + IFN(WPD > 1, 3, 0);
```

Use the IFC function for selecting a character value.

35

Financial Calculations

The SAS System includes a set of functions that cover some of the most common financial calculations. To use these functions successfully, keep these points in mind:

- The functions are expressed in terms of periods, which could be any length of time you choose. Usually, the periods should be months.
- To use monthly periods, you must express interest rates as monthly interest rates rather the more familiar annual interest rates. The monthly interest rate might be $\frac{1}{12}$ of the nominal annual interest rate.
- Although interest rates are usually written as percents, the SAS functions express them as fractional values. For example, a 6% annual interest rate is a .5% monthly interest rate, which is written as a rate of .005.

 The SAVING, COMPOUND, and MORT functions are based on formulas that involve four variables. To use the functions, supply three of the variables as arguments. Provide a missing value as the argument for the remaining variable. The function then returns the value of that variable. This is a summary of the arguments and formulas for these functions:

SAVING(f, p, r, n) $f = p\,(1 + r)\,\dfrac{(1 + r)^n - 1}{r}$

MORT(a, p, r, n) $p = r\,a\,\dfrac{(1 + r)^n}{(1 + r)^n - 1}$

COMPOUND(a, f, r, n) $f = a\,(1 + r)^n$

where

a is the initial amount
f is the final amount
n is the number of periods (months)
p is the periodic (monthly) payment amount
r is the periodic (monthly) interest rate (as a fractional value)

 To calculate the value of regular saving with compound interest, use the SAVING function with these arguments (in order):

- a missing value
- the amount saved per month
- the monthly interest rate ($\frac{1}{12}$ of the nominal annual interest rate) as a fraction
- the length of time in months (12 times the number of years)

This example is based on the scenario of saving $1,000 per month for 20 years with an interest rate of .5% per month. It calculates the value at the end of the ten-year period.

```
F = SAVING(., 1000, .005, 240);
PUT F DOLLAR14.2;
```

```
$464,351.10
```

To calculate the monthly payment on a loan, use the MORT function with these arguments:

- the amount borrowed (the principal)
- a missing value
- the monthly interest rate ($\frac{1}{12}$ of the nominal annual interest rate) as a fraction
- the length of time in months (12 times the number of years)

This example calculates the monthly payment amount for a ten-year loan of $58,145 with an interest rate of .625% per month.

```
P = MORT(58145, ., .00625, 120);
PUT P DOLLAR9.2;
```

```
$690.19
```

To calculate the total payments on a loan, multiply the monthly payment by the number of months. To calculate the total interest payments, subtract the principal from the total payments.

This example shows these calculations for a 30-year loan of $115,000 at an interest rate of 0.6875% per month (an effective annual rate of 8.5692%).

```
A = 115000;
N = 360; * 30 years;
P = MORT(A, ., .006875, N);
TOTAL = P*N;
INTEREST = TOTAL - A;
PUT 'Principal' @16 A DOLLAR11.2
  / 'Interest' @16 INTEREST DOLLAR11.2
   / @16 '-----------'
   / 'Total Payments' @16 TOTAL DOLLAR11.2
   ;
```

```
Principal       $115,000.00
Interest        $196,024.37
                -----------
Total Payments $311,024.37
```

Use the COMPOUND function to compute the effects of compound interest. Use these arguments:

- the initial amount saved
- a missing value
- the effective annual interest rate, as a fraction
- the length of time in years

This example calculates the value of $25,000 saved for 50 years with an effective annual interest rate of 6%.

```
F = COMPOUND(25000, ., .06, 50);
PUT F DOLLAR13.2;
```

    $460,503.86

To compute the amount you need to save now in order to have a specific amount of money at a specific time in the future, use the COMPOUND function with arguments:

- a missing value
- the final amount required
- the effective annual interest rate, as a fraction
- the length of time in years

This example calculates the amount that, saved for a period of 50 years with an effective annual interest rate of 6%, results in a value of $1,000,000.

```
F = COMPOUND(., 1000000, .06, 50);
PUT F DOLLAR13.2;
```

    $54,288.36

The purpose of depreciation functions is to estimate for an asset the decline in its value that results from the passage of time. They compute depreciation using several depreciation methods, which provide specific formulas for the decline in value.
The names of the depreciation functions are formed of a prefix and a suffix.

The prefix indicates the kind of value returned.

- DEP functions return the depreciation for a single year or period.
- DACC functions return the accumulated depreciation through a specific point in time.

The suffix indicates the depreciation method.

- SL is the straight line method.
- DBSL is the declining balance method, switching to the straight line method.
- DB is the declining balance method.
- TAB is a depreciation table.
- SYD is the sum of years digits method.

All the depreciation functions have the same first two arguments. The first argument is the age of the asset, or the time elapsed since depreciation began. The second argument is the original value of the asset.

The remaining arguments are parameters that depend on the depreciation method. For the SL and SYD methods, the parameter argument is the recovery period, the period during which the value of the asset declines to 0. For the DB and DBSL methods, the parameter arguments are the recovery period and a rate, or factor. For the TAB method, the parameter arguments are depreciation rates for each of the depreciation periods. The sum of these rates should be 1 to completely depreciate an asset. The number of rates determines the recovery period of the asset.

If you use a fractional value for the age argument, the depreciation functions use linear interpolation to determine their result. This may or may not be correct, depending on the accounting conventions you are following.

To determine how much an asset has depreciated after a certain number of years according to the straight line depreciation method, use the DACCSL function with these arguments (in order):

- the number of years
- the original value of the asset
- the recovery period of the asset

For example, if the original value is 279 and the recovery period is 3 years, then this expression returns the amount of depreciation in the first 2 years:

DACCSL(2, 279, 3)

To compute the depreciated value, also known as the book value, of an asset, subtract the depreciation from the original value, as shown here.

(279 - DACCSL(2, 279, 3))

To calculate the depreciation of an asset in a particular year using the straight line method, write that year as the first argument of the DEPSL function. The remaining arguments are the original value and recovery period, the same as for the DACCSL function.

This example uses a DO loop to display the depreciation, accumulated depreciation, and depreciated value of the asset described above for each of the three years of depreciation.

```
DATA _NULL_;
  ORIGINAL = 279;
  PUT 'Year' +2 'Depreciation' +2 'Accumulated' +7 'Value' / ;
  DO YEAR = 1 TO 3;
    DEP = DEPSL(YEAR, ORIGINAL, 3);
    ACC = DACCSL(YEAR, ORIGINAL, 3);
    BOOK = ROUND(ORIGINAL - ACC, .01);
    PUT YEAR F4. +4 DEP COMMA10.2 +3 ACC COMMA10.2 +2 BOOK COMMA10.2;
  END;
```

RUN;

Year	Depreciation	Accumulated	Value
1	93.00	93.00	186.00
2	93.00	186.00	93.00
3	93.00	279.00	0.00

 To calculate depreciation using the double declining balance method switching to the straight line method, use the DACCDBSL and DEPDBSL functions with the recovery period as the third argument and 2 as the fourth argument.

The expression below calculates the depreciated value of an asset after 3 years, based on an original value of 5,000 and using the double declining balance method switching to the straight line method with a recovery period of 7 years.

(5000 - DACCDBSL(3, 5000, 7, 2))

 To calculate depreciation using rates from a depreciation table, use the DACCTAB and DEPTAB functions with the depreciation rates as arguments.

The example below computes depreciation amounts for an asset with a value of 38,017, using rates from a depreciation table for 200% declining balance switching to straight line with a half-year convention for a recovery period of seven years starting in 2003. Because of the half-year convention, the depreciation amounts cover eight years. This is reflected in eight rate arguments in the depreciation functions.

```
DATA _NULL_;
  ORIGINAL = 38017;
  PUT 'Year' +2 'Depreciation' +2 'Accumulated' +7 'Value' / ;
  DO YEAR = 2003 TO 2010;
    N = YEAR - 2002;
    DEP = DEPTAB(N, ORIGINAL,
      .1429, .2449, .1749, .1249, .0893, .0892, .0893, .0446);
    ACC = DACCTAB(N, ORIGINAL,
      .1429, .2449, .1749, .1249, .0893, .0892, .0893, .0446);
    BOOK = ROUND(ORIGINAL - ACC, .01);
    PUT YEAR F4. +4 DEP COMMA10.2
      +3 ACC COMMA10.2 +2 BOOK COMMA10.2;
  END;
RUN;
```

Year	Depreciation	Accumulated	Value
2003	5,432.63	5,432.63	32,584.37
2004	9,310.36	14,742.99	23,274.01
2005	6,649.17	21,392.17	16,624.83
2006	4,748.32	26,140.49	11,876.51
2007	3,394.92	29,535.41	8,481.59
2008	3,391.12	32,926.52	5,090.48
2009	3,394.92	36,321.44	1,695.56
2010	1,695.56	38,017.00	0.00

■ 36
Time Conversions

Time is measured in so many different units that you can count on having to convert from one unit to another. SAS includes functions for many kinds of time conversions; others can be done with mathematical expressions.

Points in Time

Converting between points in time means converting to and from SAS date values and SAS time values. There are functions to extract calendar and clock elements or to assemble values from calendar or clock elements.

In the code models below, the name DATE represents a SAS date value; DATETIME is a SAS datetime values; and TIME is a SAS time value. Similarly, names such as HOUR, MONTH, and YEAR represent specific calendar and clock elements.

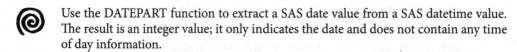 Use the DATEPART function to extract a SAS date value from a SAS datetime value. The result is an integer value; it only indicates the date and does not contain any time of day information.

```
DATE = DATEPART(DATETIME);
```

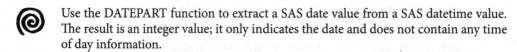 Use the TIMEPART function to extract the time of day from a SAS datetime value. The result is a SAS time value.

```
TIME = TIMEPART(DATETIME);
```

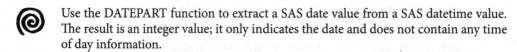 To extract calendar elements such as the year and month from a SAS date value, use a separate function for each calendar element. The function names indicate the calendar elements that are extracted.

```
YEAR = YEAR(DATE);
MONTH = MONTH(DATE);
DAY = DAY(DATE);
QUARTER = QTR(DATE);
WEEKDAY = WEEKDAY(DATE);
```

The WEEKDAY function returns the number of the day of the week. The days of the week are numbered starting from Sunday, which is day 1.

To extract calendar elements from a SAS datetime value, start by extracting a SAS date value with the DATEPART function. Then use functions for SAS date values to extract calendar elements.

```
YEAR = YEAR(DATEPART(DATETIME));
MONTH = MONTH(DATEPART(DATETIME));
DAY = DAY(DATEPART(DATETIME));
QUARTER = QTR(DATEPART(DATETIME));
WEEKDAY = WEEKDAY(DATEPART(DATETIME));
```

To extract clock elements from a SAS time value or SAS datetime value, use the HOUR, MINUTE, and SECOND functions.

```
HOUR = HOUR(TIME);
MINUTE = MINUTE(TIME);
SECOND = SECOND(TIME);
HOUR = HOUR(DATETIME);
MINUTE = MINUTE(DATETIME);
SECOND = SECOND(DATETIME);
```

The SECOND function includes any fraction of a second.

Use the MDY function to assemble a SAS date value from calendar elements. The function's arguments are reflected in the letters of its name: the month number, day of the month, and year.

```
DATE = MDY(MONTH, DAY, YEAR);
```

Use either the four-digit year number or a two-digit year number as the argument.
To indicate a year as a SAS date value, use 1 as the month and day:

```
DATE = MDY(1, 1, YEAR);
```

To indicate a month as a SAS date value, use 1 as the day:

```
DATE = MDY(MONTH, 1, YEAR);
```

Use the YYQ function to compute a calendar quarter as a SAS date value. The arguments are the year number and quarter number.

```
DATE = YYQ(YEAR, QUARTER);
```

To assemble a SAS time value from clock elements, use the HMS function. The arguments are the hour, minute, and second. Use the hour of the 24-hour clock, a number from 0 to 23.

```
TIME = HMS(HOUR, MINUTE, SECOND);
```

Usually, a time of day is recorded only as the hour and minute, and you can use 0 for the second:

```
TIME = HMS(HOUR, MINUTE, 0);
```

To convert between a SAS datetime value and a SAS date value, you can either use the conversion factor of 86,400 or function calls.

Multiply by 86,400 to convert a SAS date value to a SAS datetime value.

```
DATETIME = DATE*86400;
```

Alternatively, use the DHMS function. This function creates a SAS datetime value with both date and time of day information. The first argument is a SAS date value that provides the date. The next three arguments are the hour, minute, and second of the time of day — the same arguments used in the HMS function.

```
DATETIME = DHMS(DATE, HOUR, MINUTE, SECOND);
```

To convert a SAS datetime value to a SAS date value while retaining the time of day information, divide by 86,400.

```
DATE = DATETIME/86400;
```

Use the DATEPART function to create a SAS date value without any time of day information.

```
DATE = DATEPART(DATETIME);
```

Alternatively, use the FLOOR function to convert the SAS date value to an integer value, as shown here:

```
DATE = FLOOR(DATETIME/86400);
```

The day of the year of a SAS date value can be computed by comparing the date to the first day of the year, which can be obtained from the MDY function. The expression shown here provides the day of the year:

```
YEARDAY = DATE - MDY(1, 1, YEAR(DATE)) + 1;
```

To create a SAS datetime value from a SAS date value and a SAS time value, convert the integer part of the SAS date value to a SAS datetime value, then add the SAS time value, as shown here:

```
DATETIME = FLOOR(DATE)*86400 + TIME;
```

To assemble a SAS datetime value from calendar and clock elements, use the MDY and DHMS functions together, as shown here:

DATETIME = DHMS(MDY(MONTH, DAY, YEAR), HOUR, MINUTE, SECOND);

 Use this expression to determine the quarter based on the month number:

QUARTER = FLOOR((MONTH - 1)/3) + 1;

 Both numbers and names identify months and days of the week. The functions described here use the numbers. To convert numbers to names, use value formats. Similarly, use value informats to convert names to numbers. Programs to create informats and formats for this purpose can be seen in chapter 18, "Format Catalogs and Control Datasets."

 There are three variables involved when you convert between the 24-hour clock and the 12-hour clock: the hour of the 12- or 24-hour clock, and the day half. Convert from the 24-hour clock to the 12-hour clock this way:

HOUR12 = MOD(HOUR24 + 11, 12) + 1;
IF HOUR24 < 12 THEN DAYHALF = 'AM';
ELSE DAYHALF = 'PM';

Convert from the 12-hour clock to the 24-hour clock this way:

HOUR24 = MOD(HOUR12, 12) + IF(DAYHALF = 'PM', 12, 0);

Duration

 Elapsed time can be measured in any unit of the calendar or clock. If two measurements are made with different units of time, you have to convert them to the same unit before you can compare or combine them. In SAS, this usually means converting to seconds or days.

Do the conversion by multiplying or dividing by a conversion factor. For example, there are 60 seconds in a minute, so to convert minutes to seconds, multiply by 60; to convert seconds to minutes, divide by 60. The table below shows factors for converting between days and seconds and the other common time units.

TIME CONVERSION FACTORS				
	seconds per	days per	minutes per hour	60
second	1	1/86400	minutes per day	1440
minute	60	1/1440	hours per day	24
hour	3600	1/24	hours per week	168
day	86400	1	weeks per month	4.348125
week	604800	7	weeks per quarter	13.044375
month	2629746	30.436875	weeks per year	52.1775
quarter	7889238	91.310625	months per quarter	3
year	31556952	365.2425	months per year	12

Time conversion factors for units of the calendar longer than a week are averages based on the definition of the Gregorian calendar. In many cases, it is appropriate to convert units based on these averages. In other cases, it is necessary to determine the actual number of days involved.

Many of the routines that work with SAS time values also work with duration values measured in seconds. For example, you can use the TIME format to write these values in hours, minutes, and seconds.

Use the DATEPART, HOUR, MINUTE, and SECOND functions to divide a duration value into days, hours, minutes, and seconds. This works correctly only with positive values.

```
DAYS = DATEPART(DURATION);
HOURS = HOUR(DURATION);
MINUTES = MINUTE(DURATION);
SECONDS = SECOND(DURATION);
```

To divide a value into hours, minutes, and seconds, combine the days and hours as shown here:

```
HOURS = DATEPART(DURATION)*24 + HOUR(DURATION);
```

Picture formats work only for durations between 0 and 24 hours because the picture directive for hours is limited to values between 0 and 23. See chapter 22, "Picture Formats for Time," for details.

Use the HMS and DHMS functions to compute a duration value in seconds from separate clock elements. When you use the DHMS function for this purpose, the first argument indicates the number of days. For example, this function call returns the number of seconds in 2 days, 5 hours:

```
DHMS(2, 5, 0, 0)
```

Clock Issues

Ideally, a set of time measurements is made in reference to a single clock in continuous operation. If a combination of clocks must be used, the clocks or the measurements they provide may have to be adjusted to produce more accurate measurements. One ore more of the following might be required.

- Set clocks to standard time.
- Designate a master clock and set all other clocks to match it.
- Adjust time values measured by a clock by subtracting the clock error from the time measurement, as shown here:

  ```
  TRUE_DATETIME = CLOCK_DATETIME - SYNC_ERROR;
  ```

- Estimate sync errors among a set of clocks by examining the way related events are recorded by different clocks.

Time zones present a different synchronization issue. Points in time from different time zones cannot be used together for comparisons or computations. To use these values, convert them all to the same time zone. The time zone you select could be the predominant time zone found in the data. Another good choice would be Greenwich Mean Time (GMT), also known as Universal Time (UT), the international standard for measuring time.

To convert a SAS datetime value of a specific time zone to GMT, subtract the time zone differential from the value. Write the time zone differential as a SAS time constant in hours and minutes (this would be negative for a time zone in the Western Hemisphere). For example, Atlantic Time (or Eastern Daylight Time) is time zone –4:00, which you would write as the constant value '-4:00'T. The example below converts SAS datetime values of several time zones to GMT.

```
SELECT (ZONE);
  WHEN ('AT', 'EDT') DT_UNIVERSAL = DT_LOCAL - '-4:00'T;
  WHEN ('ET', 'CDT') DT_UNIVERSAL = DT_LOCAL - '-5:00'T;
  WHEN ('CT', 'MDT') DT_UNIVERSAL = DT_LOCAL - '-6:00'T;
  WHEN ('MT', 'PDT') DT_UNIVERSAL = DT_LOCAL - '-7:00'T;
  WHEN ('PT') DT_UNIVERSAL = DT_LOCAL - '-8:00'T;
  OTHERWISE ;
  END;
```

Daylight time is a seasonal one-hour change in clock settings. In areas that use daylight time, times recorded at the same location can mean different things, depending on the time of year. Other than this, daylight time can be addressed as a time zone issue.

SPHERICAL COORDINATES

Like clock time, arcs and angles are also measured in parts of 60. A complete circle is divided into 360 degrees. Each degree is 60 minutes, and each minute is 60 seconds. It is standard to use degrees, minutes, and seconds to write spherical coordinates, such as the longitude and latitude that locate places on Earth. SAS time routines can simplify some computations involving degrees, minutes, and seconds.

To write a degree measurement in degrees, minutes, and seconds, multiply the value by 3600 and write it with the TIME format. Use a width of 7 to write degrees and minutes or 10 for degrees, minutes, and seconds. After writing the value, write symbols for degrees, minutes, and seconds. The standard symbols are °, ′, and ″, but these are not ASCII characters, so the lowercase letters d, m, and s are more often used in computer output.

```
DEGREES = 39.875;
ARC = DEGREES*3600;
PUT ARC TIME7. +(-3) 'd' +2 'm';
PUT ARC TIME10. +(-6) 'd' +2 'm' +2 's';
```

```
39d52m
39d52m30s
```

To extract the degrees, minutes, and seconds from an arc measurement in degrees, multiply the degrees by 3600, then use the MINUTE and SECOND functions to extract minutes and seconds. These functions work correctly only with a positive value, so use the ABS and SIGN functions to separate the magnitude and sign of the value. Use the INT function to get the whole degrees. The code model below uses this logic to create the variables ARC_D, ARC_M, and ARC_S, with arc degrees, minutes and seconds, from the variable DEGREES, a measurement in degrees.

```
ARC = ABS(DEGREES*3600);
SIGN = SIGN(DEGREES)
ARC_D = INT(DEGREES);
ARC_M = MINUTE(ARC)*SIGN;
ARC_S = SECOND(ARC)*SIGN;
```

■ 37
Time Arithmetic

Time measurements in SAS are based on standard units such as seconds and days. This makes it possible to do time arithmetic using ordinary numeric operators. There are also functions for specialized kinds of time arithmetic.

Most of the actions in time arithmetic fit one of these descriptions:

- Add time units to a point in time to get a later point in time;
- Subtract time units from a point in time to get an earlier point in time.
- Subtract one point in time from another to get the elapsed time between the two points.

 Before you do time arithmetic, you might have to convert values so that they use a common time unit. If you use seconds as the time unit, convert

- SAS date values and SAS time values to SAS datetime values
- all SAS datetime values to the same time zone
- all durations to seconds

If you use days as the time unit, convert

- SAS datetime values to SAS date values
- all durations to days

Most of these conversions can be done with functions. See the previous chapter, "Time Conversions," for details.

 Calculate a later day by adding days to a SAS date value. Calculate an earlier day by subtracting days from a SAS date value. This example obtains the current date from the DATE function, then adds and subtracts 1 day to compute the dates of tomorrow and yesterday.

```
TODAY = DATE();
TOMORROW = TODAY + 1;
YESTERDAY = TODAY - 1;
```

Calculate a later time by adding seconds to a SAS datetime value. Calculate an earlier time by subtracting seconds from a SAS datetime value. If DT is a SAS datetime value, DT + 120 is a value 120 seconds, or 2 minutes, later.

 When you add hours and minutes to a SAS datetime value, you can write the added time as a SAS time constant. The expression DT + '24:00:00'T adds 24 hours to DT to get the same time of day, 1 day later.

 If you do arithmetic operations with SAS time values, make sure they do not result in a value that is less than 0 or greater than or equal to 86,400.

Comparisons

When two points in time are compared, there are three possible results: one or the other is earlier or they are the same time. With SAS date values or SAS datetime values, you can use the usual comparison operators to make these comparisons. For example, (TIME1 > TIME2) tests whether TIME1 is later than TIME2.

 To test whether a time falls into a time period, compare it to both the beginning and ending points of the period. If EFFECT and EXPIRE are the start and end dates of a time period, the expression (EFFECT <= DATE <= EXPIRE) tests whether DATE falls into that time period:

 When comparisons are made with SAS time values, they determine whether one value is earlier or later in the day than the other value or at the same time of day as the other value. If you know the two events occurred on the same day, then this indicates which event is earlier in absolute terms. However, if the two events occurred on different days, then to determine which occurred first, you must compare days rather than times of day.

 Sorting by a SAS date or SAS datetime variable puts observations in chronological order. The earliest observations are positioned first in the sorted data; the latest observations are last.

Rounding

 Round down with the FLOOR function to remove the fractional part of a SAS date value. A fractional part of a SAS date value represents the time of day. An integer SAS date value only indicates the day, with no indication of the time of day. Remove the fractional part to compare days. Two fractional SAS date value could fall on the same day without being equal. If two integer SAS date values represent the same day, then they are equal.

 Round down with the FLOOR function to remove the fractional seconds from SAS datetime values or SAS time values.

Round with the ROUND function to round a duration value to the nearest second, minute, or hour.

To round to the nearest second, use the ROUND function with only one argument. This expression rounds the duration value DURATION to the nearest second:

ROUND(DURATION)

To round to the nearest minute, use 60 (or '0:01'T) as the third argument of the ROUND function. This expression rounds DURATION to the nearest minute:

ROUND(DURATION, 60)

To round to the nearest hour, use the ROUND function with 3600 (or '1:00'T) as the roundoff unit. This expression rounds DURATION to the nearest hour:

ROUND(DURATION, 3600)

Use other roundoff unit values to round in other ways. For example, use 360 to round to the nearest tenth of an hour or 1800 to round to the nearest half hour.

Time Loops

For time loops — where the purpose of a loop is to repeat the same action for different times — it is usually simplest to use time values as the index variable of the loop.

Use SAS date values for the index variable of a DO loop that repeats actions for a sequence of days. This example demonstrates how this can work.

```
STARTDATE = '31JUL2002'D;
STOPDATE = '15AUG2002'D;
DO DAY = STARTDATE TO STOPDATE;
  PUT DAY : YYMMDD10. @;
  END;
```

```
2002-07-31 2002-08-01 2002-08-02 2002-08-03 2002-08-04 2002-08-05
2002-08-06 2002-08-07 2002-08-08 2002-08-09 2002-08-10 2002-08-11
2002-08-12 2002-08-13 2002-08-14 2002-08-15
```

Use an increment value of 7 to repeat the actions of the loop once for each week, as shown here:

```
STARTDATE = '31JUL2002'D;
STOPDATE = '15AUG2002'D;
DO DAY = STARTDATE TO STOPDATE BY 7;
  PUT DAY : YYMMDD10. @;
  END;
```

```
2002-07-31 2002-08-07 2002-08-14
```

Similarly, use a SAS datetime variable as an index variable with increment values measured in seconds. This DO statement creates an index variable to repeat actions twice for each day, at midnight and noon, over a period of time:

```
DO DT = '31JUL2002 00:00'DT TO '15AUG2002 23:59'DT BY '12:00'T;
```

Use SAS time values for an index variable in a DO loop that repeats for different times of day. This DO statement repeats actions for five-minute intervals from midnight to midnight:

```
DO TIME = '00:00'T TO '23:59'T BY '0:05'T;
```

To repeat an action for every month of a year, use the month number as the index variable, as shown here:

```
DO MONTH = 1 TO 12;
   DATE = MDY(MONTH, 1, 2006)
   PUT DATE DATE9. +1 @;
   END;
```

```
01JAN2006 01FEB2006 01MAR2006 01APR2006 01MAY2006 01JUN2006
01JUL2006 01AUG2006 01SEP2006 01OCT2006 01NOV2006 01DEC2006
```

To repeat an action for every quarter of a year, use the quarter number as the index variable.

```
DO QUARTER = 1 TO 4;
   DATE = YYQ(2006, QUARTER);
   PUT DATE DATE9. +1 @;
   END;
```

```
01JAN2006 01APR2006 01JUL2006 01OCT2006
```

If an array contains values for a specific sequence of consecutive days, use the SAS date values as the subscript values for the array. The ARRAY statement does not allow SAS date constants as boundary values, so write the values as regular numeric constants. Write the date values in a comment so you know what dates are involved. This statement defines the array CLS with subscripts for February 1 to 29, 2008:

```
ARRAY CLS{17563:17591}; * '01FEB2008'D : '29FEB2008'D ;
```

A reference to the array could be:

```
CLS{'15FEB2008'D}
```

Time Interval Arithmetic

The INTCK and INTNX functions are designed for a different kind of time arithmetic based on the time intervals that define the calendar and clock. These functions work with SAS date values, SAS datetime values, and SAS time values. You identify the kinds of values and the time interval by using a code as the first argument of the function. For example, use the code value MONTH for month calculations with SAS date values.

Working with fixed time intervals means that the INTCK and INTNX functions consider only the beginning points of time intervals in their calculations. For example, with the MONTH code, the functions consider the beginnings of months. This means:

- The difference between January 5, 1998 and January 19, 1998 is 0 months because the two values are in the same month.
- The difference between January 31, 1998 and February 2, 1998 is 1 month because the two values are in consecutive months.
- Two months after February 10, 1998 is April 1, 1998, because April is the second month after February.

These are the time interval names that can be used with SAS date values, listed from shortest to longest:

DAY WEEKDAY WEEK TENDAY SEMIMONTH
MONTH QUARTER SEMIYEAR YEAR

These are the time interval names that can be used with SAS datetime values, from shortest to longest:

SECOND MINUTE HOUR
DTDAY DTWEEKDAY DTWEEK DTTENDAY DTSEMIMONTH
DTMONTH DTQUARTER DTSEMIYEAR DTYEAR

These time interval names can also be used with SAS time values:

SECOND MINUTE HOUR

Use the INTCK function to calculate the difference between two points in time. Write the time interval code as the first argument and the points in time as the next two arguments. The function counts the number of time intervals between the two points in time.

For example, INTCK('DAY', DATE1, DATE2) counts the number of days between the SAS date values DATE1 and DATE2.

Be sure to use the DT prefix for calendar intervals of SAS datetime values. This function call counts the days between the SAS datetime values DT1 and DT2:

INTCK('DTDAY', DT1, DT2)

Use a constant value as the first point in time in the INTCK function to count the elapsed time since that point in time. This function call counts the number of months from March 2002 to the value of DATE, a SAS date value:

INTCK('MONTH', '01MAR2002'D, DATE)

Use a constant value as the second point in time to count the time remaining before a deadline or event. This function call counts the number of hours from the value of DT, a SAS datetime value, till the end of 1999, which is the same as the beginning of 2000:

```
INTCK('HOUR', DT, '01JAN2000 00:00'DT)
```

If the INTCK function returns 0, it means that the two values are in the same time interval. You can use the function in the condition of an IF-THEN statement, as demonstrated here:

```
IF INTCK('DTWEEK', DT1, DT2) = 0 THEN
  PUT 'The two events occurred during the same week.';
```

Use the INTNX function to find a time period by counting forward or backward from a point in time. The third argument of the INTNX function is an offset, the number of time intervals to count from the initial point in time, which is the second argument.

For example, this function call counts 4 months forward from June 2003:

```
INTNX('MONTH', '12JUN2003'D, 4)
```

The return value is '01OCT2003'D.

Use an offset of 0 to find the beginning of the time period that contains a value. If DAY is a SAS date value, INTNX('YEAR', DAY, 0) returns the first day of the year that contains DAY, and INTNX('MONTH', DAY, 0) returns the first day of the month. If DT is a SAS datetime value, INTNX('DTDAY', DT, 0) returns midnight at the beginning of the same day.

Use an offset of 1 to find the beginning of the next time period. INTNX('DTDAY', DT, 1) returns midnight at the end of the day, or the beginning of the next day.

Use a negative offset in the INTNX function to count backward from the starting point. INTNX('QUARTER', TRANDATE, -1) returns the starting date of the quarter before the quarter that contains the SAS date TRANDATE.

To repeat a set of actions for a sequence of time periods such as months or quarters, use the index variable of a DO loop as the offset of the INTNX function. In the DO loop below, the INTNX function generates the months from July 2005 to July 2007.

```
DO M = 0 TO 24;
  MONTH = INTNX('MONTH', '01JUL2005'D, M);
  PUT MONTH : MONYY7. @;
  END;
```

```
JUL2005 AUG2005 SEP2005 OCT2005 NOV2005 DEC2005 JAN2006 FEB2006 MAR2006
APR2006 MAY2006 JUN2006 JUL2006 AUG2006 SEP2006 OCT2006 NOV2006 DEC2006
JAN2007 FEB2007 MAR2007 APR2007 MAY2007 JUN2007 JUL2007
```

Use the INTNX and INTCK functions together to calculate the number of time periods elapsed since the beginning of a larger time period — for example, the number of weeks since the beginning of the year. Use 0 as the offset in the INTNX function and write this function call as the argument to the INTCK function.

This function call returns the number of weeks between the beginning of the current year and today:

INTCK('WEEK', INTNX('YEAR', DATE(), 0), DATE())

This counts the first week of the year as week 0. To number the weeks of a year starting with week 1 for the first week of the year, add 1 to the result, as shown here:

WEEKNO = INTCK('WEEK', INTNX('YEAR', DATE(), 0), DATE()) + 1;

 The WEEKDAY time interval code counts the days Monday through Friday, but you can use a suffix with this code to count any combination of days of the week. Write the suffix as day numbers followed by W. For example, the time interval name WEEKDAY15W counts days 1 and 5 of the week: Sundays and Thursdays.

 The time interval code names of the INTCK and INTNX functions can be modified with multiplier and shift arguments. Write a multiplier as a numeric suffix for the time interval. For example, MONTH2 is a two-month time interval.

Write a shift argument after a period at the end of the time interval. Write a shift argument greater than 1 to change the starting point of the time interval. For example YEAR2 (or YEAR2.1) is a two-year interval that begins in even years, but YEAR2.2 is a two-year time interval that begins in odd years.

Age

 Use the YRDIF function to calculate a person's age on certain date. Write the person's birthdate as the first argument, the date as the second argument, and the code value Actual as the third argument. If the day is the SAS date DATE and a person's birthdate is BIRTH, then this statement calculates the person's age in years:

AGE = YRDIF(BIRTH, DATE, 'Actual');

With the Actual code argument, the YRDIF function counts each day as $1/365$ or $1/366$ year, depending on the number of days in the year. To state a person's age as a whole number of years, as is usually done, use the FLOOR function to get the whole number:

AGE = FLOOR(YRDIF(BIRTH, DATE, 'Actual'));

 Another way to calculate age in years is to subtract the birth year from the current year, then adjust the result based on whether the current date is before or after the birthday. An expression to calculate the age this way is shown in this statement.

AGE = YEAR(DATE) - YEAR(BIRTH)
  - (MONTH(DATE) < MONTH(BIRTH) OR
  MONTH(DATE) = MONTH(BIRTH) AND DAY(DATE) < DAY(BIRTH));

■ 38

Extending the Observation Loop

A data step automatically repeats as long as there is input data. An automatic loop repeats the actions of the data step, stopping only when the end of data is reached. This automatic loop can be called the observation loop because each repetition of the loop processes the data of one observation. However, this automatic feature of the data step does not have to dictate the control flow you can use in a data step. You can modify and extend the flow of the observation loop in any way you need to.

The observation loop ends when it reaches a statement that reads input data and this statement finds the end of the data it has been reading. To end the observation loop sooner, use a conditional STOP statement. This example shows a statement that will stop a data step as soon as the value for TOTAL exceeds 1,000,000.

```
IF TOTAL > 1000000 THEN STOP;
```

To prevent the repetition of the observation loop, write an unconditional STOP statement after the last statement to execute. In the example below, the STOP statement ensures that the step processes only one observation of MAIN.CONTROL.

```
DATA MAIN.CONTROL;
   SET MAIN.CONTROL;
   SESSION + 1;
   CALL SYMPUT('SESSION', TRIM(LEFT(PUT(SESSION, F12.))));
   OUTPUT;
   STOP;
RUN;
```

Sometimes, as in this example, it is important to write an output observation before you stop the data step. Execute an OUTPUT statement before the STOP statement. With the OUTPUT statement and the STOP statement, this step rewrites MAIN.CONTROL with only one observation, even if it happens to contain multiple observations before the step executes.

If a condition occurs that makes it necessary to stop the entire SAS program from running, use the ABORT statement instead of the STOP statement. Use the ABORT statement to stop a program early if you find that it has failed or that the input data is defective in a way that prevents the program from reaching its objectives. This example stops the program if a value for TEMP is invalid.

IF TEMP < -273 THEN ABORT;

The effects of the ABORT statement vary, depending mainly on the mode of the SAS session. In batch mode, the ABORT statement stops the SAS session immediately. In interactive mode, the ABORT statement is the same as a semantic error; it stops the current step from running, but execution continues with the next step.

A data step expects input data for every observation. If there is input data in a data step, the programming logic of the data step must provide input data in every repetition of the observation loop. If a repetition of the observation loop completes without executing a statement that could read input data, the data step ends immediately with an error condition and this descriptive log message:

NOTE: DATA STEP stopped due to looping.

This feature keeps some steps from looping indefinitely, but it could also limit the way you write the programming logic for some data steps. For example, if you want to write each observation twice, you cannot do so by reading an observation in every other repetition of the observation loop, as shown here:

```
DATA NUMBERS;
  INFILE N;
  IF MOD(_N_, 2) = 1 THEN DO;
    INPUT NUMBER;
    X = 0;
    END;
  ELSE X = 1;
RUN;
```

NOTE: DATA STEP stopped due to looping.

Instead, use a DO loop to execute an OUTPUT statement more than once, as shown here:

```
DATA NUMBERS;
  INFILE N;
  INPUT NUMBER;
  DO X = 0, 1;
    OUTPUT;
    END;
RUN;
```

Use the condition _N_ = 1 for actions that are taken only once at the beginning of the execution of the data step. _N_ is an automatic variable that counts repetitions of the observation loop. Its value is always 1 for the first repetition of the observation loop.

For actions that are taken once at the end of the data step, use the option END=LAST on the INFILE, SET, MERGE, MODIFY, or UPDATE statement. Then use LAST as the condition for the actions. The END= option designates a numeric variable that indicates the end of the input data. The variable's value is 0 until the last input record or observation is reached. Then, the value of the variable changes to 1.

Control flow for actions at the beginning and end of a data step is summarized in the code model below, which uses a SET statement as an example of a statement that provides input data.

```
DATA output SAS dataset;
  IF _N_ = 1 THEN DO;
    initialization actions
    END;
  SET SAS dataset END=LAST;
  actions for each observation
  IF LAST THEN DO;
    termination actions
    END;
RUN;
```

The END= option works only if it is possible to determine the last record or observation of input. This is possible when the input data is sequential and buffered. The END= option does not work, for example, with the POINT= option, SAS datasets that use sequential engines, text files on tape volumes, or pipes.

If a data step reads input data from an unbuffered text file, use the EOF= option on the INFILE statement to control actions that occur at the end of the data step. The EOF= option indicates a statement label; when an INPUT statement cannot read data because it has reached the end of the file, it transfers control to that statement label.

Write that statement label after a RETURN statement at the end of the data step. After the statement label, write statements for actions to take at the end of the data step. Then write a STOP statement. The code model below shows these aspects of using the EOF= option to take additional actions at the end of the execution of a data step.

```
DATA . . . ;
  INFILE fileref EOF=label;
  INPUT . . .
  . . .
  RETURN;
label:
  actions at end of data
  STOP;
RUN;
```

To stop processing of an individual observation, use a RETURN, DELETE, or subsetting IF statement.

Write a RETURN statement as a separate unconditional statement or as the action of an IF-THEN statement. A RETURN statement stops processing the current observation and proceeds to the beginning of the next observation. However, the RETURN statement also has these special features:

- After a LINK statement or similar branching action, the RETURN statement has a completely different meaning. It returns control to the point of the original branching.
- If there is no statement to write an output observation in the step, such as an OUTPUT statement, the RETURN statement also implies writing an output observation.

A DELETE statement also stops processing the current observation and proceeds to the beginning of the next observation. However, it does not have either of the special features of the RETURN statement. A DELETE statement is almost always written in an IF-THEN statement.

A subsetting IF statement is an IF statement with no THEN clause. A subsetting IF statement continues processing with the next statement if the condition is true. Otherwise, it stops processing the current observation, the same as a DELETE statement. That is, the statement

IF *condition*;

is equivalent to

IF *condition* THEN ;
ELSE DELETE;

or

IF NOT (*condition*) THEN DELETE;

■ 39
Loops

Use loops to program repetitive actions in data steps. The data step automatically repeats in order to process all the observations of its input data. Inside a data step, a DO loop can repeat a sequence of actions on a smaller scale.

 Sometimes you can choose between a DO loop and the observation loop for a repetitive process. In general, use the observation loop to read input records or observations, to form observations from input data, or to process input data that has a similar repetitive structure. Use the observation loop when the number of repetitions of the loop is determined by the extent of the input data and is unknown to the program. Use DO loops to process arrays and for processes that have a predetermined number of repetitions.

There is no significant difference in performance between the DO loop and observation loop, so choose the one that is more convenient for you. Use the kind of loop that makes the program easy to read or that gives you the necessary control over the repetitive process.

 To write a DO loop, write a DO statement, action statements, and an END statement. In the DO statement, write an index variable, the starting value, the word TO, and the stopping value. This is the form of a DO loop with the index variable I:

DO I = *start* TO *stop*;
  actions
  END;

The DO loop repeats the actions for various values of the index variable, starting at the starting value and incrementing by 1 until it passes the stopping value. For example, with this DO statement:

DO I = 5 TO 8;

the index variable I takes on the values 5, 6, 7, and 8.

10 Ways to End a DO Loop

The purpose of a DO loop is to repeat, but you don't want it to repeat forever! Every DO loop has to have a way to stop repeating. This is a summary of the ways a DO loop can end.

 Index variable. An index variable takes on a different value for each repetition of the loop. When the end of the set or range of values is reached, the loop ends.

For example, with this DO statement, the index variable is I and the loop repeats four times:

DO I = 4, 5, 7, 8;

With this DO statement, the loop repeats with values of I that go from 1 to 10, and stops when I is 11:

DO I = 1 TO 10;

 Stopping condition. A WHILE or UNTIL condition in a DO statements controls loop stopping. The loop repeats as long as a WHILE condition remains true, or it repeats until an UNTIL condition becomes true.

With this DO statement, the loop repeats as long as N is less than 1,000:

DO WHILE (N < 1000);

A stopping condition can be used separately or in combination with an index variable.

 LEAVE. A LEAVE statement appears inside a loop and exits the loop when it executes.

 GOTO. A GOTO statement inside a loop ends the loop if the statement label that it branches to is outside the loop.

 CONTINUE. A CONTINUE statement continues processing with the next repetition of the loop, but it ends the loop if it executes in the last repetition of the loop.

 Change index value. When there is an index variable with a range, you can stop the loop after the current repetition by assigning a value to the index variable that is beyond the stopping value of the index range.

 Logical variable. If you don't want to end the loop immediately when you discover a condition for ending the loop, use a logical variable as a condition of ending the loop. These statements in a loop use the variable OVER for this purpose:

OVER = 0;

. . .

IF DATE > DATE() THEN OVER = 1;

. . .

IF OVER THEN LEAVE;

 Logical variable as stopping condition. A logical variable can be used as the WHILE condition. Initialize the variable to 1 before the loop, and set it to 0 inside the loop in order to stop the loop after the current repetition. This example uses the variable GO:

GO = 1;
DO WHILE (GO);

. . .

IF . . . THEN GO = 0;

. . .

 End of observation. A subsetting IF, DELETE, or RETURN statement can end processing of an observation, and that also ends the DO loop.

 End of data step. A statement that ends the data step, such as a STOP statement, also ends the DO loop.

To use an increment value other than 1, add a BY clause after the stopping value. For example, with this DO statement:

DO I = 1 TO 10 BY 2.5;

the index variable takes on the values 1, 3.5, 6, and 8.5.

In addition to or in place of the index variable, you can use a WHILE or UNTIL condition in the DO statement to stop the loop. Write the word WHILE or UNTIL and a condition in parentheses at the end of the DO statement. The loop stops repeating as soon as the WHILE condition is false or when the UNTIL condition becomes true. These are examples:

DO I = 1 TO 1000 UNTIL (N > 10);

DO UNTIL (N > 1000);

DO WHILE (N <= 1000);

It is also possible to write a list of values for the index variable in the DO statement, for example:

DO I = 1, 2, 5;

The DO loop executes once for each value listed. With this approach it is possible for the index variable to be a character variable with a list of character values, for example:

DO LETTER = 'A', 'B', 'C', 'D', 'E', 'F', 'G';

Only action statements are repeated in a DO loop. The DO loop has no effect on declaration statements. To make this clear when you write data steps, do not write declaration statements inside DO loops.

Use the LEAVE and CONTINUE statements to cut short the processing of a DO loop. The CONTINUE statement stops processing of the current repetition of the loop; execution continues with the next repetition. The LEAVE statement stops processing of the loop; execution continues with the statement that follows the loop's END statement.

To create an infinite loop, one that has no limit on the number of times it repeats, use this DO statement:

DO WHILE (1);

Write a conditional LEAVE statement inside the loop to stop the loop.

Whenever you write a DO loop without an index variable, analyze the logic of the loop carefully to make sure that the loop eventually will end, no matter what the data values are. This is also a concern if a loop with an index variable contains statements that assign values to the index variable.

 If you are not certain a DO loop will end the way you expect, use an index variable to limit the number of repetitions of the loop. For example, with this DO statement:

DO I = 1 TO 200000 WHILE (N < 1000);

the loop executes until the variable N reaches a value of 1,000 or more, but it stops after 200,000 repetitions even if N is still less than 1,000.

REPETITIVE STATEMENTS OR LOOPS?

Another way to code repetitive processing is to write repetitive statements. For example, to set five variables to missing, you might write:

```
PROSUM = .;
SPENDSUM = .;
ADCT = .;
XCT = .;
EXPSUM = .;
```

Each statement does the same action with a different variable. There is no significant performance difference between repetitive statements and loop processing, so feel free to code with repetitive statements if it is easier to do so. However, if the same list of variables is used more than once, you can make the program easier to read by coding with arrays and loops. Consider this example:

```
IF FIRST.CUSTOMER THEN DO;
    PROSUM = .;
    SPENDSUM = .;
    ADCT = .;
    XCT = .;
    EXPSUM = .;
    END;
PROSUM + PRO;
SPNDSUM + SPEND;
ADCT + AD;
XCT + X;
EXPSUM + EXP;
```

This code is easy to grasp if you have seen this pattern before. Sum variables are set to missing at the beginning of a BY group. Values are added to the sums in each observation. But what might be overlooked is the misspelled variable name I wrote in the ninth line. If you missed this, look again. The misspelled name is a logical error that prevents the program from doing what it is intended to do. This kind of error is hard to see because human perception avoids repetition — a human limitation that becomes more of a concern when a set contains more than five objects.

If the code is rewritten with arrays and loops, as shown below, it becomes easier to read. The variable names appear only in the ARRAY statement, so the possibility of inconsistency is eliminated.

```
ARRAY VARS{*} PRO SPEND AD X EXP;
ARRAY SUMS{*} PROSUM SPENDSUM
    ADCT XCT EXPSUM;
IF FIRST.CUSTOMER THEN DO I =
    LBOUND(SUMS) TO HBOUND(SUMS);
    SUMS{I} = .;
    END;
DO I = LBOUND(SUMS)
    TO HBOUND(SUMS);
    SUMS{I} + VARS{I};
    END;
```

To process an array in a DO loop, use the index variable of the DO loop as the subscript of the array. Use the LBOUND and HBOUND functions to form the range of the index variable. The example below assigns missing values to the elements of an array.

```
ARRAY SUMS{*} PROSUM SPENDSUM ADCT XCT EXPSUM;
DO I = LBOUND(SUMS) TO HBOUND(SUMS);
  SUMS{I} = .;
  END;
```

Most array subscript ranges start at 1. For those arrays, you can write 1 and the DIM function for the range of the index variable, as shown here:

```
DO I = 1 TO DIM(SUMS);
```

When you process an array in a DO loop, it is also possible to use constant values for the range of the index variable, as:

```
DO I = 1 TO 5;
```

If you do this, make sure ranges in the DO and ARRAY statements are the same. If you change the number of elements in the array, you must change the DO statement so that it matches.

If you use a DO loop with an index variable, do not store the index variable in a SAS dataset. If the data step creates a SAS dataset, use the KEEP= or DROP= dataset option to control the variables that are stored in the SAS dataset.

To process a multidimensional array in a DO loop, use nested loops — one loop inside another. Use a separate index variable for each dimension of the array.

The example below checks the elements of the two-dimensional array NOM, changing negative and missing values to zeros. The index variables I and J are used as the two subscripts of the array.

```
ARRAY NOM (5, 4);
DO I = LBOUND(NOM, 1) TO HBOUND(NOM, 1);
  DO J = LBOUND(NOM, 2) TO HBOUND(NOM, 2);
    IF NOM{I, J} < 0 THEN NOM{I, J} = 0;
    END;
  END;
```

Whenever you nest DO loops, be certain that each loop uses a different index variable. For example, if you use I as the index variable for the first loop, use a different variable such as J as the index variable for the second loop.

Inside nested loops, the LEAVE and CONTINUE statements affect the innermost loop that contains them. If you need to exit two or more loops at once, use a GOTO statement.

■ 40

Character Loops

If a process involving a character value cannot be done with the techniques described in chapters 24, "Strings," 25, "Parsing," and 28, "Codes," it can usually be done by considering each separate character of the value in a DO loop.

Programming with character loops uses these objects and elements of syntax:

- *A character string variable.* The character loop processes each character of this variable separately.
- *DO statement.* This statement marks the beginning of the DO loop. It names the index variable and controls the iterations of the loop.
- *An index variable.* This variable is controlled by the DO loop and may take on values from 1 to the length of the character variable.
- *The VLENGTH function.* This function returns the length of a character variable and is the most convenient way to set the upper limit of the index range.
- *The SUBSTR function.* This function extracts each individual character of the character string. It is also used to modify individual characters in the character string variable.
- *A one-character variable.* This variable holds the value of each individual character for processing.
- *Counters.* These numeric variables count occurrences in the character string.
- *LEAVE statement.* This control flow statement lets you exit a loop early.
- *END statement.* This marks the end of the loop.

The example below demonstrates the use of these elements.

Program	Output
| ```
LENGTH CHAR $ 1;
STRING = 'This is it.   ';
SPACES = 0;
DO C = 1 TO VLENGTH(STRING);
  CHAR = SUBSTR(STRING, C, 1);
  IF CHAR = ' ' THEN SPACES + 1;
  PUT 'Character ' C 'is ' CHAR +(-1) '.';
  IF CHAR IN ('.', '!', '?') THEN LEAVE; * End of sentence. ;
  END;
PUT 'The sentence contains ' SPACES 'spaces.';
``` | ```
Character 1 is T.
Character 2 is h.
Character 3 is i.
Character 4 is s.
Character 5 is  .
Character 6 is i.
Character 7 is s.
Character 8 is  .
Character 9 is i.
Character 10 is t.
Character 11 is ..
The sentence contains 2 spaces.
``` |

In this example, the loop processes the character variable STRING, extracting each character in turn and assigning it to the variable CHAR. The loop is driven by the index variable C, which covers the range from 1 to the length of the string variable, provided by the VLENGTH function. In this example, the LEAVE statement stops processing when it finds a character that marks the end of the sentence.

A character loop technique is the easiest way to do some kinds of censorship. In some applications, certain sensitive information cannot be shown in certain documents and reports. The objective in this example is to replace the first 12 digits of a credit card number with asterisks. The program looks for the text Credit card: and changes the next 12 digit characters it finds.

```
LENGTH CHAR $ 1;
DIGITS = 0;
ICAPTION = INDEX(UPCASE(LINE), 'CREDIT CARD:');
IF ICAPTION THEN DO C = ICAPTION + 12 TO LENGTH(LINE);
  CHAR = SUBSTR(LINE, C, 1);
  IF INDEXC(CHAR, '0123456789') THEN DO;
    DIGITS + 1;
    SUBSTR(LINE, C, 1) = '*';
    END;
  IF DIGITS >= 12 THEN LEAVE;
  END;
```

The INDEX function call returns the location of the label text Credit card:, ignoring case. If the text is not found, the function returns 0 and the DO loop is not executed. The call to the function INDEXC is checking to see if the character is a digit. If it is, the digit is counted. Then, in the assignment statement that uses the SUBSTR function as the target of the assignment, the digit is changed to an asterisk. The LEAVE statement is executed after 12 digits have been counted and changed.

If the value of the variable LINE is

```
Credit card: 6011 0000 0000 1234
```

the program changes it to

```
Credit card: **** **** **** 1234
```

Character loops are often used to apply translations or other transformations to strings. This usually requires two string variables: one to contain the original value before the translation and a second one to contain the translated value. For the two string variables, there are two corresponding character index variables. One of them, usually the character index variable for the original string, is used as the loop index. The other one is calculated in the program logic.

The example below shows a process of extracting the digits of a written telephone number. The program keeps all digits except for any 0s and 1s at the beginning of the value. It discards all punctuation. If letters are present, it translates them to digits.

```
DIGITS = 0;
C2 = 0;
```

```
DO C1 = 1 TO LENGTH(PPHONE);
  CHAR = SUBSTR(PPHONE, C1, 1);
  CHAR = TRANSLATE(UPCASE(CHAR),
    '22233344455566677778888999', 'ABCDEFGHIJKLMNOPQRSTUVWXYZ');
  IF INDEXC(CHAR, '23456789') THEN DIGITS = 1;
  IF DIGITS AND INDEXC(CHAR, '0123456789') THEN DO;
    C2 + 1;
    SUBSTR(PHONE, C2, 1) = CHAR;
    END;
  END;
```

C2 is the character index of the new string, PHONE. It is initialized to 0, then incremented every time a character is added to PHONE.

Adding a space between each character of a string is one way to stretch out a string. This can be useful, for example, for a header that should occupy a certain amount of horizontal space in a report or graph. To expand a string this way, copy each character, one at a time, from the original string to the expanded string.

This example creates the variable EXPANDED, which is an expanded form of the text in the variable TEXT. Each character extracted from TEXT is copied to a computed position in EXPANDED.

```
DATA _NULL_;
  LENGTH TEXT $ 14 EXPANDED $ 29;
  TEXT = "Base Period";
  EXPANDED = "";
  DO C = 1 TO VLENGTH(TEXT) MIN (VLENGTH(EXPANDED)/2);
    SUBSTR(EXPANDED, C*2, 1) = SUBSTR(TEXT, C, 1);
    END;
  PUT EXPANDED;
RUN;
```

```
B a s e   P e r i o d
```

The upper bound of the loop in this example is an expression designed to stop the loop if the end of either string variable has been reached.

Word wrap, also called text wrap, divides text into lines short enough to fit into a column or table cell. To wrap text, identify the starting and ending point of each segment and extract the segments with the SUBSTR function. Unlike most character loop applications, the algorithm starts at the last potential character of the line and works backward from there until it finds a break point, such as a space between two words.

```
DATA _NULL_;
  RETAIN TEXT
    "If you don't have a plan for your life, someone else does."
    LINELEN 25;
  LENGTH FRAGMENT $ 3;
  ARRAY TEXTLINE{4} $ 25;

  C = 1;
  LENGTH = LENGTH(TEXT);
```

```
* Find lines of text. ;
DO I = 1 TO DIM(TEXTLINE);
  TEXTLINE{I} = '';
  IF C >= LENGTH THEN CONTINUE;

  * Skip spaces to find start of line. ;
  DO WHILE(SUBSTR(TEXT, C, 1) = ' ');
    C + 1;
    END;
  START = C;
  * Find end of line at space, hyphen, or dash. ;
  END = 0;
  IF START + LINELEN <= LENGTH THEN
    DO C = START + LINELEN - 1 TO START BY -1
    UNTIL (END);
    FRAGMENT = SUBSTR(TEXT, C);
    IF SUBSTR(FRAGMENT, 2, 1) = ' ' OR
      SUBSTR(FRAGMENT, 2, 2) = '--' OR
      (SUBSTR(FRAGMENT, 1, 1) = '-' AND
      SUBSTR(FRAGMENT, 2, 1) NE '-') THEN END = C;
    END;
  IF END THEN DO;
    TEXTLINE{I} = SUBSTR(TEXT, START, END - START + 1);
    C = END + 1;
    END;
  ELSE DO;
    TEXTLINE{I} = SUBSTR(TEXT, START);
    C = START + LINELEN;
    END;
  END;

* Show results. ;
DO I = 1 TO DIM(TEXTLINE);
  IF TEXTLINE{I} NE '' THEN PUT TEXTLINE{I};
  END;
RUN;
```

```
If you don't have a plan
for your life, someone
else does.
```

The FRAGMENT variable contains three characters at the point being considered for a line break. Making this a separate variable ensures that the SUBSTR function works correctly.

This example wraps a sentence of less than 80 characters in a line length of 25, forming three lines. However, the process works the same way with a larger line length, a longer text value, or a potentially greater number of text lines.

41

Subsetting and Sampling

A SAS dataset often contains more observations than you need to use for a particular purpose. In this situation, you want to use some of the observations of the SAS dataset and disregard the other observations. This might be because:

- Some of the observations are relevant in a particular process and the others are not. For example, if you are using transaction data to study currency conversion, you might limit your focus to transactions involving foreign customers, disregarding the transactions that involve domestic customers.
- You want to focus on a particular part of the data. For example, in a set of events, you might want to look only at the events of the last few days. Or, in a set of patients in a clinical trial, you might want to look at the patients of one specific clinic.
- There are too many observations to do the kind of statistical analysis you want to do, and you can get useful results by analyzing a smaller set of data.
- You are testing or debugging a program and you want to make it run faster during the testing by using a much smaller set of data.
- You want to try something with a smaller group. For example, in direct marketing, you might test the effectiveness of several marketing pieces by sending each one to 1,000 customers selected at random.

When you select some items from a set to create a smaller set, the smaller set is a *subset*. Creating a subset is *subsetting*. When a subset will represent the entire set in some way, especially for statistical analysis, it is a *sample*, and selecting it is *sampling*.

Subsetting

 Use the WHERE= dataset option to select the observations of a SAS dataset that meet a specific condition. For example, this SET statement reads the observations of WORLD.ISLAND that have the specific values indicated for SEA and LATITUDE.

SET WORLD.ISLAND (WHERE=(SEA = 'Atlantic' AND LATITUDE = 47));

This PROC PRINT step prints the same subset of WORLD.ISLAND.

PROC PRINT DATA=WORLD.ISLAND (WHERE=(SEA = 'Atlantic' AND LATITUDE = 47));
RUN;

Alternatively, if there is only one input SAS dataset in a step or the same WHERE condition applies to all the input SAS datasets, the condition can be written in a WHERE statement. This PROC PRINT step is equivalent to the one shown above.

```
PROC PRINT DATA=WORLD.ISLAND;
   WHERE SEA = 'Atlantic' AND LATITUDE = 47;
RUN;
```

In an SQL query, the WHERE condition is usually written as a separate clause, as shown in this example.

```
PROC SQL;
SELECT * FROM WORLD.ISLAND
   WHERE SEA = 'Atlantic' AND LATITUDE = 47;
```

Use the WHERE= dataset option in the same way for an output SAS dataset to store only the observations that meet a condition. In a data step, write the WHERE= dataset option in the DATA statement, not the OUTPUT statement.

If you update a SAS dataset in a data step with a WHERE clause, use the WHEREUP= dataset option to indicate whether the WHERE clause applies on output. The WHERE clause always applies to input observations, and the step reads only observations that meet the condition. With WHEREUP=YES, it does not allow the observations to be changed so that they no longer meet the condition. With WHEREUP=NO, it is possible to change data values so that observations no longer meet the WHERE condition.

WHERE conditions can use several operators that are not used anywhere else in the SAS environment. This means that you cannot always take the expression from a WHERE clause and use it in another kind of statement.

Use the FIRSTOBS= and OBS= dataset options to select a sequence of observations based on their observation numbers. This example reads the second 100 observations from the SAS dataset WORLD.PLACE.

```
SET WORLD.PLACE (FIRSTOBS=101 OBS=200);
```

An alternative way to do subsetting in a data step is with a subsetting IF statement. This statement is an executable statement and allows subsetting to be incorporated into data step logic. The data step stops processing any observation that does not meet the condition in the subsetting IF statement. It continues processing observations that meet the condition. This is an example of the use of a subsetting IF statement.

```
SET WORLD.ISLAND;
IF SEA = 'Atlantic' AND LATITUDE = 47;
```

A data step can include any number of subsetting IF statements.

The DELETE statement, used as the action of an IF-THEN statement, has the same effect as a subsetting IF statement. But write the DELETE statement with the inverse condition — a condition for observations to discard. Observations that do not meet the condition are kept for further processing in the data step. This example is equivalent to the previous one.

```
SET WORLD.ISLAND;
IF SEA NE 'Atlantic' OR LATITUDE NE 47 THEN DELETE;
```

Use the OUTPUT statement as the action of an IF-THEN statement to write selected observations to an output SAS dataset in a data step. This approach makes it possible to select output observations based on variables that are not stored in the output SAS dataset. The statement below writes only observations that have a positive value for CHARGE or EXCHANGE to the output SAS dataset WORK.SALE.

```
IF CHARGE > 0 OR EXCHANGE > 0 THEN OUTPUT WORK.SALE;
```

If it is not important that a sample be representative of the set as a whole, the most efficient sample is selected as the first several observations using the OBS= dataset option. When you are debugging a program, you might want to use the OBS= system option rather than the dataset option. The system option affects every input SAS dataset and text file. If some of the files are very large, using an option setting such as OBS=1000 can make a program run much faster, which can help you find programming errors faster.

Sampling

A random sample of a SAS dataset is a subset containing the same variables and usually a much smaller number of observations. Usually, the random sample is stored as a separate SAS dataset. Sometimes, it is necessary to flag the observations of a random sample within the original SAS dataset.

Systematic sampling techniques can be somewhat like random sampling, but the resulting samples may not accurately represent the population from which they are drawn.

If the order of observations is random, use any arbitrary rule to select a certain number of observations. The easiest way is with the FIRSTOBS= and OBS= dataset options. The example below creates a SAS dataset of 1000 observations selected arbitrarily from the SAS dataset MAIN.BIG.

```
DATA MAIN.SAMPLE;
   SET MAIN.BIG (FIRSTOBS=2501 OBS=3500);
RUN;
```

This approach produces a random sample if the order of observations is random. It may also be useful as an efficient way to divide a large dataset into neatly defined segments.

If observations are not in random order, you can randomize them, similar to the way shuffling a deck of cards puts the cards in random order. To randomize a SAS dataset, sort by a variable whose value is a random number. The example below adds a variable RANDOM, a random number, to the SAS dataset WORK.LOCAL to create a new SAS dataset WORK.RANDOM in which the order of observations is randomized.

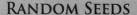

RANDOM SEEDS

Random number examples in this chapter use a small integer value, such as 5, as their seed argument. Statisticians suggest that you employ a random process, such as a table of random numbers, to generate the seed value that is written in the program. This eliminates the possibility, however remote, that using a specific seed value could introduce a bias into the sampling process.

```
DATA WORK.RANDOM;
  SET WORK.LOCAL;
  RANDOM = RANUNI(5);
RUN;
PROC SORT DATA=WORK.RANDOM;
  BY RANDOM;
RUN;
```

You can then proceed to select a random sample by using any arbitrary rule, as described above.

 Often, the reason to create a random sample is that the complete SAS dataset is too large to work with comfortably. If this is the case, then you will want to avoid sorting the complete SAS dataset. Use one of the techniques described below instead.

 To select a random sample of an approximate size, generate a random number with the RANUNI function for each observation. Keep observations whose random numbers are below a certain value. This cutoff value is the proportion of observations you want to select. For example, to select approximately one half percent of the observations, keep those that have a random number value less than .005. This is demonstrated in this example.

```
DATA WORK.SAMPLE;
  SET WORK.COMPLETE;
  IF RANUNI(5) < .005;
RUN;
```

If WORK.COMPLETE has 1,000,000 observations, WORK.SAMPLE will have around 5,000 observations. The exact number of observations in WORK.SAMPLE will vary somewhat (at random, of course). Use a different technique if you need to select a sample of an exact size.

 One way to select a sample of an exact size is to recalculate the cutoff value for every observation.

```
DATA WORK.SAMPLE;
  RETAIN NTARGET 1000 N 0;
  SET WORK.COMPLETE NOBS=NTOTAL;
  CUTOFF = (NTARGET - N)/(NTOTAL - _N_ + 1);
  IF RANUNI(5) < CUTOFF;
  N + 1;
RUN;
```

With this approach, WORK.SAMPLE will have exactly 1,000 observations (provided that

WORK.COMPLETE has at least that many). However, because of the way CUTOFF is recalculated, the sample is not a completely random sample. For most purposes, the differences between this kind of sample and a random sample are insignificant. But consecutive observations are less likely to be selected together than in a true random sample, and this could be significant in some statistical tests with some kinds of data. If you might need a true random sample, use a different technique.

To create a true random sample of a certain exact size, generate an array of random integers and use the observations that belong to those numbers. To generate the random integers, multiply the value returned by the RANUNI function by the number of observations, add 1, and find the next lower integer with the FLOOR function. Then make sure that the number is not the same as any number that you have already generated. The code model below shows how this works.

```
DATA WORK.SAMPLE (DROP=I J SIZE);
  ARRAY RAN{1000} _TEMPORARY_;
  SIZE = DIM(RAN) MIN NOBS;
  DO I = 1 TO SIZE;
    DO UNTIL (RAN{I} > 0);
      RAN{I} = FLOOR(RANUNI(5)*NOBS + 1);
      DO J = 1 TO I - 1 WHILE (RAN{I} > 0);
        IF RAN{I} = RAN{J} THEN RAN{I} = 0;
        END;
      END;
    END;
  DO I = 1 TO SIZE;
    POINT = RAN{I};
    SET WORK.COMPLETE POINT=POINT NOBS=NOBS;
    OUTPUT;
    END;
  STOP;
RUN;
```

To use this code for any specific application, change the names of the SAS datasets in the DATA and SET statements and set the sample size as the dimension of the array RAN in the ARRAY statement.

Sometimes, the right kind of sampling is *sampling with replacement*, in which items that have already been selected are available to be selected again. The same item might be selected any number of times. The code model above can be adapted for sampling with replacement by removing the logic that tests each generated random number to make sure it is unique. The change results in the much simpler code model shown below.

```
DATA WORK.SAMPLE (DROP=I);
  DO I = 1 TO 1000 MIN NOBS;
    POINT = FLOOR(RANUNI(5)*NOBS + 1);
    SET WORK.COMPLETE POINT=POINT NOBS=NOBS;
    OUTPUT;
    END;
  STOP;
RUN;
```

Often, the purpose of statistical tests is to compare groups to each other within a set of data. For some of these tests to be accurate, it may be important to have the same number, a similar number, a proportional number, or a minimum number in the sample for each group or cell. The best size for each group in the sample depends on the kind of statistical test. To create a grouped or stratified sample, first sort the SAS dataset so that it forms BY groups. Count the observations in each group and then calculate the proportion or number of observations to select from each group.

Another common approach is periodic sampling, which may be specified by a directive such as "Select every 10th observation." That is, select observation numbers 10, 20, 30, and so on. The sampling period could be any positive number *n*, so this technique has sometimes been called *n*thing. If the sampling period is a whole number, the value of the variable N, then periodic sampling can be as simple as this subsetting IF statement:

IF NOT MOD(_N_, N);

_N_ is an automatic variable that counts the repetitions of the observation loop. The MOD function is used to identify the multiples of N.

If N is not necessarily a whole number, use this statement instead:

IF MOD(_N_, N) < 1;

After selecting one group this way, it might be necessary to select a second group, consisting of the observations immediately after those of the first group, as shown here.

IF MOD(_N_ - 1, N) < 1;

This is an alternative way to write the same criterion.

IF 1 <= MOD(_N_, N) < 2;

The offset, in this case, is 1. Use an offset between 1 and N – 1 so that the new sample will not contain any of the observations of the original sample.

Periodic sampling is an example of systematic sampling, which means it selects observations by a mathematical process that is not random. Other examples of systematic sampling include sampling based on specific digits of ID codes or on checksums calculated from ID codes. Systematic sampling does not produce any kind of random sample, but can be a simpler process. This simplicity is the main reason why systematic sampling is used, as some people hope that simplicity in the selection process will protect against the possibilities of error and fraud in selecting the sample. As long as the system used for sampling is generally unrelated to the questions being studied, the resulting sample is likely to produce results that are generally similar to those of the complete set. Even so, a systematic sample cannot be used as a random sample for any kind of statistical test.

■ 42
SQL

SQL is the standard language for extracting data from databases. SAS includes a relatively complete implementation of SQL. SQL statements in the SAS environment can use SAS datasets as tables. With SAS/ACCESS, they can also connect to database management systems. If you have a collection of SQL code, it can easily be moved into the SAS environment.

SQL uses terminology from database theory. Terms used to discuss SQL are not always the same as those used in SAS. These are translations of SQL terms to the SAS environment:

- *Table:* a SAS data file.
- *Row:* an observation.
- *Column:* a variable.
- *Null:* a missing value.

Index and *view* mean the same things in SAS and SQL.

To be a proper part of the SAS environment, SQL statements must follow SAS rules for such things as names, constants, and comments. Write a semicolon at the end of every SQL statement. SQL statements use elements of the SAS environment such as title lines, system options, and librefs.

Write a PROC SQL step to execute SQL statements in a SAS program. The step starts with a PROC SQL statement and can include any number of SQL statements. The step can also include global statements. Options for SQL execution can appear in the PROC SQL statement. The ROW option, for example, adds row numbers to print output. Change options at any point in the step by writing them in a RESET statement.

This is a summary of the syntax of the SQL procedure:

```
PROC SQL options;
statements
QUIT;
```

If you need to mark the end of a PROC SQL step, write a QUIT statement. The SQL procedure does not accept the RUN statement.

7 SQL Statements You Can Use If You Don't Know SQL

You don't have to have a detailed understanding of SQL to put it to use. Here's some SQL you can use even if you never heard of SQL before. Just remember to start with a PROC SQL statement.

 Report. Printing a table as a report is one of the easiest things to do in SQL. This statement prints the SAS dataset WORK.OUT:

SELECT * FROM WORK.OUT;

Substitute any table name to print a simple report. In this statement, SELECT * means "use all columns," and the FROM clause identifies the table to read.

 More Elaborate Report. You can list specific columns, use a WHERE clause to select rows, and add an ORDER BY clause to sort the report.

SELECT A, B, C, D FROM WORK.X
WHERE A = 1 ORDER BY A, B;

Write commas between items in any list in SQL, as in the list of columns A, B, C, and D. The WHERE and ORDER BY clauses are optional, but the order of the clauses in an SQL statement is critical; the clauses must be in the right order.

 Create Table. Create a table (actually a SAS data file) from any query expression (which is what a SELECT statement really is) by turning it into a CREATE TABLE statement.

CREATE TABLE WORK.TITLES AS
SELECT * FROM DICTIONARY.TITLES;

This is is an easy way to copy the data of a view or a DICTIONARY table to a SAS data file.

 Row Count. Use COUNT(*) to count rows (observations).

SELECT COUNT(*) AS N FROM WORK.TIMES;

The modifier AS N gives the resulting column the name N.

 Number of Different Values. Use the keyword DISTINCT in the COUNT function to count the number of different values of a column (a variable). Here, the table is WORK.STUFF and the column is LOCATION.

SELECT COUNT(DISTINCT LOCATION) AS NLOC
FROM WORK.STUFF;

 Summary Report. For a summary report, use statistic functions, such as SUM, and a GROUP BY clause. COUNT(*) is also good for summary reports. Remember to select the group column, TEAM in this example.

SELECT TEAM, SUM(AMT) AS AMT, COUNT(*) AS N
FROM WORK.STUFF GROUP BY TEAM;

 Table Information. The DESCRIBE TABLE statement writes a log message that describes a table.

DESCRIBE TABLE MAIN.REGISTRY;

For a view, use the DESCRIBE VIEW statement instead.

The SELECT statement of SQL prints data in table form, similar to the output of the PRINT procedure. The SELECT statement in the example below prints all the data from the table (SAS dataset) WORK.NEW.

PROC SQL;
SELECT * FROM WORK.NEW;

The asterisk in this statement indicates all the columns of the table. In SQL terms, the SELECT clause that forms this statement is called a query expression, or query.

To create a table (a SAS data file) in SQL, write a CREATE TABLE statement with a query expression.

CREATE TABLE WORK.NEWID AS SELECT DISTINCT ID FROM WORK.NEW;

The query expression above makes a list of the distinct values of ID.

An SQL view stores a SELECT clause for later use. You can use an SQL view like a table in an SQL query expression or as a SAS dataset anywhere in the SAS environment. Write a CREATE VIEW statement to create an SQL view of a query expression:

CREATE VIEW *name* AS *query expression*;

SQL also includes statements to

- create and manage indexes and integrity contraints.
- add rows or columns to tables.
- remove rows or columns from tables.
- connect to database management systems (with SAS/ACCESS).
- delete tables, views, and indexes.

Query expressions can include terms for combining tables, grouping rows, computing statistics, counting rows, setting the name, format, and label of a column, and much more. SQL column expressions can call most SAS functions and a few additional SQL functions.

It is also possible to submit SQL statements from the SCL program of a SAS/AF application. Use a SUBMIT SQL statement in the SCL program.

In SQL, use the special libref DICTIONARY to get information about objects in the SAS environment. For example, this statement writes a table of information about all defined filerefs:

SELECT * FROM DICTIONARY.EXTFILES;

A more elaborate example of a DICTIONARY table query can be seen at the end of chapter 71, "Compression."

This is a list of DICTIONARY tables and the objects they describe:

- LIBNAMES: librefs
- EXTFILES: filerefs
- MEMBERS, TABLES, VIEWS, CATALOGS: SAS files
- MACROS: macros
- COLUMNS: columns (variables in SAS datasets)
- INDEXES: indexes (of SAS data files)
- ENGINES: engines
- FORMATS: formats
- OPTIONS, GOPTIONS: system and graphics options
- TITLES: title and footnote lines
- STYLES: ODS styles
- DICTIONARIES: columns in DICTIONARY tables
- five more tables with information about integrity constraints

For a complete list of DICTIONARY tables, run this SQL statement:

```
SELECT DISTINCT MEMNAME, MEMLABEL
FROM DICTIONARY.DICTIONARIES;
```

 To find out what columns are in a DICTIONARY table, use a DESCRIBE TABLE statement, for example:

```
DESCRIBE TABLE DICTIONARY.EXTFILES;
```

```
NOTE: SQL table DICTIONARY.EXTFILES was created like:

create table DICTIONARY.EXTFILES
  (
   fileref char(8) label='Fileref',
   xpath char(1024) label='Path Name',
   xengine char(8) label='Engine Name'
  );
```

 To get information about a specific object from a DICTIONARY table, use a WHERE clause. This example gets the path of the fileref TRANS:

```
SELECT * FROM DICTIONARY.EXTFILES WHERE FILEREF='TRANS';
```

Fileref	Path Name	Engine Name
TRANS	work.test.datsv.source	

 DICTIONARY tables can be used only in SQL, but you can make the same data available elsewhere. Write a CREATE TABLE statement to copy the DICTIONARY table to the WORK library.

43

Sorting

Sorting a SAS dataset means changing the order of observations to form a sequence that is determined by their values. When you sort a SAS dataset, you designate key variables that control the order of observations. Often, the key variables are indicated in a BY statement and are called BY variables.

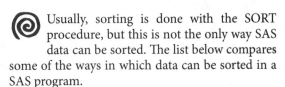 Usually, sorting is done with the SORT procedure, but this is not the only way SAS data can be sorted. The list below compares some of the ways in which data can be sorted in a SAS program.

- The SORT procedure sorts a SAS data file in place or creates a sorted copy of a SAS dataset. It can eliminate duplicate observations.
- With indexes, a SAS data file can be read in sorted order.
- A SAS dataset can be created from a text data file that is already in sorted order.
- Procedures that use CLASS statements can generate sorted summary data from unsorted detail data.
- Order and group variables in the REPORT procedure determine the sort order of table rows.
- The ORDER BY clause of SQL sorts the results of a query expression.

 The order that the sorting process creates for a variable depends on the variable's data type.

- A numeric variable is ordered from lowest to highest. Missing values come first, before the lowest numbers.

- A character variable is ordered from lowest to highest according to the binary values of the characters. Blank values usually come first, before any values that contain visible characters. In some special cases sorting a character variable results in an alphabetical sequence of values.

To sort a SAS data file in place, use the SORT procedure. Identify the SAS data file in the DATA= option of the PROC SORT statement. List the key variables for sorting in a BY statement. This example sorts the SAS data file WORK.NEW by BRANCH, OFFICER, and ACCOUNT.

```
PROC SORT DATA=WORK.NEW;
   BY BRANCH OFFICER ACCOUNT;
RUN;
```

To sort in the descending order of a key variable, write the keyword DESCENDING before the variable name in the BY statement.

If the SAS dataset is already sorted, no sorting takes place, and a log message indicates that the SAS dataset was already in sorted order.

If a SAS data file has indexes and you sort it in place, the indexes are deleted. This requires the FORCE option in the PROC SORT statement.

To create a sorted copy of a SAS dataset, use the OUT= option in the PROC SORT statement. The procedure sorts as usual, but writes the sorted data in a new SAS data file with the name you indicate. This example sorts the SAS dataset WORK.NEW to create the new SAS data file WORK.CURRENT.

```
PROC SORT DATA=WORK.NEW OUT=WORK.CURRENT;
   BY BRANCH OFFICER ACCOUNT;
RUN;
```

You can use the KEEP= and WHERE= options on the input SAS dataset in the PROC SORT statement to include only selected variables and observations in the sorted data. These options could also be used on the output SAS dataset, but it is more efficient to use them with the input SAS dataset.

```
PROC SORT DATA=WORK.NEW (KEEP=BRANCH OFFICER ACCOUNT
      WHERE=(BRANCH > '100')) OUT=WORK.CURRENT;
   BY BRANCH OFFICER ACCOUNT;
RUN;
```

To eliminate duplicate observations from a SAS dataset, use the NODUPKEY option in the PROC SORT statement and include all the key variables that identify a distinct observation in the BY statement. Usually, use the OUT= option to create a new SAS dataset. If multiple observations have the same key value, the procedure keeps only one of them.

To make a list of the distinct values of a variable in a SAS dataset, use the SORT procedure with the KEEP= dataset option, the OUT= option, and the NODUPKEY option.
This example makes a list of the values of BRANCH in WORK.NEW, saving the list as
the SAS dataset WORK.BRANCHES.

```
PROC SORT DATA=WORK.NEW (KEEP=BRANCH) OUT=WORK.BRANCHES NODUPKEY;
  BY BRANCH;
RUN;
```

To test whether a SAS dataset is sorted, use it in a data step or proc step with a BY
statement that contains the sort order clause you want to test. The step generates an
error condition and log message if the SAS dataset is not sorted.

The fastest way to test a sort order is with a SET statement in a data step. The
example below is designed to test whether WORK.NEW is sorted by BRANCH.

```
DATA _NULL_;
  SET WORK.NEW;
  BY BRANCH;
RUN;
```

If the SAS dataset is sorted, the step executes normally. If not, the step ends with
an error message. Data steps write error messages such as this for a SAS dataset that
is not sorted:

```
ERROR: BY variables are not properly sorted on data set WORK.RANDOM.
I=1 X=0.9248128491 FIRST.X=1 LAST.X=1 _ERROR_=1 _N_=1
NOTE: The SAS System stopped processing this step because of errors.
NOTE: There were 2 observations read from the data set WORK.RANDOM.
```

Proc steps verify sort order if the BYSORTED system option is in effect. If a SAS
dataset is not sorted properly in a proc step, it results in this kind of message:

```
ERROR: Data set WORK.RANDOM is not sorted in ascending sequence. The
       current by-group has X = 0.9248128491 and the next by-group has X =
       0.8504435783.
NOTE: The SAS System stopped processing this step because of errors.
NOTE: There were 2 observations read from the data set WORK.RANDOM.
```

If there is no variable or combination of variables that indicates the order in which the
observations should appear when sorted, create a variable for that purpose. Create a
code variable for sorting if the sorted order of a variable is something other than its
normal sorted order.

As an example, the provinces of Canada are sometimes listed from west to east.
To sort data in this order, create a code that indicates the west-to-east priority of each
province, and use this code variable in the sort key.

Sorting a character variable sometimes arranges it in alphabetical order. However,
the rules for alphabetical sorting are different from character sorting, and sorting a
variable that contains text values usually does not result in an alphabetical sequence.
An alphabetical sort can come about if you sort character values that contain only

alphabetic data. Usually, when a character sort produces an alphabetical sort, it is because all the values meet all of these conditions:

- All letters are uppercase.
- There is no punctuation.
- There are no leading spaces.
- Each value consists of only a single word or a single letter.

In other data it is necessary to create a separate alphabetic sort variable by transforming the text variable. For example, if the variable is WORD and its values are single words with no punctuation, this statement creates an alphabetic variable ALPHA that you can use as a sort key.

ALPHA = UPCASE(LEFT(WORD));

For details of creating an alphabetic sort key, see chapter 81, "Text Processing."

To make a list of the leading observations according to the value of a variable, sort by that variable, then use the OBS= dataset option on the resulting SAS dataset. Sort in descending order if you want to find the highest values.

This example finds the 100 top-selling records by sorting a set of records in descending order of UNITS, then selecting the first 100 observations from the result. The SAS dataset TOP100 contains the 100 observations that have the highest values for UNITS.

```
PROC SORT DATA=SALE OUT=RANK;
   BY DESCENDING UNITS;
RUN;
DATA TOP100;
   SET RANK (OBS=100);
RUN;
```

Sorting can also mean categorizing, dividing a set of objects into categories. For example, sorting eggs is accomplished by placing each egg into a size category: small, medium, large, extra large, or jumbo. In SAS data, it is usually a categorical variable that records the category to which an observation belongs. If you use the categorical variable as the sort key for the SAS dataset, you can form the categories into BY groups. If the variable BUS forms categories in the SAS dataset WORK.DRIVES, form BY groups with a step such as this:

```
PROC SORT DATA=WORK.DRIVES OUT=WORK.DRIVEGROUPS;
   BY BUS;
RUN;
```

If the categories are well defined and few in number, a faster way to separate them is to put each of them in a separate SAS dataset. For example, if BUS has the values ATA, SCSI, and USB, split the data into these three groups with a data step such as this one:

```
DATA WORK.ATADRIVES WORK.SCSIDRIVES WORK.USBDRIVES;
```

```
    SET WORK.DRIVES;
    SELECT (BUS);
      WHEN ('ATA') OUTPUT WORK.ATADRIVES;
      WHEN ('SCSI') OUTPUT WORK.SCSIDRIVES;
      WHEN ('USB') OUTPUT WORK.USBDRIVES;
      OTHERWISE ;
      END;
RUN;
```

This data step creates three SAS datasets, each of which contains a different value of BUS. To form a single SAS dataset that has these categories as BY groups, concatenate these SAS datasets, as shown in this data step:

```
DATA WORK.DRIVEGROUPS;
   SET WORK.ATADRIVES WORK.SCSIDRIVES WORK.USBDRIVES;
RUN;
```

Splitting and recombining the data creates several new SAS datasets and uses two data steps, but it is still faster than sorting with the SORT procedure — in this example, two to three times as fast.

 Sorting a large SAS dataset is one of the most time-consuming things a SAS program can do. You can sometimes make a program run much faster by finding ways to avoid sorting or to reduce the amount of data that is sorted.

 To maintain the sorted order of SAS datasets when you combine them, combine them by interleaving rather than concatenating. Write a BY statement after the SET statement that combines the SAS datasets. See chapter 51, "Combining Data," for details.

 A tag sort is an alternative sorting technique in which the key variables are sorted first, and then the remaining variables are sorted. A tag sort uses less memory and less working storage, and because of this, it is a better way to sort some kinds of SAS datasets on some kinds of computers. The tag sort technique might be faster if the total size of the file is large and the sort key is short compared to the total length of the observation. To do a tag sort, use the TAGSORT option in the PROC SORT statement.

The idea of the tag sort is demonstrate by the program below. The smaller SAS dataset KEYS, containing only the two sort keys and the original observation number from BIG, is sorted first. The other variables are then retrieved from BIG based on the observation number.

```
DATA KEYS;
   SET BIG (KEEP=KEY1 KEY2);
   OBS = _N_;
RUN;
PROC SORT DATA=KEYS OUT=KEYSORT;
   BY KEY1 KEY2;
RUN;
DATA BIGSORT;
   SET KEYS;
   SET BIG POINT=OBS;
RUN;
```

The variable OBS is not stored in the final SAS dataset BIGSORT. OBS is used in the SET statement option POINT=, so it is excluded from output SAS datasets.

Even though this algorithm was intended only to demonstrate the tag sort technique, the approach taken in this program has been found to be faster than sorting with the TAGSORT option for some kinds of SAS datasets on some kinds of computers. You can try sorting the same SAS dataset in different ways to see which way is fastest.

An alternative way to sort a SAS data file is to create an index on the key variables, then read the SAS dataset using a SET statement and a BY statement that uses the key variables. In theory, this should work nearly the same way as a tag sort. In practice, it sometimes works better, and this technique can sometimes sort a SAS data file that cannot be sorted by any other technique because of limitations of memory or working storage.

This example does the same thing as the previous example, but it uses the index KEYS in place of the SAS dataset KEYS.

```
PROC DATASETS LIBRARY=WORK NOLIST;
   MODIFY BIG;
   INDEX CREATE KEYS=(KEY1 KEY2);
RUN;
DATA BIGSORT;
   SET BIG;
   BY KEY1 KEY2;
RUN;
```

To reverse the order of observations in a SAS data file, use a SET statement with a POINT= option inside a DO loop. Use a descending observation number variable as the index variable of the DO loop. This example creates the SAS dataset DOWN with observations in the reverse order of the SAS dataset UP.

```
DATA DOWN;
   DO POINT = NOBS TO 1 BY -1;
     SET UP POINT=POINT NOBS=NOBS;
     OUTPUT;
     END;
   STOP;
RUN;
```

Be sure to include a STOP statement in a data step that gets its input from a SET statement that uses the POINT= option. Without the STOP statement, the data step would run indefinitely.

If a SAS dataset is already sorted when you create it, write the sort order clause in the SORTEDBY= dataset option. The sort order is stored with the SAS dataset. For example, the following data step creates a SAS dataset that is sorted by X1 and X2. The SORTEDBY= dataset option indicates this sort order.

```
DATA XX (SORTEDBY=X1 X2);
   DO X1 = 1 TO 6;
```

```
    DO X2 = 1 TO 6;
      OUTPUT;
      END;
    END;
RUN;
```

Procedures rely on this sorted order. For example, if you then attempt to sort XX by the same key variables, the SORT procedure notices that the SAS dataset is sorted already, and it does not do any sorting.

```
PROC SORT DATA=XX;
  BY X1 X2;
RUN;
```

```
NOTE: Input data set is already sorted, no sorting done.
```

 The SORTEDBY= dataset option can also indicate the sort order of an existing SAS dataset. Write the sort order in the SORTEDBY= dataset option for an input SAS dataset. This can be useful in the REPORT procedure and other procedures that might otherwise sort the data from the input SAS dataset.

 The SORTEDBY= dataset option is not necessary if the SAS dataset is created in a proc step with a BY or CLASS statement or a similar feature that determines the sort order. SAS automatically records the sort order in that case. In addition, a SAS-generated sort order is considered validated, and procedures rely on this sort order more strongly than they do on a sort order indicated in the SORTEDBY= dataset option.

The stored sort order information may be removed if you edit or update a SAS dataset. If necessary, sort the SAS dataset after editing, or use the SORTEDBY= dataset option if the editing did not actually affect the sort order.

 Use the CONTENTS procedure to see the sort order information of a SAS dataset. The Sort Information section of the PROC CONTENTS output shows the sort order and indicates whether this sort order is validated. If the output does not have a Sort Information section, then there is no sort order stored with the SAS dataset.

 If a SAS dataset is marked as sorted, and you want to have a procedure disregard the sort order and sort the data anyway, write _NULL_ in place of the sort order in the SORTEDBY= dataset option. The procedure will treat the SAS dataset as unsorted.

The example below uses this feature to force the SORT procedure to sort a SAS dataset that was previously marked as sorted. This results in a SAS dataset with a validated sort order.

```
PROC SORT DATA=XX (SORTEDBY=_NULL_);
  BY X1 X2;
RUN;
```

■ 44

Groups

The observations of a SAS dataset can be divided into groups that are considered separately. Groups are formed by the values of key variables; all observations that have the same key value belong to the same group. The concept of groups includes the following points:

- Every observation belongs to a group.
- It is not possible for the same observation to belong to more than one group at the same time.
- Each group is processed as a separate set of data. The way a group is processed is essentially the same as the way an entire SAS dataset is processed when groups are not defined.
- Groups are defined in statements in the SAS program. Nothing is stored in a SAS dataset to determine whether it is processed as a whole or in groups.
- Usually, when a step processes a SAS dataset in groups, it processes all of its groups. However, it is possible to use a WHERE clause to select a single group or any subset of the groups.

 Use a BY statement to indicate the key variables that form groups. If the observations are sorted in ascending order by the key variables, simply list the key variables in the BY statement, as in this example:

BY KEY1 KEY2;

If a key variable is sorted in descending order, write the word DESCENDING before the variable name in the BY statement. In this example, the key variable SIZE is sorted in descending order in order to arrange observations from largest to smallest within each SEGMENT group.

BY SEGMENT DESCENDING SIZE;

If the key values are in some kind of sorted order to form groups, but are not strictly in ascending or descending order, write the keyword NOTSORTED at the end of the BY statement.

 If you use a BY statement to indicate a sorted order of a SAS dataset, the step must be able to read the observations of the SAS dataset in that sorted order. This is possible only if the observations are sorted or if the SAS dataset has an index for the key variables. See the previous chapter, "Sorting," for information on sorting. See chapter 7, "Indexes," to create an index. If the step cannot read the SAS dataset in the order indicated in a BY statement, the step generates an error condition and stops running.

 Alternatively, for a few procedures, use a CLASS statement to indicate key variables for groups. Procedures that generate summary data use the class variables listed in the CLASS statement to form groups in the summary data.

 You can use variables in the CLASS statement regardless of the order of observations in the input SAS dataset. Class variables refer to groups in the output summary data, not in the input detail data.

 Often, you can create the same results with either class variables or BY variables. Usually, it is faster to use class variables. However, if there are very many key values compared to the amount of memory available, using class variables might run inefficiently or might not run at all. In that case, sort the SAS dataset and use BY variables.

 In a data step, a BY statement modifies a specific statement that reads data from an input SAS dataset or combines data from several input SAS datasets. Write the BY statement immediately after the SET, MERGE, MODIFY, or UPDATE statement that it modifies.

The NOTSORTED option in the BY statement can be used only with a single SAS dataset. It cannot be used to modify a statement that reads multiple SAS datasets.

 When a BY statement is used in a data step, it creates two automatic variables for each BY variable. These variables are Boolean variables that mark the beginning and end of a BY group. If KEY is a BY variable, FIRST.KEY is 1 on the first observation of a BY group of KEY; it is 0 for all other observations. Similarly, LAST.KEY is 1 on the last observation of a BY group of KEY, and 0 for all other observations.

 Use FIRST. and LAST. variables as conditions for actions that should be taken only once in each BY group. In this example, an observation is written to the output SAS dataset SKUDATA only on the last observation in a BY group for SKU.

IF LAST.SKU THEN OUTPUT SKUDATA;

 If there are several BY variables, the BY variables define a hierarchy of BY groups. That is, there are BY groups for the first BY variable, smaller BY groups for the second BY variable, and so on. A BY group for the second BY variable is contained entirely within a BY group for the first BY variable. If the FIRST. variable for a BY variable is 1, the FIRST. variables for all later BY variables are also 1. Similarly, if the LAST. variable for a BY variable is 1, the LAST. variables for all later BY variables are 1. It is never necessary to test more than one FIRST. or LAST. variable in order to find the beginning or end of a BY group.

 If the FIRST. and LAST. variables are both 1, it means that the BY group contains only one observation. This example deletes BY groups for LOCATION that contain only one observation.

IF FIRST.LOCATION AND LAST.LOCATION THEN DELETE;

The length of a character BY variable in a data step is important. Errors can occur or the resulting data can be incorrect if the variable has different lengths in different input SAS datasets.

If a variable's length is inconsistent, it is the length of the variable in the data step is that is considered for forming groups and for matching in input operations such as merging and interleaving. This is not a problem if the variable is longer in the data step than it is in the input SAS dataset. However, it can be a problem if the length of the variable in an input SAS dataset is greater than the length in the data step.

If the variable has longer values in one of the SAS datasets, the longer values are truncated before matching is done and BY groups are formed. This can result in an error with a message stating that observations are not in sorted order, even though the SAS dataset is sorted. Or it can simply result in BY groups being formed incorrectly. If this kind of problem occurs, use a LENGTH statement earlier in the data step to declare the variable with a length long enough to hold all of its values.

BY Groups in Proc Steps

When a proc step has a BY statement, the procedure does not process the input SAS dataset as a whole. Instead, it goes through most of its processing separately for each BY group.

- A statistical procedure does a separate analysis and creates separate output for each BY group.
- A reporting procedure generates a separate report for each BY group or places BY groups on separate pages.
- A graphing procedure generates a separate graph for each BY group.
- A procedure that generates output data writes the same BY groups in the output data.

The specific details of BY group processing in a proc step depend on the procedure.

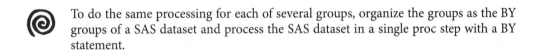

To do the same processing for each of several groups, organize the groups as the BY groups of a SAS dataset and process the SAS dataset in a single proc step with a BY statement.

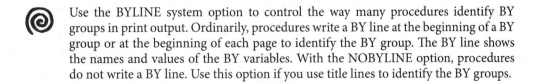

To process only selected BY groups of a SAS dataset in a proc step, write a WHERE= dataset option in the PROC statement or add a WHERE statement to the proc step.

Use the BYLINE system option to control the way many procedures identify BY groups in print output. Ordinarily, procedures write a BY line at the beginning of a BY group or at the beginning of each page to identify the BY group. The BY line shows the names and values of the BY variables. With the NOBYLINE option, procedures do not write a BY line. Use this option if you use title lines to identify the BY groups.

In a proc step with the NOBYLINE system option, use code sequences in the title lines to identify BY groups. Write the #BYLINE code in the title text to make the BY line part of the title line, or use a combination of #BYVAR and #BYVAL codes to identify specific BY variables.

This example defines a title line that contains the BY line:

TITLE1 'Spectral Components for #BYLINE';

The BY line is substituted for the #BYLINE code when the page is printed. With the BY variables ELEMENT and ISOTOPE, the substitution results in title lines such as this one.

```
Spectral Components for ELEMENT=Hydrogen ISOTOPE=2
```

For the #BYVAR and #BYVAL codes, use a numeric suffix or a variable name in parentheses to identify a specific BY variable. The #BYVAR code provides the BY variable name; the #BYVAL code provides the value of the variable (not including any leading or trailing spaces in the value). If there is only one BY variable, use the codes #BYVAR1 and #BYVAL1.

This example writes BY variable values without the variable names.

TITLE1 'Spectral Components for #BYVAL1-#BYVAL2';

```
Spectral Components for Hydrogen-2
```

The TITLE statement could also be written this way for the BY variables ELEMENT and ISOTOPE:

TITLE1 'Spectral Components for #BYVAL(ELEMENT)-#BYVAL(ISOTOPE)';

 With the NOBYLINE option, procedures write BY groups on separate pages so that you can use the title lines on each page to identify the BY groups.

Formatted Grouping

Proc steps form BY groups based on the formatted values of variables. If two consecutive BY groups have the same formatted values, the procedure combines them into one BY group. To change the way BY groups are formed, you may only need to change the format of the BY variable.

 To get the same formatted grouping behavior in the data step, write the GROUPFORMAT option at the end of the BY statement. The option affects the values of the automatic FIRST. and LAST. variables.

 The formatted grouping feature can only combine BY groups if they are consecutive. If there are multiple BY variables, formatted grouping is generally only useful for the last BY variable. If you use a format to group values together, they must be consecutive values in the data.

To form BY groups based on the initial character or first few characters of a character BY variable, format it using the $CHAR or $F format with a width argument that indicates the number of characters to consider. Apply the format in a FORMAT statement in the proc step.

The most common use of formatted grouping is to form BY groups based on intervals of a BY variable. To process intervals of values as BY groups, create a value format that defines the intervals. Use the BY variable with this format to process BY groups formed by the intervals. Write a FORMAT statement in the proc step to associate the format with the BY variable.

For example, you might not think the data below would form BY groups. The data is sorted by the variable TEMPERATURE_F, temperature, but every observation has a different temperature value.

TEMPERATURE_F	COUNT
21.4	14
27.8	3
30.3	16
32.2	11
41.4	8
41.6	10
47.0	6

With the appropriate format, though, the temperature values can form BY groups. The statements below define the format TEMPFI, which groups temperature values into two intervals.

```
PROC FORMAT;
VALUE TEMPFI LOW-32='Freezing' 32<-HIGH='Above Freezing';
RUN;
```

With the TEMPFI format, the temperature values can form two BY groups. The example below uses the format to calculate a statistic separately for the two temperature intervals.

```
PROC SUMMARY DATA=WORK.COUNT PRINT MEAN;
   BY TEMPERATURE_F;
   FORMAT TEMPERATURE_F TEMPFI.;
   VAR COUNT;
RUN;
```

In the output, shown below, there are only two BY groups, even though the data contains seven different values for the BY variable. After the format TEMPFI is applied, the seven values are reduced to two formatted values, and these formatted values form the BY groups.

```
------------------------ TEMPERATURE_F=Freezing --------------------------

The SUMMARY Procedure

Analysis Variable : COUNT
```

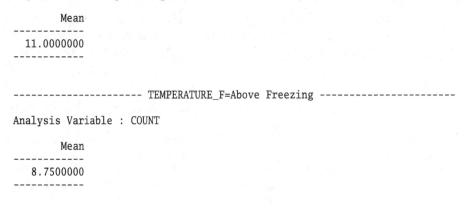

```
          Mean
       -----------
       11.0000000
       -----------



---------------------- TEMPERATURE_F=Above Freezing ----------------------

Analysis Variable : COUNT

          Mean
       -----------
        8.7500000
       -----------
```

For details of value formats, see chapter 15, "Value Formats."

Class Groups

Several procedures form groups based on class variables. Like BY variables, class variables define groups of observations. But class variables are not related in any way to the sort order of the input data. They form groups regardless of the way the data is sorted. Class groups are used in the SUMMARY and TABULATE procedures, among others.

To define class groups, list the class variables in the CLASS statement. The example below prints statistics for the variable POINTS in the SAS dataset DETAIL. Because of the CLASS statement, it calculates separate statistics for groups defined by the two class variables, SEASON and TEAM.

```
PROC SUMMARY DATA=DETAIL PRINT N MIN MEAN MAX SUM;
  CLASS SEASON TEAM;
  VAR POINTS;
RUN;
```

Processing Groups in a Data Step

To process BY groups in a data step, you have to circumvent the basic nature of data step processing. The data step is designed to process individual observations, with no provision for groups of observations. The observation loop repeats the same sequence of actions for each observation, and there is no place in the data step where actions can stand outside this loop. The data step isolates observations from each other; an automatic action resets most kinds of variables to missing between observations. If you are to process a BY group, all this has to change.

- Variables that are used in the programming logic of a BY group have to maintain their values between observations. List these variables in a RETAIN statement to keep them from being reset to missing.
- Initialize the BY group in a conditional block using the FIRST. variable as the condition. Set the group variables to missing or to other initial values if necessary.
- Take final actions for the BY group in a conditional block using the LAST. variable as the condition.

The following code model shows how to process BY groups when there is one BY variable.

```
DATA output SAS dataset;
  RETAIN variables used in group processing;
  SET SAS dataset(s);
  BY key variable;
  IF FIRST.key variable THEN DO;
    actions for beginning of group
    END;
  actions for individual observations
  IF LAST.key variable THEN DO;
    actions for end of group
    END;
RUN;
```

This kind of logic can be used to compute statistics for BY groups. This example prints the sum, maximum, and minimum of the variable VALUE in groups defined by the variable GROUP.

```
RETAIN SUM MAX MIN;
IF FIRST.GROUP THEN DO;
  SUM = 0;
  MAX = VALUE;
  MIN = VALUE;
  END;
SUM + VALUE;
IF VALUE > MAX THEN MAX = VALUE;
IF .Z < VALUE < MIN THEN MIN = VALUE;
IF LAST.GROUP THEN PUT (GROUP SUM MAX MIN) (=);
```

If there are multiple BY variables, the group logic can be extended to cover different levels of grouping. The code model for BY group processing is revised below to use two BY variables.

```
DATA output SAS dataset;
  RETAIN variables used in group processing;
  SET SAS dataset(s);
  BY key variable 1  key variable 2;
  IF FIRST.key variable 2 THEN DO;
    IF FIRST.key variable 1 THEN DO;
      actions for beginning of group for key variable 1
      END;
    actions for beginning of group for key variable 2
    END;
  actions for individual observations
  IF LAST.key variable 2 THEN DO;
    actions for end of group for key variable 2
    IF LAST.key variable 1 THEN DO;
      actions for end of group for key variable 1
      END;
    END;
RUN;
```

■ 45
Incomplete Data

Completeness is an issue for some kinds of data. With this data, you know in advance that it should contain observations and data values for a certain set of key values. If any observations or data values are absent, you might have to add them.

These are examples of kinds of data for which completeness can be important:

- *Financial statements.* Most financial statements contain a fixed set of line items. For example, an income statement may show a predetermined set of revenue and expense categories. If no transactions were recorded in a category during the time period, the line item must still be printed in the report, with a value of 0.
- *Digital audio data.* An audio file contains a fixed set of time intervals, defined by the duration and sampling frequency. For example, a 30-second audio file with a sampling frequency of 48,000 hertz has 1,440,000 intervals. Audio playback is possible only when there is a value for each time interval.
- *Key combinations.* When data includes two related key variables and you want to see how the variables are related, you might need to expand the data to include all combinations of values of the two variables.

   For example, in retail operations data, two key variables might identify the product and retail location. This data can be expanded to show every product at every retail location, filling in zero or missing values when a product is not present at a particular retail location. Having a complete set of key combinations is often important in summary data and measurement data.

To form a complete set of data when observations are missing:

1. Create a SAS dataset that contains only the key variables with the complete set of key values.
2. Merge the complete set of key values with the data.
3. If necessary, fill in values for the data variables. For example, in financial data, change the missing values to zeros.

Key Combinations and Sequences

The idea of completeness in a set of data begins with a set of key values that should be present in the data. This set is best organized as a SAS dataset that contains only the key variables and all the required key values. This complete key dataset is the starting point for completing data that is incomplete.

For some kinds of data, the key values form a regular sequence from a minimum to a maximum value. For example, simple digital signal data may use integer key values; the complete set of keys includes every integer in an interval. Another example is monthly trend data, which includes every month in a time period.

To create a complete key dataset, determine the minimum and maximum values of the interval. Define the increment, the difference between one key and the next. Then use a DO loop with an OUTPUT statement to create the observations of the dataset.

In this example, the SUMMARY procedure finds the minimum and maximum values of X in WORK.INCOMPLETE, creating the variables MIN and MAX in the SAS dataset WORK.RANGE. The data step then reads WORK.RANGE and creates the complete key dataset WORK.ALLKEY with all integer values between the minimum and maximum.

```
PROC SUMMARY DATA=WORK.INCOMPLETE;
  VAR X;
  OUTPUT OUT=WORK.RANGE MIN=MIN MAX=MAX;
RUN;
DATA WORK.ALLKEY (KEEP=X);
  SET WORK.RANGE;
  DO X = CEIL(MIN) TO MAX;
    OUTPUT;
    END;
  STOP;
RUN;
```

The program below shows an alternate way to create the same SAS dataset.

```
PROC SORT DATA=WORK.INCOMPLETE;
  BY X;
RUN;
DATA WORK.ALLKEY (KEEP=X);
  DO POINT = 1, NOBS;
    SET WORK.INCOMPLETE POINT=POINT NOBS=NOBS;
    IF POINT = 1 THEN MIN = X;
    IF POINT = NOBS THEN MAX = X;
    END;
  DO X = CEIL(MIN) TO MAX;
    OUTPUT;
    END;
  STOP;
RUN;
```

Merge the complete set of keys with the incomplete data to form a SAS dataset that has a complete set of observations. This example creates the SAS dataset WORK.COMPLETE, which contains all the data values of WORK.INCOMPLETE plus observations with any key values that are absent from WORK.INCOMPLETE.

```
PROC SORT DATA=WORK.INCOMPLETE;
  BY X;
RUN;
DATA WORK.COMPLETE;
  MERGE WORK.INCOMPLETE (IN=ACTUAL) WORK.ALLKEY (IN=REQUIRED);
  BY X;
RUN;
```

In the added observations, all variables other than the key variable X have missing values. If necessary, add other statements to fill in values for these variables in the added observations. The IN= variables in the example above can find the added observations, as shown here:

```
IF NOT ACTUAL THEN DO;
  statements to fill in values for added observations
  END;
```

The statements below would change standard missing values to zeros for numeric variables in the added observations.

```
ARRAY VALUES{*} _NUMERIC_;
IF NOT ACTUAL THEN DO I = 1 TO DIM(VALUES);
  IF VALUES{I} = . THEN VALUES{I} = 0;
  END;
```

When there are multiple key variables, having complete data might mean having an observation for every combination of values of the key variables. Start by making a list of values for each key variable. Then combine the lists of values to form a complete keys dataset.

This is easiest to do in SQL. The example below creates the table WORK.COMB with all possible combinations of the values of SIZE, COLOR, and STYLE from WORK.STOCK.

```
PROC SQL;
CREATE TABLE WORK.SIZES AS
  SELECT DISTINCT SIZE FROM WORK.STOCK;
CREATE TABLE WORK.STYLES AS
  SELECT DISTINCT STYLE FROM WORK.STOCK;
CREATE TABLE WORK.COLORS AS
  SELECT DISTINCT COLOR FROM WORK.STOCK;
CREATE TABLE WORK.COMB AS
  SELECT SIZE, STYLE, COLOR
  FROM WORK.SIZES, WORK.STYLES, WORK.COLORS
  ORDER BY SIZE, STYLE, COLOR;
QUIT;
```

Merge WORK.COMB with WORK.STOCK to form the complete dataset.

Often, the set of complete key values cannot be derived from the current data. If the values are a defined set of values, store the complete key dataset as a permanent SAS dataset, as part of the reference data of the application.

 With the SUMMARY procedure, you can fill in key values in the process of computing statistics.

- With multiple class variables, use the COMPLETETYPES option in the PROC SUMMARY statement to fill in all combinations of the class variable values. This option has no effect if there is only one class variable.
- Use the CLASSDATA= option to name a complete keys dataset for the class variables. All class values in this SAS dataset are included in the output, even if they are not in the input data. If there are multiple class variables, the procedure uses the combinations of values that it finds in the CLASSDATA= dataset.
- If you use the CLASSDATA= and EXCLUSIVE options together, the output contains all the class values from the CLASSDATA= dataset and excludes any other class values that might be found in the data.

 The TABULATE, REPORT, and FREQ procedures automatically create all combinations of two class variables when the variables are used in different dimensions in the table definition.

 A set of data might have a very large number of potential key values, but with only a small fraction of them associated with actual data. For example, an ordinary computer picture with 256 levels of red, green, and blue could contain over 16 million colors, but if you summarize the colors of an actual photograph, you might find that it contains only around 50,000 colors. This color data or similar data is called *sparse* because of the idea of long distances between one actual data point and the next. When you work with sparse data, be aware that expanding the data to include the complete set of key values could increase the size of the data by a large factor. In this example, the complete data would be over 300 times the size of the incomplete data.

 If you use the FREQ procedure with sparse data, use the LIST option in the TABLES statement to print a list-style frequency table. The list-style table can be much smaller than the usual two-dimensional table for two variables.

Interpolation

After you add observations, it might be necessary to estimate values for the new observations. You might also use estimated values to replace other missing values in a sequence of data. If the estimated values are based on the values of observations before and after the new observation, the estimating process is called interpolation.

To interpolate, you need to combine the before and after data with the observation that has the missing value. This sounds simple, but it requires multiple passes through the data.

The example here uses linear interpolation to estimate values. Linear interpolation is based on the idea that values change at a constant rate between the known values. In a graph, this appears as a straight line segment drawn to connect two consecutive points.

The key variable in this example is SEQ, sequence number; the data variable is V, which might stand for the voltage of an audio signal. The example starts with this data:

```
SEQ        V

 1       206.303
 2       218.167
 3          .
 4          .
 5      -181.918
 6       -31.593
 7          .
 8       228.836
 9          .
```

Linear interpolation provides estimates of the values for sequence numbers 3, 4, and 7, which initially show missing values.

```
PROC SORT DATA=SERIES;
  BY SEQ;
RUN;

DATA BEFORE (KEEP=SEQ BEFORE_SEQ BEFORE_V);
  SET SERIES;
  RETAIN BEFORE_SEQ BEFORE_V;
  IF V <= .Z THEN DO;
    IF BEFORE_SEQ THEN OUTPUT;
    END;
  ELSE DO;
    BEFORE_SEQ = SEQ;
    BEFORE_V = V;
    END;
RUN;

PROC SORT DATA=SERIES OUT=REVERSE;
  BY DESCENDING SEQ;
RUN;
DATA AFTER (KEEP=SEQ AFTER_SEQ AFTER_V);
  SET REVERSE;
  RETAIN AFTER_SEQ AFTER_V;
  IF V <= .Z THEN DO;
    IF AFTER_SEQ THEN OUTPUT;
    END;
  ELSE DO;
    AFTER_SEQ = SEQ;
    AFTER_V = V;
    END;
RUN;
```

```
PROC SORT DATA=AFTER;
  BY SEQ;
RUN;

DATA INTERPOL (KEEP=SEQ V SOURCE);
  MERGE SERIES BEFORE AFTER;
  BY SEQ;
  IF V > .Z THEN DO;
    SOURCE = 'A'; * Actual;
    OUTPUT;
    END;
  ELSE IF BEFORE_V > .Z AND AFTER_V > .Z THEN DO;
    SOURCE = 'I'; * Interpolated;
    V = BEFORE_V + (AFTER_V - BEFORE_V)*
      (SEQ - BEFORE_SEQ)/(AFTER_SEQ - BEFORE_SEQ);
    OUTPUT;
    END;
  ELSE DO;
    SOURCE = 'X'; * Not available;
    V = .;
    OUTPUT;
    END;
RUN;
TITLE1 'Interpolation';
PROC PRINT NOOBS HEADING=H;
RUN;
```

```
Interpolation

SEQ       V      SOURCE

 1     206.303     A
 2     218.167     A
 3      84.805     I
 4     -48.556     I
 5    -181.918     A
 6     -31.593     A
 7      98.622     I
 8     228.836     A
 9        .        X
```

The output data contains the added variable SOURCE, a one-letter code that identifies the source of each value. A indicates an actual value; I indicates a value estimated by interpolation. For the last value, the code is X to indicate that a value could not be interpolated because there was no actual value available after that observation.

 Linear interpolation is just one of many ways to estimate values. These are others:

- the most recent actual value, or the closest actual value
- cubic interpolation or other curve-fitting techniques
- values computed from other variables in the same observation
- the mean, median, or mode value

■ 46
Transposing

Transposing a SAS dataset changes the shape of data without changing the data values. Observations in the original SAS dataset become variables in a transposed SAS dataset; the original variables become observations. Usually, the groups of observations in a SAS dataset are transposed. If a SAS dataset is relatively small, it can be transposed in its entirety.

These are the most common reasons for transposing SAS datasets:

- Turning rows into columns and columns into rows in print output or an output data file.
- Turning observations into BY groups. Input variables become separate observations for a single variable in the output data.
- Turning BY groups into single observations. An input variable becomes a list of variables in the output data.

Transposing data can be described as reshaping it because it changes the structure and sequence of the data without changing the actual values. To transpose data in any of the ways mentioned here, use the TRANSPOSE procedure or data step programming.

Transposing in a Data Step

These are the main elements of data step programming to transpose data:

- arrays and DO loops to process the group of variables in an observation
- the OUTPUT statement, to create a new observation
- assignment statements, to move values from old variable to new variables
- BY variables and the automatic FIRST. and LAST. variables which form a group of observations in the input data
- the RETAIN statement, to keep a variable's value between observations

 To convert observations to BY groups in a data step, use an OUTPUT statement to create each output observation that results from an input observation. Use assignment statements, arrays, and DO loops to assign values to the output variables.

```
DATA MAIN.INT2 (KEEP=WHEN DIR COUNT);
  SET MAIN.INT1 (KEEP=WHEN N N_E N_W S S_E S_W E E_N E_S W W_N W_S);
  LENGTH DIR $3;
  DIR = 'N';
  COUNT = N;
  OUTPUT;
  DIR = 'N-E';
  COUNT = N_E;
  OUTPUT;
  DIR = 'N-W';
  COUNT = N_W;
  OUTPUT;
  DIR = 'S';
  COUNT = S;
  OUTPUT;
  DIR = 'S-E';
  COUNT = S_E;
  OUTPUT;
  DIR = 'S-W';
  COUNT = S_W;
  OUTPUT;
  DIR = 'E';
  COUNT = E;
  OUTPUT;
  DIR = 'E-N';
  COUNT = E_N;
  OUTPUT;
  DIR = 'E-S';
  COUNT = E_S;
  OUTPUT;
RUN;
```

The example at left uses traffic count data collected at an ordinary four-way intersection. The input data, in MAIN.INT1, has 12 traffic count variables. The names of these variables, N, N_E, N_W, S, and so on, indicate the 12 directions a vehicle can travel through the intersection, including left and right turns. The program transposes the data to create MAIN.INT2, which has a single traffic count variable, COUNT, and a separate variable, DIR, to indicate the direction. MAIN.INT2 has 12 observations for each one observation in the input SAS dataset.

The actions involved in transposing are repetitive, as each input variable is assigned to an output variable. The program can be shortened with the use of arrays and a DO loop, as shown below.

```
DATA MAIN.INT2 (KEEP=WHEN DIR COUNT);
  ARRAY DIRN{12} $ 3 _TEMPORARY_
    ('N' 'N-E' 'N-W' 'S' 'S-E' 'S-W' 'E' 'E-N' 'E-S' 'W' 'W-N' 'W-S');
  ARRAY DCOUNT{12} N N_E N_W S S_E S_W E E_N E_S W W_N W_S;
  SET MAIN.INT1 (KEEP=WHEN N N_E N_W S S_E S_W E E_N E_S W W_N W_S);
  DO I = 1 TO 12;
    DIR = DIRN{I};
    COUNT = DCOUNT{I};
    OUTPUT;
  END;
RUN;
```

 Some of the new observations you generate might not mean anything. For example, the clinical patient data used in medical research contains variables that measure body functions such as temperature, weight, blood pressure, and heart rate, but not every measurement is recorded for every patient visit. When clinical patient data is transposed to make each measurement a separate observation, it is not necessary to create observations for measurements that have missing values. Similarly, in data that indicates financial results, observations that have zero values can be omitted.

To leave out observations that do not represent a value, write the OUTPUT statement in an IF-THEN statement that checks whether a value is present. In clinical data, if the output variable is MEASURE, the statement might be

IF MEASURE NE . THEN OUTPUT;

To leave out both missing and zero values for the output variable AMOUNT, use the variable itself as the condition. Write a statement such as

IF AMOUNT THEN OUTPUT;

ANOTHER APPROACH

The brute force method for converting single observations to multiple observations is to read each observation multiple times. This example transposes the data from the SAS data M, converting the variables X1 and X2 to the variable X.

```
DATA MX;
  SET M (KEEP=N X1 RENAME=(X1=X) IN=N1)
      M (KEEP=N X2 RENAME=(X2=X) IN=N2)
      ;
  BY N;
  IF N1 THEN NODE = 1;
  ELSE NODE = 2;
RUN;
```

To convert BY groups to observations in a data step, assign values to the output variables and execute an OUTPUT statement only at the end of each BY group. Use a RETAIN statement to maintain the values of the output variables through the BY group.

This example reverses the transposition of the earlier traffic count example.

```
DATA MAIN.INT1;
  ARRAY DIRN{12} $ 3 _TEMPORARY_
    ('N' 'N-E' 'N-W' 'S' 'S-E' 'S-W' 'E' 'E-N' 'E-S' 'W' 'W-N' 'W-S');
  ARRAY DCOUNT{12} N N_E N_W S S_E S_W E E_N E_S W W_N W_S;
  RETAIN DCOUNT;
  SET MAIN.INT2;
  BY WHEN;
  IF FIRST.WHEN THEN DO I = 1 TO 12;
    DCOUNT{I} = .;
    END;
  DO I = 1 TO 12;
    IF DIR = DIRN{I} THEN DCOUNT{I} = COUNT;
    END;
  IF LAST.WHEN THEN OUTPUT;
RUN;
```

The TRANSPOSE Procedure

The key to transposing in a PROC TRANSPOSE step is describing how input variables are used in the transposition. Divide input variables among these categories:

- *BY variables* form the BY groups that are transposed. List BY variables in the BY statement. Each BY group is transposed separately. The output SAS dataset contains the same BY groups as the input SAS dataset. Within each BY group, each input observation becomes an output variable. Therefore, any BY group can create an output variable. The output data includes all the variables from all the BY groups.

  If there are no BY variables, then the entire SAS dataset is transposed as a unit. This is probably what you want if the SAS dataset contains only a few observations.

- *Analysis variables* are transposed. They become observations in the output data. List the analysis variables in the VAR statement. If there are no analysis variables, then nothing is transposed.

- *Copy variables* are copied to the output data without being transposed. List any copy variables in the COPY statement. Usually, there are no copy variables.

- An *ID variable* forms the names of the output variables. The value of the ID variable is converted, if necessary, to form a valid name, and when the observation is converted to a variable, this name is the name of the variable Indicate the ID variable in the ID statement. If there is no ID variable, the TRANSPOSE procedure generates variable names.

- A *label variable* forms the labels of the output variables. The value of the variable is the label of the variable that is formed when the observation is transposed. Indicate the label variable in the IDLABEL or IDL statement. If there is no label variable, the resulting labels are blank. The label variable can be the same as the ID variable.

The example below transposes the data from the SAS dataset IN to create the SAS dataset OUT. The data contains two BY groups, which are transposed separately. The SIZE variable is used in the ID and IDLABEL statements, so it provides the names and labels for the new variables. The NAME= option provides the variable COLOR for the variable that contains the input variable names.

```
TITLE1 'Input Data: Before Transposing';
PROC PRINT DATA=IN;
RUN;
PROC TRANSPOSE DATA=IN OUT=OUT NAME=COLOR;
   BY U;
   ID SIZE;
   IDLABEL SIZE;
   VAR CORAL NAVY AQUA MIDNIGHT;
   COPY X;
RUN;
TITLE1 'Output Data: After Transposing';
PROC PRINT DATA=OUT;
RUN;
```

Input Data: Before Transposing

Obs	U	SIZE	Coral	Navy	Aqua	Midnight	X
1	1025	S	6	12	3	2	1
2	1025	M	5	12	6	8	2
3	1025	L	5	9	9	6	3
4	1027	S	11	9	11	12	4
5	1027	M	2	8	14	25	5
6	1027	L	7	5	8	9	6

Output Data: After Transposing

Obs	U	X	COLOR	S	M	L
1	1025	1	Coral	6	5	5
2	1025	2	Navy	12	12	9
3	1025	3	Aqua	3	6	9
4	1025	.	Midnight	2	8	6
5	1027	4	Coral	11	2	7
6	1027	5	Navy	9	8	5
7	1027	6	Aqua	11	14	8
8	1027	.	Midnight	12	25	9

Transposing in a PROC TRANSPOSE step generates these output variables:

- *BY and copy variables* from the input data.
- *Transposed variables* that contain the values from the analysis variables.
- A *name variable* that contains the name of the analysis variable that formed an observation. The name for this variable is _NAME_. You can use the NAME= option to change the name of the variable.
- A *label variable* that contains the label of the analysis variable. The name for this variable is _LABEL_, or use the LABEL= option to provide another variable name. If the analysis variable did not have a label, then the label variable is blank. If no analysis variable has a label, then a label variable is not created.

Input observations become output variables; to limit the variables that are created, use a WHERE statement to limit the input observations.

If there is no VAR statement, all numeric variables that are not otherwise being used are used as analysis variables. If there are neither analysis variables nor COPY variables, the output SAS dataset is still created, but it has no observations.

If the analysis variables include both numeric and character variables, then the transposed variables are character variables. Numeric values of the analysis variables are converted to character values for the transposed variables. Write a FORMAT statement in the PROC TRANSPOSE step to set the formats the procedure uses to convert the numeric variables to character values.

One of the most familiar uses of transposing is to change the appearance of reports generated from a set of data. If the detail data of a SAS dataset is printed in pages, rows, and columns, you can transpose the data so that the pages are the same, but the rows become columns and the columns become rows.

- List the key variables that define the pages as BY variables.
- List the identifying variable for the original columns as the label variable in the IDLABEL statement. Use the resulting labels as the column headings in the report. For example, use the LABEL option in the PROC PRINT statement.
- Use _NAME_ or _LABEL_ or the output name or label variable to identify the rows of the table.
- If there are both numeric and character analysis variables, the TRANSPOSE procedure converts the numeric values to character values. Write a FORMAT statement in the PROC TRANSPOSE step to set the formats of the numeric variables.

The example below shows how a conventional historical report, which shows time periods as rows, can be turned into a trend report, which shows time periods as columns, by transposing.

TRANSPOSING TWICE

If you want to convert all numeric variables to character variables for reporting purposes, one gimmicky way to do so is by transposing the data twice. This also adds any missing observations in each BY group.

- Make sure there is at least one character variable among the analysis variables. Add a blank character variable if necessary. Write a FORMAT statement to set the formats of the numeric analysis variables.
- In a second PROC TRANSPOSE step, start with the output SAS dataset of the first PROC TRANSPOSE step. Use the transposed variables as analysis variables and the name variable as the ID variable.

```
TITLE1 'History';
PROC PRINT DATA=HISTORY;
RUN;
PROC TRANSPOSE DATA=HISTORY
   OUT=TREND NAME=VARIETY;
   VAR REGULAR MUSHROOM
      SAUSAGE CLASSIC;
   ID DATE;
   IDLABEL DATE;
   FORMAT DATE DATE5.;
   LABEL VARIETY='Variety';
RUN;
TITLE1 'Trend';
PROC PRINT DATA=TREND LABEL;
RUN;
```

History

Obs	DATE	REGULAR	MUSHROOM	SAUSAGE	CLASSIC
1	07JUL2003	50	9	17	8
2	08JUL2003	3	8	9	5
3	09JUL2003	19	24	8	1
4	10JUL2003	26	25	15	7
5	11JUL2003	65	9	7	11
6	12JUL2003	16	11	16	3
7	13JUL2003	71	4	14	13
8	14JUL2003	45	15	3	12
9	15JUL2003	22	8	12	7
10	16JUL2003	62	29	16	3

Trend

Obs	Variety	07JUL	08JUL	09JUL	10JUL	11JUL	12JUL	13JUL	14JUL	15JUL	16JUL
1	REGULAR	50	3	19	26	65	16	71	45	22	62
2	MUSHROOM	9	8	24	25	9	11	4	15	8	29
3	SAUSAGE	17	9	8	15	7	16	14	3	12	16
4	CLASSIC	8	5	1	7	11	3	13	12	7	3

In the PROC TRANSPOSE step, the LABEL statement provides a label for the new variable VARIETY. The procedure generates a warning message because the variable in the LABEL statement is not in the input SAS dataset. If you want to avoid this warning message, move the LABEL statement to the subsequent PROC PRINT step.

Transposing is especially useful in two-dimensional time series data, that is, data in which the same measurement is made for each of several consecutive time periods, and each such measurement is then revised at regular intervals. The loss development triangle used to forecast insurance losses is an example of this. Losses for accidents (or other covered events) that occurred in each year are added up at regular intervals over a period of several years until all the payments have been made. This data forms a triangular matrix that can be analyzed to project losses for accidents that occur in the future.

Two-dimensional time series data can be organized with each time period as a separate observation and each measurement date as a separate variable, or vice versa. Use the TRANSPOSE procedure to convert between these two ways of organizing the data. You can do calculations across one of the time dimensions, then transpose the data to do calculations across the other time dimension.

47
Frequency Tables

One of the first things to ask about a variable in a SAS dataset is the question of what kind of values it has. For a variable that has a limited number of distinct values, a good way to answer can be to list all the values. It is a short step from a list of values to a frequency table, which tells you the number of times each value occurs.

Write a PROC SORT step to create a list of the distinct values of a variable. Write:

- a DATA= option to identify the SAS dataset
- the KEEP= dataset option to select the variable
- a BY statement with the same variable
- an OUT= option to name an output SAS dataset to contain the list of values
- the NODUPKEY option to store each different key value only once

These features are summarized in the code model below.

```
PROC SORT DATA=input SAS dataset (KEEP=key)
  OUT=output SAS dataset NODUPKEY;
  BY key;
RUN;
```

Suppose the SAS dataset WORK.PLANT contains the data shown here:

TYPE	AREA	MARK	STATUS
FIR	DRIVE	005	ON ORDER
FIR	DRIVE	008	ON ORDER
APPLE	SOUTH	015	
EUCALYPTUS	FRONT	002	SCHEDULED
FIR	LOT	041	ON ORDER
FIR	LOT	042	ON ORDER
WILLOW	LOT	044	SCHEDULED

A list of the values of the variable TYPE would show four values: APPLE, EUCALYPTUS, FIR, and WILLOW.

This step creates the list of values as the SAS dataset WORK.TYPES:

```
PROC SORT DATA=WORK.PLANT (KEEP=TYPE) OUT=WORK.TYPES NODUPKEY;
  BY TYPE;
RUN;
```

A list of values might be needed in the form of either a SAS dataset or a report. A SAS dataset is required if a SAS program will combine the list with other data or if the program uses the list as a lookup table. Create a report if you are making a list for a person to review. Print the SAS dataset to create the report, as shown here:

```
TITLE1 'Current Plant Types';
PROC PRINT DATA=WORK.TYPES NOOBS
    HEADING=HORIZONTAL;
RUN;
```

```
Current Plant Types

TYPE

APPLE
EUCALYPTUS
FIR
WILLOW
```

To create a list of values in an SQL query, use the DISTINCT keyword in the query. Like the previous example, this example lists the values of TYPE.

```
PROC SQL;
SELECT DISTINCT TYPE FROM WORK.PLANT;
QUIT;
```

```
Current Plant Types

TYPE
----------
APPLE
EUCALYPTUS
FIR
WILLOW
```

If you use the same approach with multiple variables, it creates a list of the combinations of values of the variables. The example below lists the combinations of values of the variables TYPE and STATUS in the SAS dataset WORK.PLANT.

```
PROC SORT DATA=WORK.PLANT (KEEP=TYPE STATUS)
    OUT=WORK.STATUS NODUPKEY;
  BY TYPE STATUS;
RUN;

TITLE1 'Current Plant Status';
PROC PRINT DATA=WORK.STATUS NOOBS
    HEADING=HORIZONTAL;
RUN;
```

```
Current Plant Status

TYPE              STATUS

APPLE
EUCALYPTUS        SCHEDULED
FIR               ON ORDER
WILLOW            SCHEDULED
```

This SQL query accomplishes the same thing:

```
SELECT DISTINCT TYPE, STATUS FROM WORK.PLANT;
```

To create a frequency table, write a PROC SUMMARY step with:

- the NWAY option
- a CLASS statement listing one or more class variables for which the procedure will count frequencies
- the MISSING option if it is possible that any of the class variables have blank or missing values
- an OUTPUT statement with the OUT= option to name the output SAS dataset

The procedure counts the observations for each class value and places the results in the variable _FREQ_. To use a different name for the frequency variable, use the RENAME= dataset option in the OUTPUT statement to rename _FREQ_. Another output variable, _TYPE_, has no significance in this context; use the DROP= or

KEEP= dataset option in the OUTPUT statement to discard it.

The example below creates a frequency table for the variable TYPE using the same data as in the previous examples.

```
PROC SUMMARY DATA=WORK.PLANT MISSING NWAY;
   CLASS TYPE;
   OUTPUT OUT=WORK.TYPECT
      (DROP=_TYPE_ RENAME=(_FREQ_=N));
RUN;
TITLE1 'Current Plants';
PROC PRINT DATA=WORK.TYPECT NOOBS
   HEADING=HORIZONTAL;
RUN;
```

Current Plants	
TYPE	N
APPLE	1
EUCALYPTUS	1
FIR	4
WILLOW	1

The next example shows the use of two class variables:

```
PROC SUMMARY DATA=WORK.PLANT MISSING NWAY;
   CLASS TYPE STATUS;
   OUTPUT OUT=WORK.STATCT
      (DROP=_TYPE_ RENAME=(_FREQ_=N));
RUN;
TITLE1 'Current Status';
PROC PRINT DATA=WORK.STATCT NOOBS
   HEADING=HORIZONTAL;
RUN;
```

Current Status		
TYPE	STATUS	N
APPLE		1
EUCALYPTUS	SCHEDULED	1
FIR	ON ORDER	4
WILLOW	SCHEDULED	1

 Use the ORDER= option in the PROC SUMMARY statement to control the order of the class values in the step's output.

- To sort the output by the class variable values, use the option ORDER=INTERNAL. This is the default, which means it is not necessary to write the option in the PROC SUMMARY statement.
- To sort by formatted class values, use ORDER=FORMATTED. With this option, the procedure applies the variables' formats to generate formatted text before sorting.
- To sort by descending order of frequency, use ORDER=FREQ. This places the most frequent values at the beginning of the output.
- To keep the output data in the same order as the input data, use ORDER=DATA. The order of appearance of class values in the input data determines their order in the output.

 With the PRINT option in the PROC SUMMARY statement, the procedure prints a table of its results. When the PRINT option is used, the OUTPUT statement is not required.

The example shows a frequency table printed by the SUMMARY procedure.

```
PROC SUMMARY DATA=WORK.PLANT MISSING PRINT;
   CLASS TYPE;
RUN;
```

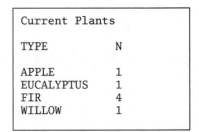

Current Plants	
The SUMMARY Procedure	
TYPE	N Obs
APPLE	1
EUCALYPTUS	1
FIR	4
WILLOW	1

The layout of the PROC SUMMARY report requires about twice as much space to display the same information. For a more compact report, create the SAS dataset and use another procedure, such as PRINT or REPORT, to print it.

The FREQ procedure is specifically designed to print frequency tables. To write a PROC FREQ step, name the input SAS dataset in the PROC FREQ statement and write a TABLES statement to describe the frequency tables.

A TABLES statement can contain a single table definition or a list of them. It can also list options for the content of the frequency tables it produces. For a frequency table for a variable, the table definition is the name of the variable. This kind of table is called a one-way frequency table.

To create a frequency table for two variables — a two-way frequency table — write the variable names with an asterisk between them in the TABLES statement. The first variable forms rows in the table; the second forms columns.

Write options after a slash at the end of the list of table definitions. The MISSING option allows missing values to be included in the frequency tables.

The step below creates four frequency tables. The two two-way tables of the variables TYPE and STATUS demonstrate the effect of the order of variables in the table definition.

```
PROC FREQ DATA=WORK.PLANT;
   TABLES TYPE STATUS TYPE*STATUS STATUS*TYPE / MISSING;
RUN;
```

TYPE	Frequency	Percent	Cumulative Frequency	Cumulative Percent
APPLE	1	14.29	1	14.29
EUCALYPTUS	1	14.29	2	28.57
FIR	4	57.14	6	85.71
WILLOW	1	14.29	7	100.00

STATUS	Frequency	Percent	Cumulative Frequency	Cumulative Percent
	1	14.29	1	14.29
ON ORDER	4	57.14	5	71.43
SCHEDULED	2	28.57	7	100.00

```
Table of TYPE by STATUS                           Table of STATUS by TYPE

TYPE       STATUS                                 STATUS      TYPE

Frequency |                                       Frequency |
Percent   |                                       Percent   |
Row Pct   |                                       Row Pct   |
Col Pct   |     |ON ORDER|SCHEDULE|  Total         Col Pct   |APPLE    |EUCALYPT|FIR     |WILLOW  |  Total
          |     |        |D       |                          |         |US      |        |        |
----------+-----+--------+--------+                ----------+--------+--------+--------+--------+
APPLE     |    1|      0 |      0 |      1          |       1 |      0 |      0 |      0 |      1
          |14.29| 0.00   | 0.00   |  14.29         |  14.29  | 0.00   | 0.00   | 0.00   |  14.29
          |100.00| 0.00  | 0.00   |                |  100.00 | 0.00   | 0.00   | 0.00   |
          |100.00| 0.00  | 0.00   |                |  100.00 | 0.00   | 0.00   | 0.00   |
----------+-----+--------+--------+                ----------+--------+--------+--------+--------+
EUCALYPTUS|    0|      0 |      1 |      1          ON ORDER  |      0 |      0 |      4 |      0 |      4
          | 0.00| 0.00   |14.29   |  14.29                   | 0.00   | 0.00   |57.14   | 0.00   |  57.14
          | 0.00| 0.00   |100.00  |                          | 0.00   | 0.00   |100.00  | 0.00   |
          | 0.00| 0.00   | 50.00  |                          | 0.00   | 0.00   |100.00  | 0.00   |
----------+-----+--------+--------+                ----------+--------+--------+--------+--------+
FIR       |    0|      4 |      0 |      4          SCHEDULED |      0 |      1 |      0 |      1 |      2
          | 0.00|57.14   | 0.00   |  57.14                   | 0.00   |14.29   | 0.00   |14.29   |  28.57
          | 0.00|100.00  | 0.00   |                          | 0.00   |50.00   | 0.00   |50.00   |
          | 0.00|100.00  | 0.00   |                          | 0.00   |100.00  | 0.00   |100.00  |
----------+-----+--------+--------+                ----------+--------+--------+--------+--------+
WILLOW    |    0|      0 |      1 |      1          Total          1        1        4        1        7
          | 0.00| 0.00   |14.29   |  14.29                    14.29    14.29    57.14    14.29   100.00
          | 0.00| 0.00   |100.00  |
          | 0.00| 0.00   | 50.00  |
----------+-----+--------+--------+
Total          1       4        2        7
           14.29   57.14    28.57   100.00
```

In addition to the frequency counts, the tables show relative frequencies as percents. In the two-way tables, the three percents shown are the percent of the total, of the row, and of the column, as indicated in the legend at the upper left corner. In the one-way tables, the last two columns show cumulative frequency and percent.

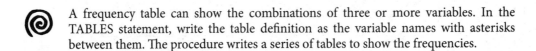

A frequency table can show the combinations of three or more variables. In the TABLES statement, write the table definition as the variable names with asterisks between them. The procedure writes a series of tables to show the frequencies.

Options in the TABLES statement can change the content or layout of the frequency table. Use the NOCUM, NOPERCENT, NOROW, and NOCOL options to remove the cumulative frequency and percents from the tables. The LIST option changes a table of two or more variables to a list-style report, similar to that produced by the SUMMARY procedure. The step below demonstrates these options.

```
PROC FREQ DATA=WORK.PLANT;
    TABLES TYPE STATUS / MISSING NOCUM;
    TABLES TYPE*STATUS / MISSING LIST NOCUM;
    TABLES TYPE*STATUS / MISSING NOPERCENT NOROW NOCOL;
RUN;
```

TYPE	Frequency	Percent
APPLE	1	14.29
EUCALYPTUS	1	14.29
FIR	4	57.14
WILLOW	1	14.29

Table of TYPE by STATUS

TYPE Frequency	STATUS	ON ORDER	SCHEDULED	Total
APPLE	1	0	0	1
EUCALYPTUS	0	0	1	1
FIR	0	4	0	4
WILLOW	0	0	1	1
Total	1	4	2	7

TYPE	STATUS	Frequency	Percent
APPLE		1	14.29
EUCALYPTUS	SCHEDULED	1	14.29
FIR	ON ORDER	4	57.14
WILLOW	SCHEDULED	1	14.29

 The FREQ procedure truncates values to 16 characters. If values are longer than this, use the SUMMARY procedure or another procedure to create a frequency table.

 The TABULATE procedure summarizes the same as the SUMMARY procedure, then creates table reports of the results, allowing detailed control of the formatting.

The CLASS statement is the same as in the SUMMARY procedure. Then write a TABLE statement to define each table. A table definition in the TABULATE procedure is divided into dimensions. For a two-dimensional table, write the definition of the rows, then a comma, then the definition of the columns. Use an asterisk to combine items in the same dimension. Use the statistic name N to indicate a frequency count. The example below creates three tables that show three likely layouts for a frequency table.

```
PROC TABULATE DATA=WORK.PLANT MISSING FORMAT=F10.;
   CLASS TYPE STATUS;
   TABLE TYPE, N;
   TABLE TYPE, STATUS;
   TABLE TYPE*STATUS, N / RTSPACE=23;
RUN;
```

	N
TYPE	
APPLE	1
EUCALYPTUS	1
FIR	4
WILLOW	1

	STATUS		
		ON ORDER	SCHEDULED
	N	N	N
TYPE			
APPLE	1	.	.
EUCALYPTUS	.	.	1
FIR	.	4	.
WILLOW	.	.	1

```
-----------------------------------
|               |           | N    |
|---------------+-----------|      |
|TYPE           |STATUS     |      |
|-----------+-----------|          |
|APPLE      |           |         1|
|-----------+-----------+----------|
|EUCALYPTUS |SCHEDULED  |         1|
|-----------+-----------+----------|
|FIR        |ON  ORDER  |         4|
|-----------+-----------+----------|
|WILLOW     |SCHEDULED  |         1|
-----------------------------------
```

The second TABLE statement does not specifically mention N, but N is the default statistic for the procedure. In the last TABLE statement, the RTSPACE= option sets a larger width for the row title space, which holds the row captions at the left side of the table. This allows each value to print on a single line in the table.

A PROC TABULATE report can also have analysis variables and statistics. See chapter 58, "Table Reports," for details.

To create a frequency table in an SQL query, use a GROUP BY clause to form groups. Use the expression COUNT(*) for the frequency count. The example below prints frequency tables with one variable and two variables.

```
PROC SQL;
SELECT TYPE, COUNT(*) AS N FROM WORK.PLANT GROUP BY TYPE;
SELECT TYPE, STATUS, COUNT(*) AS N FROM WORK.PLANT
   GROUP BY TYPE, STATUS;
QUIT;
```

TYPE	N
APPLE	1
EUCALYPTUS	1
FIR	4
WILLOW	1

TYPE	STATUS	N
APPLE		1
EUCALYPTUS	SCHEDULED	1
FIR	ON ORDER	4
WILLOW	SCHEDULED	1

The REPORT procedure can also print frequency tables. For a simple frequency table, define the report with a group variable and the statistic N, or use any combination of group and across variables. In the DEFINE statement for each variable, use the usage keyword GROUP for a variable that forms rows, ACROSS for a variable that forms columns. Features of the REPORT procedure are described in detail in chapter 58, "Table Reports."

■ 48
Descriptive Statistics

A statistic is a value or measurement that is derived from the values of a sample or other set. In mathematical terms, a statistic may be defined as a scalar function of a set of numbers. One of the most familiar statistics is the sum, which is computed by adding all the values in the sample. Another relatively simple statistic is the uncorrected sum of squares, calculated by adding the squares of all the values.

Simple statistics such as these are used to compute other statistics. The sum, for example, is needed to calculate the mean, which is the sum divided by the number of values. The mean, often called the average, is useful in describing sets. For example, if the average price of a car this year is nearly the same as the average price of a car last year, that statistical comparison suggests that prices of cars have not changed much in general, even though you see specific car prices going up or down.

Statistics are at the heart of most statistical tests. The *t* statistic, for example, is the basis of the *t* test. For a random sample of a population, the *t* test may be able to determine whether the mean of the population is different from 0.

SAS computes many statistics and provides broad support for a set of commonly used descriptive statistics, sometimes called simple descriptive statistics or summary statistics. These statistics, listed at right, can be computed in function calls, in the REPORT, SUMMARY, TABULATE, and UNIVARIATE procedures, and in many of the SAS/STAT procedures.

To use a statistic function, write the statistic name as the name of the function and the sample values as the arguments. This example calculates the standard deviation of a sample of five values.

STANDARDDEVIATION = STD(3, 4, 5, 7, 10);

The arguments to a statistic function are often variables. If they are, it can be easier to write the arguments as the keyword OF

Descriptive Statistics

You can use these simple descriptive statistics in many places in SAS.

★ **CSS** corrected sum of squares

★ **CV** percent coefficient of variation

★ **KURTOSIS** kurtosis

★ **MAX** maximum

★ **MEAN** mean

★ **MIN** minimum

★ **N** sample size (number of non-missing values)

★ **NMISS** number of missing values

★ **RANGE** range

★ **SKEWNESS** skewness

★ **STD** standard deviation

★ **STDERR** standard error of the mean

★ **SUM** sum

★ **USS** uncorrected sum of squares

★ **VAR** variance

and a variable list. The example below uses an abbreviated variable list to refer to 17 variables.

```
SMALLEST = MIN(OF SIZE1-SIZE17);
BIGGEST = MAX(OF SIZE1-SIZE17);
```

STATISTIC FORMULAS

The data step below demonstrates the computation of common statistics across observations in a data step. Use these formulas if you have a reason to compute statistics this way, or refer to them to see how these statistics may be computed mathematically.

The program computes sums of the values and their squares, cubes, and fourth powers. At the end, it derives the other statistics from these sums.

This is representative output from the program.

```
DATA _NULL_;
  RETAIN;
  SET A (KEEP=A) END=LAST;
  IF MIN = . THEN MIN = A;
  IF A <= .Z THEN NMISS + 1;
  ELSE DO;
    N + 1;
    SUM + A;
    USS + A*A;
    SC + A*A*A;
    SF + A*A*A*A;
    MIN = MIN MIN A;
    MAX = MAX MAX A;
    END;
  IF LAST THEN DO;
    IF N >= 1 THEN DO;
      RANGE = MAX - MIN;
      MEAN = SUM/N;
      CSS = USS - MEAN*SUM;
      END;
    IF N >= 2 THEN DO;
      VAR = CSS/(N - 1);
      STD = SQRT(VAR);
      STDERR = SQRT(VAR/N);
      IF MEAN THEN CV = 100*STD/MEAN;
      IF STD THEN DO;
        IF N >= 3 THEN SKEWNESS =
          (SC - 3*MEAN*USS + 2*MEAN*MEAN*SUM)
          / (VAR*STD) * N/((N - 1)*(N - 2));
        IF N >= 4 THEN KURTOSIS = (SF - 4*MEAN*SC
          + 6*MEAN*MEAN*USS - 3*MEAN*MEAN*MEAN*SUM)
          / (VAR*VAR) * N*(N + 1)/((N - 1)*(N - 2)*(N - 3))
          - 3*(N - 1)*(N - 1)/((N - 2)*(N - 3));
        T = MEAN/STDERR;
        PRT = 2*PROBT(-ABS(T), N - 1);
        END;
      END;
    PUT 'Descriptive Statistics' //
      N= / NMISS= / MIN= / MAX= / RANGE= /
      SUM= / MEAN= / USS= / CSS= / VAR= / STD= / STDERR= /
      CV= / SKEWNESS= / KURTOSIS= / T= / PRT= ;
    END;
  RUN;
```

```
Descriptive Statistics

N=10
NMISS=0
MIN=1
MAX=10
RANGE=9
SUM=55
MEAN=5.5
USS=385
CSS=82.5
VAR=9.1666666667
STD=3.0276503541
STDERR=0.9574271078
CV=55.048188256
SKEWNESS=0
KURTOSIS=-1.2
T=5.7445626465
PRT=0.000278196
```

Replace the PUT statement with an OUTPUT statement to create a SAS dataset of statistics. To create statistics from BY groups, process the groups using the FIRST. and LAST. variables, as described in chapter 44, "Groups."

Missing values do not affect the calculation of statistics; the statistics are the same as if the missing values were not present. Even the N statistic, which counts the number of values, does not count missing values. Use the NMISS statistic to get a count of the missing values in a sample.

Usually, statistics are calculated in a proc step across the observations of a SAS dataset. To print a report of statistics in the SUMMARY procedure, write the PRINT option in the PROC SUMMARY statement along with a list of statistics. List the analysis variables in the VAR statement, or use the special abbreviated variable list _NUMERIC_ for all numeric variables in the SAS dataset.

```
PROC SUMMARY DATA=CORP.DEPT PRINT N MEAN MIN MAX RANGE STD;
   VAR _NUMERIC_;
RUN;
```

Add a CLASS statement with class variables to get statistics for groups of observations.
   When it has the PRINT option and a VAR statement, the SUMMARY procedure is the same as the MEANS procedure.

A frequency variable, listed in the FREQ statement of a proc step, tells a procedure such as the SUMMARY procedure to count some observations more than once. The values of the frequency variable are counting numbers, such as 1, 2, 3, and so, telling how many times to count an observation.

To print a report of statistics in the REPORT procedure, write the statistics in the COLUMN statement, joining them to specific analysis variables with a comma. You can use parentheses to combine a list of statistics with a list of variables, as shown in this example.

```
PROC REPORT DATA=CORP.DEPT NOWD;
   COLUMN (SIZE RANK AREA), (N SUM);
RUN;
```

Add group variables to the report definition to get statistics for groups of observations. See chapter 58, "Table Reports," for more details.

The TABULATE procedure has most of the same syntax and computes most of the same statistics as the SUMMARY procedure. The use of the TABULATE procedure is described in chapter 58, "Table Reports."

SQL queries can compute statistics. Use a statistic as a function in a column expression. Write a GROUP BY clause to form groups from the input data.

The UNIVARIATE procedure computes additional statistics and prints a one-page report about each variable. Name the SAS dataset in the DATA= option of the PROC UNIVARIATE statement. List analysis variables in the VAR statement.

Creating Summary Data

Summary data is a reduced representation of data. The original dataset that contains the complete data is called detail data. Applying descriptive statistics to the detail data creates the summary data. Summary data can have just one observation, one observation for each BY group in the detail data, or one observation for each class group in the detail data.

Create a SAS dataset of summary data in a PROC SUMMARY step with an OUTPUT statement. List analysis variables in the VAR statement. In the OUTPUT statement, write an OUT= term to name the new output SAS dataset and one or more terms to define the output variables. To create output variables that have the same names as the analysis variables, write a statistic followed by an equals sign, such as SUM=. To apply different statistics to different analysis variables, list the analysis variables in parentheses after the statistic name, for example, SUM(VALUE VOLUME)= MIN(RATING)=.

If you apply more than one statistic to the same analysis variable, the output variables must have different names. Write the output variable names after the equals sign. The example below creates three output variables from the analysis variable RATING. It uses the statistics MIN, MEAN, and MAX. The output variables are RATEMIN, RATING, and RATEMAX.

MIN(RATING)=RATEMIN MEAN(RATING)= MAX(RATING)=RATEMAX

You can let the SUMMARY procedure generate the output variable names by concatenating the statistic name and the analysis variable name. In a similar way, the procedure can create labels for the output variables. To use these features, write the AUTONAME and AUTOLABEL options in the OUTPUT statement. These options must be written after a slash at the end of the statement.

This is an example of a complete PROC SUMMARY step:

```
PROC SUMMARY DATA=WORK.TRAVEL;
  VAR DISTANCE FUEL RATE;
  OUTPUT OUT=WORK.TRAVEL1 MEAN= SUM(DISTANCE FUEL)=
    MIN(RATE)= MAX(RATE)= / AUTONAME AUTOLABEL;
RUN;
```

The new SAS dataset, WORK.TRAVEL1, has one observation with these variables:

- DISTANCE_MEAN, FUEL_MEAN, and RATE_MEAN, the means of the analysis variables
- DISTANCE_SUM, the sum of the analysis variable DISTANCE
- FUEL_SUM, the sum of the analysis variable FUEL
- RATE_MIN, the minimum of the analysis variable RATE
- RATE_MAX, the maximum of the analysis variable RATE
- _TYPE_, which has the value 0
- _FREQ_, which contains a count of the observations in WORK.TRAVEL

Add a CLASS statement listing class variables to create a summary dataset with multiple observations. For the simplest use of class variables, add the NWAY, MISSING, and CHARTYPE options to the PROC SUMMARY statement. This example modifies the previous example to add class variables:

```
PROC SUMMARY DATA=WORK.TRAVEL
   NWAY MISSING CHARTYPE;
   CLASS CAR DRIVER;
   VAR DISTANCE FUEL RATE;
   OUTPUT OUT=WORK.TRAVEL2
     MEAN= SUM(DISTANCE FUEL)=
     MIN(RATE)= MAX(RATE)=
     / AUTONAME AUTOLABEL;
RUN;
```

The output SAS dataset WORK.TRAVEL2 has an observation for each class combination — each combination of CAR and DRIVER values that is actually found in the detail data. The observations are sorted by the class variables CAR and DRIVER. WORK.TRAVEL2 has the same statistic variables that are listed above for WORK.TRAVEL1. It also has:

- CAR and DRIVER, the two class variables, with the same values they have in the input data
- _TYPE_, which has the value 11
- _FREQ_, which tells you how many detail observations in each class combination are represented in the summary observation

The purpose of the NWAY option is to form summary observations using all the class variables. Without the NWAY option, the procedure also forms summary observations using all possible subsets of the class variables. The purpose of the _TYPE_ variable is to identify which class variables are used in each output observation. This is easiest to see if you use the CHARTYPE option, which makes _TYPE_ a character variable, a pseudo-array in which each character, a 1 or 0, signals the presence or absence of the corresponding class variable.

With two class variables, there are four possible values of _TYPE_:

- 00 indicates that both class variables are absent. The output observation that has this value for _TYPE_ is the observation that is produced if there are no class variables.

OPTIONS

There are so many options in the SUMMARY procedure that affect the use of class variables and the summary observations they form that it is not practical to mention all of them here. These are some of them:

- With the MISSING option, the procedure uses observations in which class variables have missing values. Without this option, it ignores those observations.
- The TYPES and WAYS statements provide two ways to select the combinations of class variables that are included in the output.
- When there are multiple class variables, the COMPLETETYPES option creates all combinations of class values, whether they are present in the detail data or not.
- The ORDER= option changes the order of class values in the output.
- The DESCENDING option reverses the order of _TYPE_ values in the output so that they go from highest to lowest. Use this option to put the grand total observation last in the output SAS dataset.
- Various options in CLASS statements can change the treatment of specific class variables.
- Without the CHARTYPE option, _TYPE_ is a numeric variable. It is a bitfield, the binary numeral value of the character _TYPE_ value.
- In the ID statement, you can list additional variables to copy to the output SAS dataset. The values of these variables are selected from one observation for each class group.
- MINID and MAXID terms in the OUTPUT statement can find minimums and maximums within a class group and add identifying variables from those observations to the output SAS dataset.
- The LEVELS option in the OUTPUT statement creates the output variable _LEVEL_. This variable provides sequential numbers for the output observations within each value of _TYPE_.

- 01 indicates that only the second class variable is used. This group of output observations contains one observation for each value of the second class variable.
- 10 indicates that only the first class variable is used. This group of output observations contains one observation for each value of the first class variable.
- 11 indicates that both class variables are used. These output observations are the same ones that are created with the NWAY option.

If n is the number of class variables, _TYPE_ has 2^n values.

When you read the SAS dataset that a PROC SUMMARY step creates, you usually want to select one specific value of _TYPE_ to read one kind of summary data. Use the WHERE= dataset option. This example selects observations in which _TYPE_ is 11:

```
SET WORK.TRAVEL2 (WHERE=(_TYPE_ = '11'));
```

To create summary data in SQL, write a CREATE TABLE statement in which the columns are defined as statistics. Add a GROUP BY clause to form groups, essentially the same as class groups. This is an example of an SQL statement to create summary data:

```
PROC SQL;
CREATE TABLE WORK.INV AS
    SELECT CAT, SUM(WEIGHT) AS WEIGHT, SUM(VOLUME) AS VOLUME
    FROM WORK.STOCK
    GROUP BY CAT;
```

DEGREES OF FREEDOM, WEIGHTS, AND THE VARIANCE DIVISOR

In statistics, a population is a complete set that is being studied. A sample is a subset of the population. Many statistics are computed differently for a population than they are for a sample. The difference is based on the concept of degrees of freedom.

The number of degrees of freedom is equal to the number of observations of a population, but it is 1 less than the number of observations in a sample. In the formula that calculates the variance, the divisor is the degrees of freedom. As a result, a population variance is computed differently from a sample variance. This also affects statistics that are computed from the variance, including the standard deviation, standard error of the mean, corrected sum of squares, percent coefficient of variation, skewness, kurtosis, and t.

The statistic functions compute sample statistics. Procedures can compute sample or population statistics, depending on the VARDEF= (variance definition) option in the PROC statement. Use the VARDEF=N option to compute population statistics. Use the VARDEF=DF option to compute sample statistics.

Some procedures also can compute weighted statistics, in which the relative importance of each observation is determined by a weight variable. Identify the weight variable in the WEIGHT statement. In the PROC statement, use the option VARDEF=WGT for weighted population statistics or VARDEF=WDF for weighted sample statistics. The additional statistic SUMWGT is the sum of the weight values. Some statistics, such as skewness and kurtosis, cannot be calculated for weighted data.

■ 49

Summary Statistics in Computations

Sometimes, the important thing to know about a value is not how much it is in absolute terms, but what part of the total it represents. The formula involved is nothing fancy — a division of the value by the total — but computing it requires two steps in the SAS program. This is because the formula depends on both detail data and a summary statistic. The same is true for various other computations you might make that use detail data and summary statistics together. Any such computation takes two steps, or two passes through the data, to:

1. Compute the summary statistics from the detail data.
2. Combine the detail data with the summary statistics to compute the final values.

 Use the SUMMARY procedure to create a SAS dataset of the summary statistics. Create distinct variable names for the summary statistics. Then write a data step with two SET statements to combine the summary statistics with the detail data and compute the resulting values.

SECTOR	GDP
Nonfarm less housing	7,480.8
Housing	796.9
Farm	79.0
Private households	13.6
Nonprofit institutions	418.4
Federal government	323.8
State and local government	760.4

The example below starts with data indicating gross domestic product (GDP) by sector, measured in billions of dollars, as shown at left. From this, it calculates the percent of GDP for each sector.

Starting with the SAS dataset WORK.SI, the program below creates the SAS dataset WORK.SECTOR, adding the variable GDPPCT, the percent of GDP.

```
PROC SUMMARY DATA=WORK.SI;
  VAR GDP;
  OUTPUT SUM=GDPSUM OUT=WORK.TOTAL;
RUN;
DATA WORK.SECTOR;
  IF _N_ = 1 THEN SET WORK.TOTAL (KEEP=GDPSUM);
```

SECTOR	GDP	GDPPCT	GDPSUM
Nonfarm less housing	7,480.8	75.771	9,872.9
Housing	796.9	8.072	9,872.9
Farm	79.0	0.800	9,872.9
Private households	13.6	0.138	9,872.9
Nonprofit institutions	418.4	4.238	9,872.9
Federal government	323.8	3.280	9,872.9
State and local government	760.4	7.702	9,872.9

```
SET WORK.SI;
GDPPCT =
    GDP/GDPSUM*100;
RUN;
```

In the program, the purpose of the condition _N_ = 1 is to execute the SET statement for the SAS dataset WORK.TOTAL only once. The one observation of summary data is used throughout the data step.

To calculate a percent, divide by the total, then multiply by 100, as shown in the assignment statement.

The resulting data is shown above. In this data, the variable SECTOR is the original ID variable, and GDP is the original detail variable. GDPSUM is the statistic that it added, the sum of GDP; as a statistic, it has the same value for every observation. GDPPCT is computed from the detail variable and the statistic.

To compute values with summary statistics of BY groups, start with a SAS dataset that is sorted in BY-group order and add a BY statement to the PROC SUMMARY step. Use a MERGE statement with the same BY statement to merge this summary data, which has an observation for each BY group, with the detail data.

The example below uses the BY variable FUND, indicating an investment portfolio. Each observation represents a particular security, with the variable VALUE indicating the value of the security. The program creates the variable SHARE to indicate each security value as a percent of the portfolio total.

```
PROC SUMMARY DATA=WORK.FUNDS;
   BY FUND;
   VAR VALUE;
   OUTPUT SUM=FUNDTOTAL OUT=WORK.TOTALS;
RUN;
DATA WORK.BALANCE;
   MERGE WORK.FUNDS
      WORK.TOTALS (KEEP=FUND FUNDTOTAL);
   BY FUND;
   SHARE = VALUE/FUNDTOTAL*100;
RUN;
```

In SQL, you can write formulas that combine detail data with summary statistics, such as X/SUM(X)*100 AS XPCT. Combining detail and summary values in a query is called a *remerge*. It is noted in the log as a possible mistake with this message:

```
NOTE: The query requires remerging summary
      statistics back with the original data.
```

COMPUTED FROM STATISTICS

These are examples of other values that are computed with summary statistics:

- *Standardized values.* These are computed by subtracting the mean, then dividing by the standard deviation. The result is a distribution with a mean of 0 and a standard deviation of 1, ready for clustering and some other statistical analyses.

- *Normalized values.* The normalized values often used in digital signal processing have a mean of 0 and fall between –1 and 1. Subtract the mean, then divide by the difference between the mean and the minimum or maximum, whichever is greater.

- *Traffic lighting.* "Traffic lights" highlight (usually with color coding) values that are especially high or low or are outside the expected range of values. For example, you might flag values that are above the 95th percentile.

■ 50

Type Conversion

Type conversion makes it possible to use a numeric value where a character value is required or a character value where a numeric value is required. It uses numeric formats and informats to convert values from one data type to the other.

- Numeric formats convert numeric values to character values.
- Numeric informats convert character values to numeric values.

AUTOMATIC TYPE CONVERSION

In data step statements, SAS automatically converts between numeric and character data types when you use an expression of one type in a context where the other type is required. The type mismatch results in an attempt at an automatic type conversion. It also generates a log note that resembles an error message.

This program demonstrates automatic type conversion, including the log messages.

```
DATA _NULL_;
  * Declare X as character and N as numeric. ;
  LENGTH X $ 12 N 8;
  X = 8;
  N = '-2.2400';
  PUT X= / N=;
RUN;
```

```
NOTE: Numeric values have been converted to character values at the places given by:
      (Line):(Column).
      4:8
NOTE: Character values have been converted to numeric values at the places given by:
      (Line):(Column).
      5:8
X=8
N=-2.24
```

Other messages are produced if the type conversion fails because a character value does not represent a number. Automatic type conversion works only in data step statements; a type mismatch anywhere else results in an error. In programs that matter, it is better not to rely on automatic type conversion; instead, use numeric informats and formats in function calls to convert between data types.

To convert a numeric value to a character value, use the PUT function with a format. Usually, use the F or BEST format. The length of the resulting character value is determined by the width argument of the format.

The assignment statement in this example converts the value of the numeric variable YEAR to a four-character value, which it assigns to the character variable YEARTEXT.

```
LENGTH YEARTEXT $ 4;
YEAR = 2002;
YEARTEXT = PUT(YEAR, F4.);
PUT YEARTEXT=;
```

```
YEARTEXT=2002
```

To convert a character value to a numeric value, use the INPUT function with an informat. Usually, use the F informat. Use a width argument equal to the length of the character value. This example extracts a numeric value from the variable YEARTEXT.

```
YEARTEXT = '2003';
YEAR = INPUT(YEARTEXT, F4.);
PUT YEAR=;
```

```
YEAR=2003
```

If a character value cannot be converted to a numeric value, the informat involved reports a data error and generates a missing value, as shown in this example.

```
YEARTEXT = 'XXXX';
YEAR = INPUT(YEARTEXT, F4.);
PUT YEAR=;
```

```
NOTE: Invalid argument to function INPUT at line 19 column 8.
YEAR=.
YEARTEXT=XXXX YEAR=. _ERROR_=1 _N_=1
NOTE: Mathematical operations could not be performed at the following
      places. The results of the operations have been set to missing values.
      Each place is given by: (Number of times) at (Line):(Column).
      1 at 19:8
```

To avoid this kind of error condition, write two question marks as an error control before the informat in the INPUT function.

```
YEARTEXT = 'XXXX';
YEAR = INPUT(YEARTEXT, ?? F4.);
PUT YEAR=;
```

```
YEAR=.
```

With the error control, the data step ignores the error condition returned by the informat.

Four more functions, INPUTC, INPUTN, PUTC, and PUTN, can be used to apply informats and formats to values. For type conversions, use INPUTN with a numeric informat and PUTN with a numeric format. These functions perform the same actions as the INPUT and PUT functions, but they obtain the informat or format from a character argument. These functions also let you supply separate numeric arguments for the width and decimal arguments of the informat or format.

CHANGING THE DATA TYPE OF A VARIABLE

There is no direct way to change the data type of a variable in a SAS dataset. The data type is an essential attribute of a variable, so it cannot be changed in place. However, it is possible to change the data type by replacing the SAS dataset.

To change the data type of a variable in a SAS dataset, use a data step that reads the existing SAS dataset and replaces it with a new SAS dataset of the same name. Use the RENAME= dataset option to avoid conflicts in the data type of the variable.

Write the RENAME= dataset option in the SET statement to change the name of the original variable. This way, the original variable name is not used for the original variable in the data step. This makes it possible to create the new variable with the original variable name.

Create the value for the new variable from the renamed original variable. Use the INPUT or PUT function, as described earlier in this chapter.

Write the DROP= dataset option in the DATA statement to remove the original variable. Be sure to use the changed variable name in the DROP= option.

This example changes the variable STATUS in the SAS dataset EVENT from a numeric variable to a one-byte character variable.

```
DATA EVENT (DROP=STATUSNO);
  SET EVENT (RENAME=(STATUS=STATUSNO));
  LENGTH STATUS $ 1;
  STATUS = PUT(STATUSNO, F1.);
RUN;
```

There is no conflict between the original numeric variable STATUS and the new character variable STATUS because the numeric variable uses the variable name STATUSNO in the data step.

The one-byte character variable created in this example uses less storage space than the numeric variable it replaces. The one-character length works, of course, only if the variable's values have only one digit.

■ 51
Combining Data

Whether it is a matter of adding new data to the old data or combining multiple sources of data to form a more complete picture, nearly every SAS application combines data. The data step makes combining data easy to do. Whenever you read multiple SAS datasets in the same data step, it results in a combination of the SAS datasets.

The two main data step statements that combine SAS datasets are the SET and MERGE statements. You might use either of these statements or a combination of statements, depending on what kind of combination of data you want to make.

- To use observations that are already formed, but are stored in multiple SAS datasets, write a SET statement.
- To form observations by drawing some variables from one SAS dataset and other variables from another SAS dataset, write a MERGE statement.
- To add variables that have the same value in every observation, add a one-observation SET or MERGE statement.

If your objective is to add variables related to key values in the data, use a table lookup technique. See the next chapter, "Table Lookup," for details.

A SET statement with multiple SAS datasets reads observations from all the SAS datasets. It can concatenate or interleave them. Used by itself, a SET statement concatenates SAS datasets. The statement

SET A B;

reads all the observations from A, then all the observations from B.

If a SET statement is followed by a BY statement, it interleaves the SAS datasets. The BY statements contains a sort order clause, and the SAS datasets must already be organized in that sort order. Then, the SET statement maintains the sorted order when it reads the observations. The statements

SET A B;
BY X;

interleave two SAS datasets, A and B, using the sort variable X. Both SAS datasets must already be in sorted order by X. The SET statement reads the observations while maintaining the sorted order, so that the results are sorted in the same way.

Concatenating and interleaving result in the same set of observations. The only difference is the order of observations.

A SET statement uses all the variables from all of the SAS datasets it reads. If one SAS dataset contains a variable that is not in the other SAS datasets, the variable has a missing value in observations that are read from the other SAS datasets.

A MERGE statement forms observations from the variables of multiple SAS datasets. After the MERGE statement, write a BY statement with the key variable or variables that are used to match observations between the SAS datasets. This process is called a match merge. As in interleaving, the SAS datasets must already be in sorted order.

The MERGE statement below forms observations with the variables from two SAS datasets, A and B, and it uses the variable X to match the observations of A with the observations of B.

MERGE A B;
BY X;

The BY statement defines BY groups in each input SAS dataset. A BY group is the consecutive observations that have the same BY value. If no other observation has the same BY value, then the BY group consists of only one observation. For more about BY groups and the BY statement, see chapter 44, "Groups."

The effect of the match merge process depends on the number of observations in each BY group.

- If each SAS dataset has only one observation in a BY group, then the MERGE statement forms the BY group with only one observation.
- If one SAS dataset has multiple observations in a BY group, and all other SAS datasets have only one observation in that BY group, then the MERGE statement forms the BY group with the multiple observations. For a variable that come from a SAS dataset that has only one observation in the BY group, the MERGE statement uses the same value in every observation of the BY group.
- If one SAS dataset does not have any observations in a BY group formed by a MERGE statement, its variables have missing values in that BY group.
- If multiple SAS datasets have multiple observations in a BY group, the MERGE statement forms a BY group with multiple observations. When it reaches the last observation of the BY group in an input SAS dataset, it repeats those values in the remaining observations of the BY group. In this situation, the MERGE statement generates a log message that states that multiple SAS datasets had multiple observations in a BY group.

When a SET or MERGE statement reads multiple SAS datasets, use the IN= dataset option to keep track of the source of observations. The IN= dataset is useful only for input SAS datasets in a data step. In the option, provide a variable name. This name is used for a numeric variable that tells you whether the SAS dataset is represented in the current observation. The variable is a Boolean variable with a value of 1 if the observation contains data from that SAS dataset, 0 if it does not. Use a different variable name for each SAS dataset.

Consider this MERGE statement:

```
MERGE A (IN=IN1) B (IN=IN2);
BY X;
```

The variables IN1 and IN2 tell you whether each BY group is found in the two input SAS datasets. If both SAS datasets contain the BY group, then both IN1 and IN2 have values of 1. If only A contains the BY group, then IN1 is 1 and IN2 is 0. Or if only B contains the BY group, then IN1 is 0 and IN2 is 1.

In a merge, you might want to keep observations only if the key value is present in a specific SAS dataset. Use a subsetting IF statement to select these observations. The example below keeps only observations that are found in A. It discards observations that are found in B, but not in A.

```
MERGE A (IN=IN1) B;
BY X;
IF IN1;
```

If a SAS dataset contains one observation and you want to add variables from this dataset to every observation in a data step, execute a SET statement to read this SAS dataset one time at the beginning of the data step. You can use the condition _N_ = 1 in an IF-THEN statement to execute the statement once.

To add the variables from the one observation of the SAS dataset WORK.PARM, use this statement:

```
IF _N_ = 1 THEN SET WORK.PARM;
```

Use this statement in addition to a SET, MERGE, or other statement that reads the primary data of the data step.

To add variables from multiple SAS datasets in this manner, either use multiple SET statements or list the SAS datasets in a MERGE statement with no BY statement.

When a data step reads multiple SAS datasets that contain the same variable, the variable must have the same data type in every SAS dataset. It is a semantic error if two variables have the same name and different data types. Use the RENAME= dataset option to rename one of the variables.

SQL includes a set of table join operators that define various other ways of combining data.

Appending is an alternative to concatenating SAS datasets. In appending, observations are added to a base dataset. The observations of the base dataset stay where they are, and observations of another SAS dataset are added to the end of the base dataset. This can be much faster than concatenating with the SET statement if the number of new observations is small compared to the number of base observations. However, appending works only if the new observations have the same variables as the base observations.

Use a PROC APPEND step to append a SAS dataset. The form of the proc step is:

PROC APPEND DATA=*new SAS dataset* OUT=*base SAS dataset*;
RUN;

Observations are read from the input SAS dataset named in the DATA= option and written to the end of the output SAS dataset named in the OUT= option.

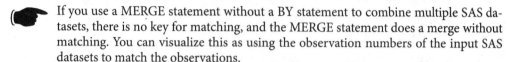

If you use a MERGE statement without a BY statement to combine multiple SAS datasets, there is no key for matching, and the MERGE statement does a merge without matching. You can visualize this as using the observation numbers of the input SAS datasets to match the observations.

A MERGE statement with only one SAS dataset is the same as a SET statement. However, this form of the MERGE statement is not officially documented. When there is only one input SAS dataset, write a SET statement to read it.

Complex combinations of data can require multiple data steps. For example, if you want to interleave two SAS datasets and merge the result with other SAS datasets, the interleaving and merging processes usually have to be done in separate data steps. Another example occurs when you want to do two merges, and the key for the second merge contains only some of the variables from the first merge.

For efficiency, run all the data steps involved within a single step by defining the intermediate SAS datasets as data step views. Add the VIEW= option to the DATA statement as shown in the example below. In the example at right, the first step interleaves SAS datasets A and B, the second step merges SAS datasets C and D, and the third step merges the results to create the SAS dataset E.

```
DATA AB / VIEW=AB;
   SET A B;
   BY X1 X2;
RUN;
DATA CD / VIEW=CD;
   MERGE C (IN=IN1)
         D (IN=IN2);
   BY X1;
   IF IN1 AND IN2;
RUN;
DATA E;
   MERGE AB CD;
   BY X1 X2;
RUN;
```

In a match merge, to ensure that a SAS dataset contains only one observation per BY group, use a separate data step before the merge to eliminate any duplicate observations. The example at right eliminates duplicates in A and B before merging them with C.

A hierarchy presents special problems in combining data. In a hierarchy, objects at each level are linked to objects at the next higher level. Hierarchical data can be easier to manage or maintain when each level is stored in a separate table. This way, there is only one observation to define each object. However, it is easier to use the data if the entire hierarchy is combined in one table with each level as a variable.

```
DATA A1 / VIEW=A1;
   SET A;
   BY X;
   IF LAST.X;
RUN;
DATA B1 / VIEW=B1;
   SET B;
   BY X;
   IF LAST.X;
RUN;
DATA D;
   MERGE A1 B1 C;
   BY X;
RUN;
```

In a well-formed hierarchy, each object is placed at one specific level and links to exactly one object in the next higher level. In describing the links between levels, the *parent* is the higher-level object; the *child* is the lower-level object. Using this terminology, each child has only one parent. To combine the various tables of the hierarchy into a single table, start at the top and merge each level with the next.

The example below is based on a taxonomy that divides organisms by order, family, genus, and species. This forms a hierarchy in which each species belongs to one genus, each genus to one family, and each family to one order. The hierarchy is defined in the SAS datasets TAX.FAMILY, which places each family in one order; TAX.GENUS, which places each genus in a family, and TAX.SPECIES, which places each species in a genus. The program combines the hierarchy to form the SAS datasets WORK.HIER3, with order, family, and genus, and WORK.HIER, which has order, family, genus, and species.

```
*
   TAX.FAMILY: ORDER, FAMILY
*;
PROC SORT DATA=TAX.FAMILY OUT=WORK.LEVEL2;
   BY ORDER;
RUN;
*
   TAX.GENUS: FAMILY, GENUS
*;
PROC SORT DATA=TAX.GENUS OUT=WORK.LEVEL3;
   BY ORDER;
RUN;
*
   WORK.HIER3: ORDER, FAMILY, GENUS
*;
DATA WORK.HIER3;
   MERGE WORK.LEVEL2 WORK.LEVEL3;
   BY ORDER;
RUN;
PROC SORT DATA=WORK.HIER3;
   BY GENUS;
RUN;
*
   TAX.SPECIES: GENUS, SPECIES
*;
PROC SORT DATA=TAX.SPECIES OUT=WORK.LEVEL4;
   BY GENUS;
RUN;
*
   WORK.HIER: ORDER, FAMILY, GENUS, SPECIES
*;
DATA WORK.HIER;
   MERGE WORK.HIER3 WORK.LEVEL4;
   BY GENUS;
RUN;
```

It would also be possible to start at the bottom of a hierarchy and merge upward; however, that approach takes longer to run. The lowest level of a hierarchy usually contains more than half of the objects in the hierarchy, so processing goes faster if the data at this level is processed no more than necessary. Similarly, it is sometimes possible to add hierarchy information to a separate set of data one level at a time; however, it is more efficient to form the hierarchy into one table before you combine it with other data.

■ 52

Table Lookup

Table lookup is a way to add a variable to a program. The program already contains a key variable, and it looks up the key variable in a table to find values for another variable. This process also works with combinations of variables. The key can be a combination of variables. The lookup can return several variables based on the same key.

There are many different ways to do table lookup in SAS programs. Each is well suited for some applications and poorly suited for others. Each is widely used. In order to write efficient SAS programs and to work with the SAS programs of others, you will need to be familiar with the full range of table lookup techniques.

 Two questions to ask when selecting a table lookup technique are:

- How large is the lookup table?
- Is the lookup table updated often?

A small lookup table that will never be updated is most efficiently done using a small-scale technique that is hard-coded into a data step. The technique might involve a SELECT block, the IN operator, an array, or a pseudo-array. These techniques are described in the rest of this chapter.

If the lookup table is large, it is most efficient when implemented as a SAS data file. Also, if the lookup table changes frequently, it is easiest to implement as a SAS data file. There are various ways to look up values in a SAS data file. These techniques are described in the next chapter, "Table Lookup From SAS Data Files."

TABLE LOOKUP EFFECTS

Table lookup is a technical way of understanding a familiar, everyday process. Depending on the context, a lookup table might be called a table, index, directory, standard, mapping, dictionary, thesaurus, chart, or list. The process of table lookup produces effects such as:

- *Categorizing or classifying*, putting something into a category or class.
- *Grading*, putting a measurement into one of several consecutive named categories. For example, ranges of test scores may be converted to letter grades A, B, C, etc.
- *Stratifying*, grouping numeric values into layers of magnitude.
- *Validating*, determining whether a code belongs to a set. This could mean making sure that a code entered by a user is an acceptable value or checking a credit card number offered by a customer to see if it is real.
- *Recoding*, replacing one code with another.
- *Standardizing*, replacing words or codes with the preferred equivalent words or codes.
- *Spell checking*, checking words against a dictionary of known words to identify words that might be misspelled.
- *Data retrieval*, finding the available data about an item. In a product catalog, for example, if you know the catalog number of an item, you can obtain such information as its name, description, and price.

A lookup table that does not change regularly and is not especially large can often be implemented effectively as a value format or value informat. This is described in chapter 54, "Value Formats for Table Lookup." Value formats are especially well suited for lookup that involves ranges of values.

Lookup Expressions

Use the IN or NOTIN operator for Boolean lookup based on a list of values. The result of the lookup is 1 or 0, depending on whether the key value is in the list or not.

For example, given the atomic number of an element, you can determine whether the element is a metal or nonmetal. The expression in this example checks an atomic number against the list of nonmetallic atomic numbers. If the number is not in that list, the element is a metal.

```
METALLIC = NUMBER NOTIN (1, 2, 5, 6, 7, 8, 9, 10,
    14, 15, 16, 17, 18, 33, 34, 35, 36, 52, 53, 54, 85, 86);
```

The value assigned to METALLIC is 1 for an element that is metallic, 0 for an element that is nonmetallic.

Use the FINDC function for Boolean lookup based on a set of characters contained in a character string, as described in chapter 27, "Foreign Data Types."

Use a comparison SELECT block for table lookup based on specific key values. Use the key variable as the SELECT expression. List the key values as the constant values in the WHEN statement. Assign the corresponding value to the resulting variable in an assignment statement that is the action of the WHEN statement. This code model shows the form of a SELECT block used for table lookup.

```
SELECT (key variable);
    WHEN (value, . . . ) variable = value;
    . . .
    OTHERWISE ;
    END;
```

This example shows a small table lookup using a SELECT block. This code fragment provides the approximate storage capacity of an audio CD in hours, minutes and seconds, based on its diameter in centimeters.

```
SELECT (DIAMETER);
    WHEN (12) CAPACITY = '1:18:00'T;
    WHEN (8) CAPACITY = '0:24:00'T;
    OTHERWISE ;
    END;
```

A comparison SELECT block can provide values for multiple variables by using a DO block in each WHEN statement, as shown in this example.

```
SELECT (DIAMETER);
    WHEN (12) DO;
        CAPACITY = '1:18:00'T;
        WEIGHT = 15;
        END;
```

LOOKUP FUNCTIONS

These SAS functions look up properties of U.S. states.

- ZIPSTATE returns the two-letter state abbreviation from the ZIP code.
- ZIPNAMEL returns the state name from the ZIP code.
- ZIPCITY returns the place name and two-letter state abbreviation from the ZIP code.
- STNAMEL returns the state name from the two-letter abbreviation.
- ZIPNAME and STNAME return the state name in uppercase letters.
- FIPSTATE, STFIPS, ZIPFIPS, FIPNAMEL, and FIPNAME translate to and from the FIPS state code.

These functions generate an error condition when they do not recognize the value you supply as the argument. If you need to avoid this, use a format instead of a function. See chapter 18, "Format Catalogs and Control Datasets," for an example that creates a value format from the ZIPSTATE function.

```
WHEN (8) DO;
  CAPACITY = '0:24:00'T;
  WEIGHT = 6;
  END;
OTHERWISE ;
END;
```

 Use a conditional SELECT block for lookup based on ranges of the key variable. This example provides the sign of a numeric value; it duplicates the effect of the SIGN function.

```
SELECT ;
  WHEN (VALUE <= .Z) SIGN = .;
  WHEN (VALUE < 0) SIGN = -1;
  WHEN (VALUE = 0) SIGN = 0;
  OTHERWISE SIGN = 1;
END;
```

It is okay when ranges overlap; the SELECT block still selects only one WHEN action. It is the first WHEN expression that is true, the first range that contains the value, that matters. Missing values are contained in the first range in this example, so the corresponding action is executed in that WHEN statement; it does not matter that missing values are also contained in the second range.

Lookup Arrays

When key values are index values, integer values that fall within a limited range, it is possible to implement table lookup as an array reference. Use the key variable as the array subscript. Array lookup is fast and deceptively simple.

```
ARRAY ELSYM {109} $ 2 _TEMPORARY_ (
  'H', 'He', 'Li', 'Be', 'B', 'C', 'N', 'O', 'F', 'Ne',
  'Na', 'Mg', 'Al', 'Si', 'P', 'S', 'Cl', 'Ar', 'K', 'Ca',
  'Sc', 'Ti', 'V', 'Cr', 'Mn', 'Fe', 'Co', 'Ni', 'Cu', 'Zn',
  'Ga', 'Ge', 'As', 'Se', 'Br', 'Kr', 'Rb', 'Sr', 'Y', 'Zr',
  'Nb', 'Mo', 'Tc', 'Ru', 'Rh', 'Pd', 'Ag', 'Cd', 'In', 'Sn',
  'Sb', 'Te', 'I', 'Xe', 'Cs', 'Ba', 'La', 'Ce', 'Pr', 'Nd',
  'Pm', 'Sm', 'Eu', 'Gd', 'Tb', 'Dy', 'Ho', 'Er', 'Tm', 'Yb',
  'Lu', 'Hf', 'Ta', 'W', 'Re', 'Os', 'Ir', 'Pt', 'Au', 'Hg',
  'Tl', 'Pb', 'Bi', 'Po', 'At', 'Rn', 'Fr', 'Ra', 'Ac', 'Th',
  'Pa', 'U', 'Np', 'Pu', 'Am', 'Cm', 'Bk', 'Cf', 'Es', 'Fm',
  'Md', 'No', 'Lr', 'Rf', 'Db', 'Sg', 'Bh', 'Hs', 'Mt');
```

For example, the array ELSYM defined in the statement at left is all you need to look up the chemical symbol of an element based on its atomic number.

As shown, use the keyword _TEMPORARY_ to create an array whose elements are temporary variables (rather than named variables). This makes the array faster and simpler.

Proofread a lookup array by printing every element of the array along with its index number. The statements below create the output shown at right.

```
DO I = LBOUND(ELSYM) TO HBOUND(ELSYM);
  PUT I ELSYM{I};
  END;
```

```
 1 H
 2 He
 3 Li
 4 Be
 5 B
 6 C
 7 N
 8 O
 9 F
10 Ne
11 Na
12 Mg
13 Al
14 Si
15 P
16 S
17 Cl
18 Ar
19 K
20 Ca
21 Sc
22 Ti
23 V
24 Cr
. . .
```

To look up a chemical symbol, use a reference to the ELSYM array with the atomic number as the array subscript.

```
NUMBER = 10;
SYMBOL = ELSYM{NUMBER};
PUT SYMBOL=;
```

SYMBOL=Ne

Use the same kind of array to look up an index number based on an array value. To look up an atomic number based on a chemical symbol, use a DO loop to check every element of the ELSYM array until one matches.

```
NUMBER = .;
SYMBOL = 'Zn';
DO I = LBOUND(ELSYM) TO HBOUND(ELSYM) UNTIL(NUMBER);
  IF SYMBOL = ELSYM{I} THEN NUMBER = I;
  END;
PUT SYMBOL= NUMBER=;
```

SYMBOL=Zn NUMBER=30

The UNTIL clause in the DO statement stops the DO loop after a value is found for NUMBER. The LBOUND and HBOUND functions provide the subscript range of the array. When a matching value is found in the array, the corresponding index value is assigned to the variable NUMBER. If a matching value is not found, no value is assigned to NUMBER.

When two lookup arrays are both based on the same key index values, you can use a combination of the techniques mentioned above to translate from one array value to another. For example, you could use this approach to get the name of an element from its chemical symbol, as shown here. (The lookup tables are reduced to 10 elements to make the example shorter.)

```
ARRAY ELSYM {10} $ 2 _TEMPORARY_ (
  'H', 'He', 'Li', 'Be', 'B', 'C', 'N', 'O', 'F', 'Ne');
ARRAY ELNAME {10} $ 17 _TEMPORARY_ (
  'Hydrogen', 'Helium', 'Lithium', 'Beryllium', 'Boron',
  'Carbon', 'Nitrogen', 'Oxygen', 'Fluorine', 'Neon');

NUMBER = .;
SYMBOL = 'O';
NAME = '            ';
DO I = LBOUND(ELSYM) TO HBOUND(ELSYM) UNTIL(NUMBER);
  IF SYMBOL = ELSYM{I} THEN DO;
    NUMBER = I;
    NAME = ELNAME{NUMBER};
    END;
  END;
PUT SYMBOL= NUMBER= NAME=;
```

SYMBOL=O NUMBER=8 NAME=Oxygen

Table lookup using two arrays is possible even when there is no key index variable to tie things together. Associate arbitrary index values with the key values.

A lookup table can also be set up as a pseudo-array using the character index as the key. This can be a quicker, simpler technique when the index values start at 1 and the lookup values are single letters or other one-byte values. Use the SUBSTR function to look up a value. See chapter 27, "Foreign Data Types," for pseudo-array techniques.

Most table lookup is designed to return a single result. However, there is occasionally a need to look for multiple resulting values in table lookup. This can be done with arrays, but it requires slightly different logic. Instead of stopping when one result is found, check for the possibility of additional results. Act on each result you find. If you need to consider all the results together, use an array to hold the results of the lookup.

Hash Objects for Lookup

The hash component object is designed to support table lookup on any scale. It offers speed and flexibility in exchange for the more technical coding required to set it up.

If you can, store the lookup table containing the hash data as a SAS data file, as described in the next chapter. If you want to write the hash data into a data step, the easiest way is to write the data as one or more arrays, then load the data from the arrays into the hash.

These statements set up the hash ELEMENT from the ELSYM and ELNAME arrays shown in the previous examples.

```
DECLARE HASH ELEMENT(ORDERED: 'A');
ELEMENT.DEFINEKEY('NUMBER');
ELEMENT.DEFINEDATA('NUMBER', 'SYMBOL', 'NAME');
ELEMENT.DEFINEDONE();
DO NUMBER = LBOUND(ELSYM) TO HBOUND(ELSYM);
  SYMBOL = ELSYM{NUMBER};
  NAME = ELNAME{NUMBER};
  ELEMENT.ADD();
  END;
```

Look up data in the hash by assigning a value to the key variable, then calling the FIND method of the object:

```
NUMBER = 4;
ELEMENT.FIND();
PUT (NUMBER SYMBOL NAME) (=);
NUMBER = 8;
ELEMENT.FIND();
PUT (NUMBER SYMBOL NAME) (=);
```

```
NUMBER=4 SYMBOL=Be NAME=Beryllium
NUMBER=8 SYMBOL=O NAME=Oxygen
```

53

Table Lookup From SAS Data Files

A SAS data file is the natural starting point for the data you use in a SAS table lookup. You can use the SAS dataset itself as a lookup table or load its data into a hash object. Either approach is practical for a lookup table of any size. There can be a single variable or a combination of variables as a key, and the lookup can provide values for any number of variables.

It takes several statements at the start of the data step to create a hash object and load data from the SAS dataset. These statements name the hash object and identify the SAS dataset, the key variables, and the data variables that will be looked up. Often it is helpful to list the key variables as data variables also. This example creates the hash object STATECAPITAL using the variables STATE and CAPITAL from the SAS dataset MAIN.STATES.

```
IF _N_ = 1 THEN DO;
  DECLARE HASH STATECAPITAL(DATASET: 'MAIN.STATES', ORDERED: 'A');
  STATECAPITAL.DEFINEKEY('STATE');
  STATECAPITAL.DEFINEDATA('STATE', 'CAPITAL');
  STATECAPITAL.DEFINEDONE();
  END;
```

The DECLARE statement declares the object and identifies the SAS dataset that provides its data. The subsequent statements call methods of the object to define the key and data variables. The condition _N_ = 1 ensures that the statements execute only once at the beginning of the data step.

After the hash object is initialized, look up data by assigning the key value to the key variable, then calling the FIND method. The hash object supplies a value for the data variables. If it does not find the key value, it returns a nonzero error code. Check this return value to see if data was found. If it is nonzero, assign default values to the lookup variables.

The following example creates the SAS dataset WORK.OUTER of observations from WORK.LOCATE in which the value of CITY differs from the value of CAPITAL found in the hash object. WORK.LOCATE also supplies the key variable, STATE. The subsetting IF statement at the end of the data step keeps only those observations that meet this test. The DROP= dataset option in the DATA statement drops the variable RC, which is not needed in the output data.

```
DATA WORK.OUTER (DROP=RC);
  IF _N_ = 1 THEN DO;
    DECLARE HASH STATECAPITAL(DATASET: 'MAIN.CAPITALS', ORDERED: 'A');
    STATECAPITAL.DEFINEKEY('STATE');
    STATECAPITAL.DEFINEDATA('STATE', 'CAPITAL');
    STATECAPITAL.DEFINEDONE();
    END;
  SET WORK.LOCATE;
  RC = STATECAPITAL.FIND();
  IF RC THEN DO;
    CAPITAL = '';
    END;
  IF CAPITAL NE CITY;
RUN;
```

These are common variations on the lookup process:

- There could be two or more key variables. The hash object looks for a row that matches the current values of all of the key variables.
- Create a hash with no data variables if your objective is to check whether key values are in a list. Use the CHECK method in place of the FIND method.
- There can be any number of data variables. To use all the variables of the SAS dataset as data variables, use the method DEFINEDATA(ALL: 'YES').
- Use multiple hash objects to look up several unrelated variables in the same data step.

If you create a SAS data file to be used directly as a lookup table, include these features:

- Include only key variables and lookup variables; do not include any extra variables. Use the KEEP= dataset option, if necessary, when you create the SAS data file.
- Do not compress the SAS data file. Use the COMPRESS=NO dataset option or system option when you create the SAS data file.
- Create an index on the key variable or variables. Use the INDEX= option when you create the SAS data file. See chapter 7, "Indexes," for the details of creating an index.

The KEY= option of the SET statement is designed to do ordinary indexed lookup. However, the lookup process is not as simple as using this option with the correct index name. To make the lookup process work correctly, you need to:

- Make sure the key variables have the key values you want before the SET statement executes.
- Use the KEEP= dataset option in the SET statement to list the variables you read from the SAS data file.

- Use the /UNIQUE option in the SET statement. Without this option, the lookup process may fail if you happen to look for the same key value two times in succession.
- After the SET statement, check the value of the automatic variable _IORC_. If the lookup fails because the key value is not found, this variable will have a nonzero value. In that case, you need to assign missing values to all the lookup variables (but not to the key variables). Also assign 0 values to the automatic variables _IORC_ and _ERROR_ so that no error messages will result.

The following code model puts these elements together for a lookup with one key variable and one lookup variable.

```
key variable = key value;
SET lookup table (KEEP=variables) KEY=key variable/UNIQUE;
IF _IORC_ THEN DO; * Not found. ;
  lookup variable = missing value;
  _IORC_ = 0;
  _ERROR_ = 0;
  END;
```

The effect of these statements is to obtain a value for the lookup variable from the lookup table if the key value is found there.

The following example looks up the capital of a state.

```
STATE = 'OH';
SET MAIN.STATES (KEEP=STATE CAPITAL) KEY=STATE/UNIQUE;
IF _IORC_ THEN DO; * Not found. ;
  CAPITAL = '';
  _IORC_ = 0;
  _ERROR_ = 0;
  END;
PUT CAPITAL=;
```

```
CAPITAL=Columbus
```

This example uses the lookup table MAIN.STATES, which contains the variables STATE and CAPITAL and has an index on STATE. The lookup table contains an observation in which STATE is OH and CAPITAL is Columbus.

The example below shows how the lookup process differs when there are two key variables. The lookup table CENSUS has an index STYR on the two key variables STATE and YEAR.

```
STATE = 'OH';
YEAR = 1990;
SET CENSUS (KEEP=STATE YEAR POP) KEY=STYR/UNIQUE;
IF _IORC_ THEN DO; * Not found. ;
  POP = .;
  _IORC_ = 0;
  _ERROR_ = 0;
  END;
```

Sometimes the purpose of a lookup is not to add a new variable, but just to find out whether the key value is found in the lookup table. In this case, the main focus is on the variable _IORC_. This variable is 0 if the key is found, but it is a nonzero value if the key is not found.

The example below looks up an expense code, XCODE, in a list of approved expense codes in the SAS data file CORP.EXPLIST. It assigns a 1 to the variable OK if the code is found in the list, or 0 if it is not.

```
SET CORP.EXPLIST (KEEP=XCODE) KEY=XCODE/UNIQUE;
IF _IORC_ THEN DO; * Not found. ;
  OK = 0;
  _IORC_ = 0;
  _ERROR_ = 0;
  END;
ELSE OK = 1; * Found. ;
```

A lookup table can be created without a key variable if the observation numbers can be used as the key. This is an especially fast technique when the key values are positive integers.

The data at right is an example of a part of a lookup table that uses observation number lookup. The column Obs, produced by the PRINT procedure, shows observation numbers, which indicate the atomic numbers of the elements in the data.

Use the SET statement with the POINT= option to read the specific observation in the lookup dataset. In the POINT= option, write the name of the key variable.

The POINT= option only works for observation numbers between 1 and the number of observations in the SAS data

Obs	SYMBOL	NAME
1	H	Hydrogen
2	He	Helium
3	Li	Lithium
4	Be	Beryllium
5	B	Boron
6	C	Carbon
7	N	Nitrogen
8	O	Oxygen
...		

file. If necessary, use the NOBS= option in the SET statement to create a variable that contains the number of observations, and compare this variable to the key value before the lookup.

This example uses the lookup table shown above to get the chemical symbol and name of an element from its atomic number.

```
NUMBER = 8;
IF 1 <= NUMBER <= NOBS THEN SET MAIN.ELEMENT POINT=NUMBER NOBS=NOBS;
ELSE DO;
  SYMBOL = '';
  NAME = '';
  END;
PUT (NUMBER SYMBOL NAME) (=);
```

```
NUMBER=8 SYMBOL=O NAME=Oxygen
```

The observation number lookup is so fast that it may be worth considering even if the highest key value is relatively large compared to the number of key values. For example, if there are 5,000 key values ranging from 1 to 1,000,000, it may still be faster to create a 1,000,000-observation lookup table based on observation numbers than to do indexed lookup using the 5,000-observation lookup table.

To create a lookup table based on observation numbers from one based on a key variable that has integer values, first use the SUMMARY procedure to determine the maximum key value. Create a view with values from 1 to this number, and merge this view with the lookup table to create the new lookup table. This process is shown here with a key variable KEY and an indexed lookup table TABLE1, creating a new lookup table TABLE2.

```
PROC SUMMARY DATA=TABLE1;
  VAR KEY;
  OUTPUT OUT=MAXKEY MAX=MAX;
RUN;
DATA N (KEEP=KEY) / VIEW=N;
  SET MAXKEY;
  DO KEY = 1 TO MAX;
    OUTPUT;
    END;
RUN;
DATA TABLE2 (DROP=KEY);
  MERGE N TABLE1 (IN=IS);
  BY KEY;
  IF FIRST.KEY;
  VALID = IS;
  LENGTH VALID 3;
RUN;
```

In the new lookup table, TABLE2, VALID is a Boolean lookup variable that indicates that the key value is present in the lookup table. The statement IF FIRST.KEY; ensures that duplicate values are not included in the data.

Usually, a lookup returns a single result. For example, for a state, there is only one state capital; for an employee, there can be no more than one Social Security Number. Sometimes, though, a lookup process looks for a set of results. A state could have multiple retail locations; a driver could own any number of cars.

To allow for multiple results in table lookup from a SAS data file, use the SET statement with the KEY= option, but with these changes:

- Do not use the /UNIQUE option.
- Use a DO loop to execute the SET statement repeatedly until _IORC_ has a nonzero value.
- Process or store each value the SET statement provides as long as until _IORC_ is 0.
- You must be sure the key value has changed between observations. If you look up the same key value in two consecutive observations without the /UNIQUE option, only the first observation will find the lookup values.

If a SAS data file used as a lookup table is relatively small and is heavily used, the program might run much faster if the SAS data file is loaded into memory with the SASFILE statement. This technique works if there is enough extra memory to hold the entire SAS data file. The SASFILE statement was introduced in release 8.1.

Memory is about a thousand times as fast as storage, so this technique can produce dramatic speed increases for some applications. On the other hand, if you use too much of the available memory for a SAS file, a program might run out of memory and be unable to execute. Also, the speed increases associated with memory occur only if there is sufficient physical memory. If the computer is using virtual memory, moving a lookup table from storage to memory might not result in any increase in speed.

To load a SAS data file into memory, use the SASFILE statement with the LOAD option before the step that uses the file. After the step or steps that use the file, use the SASFILE statement with the CLOSE option to close the file and release the block of memory that it occupied. The process is shown in this code model.

```
SASFILE SAS dataset LOAD;
step that uses the SAS dataset
. . .
RUN;
SASFILE SAS dataset CLOSE;
```

If the data acquired from a lookup table is most of the data used in a data step, the sort-merge technique could be the most efficient table lookup technique. This technique, although somewhat complex, is widely used even when it is not efficient because it is widely taught and was previously the only lookup technique to be supported by the SAS language.

To set up for the sort-merge technique, create a SAS data file of the base data involved. Use the SORT procedure to sort this SAS data file by the key variable. Use the MERGE statement with a BY statement to merge the base data with the lookup table. Finally, if necessary, sort the resulting data to put it back in the intended order.

The IN= dataset option can be useful in a sort-merge. Use a dataset option such as IN=BASE for the base dataset in the MERGE statement. Then, after the BY statement, write the subsetting IF statement

```
IF BASE;
```

This prevents the lookup table from adding observations that are not already present in the base data.

If the base data contains a large number of variables, it can take a long time to sort it by the key variables of the lookup, then sort again by the base data's own key variables after the lookup to restore the order of the data.

To speed up the process, create a smaller dataset that contains only key variables, and use it as the base dataset for the sort-merge. Merge the results of the sort-merge with the original base data to form the complete dataset.

A table lookup can also be done in an SQL query using a left join of the base data and the lookup table. SQL syntax does not let you indicate how the table lookup process will be carried out, so SAS could execute it efficiently or inefficiently.

■ 54
Value Formats for Table Lookup

Although designed for writing text data, value formats provide an easy way to do table lookup. Value informats work the same way and can create numeric values and error conditions. Value informats and formats are especially useful for lookup based on ranges of values; they can handle this as easily as they handle lookup based on individual key values.

 These are the key points to follow in the technique of creating and using a value format for table lookup.

- Make sure there are no duplicate key values.
- Create the value format in the VALUE statement of a PROC FORMAT step. Alternatively, create a control dataset and name it in the PROC FORMAT statement to create the value format.
- In the definition of the value format, use key values as ranges and lookup values as labels.
- Use the PUT function to apply the value format in a data step.

The example below converts numbers to names for four U.S. time zones. The time zones, numbered from –5 to –8, are named Eastern, Central, Mountain, and Pacific. This step creates the value format USTZN to do the mapping from numbers to names.

```
PROC FORMAT;
VALUE USTZN
  -5 = 'Eastern'
  -6 = 'Central'
  -7 = 'Mountain'
  -8 = 'Pacific'
  ;
```

This data step statement creates the variable ZONENAME, with the name of the time zone, from the variable ZONE, with the time zone number.

```
ZONENAME = PUT(ZONE, USTZN.);
```

Table lookup with a value informat is the same except that it uses the INVALUE statement and the INPUT function. The example below uses the informat LIST to obtain prices based on catalog numbers. This step creates the value informat.

```
PROC FORMAT;
INVALUE LIST
  '56012' - '56037' = 2.89
  '56088' - '56114' = 1.79
  OTHER = .
  ;
```

In this example, multiple catalog numbers have the same price. All catalog numbers from 56012 to 56037 have one price, and another interval of catalog numbers is given another price. The special range OTHER lets the informat provide a value — in this example, a missing value — if any other catalog number is supplied.

These data step statements demonstrate the use of the informat to look up a price.

```
CAT = '56025';
PRICE = INPUT(CAT, LIST.);
PUT PRICE=;
```

```
PRICE=2.89
```

Is it better to use a value format or a value informat? In most cases, either will work, but one might be slightly easier or more efficient than the other. These are some factors to consider.

- To map character values to character values, use a character value format or a character value informat.
- To map numeric values to character values, use a numeric value format.
- To map character values to numeric values, use a numeric value informat.
- To map numeric values to numeric values, use a format (such as F) to convert the key values to character values and use a numeric value informat. Alternatively, use a numeric value format and use an informat (such as F) to convert the resulting values to numeric values.
- Use a value informat if the UPCASE and JUST informat options or the special range _ERROR_ can be used to advantage.
- Using a value format, it is possible to do table lookup in a proc step, and this can sometimes eliminate the need for a data step. For example, by associating the lookup format with the key variable in the REPORT procedure, you can print the lookup value without having to create a separate lookup variable.

To do a validation process that checks a key value against a set of values, create a Boolean value informat. Use the value 1 as the label for all the key values in the set. Use the value 0 as the label for the special range OTHER.

This example creates the value informat PRCOL that tests to see whether a color is one of the primary colors of light.

```
PROC FORMAT;
INVALUE PRCOL (UPCASE JUST)
```

```
'RED', 'GREEN', 'BLUE' = 1
' ' = .
OTHER = 0
;
```

The informat returns 1 if the value supplied to it is one of the primary colors red, green, or blue. It returns 0 for any other word, or a missing value if a blank value is supplied. The UPCASE and JUST informat options allow the informat to recognize words that are not capitalized or that have leading spaces.

An INPUT function call that uses this kind of informat returns a Boolean value that can be used directly in a control flow statement, as shown in this example.

```
DO COLOR = 'Red ', 'White', 'Blue';
  IF INPUT(COLOR, PRCOL.) THEN PUT COLOR 'is a primary color of light.';
  ELSE PUT COLOR 'is not a primary color of light.';
  END;
```

```
Red is a primary color of light.
White is not a primary color of light.
Blue is a primary color of light.
```

 If data values are already in a data file, use that file to create a control dataset, and create the value format from that. Control datasets use specific variables to define a format. Use these variable names:

- TYPE: A one-letter code indicating the type of routine. Use F for a numeric value format, C for a character value format, I for a numeric value informat, J for a character value informat. (You can omit this variable if you are creating a numeric value format.)
- FMTNAME: The name of the format or informat. Include the dollar sign at the beginning of the name of a character format or informat.
- START: The range value, or the low endpoint of an interval.
- END: The high endpoint of an interval.
- SEXCL: Use the code value Y to exclude the start value from the interval.
- EEXCL: Use the code value Y to exclude the end value from the interval.
- LABEL: The label value.
- HLO: A character value containing one or more letters as codes. Use U for the UPCASE option, J for the JUST option, H, L, and O for the special range keywords HIGH, LOW, and OTHER.

Name the control dataset in the CNTLIN= option of the PROC FORMAT statement. See chapter 18, "Format Catalogs and Control Datasets."

This example creates formats to look up the symbol and name of a chemical element based on its atomic number. The formats are created from control datasets constructed from the SAS dataset ELEMENT, a SAS dataset of chemical elements with the variables NUMBER, SYMBOL, and NAME.

```
*
  Create value format ELNAME for name of chemical element.
*;
DATA CNTL1 / VIEW=CNTL1;
```

```
    RETAIN FMTNAME 'ELNAME';
    SET ELEMENT (KEEP=NUMBER NAME RENAME=(NUMBER=START NAME=LABEL));
RUN;
PROC FORMAT CNTLIN=CNTL1;
RUN;
*
  Create value format ELSYM for symbol of chemical element.
*;
DATA CNTL2 / VIEW=CNTL2;
    RETAIN FMTNAME 'ELSYM';
    SET ELEMENT (KEEP=NUMBER SYMBOL
       RENAME=(NUMBER=START SYMBOL=LABEL));
RUN;
PROC FORMAT CNTLIN=CNTL2;
RUN;
```

The VIEW= option in this program creates the control datasets as views. This simplifies the execution of the program and saves a small amount of time and storage space.

The code fragment below demonstrates the use of these two formats.

```
DO NUMBER = 104 TO 109;
    NAME = PUT(NUMBER, ELNAME.);
    SYMBOL = PUT(NUMBER, ELSYM.);
    PUT NUMBER 4. +2 SYMBOL $CHAR5. NAME $CHAR24.;
    END;
```

```
    104   Rf   Rutherfordium
    105   Db   Dubnium
    106   Sg   Seaborgium
    107   Bh   Bohrium
    108   Hs   Hassium
    109   Mt   Meitnerium
```

 The way a value format is defined, it has only one key variable. If you have to create a value format to work with a combination of key variables, you can concatenate the key variables (forming a structure — see chapter 27, "Foreign Data Types"). This is a complicated approach, but there is one situation in which it might make sense. If a lookup table uses two or more variables and involves ranges of one of the variables, you can make the lookup table a value informat using a concatenation of variables as the key. An example of this is a price list in which the price points depend on quantity ranges; the unit price for the sale of 50–99 units might be less than the unit price for a sale of 1–49 units. Make the variable that forms ranges the last part of the key.

55
Calendars

 Calendar information is often used as program parameters, macro variables that control an aspect of the actions of a program. This is usually the case when a program runs on a regular cycle, such as monthly, with new data files or libraries each time. You can use one date parameter for a program, and use it to compute a set of macro variables with calendar information. The example below starts from a date in the macro variable DATEPARM and creates a dozen other macro variables that could be useful in the program: a SAS date constant, the year, month, and day numbers, the two-digit year, and more.

For more information on how the parts of this work, see these chapters:

- chapter 64, "Program Parameters"
- chapters 36, "Time Conversions," and 37, "Time Arithmetic"
- chapters 61, "Macro Variables," and 63, "Macro Programming"

```
%LET DATEPARM = 11JUL2002;

%LET DATE = "&DATEPARM"D;
%LET YEAR = %SYSFUNC(YEAR(&DATE));
%LET M = %SYSFUNC(MONTH(&DATE), Z2.);
%LET D = %SYSFUNC(DAY(&DATE), Z2.);
%LET Y2 = %SYSFUNC(MOD(&YEAR, 100), Z2.);
%LET MONTH = %SYSFUNC(INTNX(MONTH, &DATE, 0), DATE9.);
%LET NEXTMONTH = %SYSFUNC(INTNX(MONTH, &DATE, 1), DATE9.);
%LET LASTMONTH = %SYSFUNC(INTNX(MONTH, &DATE, -1), DATE9.);
%LET MONTHDAYS = %SYSEVALF("&NEXTMONTH"D - "&MONTH"D);
%LET NEXTYEAR = %EVAL(&YEAR + 1);
%LET LASTYEAR = %EVAL(&YEAR - 1);
%LET YEARDAYS =
   %SYSEVALF("01JAN&NEXTYEAR"D - "01JAN&YEAR"D);

%PUT _USER_;
```

```
GLOBAL DATEPARM 11JUL2002
GLOBAL NEXTMONTH 01AUG2002
GLOBAL MONTH 01JUL2002
GLOBAL Y2 02
GLOBAL NEXTYEAR 2003
GLOBAL DATE "11JUL2002"D
GLOBAL M 07
GLOBAL YEARDAYS 365
GLOBAL YEAR 2002
GLOBAL LASTMONTH 01JUN2002
GLOBAL MONTHDAYS 31
GLOBAL D 11
GLOBAL LASTYEAR 2001
```

With these macro variables, you can write statements that depend on the calendar. For example, to define an array with one element for each day of the current month, use a statement such as:

```
ARRAY RETURN{&MONTHDAYS};
```

5 Kinds of Calendars

A calendar is a list of days and events, but there are several kinds of calendars. When you design a calendar, organize it according to the way it is used and the data it contains.

Sometimes it appears that a calendar should be more than one of the kinds described below. In that case, you might need to design two or more SAS datasets to contain the different kinds of information that are in the calendar.

 A schedule or other list of events. In this kind of calendar, there could be multiple events on the same day. A SAS date variable might indicate the date of the event, or if the time of day is significant, it could be a SAS datetime value. Other variables describe or measure the event. There could be an additional SAS date or SAS datetime variable to indicate the end of the event. This kind of data can have multiple events on the same day.

```
DATE       LOC   OPPONENT

13APR2002  AWAY  ATLANTA
27APR2002  AWAY  NEW YORK
04MAY2002  HOME  BOSTON
11MAY2002  HOME  WASHINGTON
19MAY2002  AWAY  SAN DIEGO
25MAY2002  AWAY  CAROLINA
. . .
```

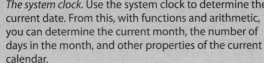 *The properties of days.* This kind of calendar lists a sequence of days, with additional variables to indicate the properties of days. There is one and only one observation for each day in the time period that the calendar covers. In a business application, there might be flags to indicate the days on which the business or parts of it are open or operating.

```
DATE       OPEN

01JAN2002  N
02JAN2002  Y
03JAN2002  Y
04JAN2002  Y
05JAN2002  N
. . .
```

A list of changes. Some values that are parameters in a program change from time to time; for example, an interest rate might change frequently, but not every day. The variables in this kind of calendar are the new value and the effective date of the change.

```
EFFECTIVE   RATE

02JUL1990   8.35
03JUL1990   8.32
09JUL1990   8.33
10JUL1990   8.34
11JUL1990   8.01
12JUL1990   8.29
13JUL1990   8.18
16JUL1990   8.07
. . .
```

A job schedule. This kind of calendar tells programs to do certain things on certain days. The calendar has one observation for each day the programs run. It may contain a series of flags that control specific actions of the programs.

The system clock. Use the system clock to determine the current date. From this, with functions and arithmetic, you can determine the current month, the number of days in the month, and other properties of the current calendar.

 A business operations calendar is usually maintained by an interactive application. This allows users to change the calendar data to reflect operating decisions that are made each year or from time to time. To make things easier for the users, you can initialize the calendar with weekends and holidays that are expected to affect operations.

This example sets up a 12-year calendar with values of 0, meaning closed, on Saturday, Sunday, and six U.S. holidays, and 1, meaning open, on all other days.

```
DATA CORP.CALENDAR (KEEP=DATE OPENDAY INDEX=(DATE) COMPRESS=NO);
  LENGTH DATE 4 OPENDAY $ 1;
  FORMAT DATE DATE9.;
  DO DATE = '01JAN2003'D TO '31DEC2014'D;
    MONTH = MONTH(DATE);
    DAY = DAY(DATE);
    WEEKDAY = WEEKDAY(DATE);
    OPEN = WEEKDAY NOTIN (1, 7);

    * U.S. holidays. ;
    * New Year's Day ;
    IF MONTH = DAY = 1 THEN OPEN = 0;
    * Memorial Day ;
    IF MONTH = 5 AND 25 <= DAY <= 31 AND WEEKDAY = 2 THEN OPEN = 0;
    * Independence Day ;
    IF MONTH = 7 AND DAY = 4 THEN OPEN = 0;
    * Labor Day ;
    IF MONTH = 9 AND 1 <= DAY <= 7 AND WEEKDAY = 2 THEN OPEN = 0;
    * Thanksgiving ;
    IF MONTH = 11 AND 22 <= DAY <= 28 AND WEEKDAY = 5 THEN OPEN = 0;
    * Christmas ;
    IF MONTH = 12 AND DAY = 25 THEN OPEN = 0;

    OPENDAY = PUT(OPEN, F1.);
    OUTPUT;
    END;
RUN;
```

The resulting calendar, in the SAS data file CORP.CALENDAR, has 4,383 observations, one for each day in the years 2003 to 2014. The INDEX= option creates an index on the variable DATE so that a data step can find a specific date in the calendar. The COMPRESS= option ensures that the SAS data file is not compressed; compression would not save any space in this SAS dataset, which has a total length of variables of only 5 bytes, and it would slow down indexed access to the observations.

OPENDAY in the example above is a character variable of length 1. The compactness of this variable, compared to a numeric variable, is not crucial in this example, but it can make a difference if you create a calendar that has many flags for each day. Each flag can be a separate variable, or you can create a single character variable in which each character is a separate flag. This use of a character variable is a pseudo-array; see chapter 27, "Foreign Data Types," for pseudo-array techniques.

To look up a day in a day calendar SAS dataset, use a SET statement with the KEY= option. The example below looks up December 31, 2005, to see if that day is scheduled to be open. For more information about this technique, see chapter 53, "Table Lookup From SAS Data Files."

```
DATE = '31DEC2005'D;
SET CORP.CALENDAR (KEEP=DATE OPENDAY) KEY=DATE/UNIQUE;
IF _IORC_ THEN DO; * Date not in calendar. ;
  _IORC_ = 0;
  _ERROR_ = 0;
  OPENDAY = ' ';
  END;
```

```
PUT DATE : WEEKDATE. +(-1) ': ' @;
IF OPENDAY = '1' THEN PUT 'OPEN';
ELSE IF OPENDAY = '0' THEN PUT 'CLOSED';
```

```
Saturday, December 31, 2005: CLOSED
```

The most familiar look of a calendar is a two-dimensional array showing a single month, with each week in a separate row and each day of the week located in a specific column. If you choose to convert a calendar to this layout for a user to edit or to prepare a report, you need to create two arrays, one with the days of the month and the other with the values for the user to edit. Define each array with 6 rows and 7 columns, as shown here:

```
ARRAY DAYS{6, 7} $ 2;
ARRAY FLAG{6, 7} $ 1;
```

Converting a standard calendar dataset with one observation per day to the visual form that has one observation per month is a special kind of transposing. See chapter 46 for a general discussion of transposing. The program below converts from CORP.CALENDAR, with the variables DATE and OPENDAY, to WORK.MONTH, with 86 variables.

```
DATA WORK.YM / VIEW=WORK.YM;
  SET CORP.CALENDAR;
  BY DATE;
  YEAR = YEAR(DATE);
  MONTH = MONTH(DATE);
RUN;

DATA WORK.MONTH (KEEP=YEAR MONTH DAYS1-DAYS42 FLAG1-FLAG42);
  SET WORK.YM;
  BY YEAR MONTH;
  ARRAY DAYS{6, 7} $ 2;
  ARRAY FLAG{6, 7} $ 1;
  RETAIN DAYS ' ' FLAG ' ' WEEK 1;

  WEEKDAY = WEEKDAY(DATE);
  IF FIRST.MONTH THEN DO;
    DO W = 1 TO 6;
      DO D = 1 TO 7;
        DAYS{W, D} = ' ';
        FLAG{W, D} = ' ';
        END;
      END;
    WEEK = 1;
    END;
  ELSE IF WEEKDAY = 1 THEN WEEK + 1;

  DAYS{WEEK, WEEKDAY} = PUT(DAY(DATE), F2.);
  FLAG{WEEK, WEEKDAY} = OPENDAY;

  IF LAST.MONTH THEN OUTPUT;
RUN;
```

In WORK.MONTH, each observation contains all the variables necessary to display an entire month for editing. After editing, the program below converts the results back to a standard calendar dataset.

```
DATA CORP.CALENDAR (KEEP=DATE OPENDAY INDEX=(DATE));
  SET WORK.MONTH;
  ARRAY DAYS{6, 7} $ 2;
  ARRAY FLAG{6, 7} $ 1;
  WEEK = 1;
  DO DAY = 1 TO 31;
    DATE = MDY(MONTH, 1, YEAR) + DAY - 1;
    IF MONTH(DATE) > MONTH THEN DELETE;
    WEEKDAY = WEEKDAY(DATE);
    IF DAY > 1 AND WEEKDAY = 1 THEN WEEK + 1;
    OPENDAY = DAYFLAG{WEEK, WEEKDAY};
    OUTPUT;
    END;
RUN;
```

A list of changes, such as the list of rates and effective dates shown at the beginning of the chapter, can sometimes be made easier to use by converting it to a day calendar. The conversion requires a data step to fill in the dates between the effective dates of the changes.

The example converts a list of changes and effective dates, in WORK.CHANGES, to a list of days, in WORK.EOD. The program works correctly only if WORK.CHANGES is already sorted in chronological order.

```
DATA WORK.EOD (KEEP=DATE LATESTRATE
   RENAME=(LATESTRATE=RATE) INDEX=(DATE));
  LENGTH DATE 4;
  RETAIN PREVIOUSDATE LATESTRATE;
  SET WORK.CHANGES;
  BY EFFECTIVE;
  * Fill in dates between changes. ;
  IF FIRST.EFFECTIVE AND EFFECTIVE > PREVIOUSDATE > .Z THEN
     DO DATE = PREVIOUSDATE + 1 TO EFFECTIVE - 1;
     OUTPUT;
     END;
  IF LAST.EFFECTIVE THEN DO;
     DATE = EFFECTIVE;
     LATESTRATE = RATE;
     OUTPUT;
     PREVIOUSDATE = EFFECTIVE;
     END;
RUN;
```

DATE	RATE
02JUL1990	8.35
03JUL1990	8.32
04JUL1990	8.32
05JUL1990	8.32
06JUL1990	8.32
07JUL1990	8.32
08JUL1990	8.32
09JUL1990	8.33
10JUL1990	8.34
11JUL1990	8.01
12JUL1990	8.29
13JUL1990	8.18
14JUL1990	8.18
15JUL1990	8.18
16JUL1990	8.07
. . .	

If the input SAS dataset WORK.CHANGES is the SAS dataset shown earlier, the output SAS dataset WORK.EOD contains the data shown at right.

For the reverse conversion, use a program such as the one below. Again, the program requires the input SAS dataset to be sorted in chronological order.

```
DATA WORK.CHANGES2 (RENAME=(DATE=EFFECTIVE) INDEX=(EFFECTIVE));
  SET WORK.EOD;
  BY RATE NOTSORTED;
  IF FIRST.RATE;
RUN;
```

 The CALENDAR procedure is designed to print date-oriented data in the form of a monthly calendar. The START statement in the proc step identifies the variable that indicates the date of an event. For an event that lasts longer than one day, the FIN statement identifies the end date variable. List the name or description of the event and other variables to print in the VAR statement.

The example below shows a SAS dataset, WORK.EVENTS, with three observations. The observations are events starting on January 16, 17, and 21, 2003, as indicated in the variable DATE. The last event runs three days, finishing on January 24; this value is indicated in the variable ENDDATE. Two variables, WORK and STAFF, are shown for each event, with a slash separating the variables. In the PROC CALENDAR statement, the WEEKDAYS option is used to show only weekdays.

```
PROC CALENDAR
  DATA=WORK.EVENTS
  WEEKDAYS;
  START DATE;
  FIN ENDDATE;
  VAR WORK STAFF;
RUN;
```

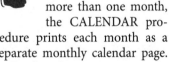 If the data extends to more than one month, the CALENDAR procedure prints each month as a separate monthly calendar page. With the FILL option in the PROC statement, the procedure prints all months from the first month to the last month, whether the intervening months contain observations or not.

```
------------------------------------------------------------------------
                              January  2003
------------------------------------------------------------------------
   Monday  |   Tuesday  |  Wednesday  |   Thursday  |    Friday
-----------+------------+-------------+-------------+------------------
           |            |      1      |      2      |      3
           |            |             |             |
           |            |             |             |
           |            |             |             |
-----------+------------+-------------+-------------+------------------
     6     |     7      |      8      |      9      |     10
           |            |             |             |
           |            |             |             |
           |            |             |             |
-----------+------------+-------------+-------------+------------------
    13     |    14      |     15      |     16      |     17
           |            |             |             |
           |            |             | +=INSTALL/1=+|+TEST,DEMO/3+
-----------+------------+-------------+-------------+------------------
    20     |    21      |     22      |     23      |     24
           |            |             |             |
           | +==============TRAINING/17==============+
-----------+------------+-------------+-------------+------------------
    27     |    28      |     29      |     30      |     31
           |            |             |             |
           |            |             |             |
           |            |             |             |
------------------------------------------------------------------------
```

■ 56
Multiple Text Files

The same SAS language features you use to read or write a single text file in a data step also let you read and write multiple text files.

Input

It is usually possible to concatenate, interleave, or merge data from input text files without using any special data step logic. Input text files can be concatenated in the FILENAME statement. The data from input text files can be concatenated, interleaved, or merged by creating SAS datasets from the data and combining them in a subsequent data step.

 Use the FILENAME statement to concatenate input text files. List the physical file names in parentheses in the FILENAME statement. This example defines the fileref NEW as a concatenation of four text files.

FILENAME NEW ('new1.txt' 'new2.txt' 'new3.txt' 'new4.txt');

In a data step, use the fileref NEW in an INFILE statement, for example:

INFILE NEW;

INPUT statements in the data step read the records of the four files the same way as if the records were all contained in one input text file.

 If you need to keep track of which input text file each record comes from, use the FILENAME= option in the INFILE statement. The FILENAME= option names a character variable; when an INPUT statement reads a record, it gives this variable the physical file name of the input text file from which the record is read. Use an earlier LENGTH statement to declare the variable with a length sufficient to hold the physical file name. In this example, the variable FILE contains the physical file name of the input file.

LENGTH FILE $ 64;
INFILE NEW FILENAME=FILE;

A variable created with the FILENAME= option is not stored in any output SAS dataset. To store the value, assign it to another variable. This statement assigns the value of FILE to the variable SOURCE.

```
SOURCE = FILE;
```

If the physical file names are long and not very meaningful, consider converting them to one-letter codes that indicate the source of data.

If input text files do not have the same record layout, read them in separate data steps. Create a data step view in each data step. Then concatenate the views in a SET statement in another data step.

The code model below concatenates the data in the input files NEW1 and NEW2 to create the SAS dataset WORK.NEW.

```
DATA WORK.NEW1 / VIEW=WORK.NEW1;
   INFILE NEW1;
   INPUT variables;
RUN;
DATA WORK.NEW2 / VIEW=WORK.NEW2;
   INFILE NEW2;
   INPUT variables;
RUN;
DATA WORK.NEW;
   SET WORK.NEW1 WORK.NEW2;
RUN;
```

> ## DATA STEP TECHNIQUES
>
> If you need maximum flexibility and maximum efficiency in combining text data files, you can combine with data step logic in a single data step. If you want to attempt this, these features and techniques are helpful:
>
> - A separate INFILE statement for each input file.
> - A separate key variable for each file. Compare the key variables to each other to find matching records.
> - The EOF= option in the INFILE statement to respond to the end of the file.
> - End of file variables to keep track of which files you have finished reading.
> - Statement labels to mark points in the data step for branching.
> - A variable used as a file index or counter to keep track of what file you are reading from. Use this variable in a SELECT block to select and read a record from one file.
> - The KEEP= dataset option to keep only the relevant data variables in the output SAS dataset.

Use the same approach to interleave or merge data from input text files. To interleave sorted data, add a BY statement after the SET statement. To merge sorted data, change the SET statement to a MERGE statement and add a BY statement.

Output

As easily as a data step can create one output text file, it can create a second one. Use a separate FILE statement for each output text file. This example writes the same data to two different files.

```
DATA _NULL_;
   SET PRODUCT;
   FILE OUTC DLM=',' DSD;
   PUT CODE DESCRIPTION;
   FILE OUTFIX;
   PUT CODE $CHAR12. DESCRIPTION $CHAR48.;
RUN;
```

To write different observations in different output files, use control flow statements (such as IF-THEN) to control the FILE and PUT statements.

 Occasionally, there is a need to write the BY groups of a SAS dataset as separate text files. Usually, the reason for this is that each BY group represents the responsibility of a different person, department, or location, and each text file contains the data to be delivered separately to each place. Another possible reason is that each BY group is being presented in a separate web page.

To write each BY group of a SAS dataset as its own text file, use the FILEVAR= option of the FILE statement. The value of the character variable named in the option determines what file a PUT statement writes to. Change the value of the variable to write to a different file. Construct names for the files based on the key values that form the BY groups. When the FILE statement has the FILEVAR= option, use a fileref that has not been previously defined in a FILENAME statement.

The example below writes a separate file for each location in a set of data, as indicated by the value of the variable LOCATION.

```
DATA _NULL_;
  LENGTH DSN $ 256;
  RETAIN DSN;
  SET WORK.ER;
  BY LOCATION;
  IF FIRST.LOCATION THEN
    DSN = '/My Documents/new/' || COMPRESS(LOCATION, '/ :\+;') || '.txt';
  FILE OUT FILEVAR=DSN DLM=',' DSD;
  PUT EMPLOYEE NAME ACTION EFFDATE;
RUN;
```

The program might write any number of output text files, depending on the number of BY groups. Each output file is noted in the log with messages such as these:

```
NOTE: The file OUT is:
      File Name=C:\My Documents\new\Allentown.txt,
      RECFM=V,LRECL=256

NOTE: The file OUT is:
      File Name=C:\My Documents\new\Dover.txt,
      RECFM=V,LRECL=256

NOTE: The file OUT is:
      File Name=C:\My Documents\new\EastRutherford.txt,
      RECFM=V,LRECL=256

NOTE: 12 records were written to the file OUT.
      The minimum record length was 33.
      The maximum record length was 39.
NOTE: 4 records were written to the file OUT.
      The minimum record length was 31.
      The maximum record length was 42.
NOTE: 7 records were written to the file OUT.
      The minimum record length was 35.
      The maximum record length was 42.
NOTE: There were 23 observations read from the data set WORK.ER.
```

■ 57
Print Files

A print file is a text file for people to read. Most SAS programs create print files to present their results. The text that a program writes in a print file is called print output. Print output is a fundamental part of the way the SAS environment works. Print files can be printed on paper or viewed on the computer screen.

Print files have these special qualities:

- *Pages.* A print file is divided into pages. A special print control character marks the beginning of each page.
- *Lines.* Each record of a print file is displayed as a separate line.
- *Monospaced font.* A print file is properly displayed using a monospaced font, in which all characters have the same width. The use of a monospaced font makes it possible to control the specific locations at which characters appear on the page.
- *Line size.* The line size of a print file is a fixed maximum number of characters that can appear in a line.
- *Page size.* The page size is a fixed maximum number of lines that can appear on a page.
- *Title lines.* Title lines are lines that are repeated at the top of each page of print output. They usually contain identifying information, such as a title.
- *Page numbers.* Pages in a print file are numbered sequentially, and the page numbers are usually written at the end of the first title line.

It is possible for a print file to have these additional qualities, but they are used only occasionally:

- *Footnote lines.* Footnote lines are lines that are repeated at the bottom of each page. They usually contain explanatory notes. They might also identify the source of the data or the program that created the print output.
- *Extended character set.* Most print files contain only ASCII text characters, but it is possible to create a print file that uses an extended character set such as Unicode.
- *Overprinting.* Overprinting is a feature of some printers, especially impact printers, that allow two characters to be placed in the same character position. This makes it possible to underline words by writing underscores at the same character positions. On some printers, it is possible to add emphasis by repeating the same characters at the same positions.

- *Top margin.* It is possible to leave several blank lines at the top of each page in a print file.

You might hope for or expect print files to have these qualities, but they do not:

- *Character formatting.* When you create a print file, you do not control the size, typeface, color, or style of the text.
- *Table formatting.* The SAS environment does not provide specific support for tables in print files. Instead, tables are displayed by placing column headers and fields at specific character positions in each line.

For this kind of formatting, use the object-oriented output of ODS instead.

Print Files in the SAS Environment

SAS provides special support for two print files. These two files, the log and standard print file, are automatically created in every SAS session. Use these two print files for most print output from SAS programs.

Use the log to write short notes and information about the execution of the program. The SAS supervisor and procedures write messages in the log about every step in a SAS program and various other events in a SAS session. For more about the log, see chapter 1, "The Log."

Use the standard print file for pages of results from the program. Procedures that write print output write it in the standard print file.

Use the LOG fileref to refer to the log. If you do not specify a fileref for text output in a data step, PUT statements write to the log by default.

Use the PRINT fileref to refer to the standard print file. For example, use this statement in a data step to direct text output to the standard print file:

FILE PRINT;

Use system options to control the general qualities of print output. Many of the options affect both the log and the standard print file. Use these options:

- LINESIZE= to set the line size
- PAGESIZE= to set the page size
- SKIP= to leave blank lines at the top of every page
- NUMBER to write the page number in the first title line, or NONUMBER to omit the page number
- PAGENO=1 to reset the page number
- CENTER to center title lines and many other elements of print output, or NOCENTER to left-align
- DATE to write the date in the first title line, or NODATE to omit the date

Create other print files when a program must create more than one file of results. Usually, this is because different parts of the results from a program are printed on different printers or delivered to different people. Use any available fileref for these other print files.

Use the PRINT option in the FILE statement to write to a print file in a data step. The PRINT option is not necessary for the PRINT or LOG filerefs. These other FILE statement options are useful for some print files:

- TITLE to write title lines, or NOTITLE to not write title lines
- FOOTNOTE to write footnote lines along with the title lines, or NOFOOTNOTE to not write footnote lines even though title lines are used
- LINESIZE= to set the line size
- PAGESIZE= to set the page size
- N=PS to give the PUT statement access to all the lines on the page, allowing the use of the # line pointer control, or N=1 to have a PUT statement only write one line at a time, not allowing the use of the # pointer control

These additional FILE statement options create numeric variables to help you keep track of the pointer location.

- LINE= creates a numeric variable that indicates the line number.
- COLUMN= creates a numeric variable that indicates the column number (the character position within the current line).
- LINESLEFT= creates a numeric variable that tells how many lines remain on the page, including the current line.

Variables created by these options, or any I/O statement options, cannot be stored in output SAS datasets.

 Use the PRINTTO procedure to redirect standard print output to a different fileref. Name the fileref in the PRINT= option of the PROC PRINTTO statement. For example, this step redirects print output to the GENERAL fileref:

```
PROC PRINTTO PRINT=GENERAL;
RUN;
```

Print output from subsequent proc steps goes to the GENERAL fileref instead of the standard print file. Output that data steps write to the PRINT fileref is also redirected to the GENERAL fileref.

 To direct the standard print file back to its own file, use this step:

```
PROC PRINTTO PRINT=PRINT;
RUN;
```

After this step executes, standard print output from subsequent steps goes to the standard print file.

 You can also use the PRINTTO procedure to redirect the log. Name a new fileref to direct the log to in the LOG= option in the PROC PRINTTO statement. The redirection of the log affects SAS messages, log output generated in a data step, and lines written by the %PUT statement.

To direct log messages back to the log, use this step:

```
PROC PRINTTO LOG=LOG;
RUN;
```

If you read a print file in a data step, you have a choice about how the print control characters in the print file are treated. Use the PRINT option in the INFILE statement, and SAS interprets the print control characters and provides the text of each line to the INPUT statement as if it were a record from a standard text data file. If you would rather read the print control characters as part of the data, use the NOPRINT option in the INFILE statement.

Title and Footnote Lines

Title and footnote lines are lines that are repeated on each page of print output. Title lines appear at the top of the page. Footnote lines appear at the bottom of the page.

There can be just one title line or as many as ten. The title lines are counted from the top. The first title line at the top of the page is title line 1.

Define title lines in TITLE statements. In the TITLE statement, identify the title line with a numeric suffix on the word TITLE. Start with a TITLE1 statement to define the first title line. Add a TITLE2 statement for a second title line, a TITLE3 statement for a third title line, and so on for as many title lines as you define. Write the title text for each TITLE statement as a character constant.

This example defines three title lines.

```
TITLE1 'National Weather Task Force';
TITLE2 'ICE Project';
TITLE3 'Integrated Precipitation Effects Model';
```

```
National Weather Task Force
ICE Project
Integrated Precipitation Effects Model
```

These statements replace any previous title lines. Each TITLE statement replaces the title line it refers to and clears all higher-numbered title lines. The TITLE1 statement replaces the first title line and clears all other title lines.

TITLE statements have to be written in order. If they are out of order, the lower-numbered TITLE statements supersede any higher-numbered TITLE statements that came before. This effect is demonstrated in the example below. There is only one title line because the TITLE1 statement supersedes the TITLE statements that precede it.

```
TITLE3 'Integrated Precipitation Effects Model';
TITLE2 'ICE Project';
TITLE1 'National Weather Task Force';
```

```
National Weather Task Force
```

The CENTER system option affects title lines. Use the CENTER option to center title lines. Use the NOCENTER option to left-align the title lines. The examples in this book use the NOCENTER option.

To clear title lines, use a TITLE statement with no title text. This clears the indicated title line and all title lines below it. To clear all title lines other than the first, use this statement:

TITLE2;

There is always at least one title line. The default text of the first title line identifies the SAS System as the source of the print output. Use this statement to restore the default title line:

TITLE1;

Use this statement to make the first title line blank:

TITLE1 ' ';

The numeric suffix can be omitted from the TITLE1 statement. That is, you can write the word TITLE in place of TITLE1. Most programmers write TITLE statements this way in applications that use only a single title line.

Write TITLE statements, like all global statements, between steps. If TITLE statements apply to a specific step, write them before that step. In run-group procedures, you can change title lines between run groups; write TITLE statements at the beginning of the run group.

If TITLE statements are affecting the previous step, it is because you did not write a RUN statement at the end of that step. Add the RUN statement in the previous step. Make it a habit to write RUN statements at the end of the steps you write.

In proc steps, title lines can display BY variables. See chapter 44, "Groups," for details. This feature is not available in data steps.

In data steps, title lines are optional. Use the NOTITLE option in the FILE statement to write a print file without title lines.

Footnote lines work like title lines, but are located at the bottom of the page. If there are footnote lines, there can be as many as ten of them. Like title lines, footnote lines are counted from the top. Footnote line 2 appears below footnote line 1, and so on.

Use FOOTNOTE statements, written like TITLE statements, to define or clear footnote lines. To clear all footnote lines, use this statement:

FOOTNOTE1;

Print Output in Data Steps

In data steps, print files are treated as text files. Use the FILE statement to identify the print file and the PUT statement to write lines of print output. In addition, there are data step features specifically for print files.

In a PUT statement, use the _PAGE_ keyword to advance to a new page. This example advances to a new page at the beginning of a BY group:

IF FIRST.STATE THEN PUT _PAGE_ @;

PAGE writes a print control character that marks the beginning of a page. If you think of _PAGE_ as indicating the end of a page or the division between pages, you might get results you do not expect.

The _PAGE_ keyword will not write a blank page at the beginning of a print file. To do that, use the _BLANKPAGE_ keyword instead. Anywhere else in the file, _BLANKPAGE_ and _PAGE_ are equivalent.

If you write page headers or column headers, use the LINESLEFT= (or LL=) option of the FILE statement to determine when to start a new page. For example, the FILE statement might be:

FILE PRINT LINESLEFT=LL;

The LL variable, then, tells you how many lines are left on the page. Use an IF-THEN statement to test this variable. If the value is less than or equal to the number of lines required to write an observation, then you need to start a new page before you write that observation. Use a single PUT statement or a DO block containing PUT statements to start the new page and write any necessary headers on the page.

This example starts a new page and writes headers. The headers include a page number, which is counted in the same DO block.

```
FILE PRINT LINESLEFT=LL;
IF _N_ = 1 THEN LL = 0;
IF LL <= 1 THEN DO;
   PAGENO + 1;
   PUT _PAGE_ @32 'Final List' @67 'Page:' PAGENO F4.
     / @7 'Material' @52 'Hardness' @64 'Opacity'
     / ;
   END;
PUT @7 MATERIAL $CHAR44. @52 HARDNESS BEST8. @64 OPACITY BEST7.;
```

The first IF-THEN statement checks the value of the automatic variable _N_ in order to start the first page for the first observation. In some programs, you might want to check in a similar way for the beginning of a BY group.

If you use the N=PS option in the FILE statement, you can use the # line pointer control to move to any line on the page. For example, this statement moves to the second line on the page:

PUT #2 @;

The number of lines is the same as the page size only if you use the NOTITLE option. If the page uses title lines, the number of lines you can write with the PUT statement is reduced.

 Use the HEADER= option to branch to statements that execute when a print file reaches a new page. Write the HEADER= option with a statement label in the FILE statement. At the end of the data step, write a RETURN statement, the statement label, statements to execute at the point in the middle of a PUT statement when it advances to a new page, and another RETURN statement. One possible use of this feature is to create a separate file that indicates what the pages of print output contain.

 The name of the HEADER= option might lead you to try to use it to execute statements that write in the print file itself, such as a page header, but various problems can result with this approach. If you use the HEADER= option to write column headers, the program may write the column headers on an otherwise blank page at the end of the report. If you use it to write values of variables, the program may write values that belong to the wrong observations. If you attempt to use the HEADER= option to write lines at the bottom of the page, the lines may appear on a different page from the one you were thinking of and may be overwritten by later PUT statements. To keep things simple and avoid all these problems, write column headers and other page text in the same PUT statement that contains the _PAGE_ keyword to start the new page, as described above.

Print Output in Proc Steps

Most procedures write output in the standard print file. Options and statements in the proc steps determine the details of the output.

 Output from proc steps does not go directly from the procedure to the standard print file. Instead, the proc steps produce what are called output objects. ODS, the Output Delivery System, converts the output objects to text that it writes in the standard print file. The ODS statement is a global statement that sets options for this process. There are thousands of possible options, which can change the way the output object is converted to text. With the right ODS drivers and options, you can also convert output to many other formats, from SAS datasets to web pages.

 The FORMCHAR string is a set of table formatting characters used by procedures that write tables. The string can be set in the FORMCHAR= system option and the FORMCHAR= option in the PROC statement of a few procedures. Individual characters in the FORMCHAR string are used at specific points in the boundaries and rules that form tables in print files. Change the appearance of a table by changing these characters. The default FORMCHAR string is:

OPTIONS FORMCHAR='|----|+|---+=|-/\<>*';

The first 11 characters of this string are used to form tables.

The following table shows several examples of FORMCHAR values for tables.

Default

FORMCHAR='|----|+|---+=|-/\<>*'

```
 -------------------------------
|           |        X          |
|           |-------------------|
|           |    3    |    4     |
|-----------+---------+----------|
| STATE     |         |          |
|-----------|         |          |
|1          |    1.00 |    1.00  |
|-----------+---------+----------|
|2          |    1.00 |    1.00  |
 -------------------------------
```

Horizontal Rules Only

FORMCHAR=' ----------'

```
 -------------------------------
                      X
            -----------------------
               3           4
 STATE
 ------------------
 1             1.00        1.00
 -------------------------------
 2             1.00        1.00
 -------------------------------
```

Shorter Horizontal Rules

FORMCHAR=' - - - -'

```
    -----------------------------
                    X
    ----------------------------
        3            4
 STATE
 ----------------
 1              1.00         1.00
 ---------------------------------
 2              1.00         1.00
    -----------------------------
```

Horizontal Rules Within Columns

FORMCHAR=' -'

```
     ----------------  ----------------------
                          X
                     ------------  ------------
                        3            4
 ---------------     ------------  ------------
 STATE
 ----------------
 1                      1.00         1.00
                     ------------  ------------
 2                      1.00         1.00
     ----------------  ------------  ------------
```

Vertical Rules

FORMCHAR='| |||||||||'

```
|           |         X          |
|           |         |          |
|           |    3    |    4     |
|           |         |          |
|           |    N    |    N     |
|           |         |          |
| STATE     |         |          |
|1          |         |          |
|           |    1.00 |    1.00  |
|           |         |          |
|2          |    1.00 |    1.00  |
|           |         |          |
```

Shorter Vertical Rules

FORMCHAR='| |||'

```
|           |         X          |
|           |         |          |
|           |    3    |    4     |
|           |         |          |
|           |    N    |    N     |
|           |         |          |
| STATE     |         |          |
|1          |         |          |
|           |    1.00 |    1.00  |
|           |         |          |
|2          |    1.00 |    1.00  |
|           |         |          |
```

Vertical Rules Plus Horizontal Rules Within Columns

FORMCHAR='|-|||||||||'

Tables Without Rules

FORMCHAR=' '

58
Table Reports

The most common task in reporting is to generate a table report with data arranged in rows and columns. SAS prints tables with observations as rows and variables as columns.

PRINT

Use a PROC PRINT step to generate a basic table report. Write:

- the PROC PRINT statement with the DATA= option to identify the input SAS dataset, the HEADING=HORIZONTAL (or HEADING=H) option to orient the column headers horizontally, and the NOOBS option (if you choose) to remove the observation number column from the report.
- a VAR statement listing variables to use as columns in order from left to right.
- a FORMAT statement to set formats for any or all of the variables.

The example below demonstrates these components of a PROC PRINT step.

```
PROC PRINT DATA=WORK.VOLCANO HEADING=HORIZONTAL NOOBS;
   VAR NAME LATITUDE LONGITUDE ELEVATION;
   FORMAT LATITUDE LONGITUDE F7.2 ELEVATION COMMA7.;
RUN;
```

NAME	LATITUDE	LONGITUDE	ELEVATION
Arenal	10.50	-84.70	1,656
Irazu	9.98	-83.85	3,431
Poas	10.20	-84.20	2,703
Rincon de la Vieja	10.20	-85.50	1,915

Use these features to provide labels for the columns of the report.

- the LABEL option in the PROC PRINT statement to use labels, rather than variable names, as the column headers
- a LABEL statement to set labels for variables
- the SPLIT= option to set the split character, if the labels are multiple lines and a specific character indicates a line break in a label

Use global statements to control general features of the print output, such as title lines, page numbers, and page size. See the previous chapter, "Print Files," for details.

To limit the observations that are used, use the OBS= or WHERE= dataset option. You might do this, for example, to make sure the report is formatted correctly before generating the entire report. See chapter 6, "Dataset Options," for details.

These are other statements you can use for a PROC PRINT report:

- The ID statement lists variables that appear as columns at the left side of the page.
- The SUM statement displays sums of the selected numeric variables.
- The BY statement displays BY variables in a BY line, which appears at the beginning of each BY group or page. The PAGEBY statement indicates one of the BY variables to force BY groups to appear on separate pages. The SUMBY statement indicates a BY variable and shows sums for BY groups.

REPORT

To have greater control over the format of a table report, use the REPORT procedure. A basic PROC REPORT step consists of the PROC statement, a COLUMN statement to list the columns of the report, and a DEFINE statement for each column.

In the PROC statement, write the DATA= option to identify the input SAS dataset, the NOWD option to suppress the proc's interactive features, and any of various formatting options that might apply. The most important formatting options are HEADLINE, HEADSKIP, SPLIT=, and NOHEADER, which affect the formatting of column headers; COLWIDTH= and SPACING=, which set the default width and spacing for columns; PANELS=, to divide the width of the page into panels; and PSPACE=, for the spacing between panels.

In the COLUMN statement, list the columns of the report in order from left to right. Often, this is just a list of variables.

In the DEFINE statement for each column, write the column name or the alias if there is one. Then write a slash and any options for the column. Options can include:

- A character constant to use as the column header. To define multiple lines for the header, write each header line as a separate constant value in the DEFINE statement.
- The FORMAT= option to set the format for the column.
- The WIDTH= option to set the column width.
- The SPACING= option to set the spacing to the left of the column.
- A keyword to indicate the usage of the variable in the column, such as ORDER, DISPLAY, or ANALYSIS.
- An alignment option: LEFT, CENTER, or RIGHT.
- A statistic keyword such as SUM, MEAN, or MAX. Statistics are used only for analysis columns.

The usage of the variables determines the structure of the report. The default usage is DISPLAY for a character variable and ANALYSIS for a numeric variable. The main difference is that it is possible to compute statistics for an analysis variable. The ORDER usage for columns at the left side of the page means that the variables determine the order of the rows in the report. Each value of an order column appears only once on the page, even if the value is repeated in several consecutive rows.

This example creates a simple report using four variables from the SAS dataset WORK.VOLCANO, the same SAS dataset shown in the earlier PROC PRINT example.

```
PROC REPORT DATA=WORK.VOLCANO NOWD SPACING=3;
   COLUMN NAME LATITUDE LONGITUDE ELEVATION;
   DEFINE NAME / 'Volcano' ORDER WIDTH=20 LEFT SPACING=8;
   DEFINE LATITUDE / 'Latitude' DISPLAY FORMAT=8.2;
   DEFINE LONGITUDE / 'Longitude' DISPLAY FORMAT=9.2;
   DEFINE ELEVATION / 'Elevation' FORMAT=COMMA9.;
RUN;
```

```
         Volcano               Latitude   Longitude   Elevation
         Arenal                   10.50      -84.70       1,656
         Irazu                     9.98      -83.85       3,431
         Poas                     10.20      -84.20       2,703
         Rincon de la Vieja       10.20      -85.50       1,915
```

These are restrictions on usage in a PROC REPORT step:

- A table report must include at least one order or display column. If a report has only analysis variables, it displays as a summary report with only one row.
- The order columns must be listed first in the COLUMN statement. In a summary report, the group variables must be listed first.

If you use the same variable for multiple columns in a PROC REPORT step, assign an alias to each column. Write an equals sign and the alias after the variable name in the COLUMN statement. Use the alias to identify the column in the DEFINE statement. In the example below, AMOUNT and LEVEL are aliases for RESULT.

```
COLUMN PLACE RESULT=AMOUNT RESULT=LEVEL;
```

One reason to show a column twice is to display it with two diffferent formats.

A label can span two or more columns. Write the label and columns in parentheses in the COLUMN statement. If the first and last characters of a label are hyphens or any of various pairs of symbols, the label is extended on both sides to fill the space available.

Another usage for a column is COMPUTED. A computed variable is computed from variables that appear before it in the COLUMN statement. The code segment that does the computation appears between COMPUTE and ENDCOMP statements in what is called a COMPUTE block.

The COMPUTE statement names the variable it computes. For a character variable, the statement must also indicate the type and length of the variable. After a slash, write CHARACTER to indicate the character data type and LENGTH= with the length of the variable.

A code segment can use most data step statements. It assigns a value to the computed variable. It can also create other variables. A variable created in a code segment is also available in later code segments.

A code segment can use variables that are not shown in the report. List these variables to the left of the computed variable in the COLUMN statement. Use the NOPRINT option in the DEFINE statement to hide the column.

If a column is defined with an alias, you must use the alias to refer to the variable in a code segment.

When you refer to an analysis variable that does not have an alias in a code segment, the reference must combine the variable name and the statistic in this syntax:

variable.statistic

Remember that ANALYSIS is the default usage for a numeric variable. The default statistic is SUM.

Write a BREAK or RBREAK statement to add a summary line at the beginning or end of the report or each page or a group defined by an order variable. The form of the statement is one of the following:

RBREAK BEFORE / *break options*;
RBREAK AFTER / *break options*;
BREAK BEFORE *variable* / *break options*;
BREAK AFTER *variable* / *break options*;
BREAK BEFORE _PAGE_ / *break options*;
BREAK AFTER _PAGE_ / *break options*;

Break options include SUMMARY for a summary line, OL, DOL, UL, and DUL for lines above and below, and SKIP for a blank line below the summary line.

The example below demonstrates some of the more advanced features of the REPORT procedure. It shows the same data as the earlier example, but with changes in the appearance of the report. The computed LONGX and LATX variables show longitude and latitude variables formatted in a more readable way. The computed variable ELEVATIONFT converts elevation to feet. Two spanning headers identify groups of columns. The summary line, created by the RBREAK statement, shows the MEAN statistic computed for the one analysis variable, along with a computed variable.

```
PROC REPORT DATA=WORK.VOLCANO NOWD SPACING=3 HEADLINE;
   COLUMN NAME ('- Location -' LATITUDE LATX LONGITUDE LONGX)
      ('Elevation' ELEVATION ELEVATIONFT);
   DEFINE NAME / 'Volcano' ORDER WIDTH=22 LEFT SPACING=5;
   DEFINE LATITUDE / NOPRINT DISPLAY FORMAT=8.2;
   DEFINE LATX / 'Latitude' COMPUTED WIDTH=9 RIGHT;
   DEFINE LONGITUDE / NOPRINT DISPLAY FORMAT=9.2;
   DEFINE LONGX / 'Longitude' COMPUTED WIDTH=9 RIGHT SPACING=2;
   DEFINE ELEVATION / '(meters)' MEAN FORMAT=COMMA8.;
   DEFINE ELEVATIONFT / '(feet)' COMPUTED FORMAT=COMMA8. SPACING=0;
   COMPUTE LATX / CHARACTER LENGTH=9;
      IF LATITUDE > .Z THEN DO;
         LATX = PUT(ABS(LATITUDE), F6.2);
         IF LATITUDE > 0 THEN SUBSTR(LATX, 8) = 'N.';
         ELSE IF LATITUDE < 0 THEN SUBSTR(LATX, 8) = 'S.';
         END;
      ENDCOMP;
   COMPUTE LONGX / CHARACTER LENGTH=9;
      IF LONGITUDE > .Z THEN DO;
```

```
   LONGX = PUT(ABS(LONGITUDE), F6.2);
   IF LONGITUDE > 0 THEN SUBSTR(LONGX, 8) = 'E.';
   ELSE IF LONGITUDE < 0 THEN SUBSTR(LONGX, 8) = 'W.';
   END;
  ENDCOMP;
 COMPUTE ELEVATIONFT;
  ELEVATIONFT = ELEVATION.MEAN/.3048;
  ENDCOMP;
 RBREAK AFTER / SUMMARIZE OL;
RUN;
```

Volcano	---- Location ---- Latitude	Longitude	Elevation (meters)	(feet)
Arenal	10.50 N.	84.70 W.	1,656	5,433
Irazu	9.98 N.	83.85 W.	3,431	11,257
Poas	10.20 N.	84.20 W.	2,703	8,868
Rincon de la Vieja	10.20 N.	85.50 W.	1,915	6,283
			2,426	7,960

Another example of a PROC REPORT step can be seen at the end of chapter 71, "Compression."

Summary Reports

Most summary reports also are organized in table form. In a summary report, each row represents the summary of a group of observations.

The columns of a summary report are key variables and analysis variables. The key variables identify the group. Analysis variables are numeric variables summarized with descriptive statistics for the observations that form the group. In most business reports, the only statistic used is the sum, computed by simply adding the detail data together.

One way to print a summary report is to summarize the data to create a summary dataset, then print the summary dataset. Chapter 48, "Descriptive Statistics," tells how to create summary data with the SUMMARY procedure.

Another approach is to use the REPORT or TABULATE procedure to compute and print the summary report in a single step. The REPORT procedure can create summary reports in nearly the same way as detail reports. The TABULATE procedure is designed exclusively for printing summary tables. It allows detailed control over the layout of the report.

If you only want to show counts of observations, what you need is a frequency table; see chapter 47.

Creating a summary report in the REPORT procedure depends on the usage of each column. In the DEFINE statement, indicate the GROUP usage for variables that form groups and the ANALYSIS usage for variables used to compute statistics. For an analysis column, list a statistic. SUM is the default statistic.

This example shows a summary report with one group variable, AMAGN. It produces one row for each value of the group variable. The other columns show the statistic N and five analysis variables.

```
PROC REPORT DATA=WORK.PHA NOWD SPACING=2 HEADLINE;
  COLUMN AMAGN N DIAMETER
    ('- Orbit -' PERIHELION APHELION ECCENTRICITY) SM_AXIS;
  DEFINE AMAGN / 'Magnitude' GROUP F=F9. SPACING=0;
  DEFINE N / 'Count' F=5.;
  DEFINE PERIHELION / 'Perihelion' MEAN F=F10.3;
  DEFINE APHELION / 'Aphelion' MEAN F=F8.3;
  DEFINE DIAMETER / 'Diameter' MEAN F=F9.3;
  DEFINE ECCENTRICITY / 'Ecc.' MEAN F=F6.3;
  DEFINE SM_AXIS / 'Semimajor' 'Axis' MEAN F=F9.3;
  RBREAK AFTER / SUMMARIZE OL;
RUN;
```

Magnitude	Count	Diameter	Perihelion	--------- Orbit ---------- Aphelion		Ecc.	Semimajor Axis
14	3	5.333	0.529	3.339	16.300	0.717
15	5	3.812	0.714	3.770	15.560	0.703
16	20	2.359	0.798	2.850	18.540	0.539
17	40	1.511	0.785	3.498	17.880	0.536
18	55	0.967	0.747	2.613	13.638	0.523
19	72	0.619	0.737	2.565	10.197	0.517
20	81	0.388	0.756	2.530	9.093	0.506
21	70	0.250	0.728	2.273	8.411	0.477
22	26	0.172	0.682	2.342	7.681	0.530
	372	0.790	0.744	2.632	11.349	0.516

TABULATE

The TABULATE procedure gives you detailed control over summary table reports. To write a PROC TABULATE step, start with statements to identify the variables. List class variables, those that form groups of observations, in the CLASS statement. List analysis variables, numeric variables used for statistics, in the VAR statement. Write a TABLE statement using these variables to define the table layout.

A table definition consists of two or three dimension definitions which are separated by commas. The last dimension is the column dimension, defining the columns of the table. The next to last dimension is the row dimension. If there are three dimensions, the first is the page dimension; it defines the pages of the report.

A dimension definition combines elements in two different ways.

- If there is a space between two elements, the two elements appear next to each other.
- If there is an asterisk between two elements, the elements are combined in the same column, row, or page. The item on either side of the asterisk can be a list of elements in parentheses. All items in the list are combined with the other element.

The complete definition of a table cell can include any number of class variables and the following elements, each of which can be used only once:

- an analysis variable.
- a statistic. Statistics are used only with analysis variables, except that N and related statistics are usually used without an analysis variable.

• a format, preceded by F=.

It is usually best to place statistics and formats in the column dimension because the format determines the width of the column. The keyword ALL can be used in the definition of a cell in place of a class variable. ALL provides an unclassified summary. The example below demonstrates most of the features mentioned so far and a few more.

```
PROC TABULATE DATA=WORK.PHA F=BEST6.;
   CLASS AMAGN;
   VAR DIAMETER ECCENTRICITY SM_AXIS;
   TABLE AMAGN, N (DIAMETER*F=F6.3 ECCENTRICITY*F=F6.1
      SM_AXIS*F=F7.3)*(MIN MAX)
      / RTSPACE=20 BOX='Potentially Hazardous Asteroids';
   LABEL AMAGN='Absolute Magnitude' DIAMETER='Diameter'
      ECCENTRICITY='Eccentricity' SM_AXIS='Semi-Major Axis';
   KEYLABEL N='Count' MIN='Min' MAX='Max';
RUN;
```

```
-----------------------------------------------------------------------------
|Potentially        |      |     | Diameter    |Eccentricity |Semi-Major Axis|
|Hazardous          |      |     |-------------+-------------+---------------|
|Asteroids          |Count | Min | Max | Min | Max | Min | Max |
|-------------------+------+------+------+------+------+------+------|
|Absolute Magnitude |      |     |     |     |     |     |     |
|-------------------|      |     |     |     |     |     |     |
|14                 |     3| 5.006| 5.751|  6.8| 24.4| 0.636| 0.859|
|-------------------+------+------+------+------+------+------+------|
|15                 |     5| 3.302| 4.564|  0.5| 38.8| 0.634| 0.890|
|-------------------+------+------+------+------+------+------+------|
|16                 |    20| 1.986| 3.010|  2.8| 64.0| 0.299| 0.773|
|-------------------+------+------+------+------+------+------+------|
|17                 |    40| 1.250| 1.896|  1.4| 53.3| 0.144| 0.947|
|-------------------+------+------+------+------+------+------+------|
|18                 |    55| 0.788| 1.194|  1.4| 39.9| 0.075| 0.927|
|-------------------+------+------+------+------+------+------+------|
|19                 |    72| 0.496| 0.752|  0.1| 50.7| 0.090| 0.888|
|-------------------+------+------+------+------+------+------+------|
|20                 |    81| 0.312| 0.474|  1.0| 52.2| 0.132| 0.814|
|-------------------+------+------+------+------+------+------+------|
|21                 |    70| 0.197| 0.298|  0.6| 30.0| 0.065| 0.865|
|-------------------+------+------+------+------+------+------+------|
|22                 |    26| 0.149| 0.188|  0.4| 27.8| 0.248| 0.869|
-----------------------------------------------------------------------------
```

To understand how the TABULATE procedure works, look for the connections between the table definition in the TABLE statement and the labels for the rows and columns. The rows represent all the values of the class variable AMAGN. The columns are the statistics and variables from the column dimension of the table definition.

The KEYLABEL statement provides labels for statistics. In the PROC TABULATE statement, the F= option provides a default format for the table cells. At the end of the TABLE statement, the BOX= option provides text for the box in the upper left corner of the table. The RTSPACE= option sets the width of the row title space, which is used in this example for the variable AMAGN, the only item in the row dimension.

The FORMCHAR= system option controls the rules that the TABULATE procedure prints between cells. See chapter 57, "Print Files," for details.

ODS

ODS, the Output Delivery System, is what converts the output objects from a proc step to print output. With options set in the ODS statement, ODS can also create numerous other formats.

Output objects are primarily tables. They contain data values and formatting, which can include fonts, text formatting, colors, and page layout. When output objects are used to create web pages, they can also contain links.

Data steps also create output objects; see the next chapter, "Data Step Report Programming," for details.

ODS drivers create the various destination formats of ODS. The default Listing destination contains the usual print output. The HTML destination creates web pages, and the Output destination converts tables to SAS data files. There are several more destination formats.

ODS statements turn each destination format on and off and set options for each driver. The following examples describe and show code for common objectives of ODS.

Web page

Open the HTML destination and indicate the file name of the HTML file to create (newpage.html in this example). Then execute the steps that create the output. ODS converts the output to a web page and stores it in the HTML file. Close the HTML destination, and ODS writes the end tags in the HTML file and closes the file.

```
ODS LISTING CLOSE;
ODS HTML FILE="newpage.html";
steps to create output objects
ODS HTML CLOSE;
ODS LISTING;
```

Selected objects

List the objects to include in the ODS SELECT statement before the step that creates the objects. Afterward, reset the list with the keyword ALL. This example prints only the Attributes component of the PROC CONTENTS output for the SAS dataset MAIN.CURRENT.

```
ODS SELECT ATTRIBUTES;
PROC CONTENTS
    DATA=MAIN.CURRENT;
RUN;
ODS SELECT ALL;
```

Tracing

Use the ODS TRACE statement to trace ODS output. Tracing tells you the names of output objects so that you can list them in the ODS SELECT statement. With the Listing destination open, turn tracing on and run the steps that create the output objects. Tracing writes log notes to identify all ODS objects created in the steps. The LISTING option labels the objects in the Listing destination.

```
ODS TRACE ON / LISTING;
steps to create output objects
ODS TRACE OFF;
```

SAS data file

Write an ODS OUTPUT statement to create a SAS data file from an ODS table. Indicate the object name, an equals sign, and the SAS dataset name. Close the Output destination after the object is created.

```
ODS OUTPUT object=SAS dataset;
step to create output table object
ODS OUTPUT CLOSE;
```

■ 59
Data Step Report Programming

A data step can create a report using the FILE and PUT statements — the same statements that create text data files. A data step can produce quick, simple reports with relatively little programming, or you can use data step logic to control every detail of a report.

ODS Tables

Even if you want to create the traditional print output, the easy way to create a simple table in a data step is to create an ODS table. ODS also makes it possible to convert the table to another format, such as HTML.

 To create an ODS table in a data step, define the table columns in the FILE statement and use PUT statements to add rows or cells to the table. In the FILE statement, indicate the PRINT fileref and use the ODS= option to set ODS options that define the table columns. The easiest way to define the columns is as a list of variables. Use the VARIABLES= option to list the variables in order from left to right. You can also set options, such as formats, for each variable. In the PUT statement, the keyword _ODS_ creates a table row and places the value of each ODS variable in its respective column in the table.

The example below computes a loan payment schedule and creates an ODS table of it. Most of the statements in this example are ordinary data step statements to compute the values of the loan table. Only the FILE and PUT statements refer to ODS.

```
DATA _NULL_;
  FILE PRINT ODS=(VARIABLES=(MONTH (FORMAT=F5.)
    PRINCIPAL (FORMAT=COMMA10.2)
    PAYMENT (FORMAT=COMMA8.2) RATE (FORMAT=F8.6)
    INTEREST (FORMAT=COMMA8.2)));
  PRINCIPAL = 100000;
  RATE = .006250;
  N = 12;
  PAYMENT = MORT(PRINCIPAL, ., RATE, N);

  DO MONTH = 1 TO N;
    INTEREST = PRINCIPAL*RATE;
    PUT _ODS_;
```

```
        PRINCIPAL = PRINCIPAL - PAYMENT + INTEREST;
        END;
RUN;
```

MONTH	PRINCIPAL	PAYMENT	RATE	INTEREST
1	100,000.00	8,675.74	0.006250	625.00
2	91,949.26	8,675.74	0.006250	574.68
3	83,848.20	8,675.74	0.006250	524.05
4	75,696.51	8,675.74	0.006250	473.10
5	67,493.87	8,675.74	0.006250	421.84
6	59,239.97	8,675.74	0.006250	370.25
7	50,934.47	8,675.74	0.006250	318.34
8	42,577.07	8,675.74	0.006250	266.11
9	34,167.44	8,675.74	0.006250	213.55
10	25,705.24	8,675.74	0.006250	160.66
11	17,190.16	8,675.74	0.006250	107.44
12	8,621.86	8,675.74	0.006250	53.89

Instead of using the keyword _ODS_ to write a defined set of variables, you can specify the variables to write in the cells of the ODS table row. This also makes it possible to leave a table cell without a value.

The variables you write do not have to be the same ones listed in the VARIABLES= option, but you can only write variables in an ODS table. You cannot write constant values. To add a constant value to an ODS table, assign it to a variable first.

Column pointer controls in ODS refer to table columns rather than character columns. For example, @5 means table column 5; +1 means skip a table column.

You can modify the example above to write the variable RATE only in the first row of the table, leaving the remaining cells in that column with missing values. Replace the PUT statement with these two statements:

```
IF MONTH = 1 THEN PUT MONTH PRINCIPAL PAYMENT RATE INTEREST;
ELSE PUT MONTH PRINCIPAL PAYMENT +1 INTEREST;
```

Text Tables

Print output is limited to just text, but it gives you the greatest control over the layout of the page. At the same time, the data step gives you complete control over the data values, labels, and spacing that make up the report. When you use a data step to create print output, you can place any character in any position on the page for any reason. With the flexibility that the data step gives you, a table report can be much more than just a simple table divided into pages.

These FILE statement options are useful for writing print files:

- *PRINT.* This option indicates that the file is a print file. It adds print control characters to the file and allows you to address the pages that make up the file. (When you use the PRINT fileref for the standard print file, the PRINT option is the default, so you don't have to write PRINT twice in a FILE statement.)

- *COLUMN=.* This option creates a variable that tells you the current column pointer position in the file.
- *TITLES or NOTITLES.* Use one of these options to include title lines in the file or exclude them.
- *FOOTNOTES.* If you use the TITLES option, you can also use the FOOTNOTES option to include footnote lines.
- *OLD or MOD.* If the file already exists, the OLD option tells the data step to replace the previous contents of the file. The MOD option adds more pages to the end of the file.
- *LINESLEFT= or LL=.* This option creates a variable that tells you how many lines are left on the current page, including the current line.

The N=PS (or N=PAGESIZE) option in the FILE statement gives the PUT statement a buffer as large as the entire page instead of the usual single-line buffer. This lets you move around the entire page, from one line to another; you don't have to write the various elements of the page in any particular order.

With the N=PS option, you can use the # pointer control with a numeric value to go to a specific line on the page. In the FILE statement, you can use the LINE= option to create a variable that tells you the current line on the page.

Use the _PAGE_ keyword in the PUT statement to start each new page. Several other actions are necessary for each new page. If you are using page numbers, you must count the new page for page numbering purposes. After it starts the new page, the PUT statement must write the column headers and any other constant text on the page. If the program does any processing of pages, statements that initialize variables for the page must execute at the same time. All these new page actions can be contained in a DO block, as shown in this code model:

```
DO;
  PAGENO + 1;
  PUT _PAGE_ headers ;
  other statements to initialize page
  END;
```

The program must keep track of its position on the page and advance to a new page before it reaches the end of the page. Otherwise, the PUT statement might automatically advance to a new page when it reaches the end of a page. If this happens, the new page would not contain the headers it needs, and the page numbers and other page processing would be incorrect.

If each observation appears as one line in the report, you can use the LL= variable in the condition for starting a new page. Write the option LL=LL in the FILE statement, then use this page break logic:

```
IF _N_ = 1 OR LL <= 1 DO;
  PAGENO + 1;
  PUT _PAGE_  . . . ;
  . . .
  END;
```

In the condition, _N_ = 1 checks for the first observation in order to write headers and other page text on the first page.

For some reports, other conditions are necessary to control page breaks.

- If each observation takes more than one line, compare LL to the number of lines needed. For example, use this condition if the observation takes 2 lines.

  LL <= 2

- To put BY groups on separate pages in the report, add the FIRST. variable to the condition, for example:

  FIRST.GROUP OR LL <= 1

- If there are lines for totals at the end of the BY group, add those lines to the number needed for the last observation in the BY group. If the totals take 2 lines, you might use this condition:

  LL <= 1 + LAST.GROUP*2

- Sometimes the idea is not to put BY groups on separate pages, but to put each BY group on a single page whenever possible. To do this, you need to have a variable that indicates the number of lines the BY group requires — which is usually the number of observations in the BY group. For an explanation of the steps required to create such a variable, see chapter 49, "Summary Statistics in Computations." If GROUP is the BY variable, GRPSIZE is the number of lines needed for the group, and 43 is the number of lines available on a page, then use a condition such as this one:

  LL <= 1 OR (FIRST.GROUP AND GRPSIZE < 43 AND GRPSIZE < LL)

- If you use the PUT statement to write footnotes or other text at the bottom of the page, save lines for the footnotes, including a blank line above the footnotes. Advance to the next page before you get to the footnotes. If the observation takes one line and you want to save 5 lines for footnotes, use this condition:

  LL <= 6

  This is necessary only if you use the data step to write the footnotes; if you use FOOTNOTE statements and the FOOTNOTES option to write the same footnote lines on every page, those lines are not available to the PUT statement and are not counted in the LL= variable.

With the approach described above for page breaks, a table row cannot be written on the last line of the page. If it is important to use the last line of the page, use one of the following approaches:

- Write a trailing @ at the end of the PUT statement and use the / pointer control at the beginning of the PUT statement to advance to the next line.
- Use the last line and allow the PUT statement to advance automatically to the next page. Check the LINE= variable for a value of 1 and initialize the page (without writing a page break) if this condition is true. This approach works only when each observation provides only one line of the report.

The statement that writes the headers on the page can write other elements anywhere on the page, including:

- titles, identifying information, and BY group variables at the top of the page
- footnotes and other notes at the bottom of the page
- page numbers
- rules

At the end of the statement that writes the page elements, move the pointer so that it will be in position to write the first table row. For example, if the first table row is on line 5, you could end the statement that writes the page elements with:

#4;

The pointer, positioned on line 4, automatically advances to the next line, line 5, at the end of the PUT statement.

It makes it easier to set up a table if you use variables for the column pointer locations. Examples in this chapter use the letters A, B, C, etc., similar to the way these letters identify the columns of a spreadsheet. Define the column locations in a RETAIN statement, for example:

RETAIN A 1 B 11 C 25 D 39 E 53 F 67;

In the PUT statement, use the column-location variables with the @ pointer control. For example, this term writes the variable CHANGE in the third column of the table:

@C CHANGE F8.2

With this approach, if you need to adjust the locations of the columns, you only need to change the RETAIN statement.

To create an ordinary table, use a PUT statement to write the table cells for each observation and write the page breaks and page text as described above.

The example below prints a standard table of data from the SAS dataset WORK.SETUP with column headers on each page.

```
DATA _NULL_;
  RETAIN A 8  B 19  C 32  D 42  E 52;
  SET WORK.SETUP;
  FILE PRINT N=PS LL=LL LINE=LINE;
  * Page break and header ;
  IF LL <= 1 OR _N_ = 1 THEN PUT _PAGE_ @D 'Setup'
    / @A 'Section' @B 'Equipment' @C ' Power' @D ' Time' @E 'Weight'
    /;
  * Table row ;
  PUT @A DEPT $CHAR8. @B EQUIP $CHAR10. @C POWER F6.
    @D SETUP F5. @E WEIGHT F6.;
RUN;
```

Section	Equipment	Power	Setup Time	Weight
Audio	FOH	9300	8	2500
Audio	Monitor	1800	2	500
Audio	Fill	800	2	200
Audio	Stage	400	9	500
Lights	Overhead	32500	9	1400
Lights	Stage	10000	4	500
Lights	House	40000	0	0
Video	Projector	5000	1	100
Video	Playback	100	1	100

The column headers are written in a single PUT statement. Column D has two lines of headers. Notice the leading spaces in some of the header text to make those column headers line up with the right side of the table columns. The blank line after the column headers is produced by the / at the end of the statement.

The statement that writes the header could also be written as:

```
IF LINE = 1 THEN PUT @D 'Setup'
  / @A 'Section' @B 'Equipment' @C ' Power' @D ' Time' @E 'Weight'
  /;
```

When this statement is written this way, the data step can write a table row on the last line of the page.

 Most data steps that create reports use the special SAS dataset name _NULL_ in the DATA statement to indicate no output SAS dataset for the data step. Use the name _NULL_ in the DATA statement whenever a data step does not create a SAS dataset.

 There is little reason to create a simple table, such as the one in the previous example, as a text table because it is easier to create the table as an ODS table, as described at the beginning of the chapter. Create a text table in order to add other features to the table, such as those shown in the example below. This example adds page numbers and subtotals for BY groups.

```
DATA _NULL_;
  RETAIN A 8  B 19  C 32  D 42  E 52;
  SET WORK.SETUP;
  BY DEPT;
  IF FIRST.DEPT THEN DO;
    SP = 0;
    SS = 0;
    SW = 0;
    END;
  FILE PRINT N=PS LL=LL LINE=LINE;
  IF _N_ = 1 OR LL <= 1 + 2*LAST.DEPT THEN DO;
    PAGENO + 1;
    PUT _PAGE_ 'Show Setup' / 'Page ' PAGENO
      // @D 'Setup'
      / @A 'Section' @B 'Equipment' @C ' Power' @D ' Time' @E 'Weight'
      /;
    END;
  IF FIRST.DEPT OR LINE <= 7 THEN PUT @A DEPT $CHAR8. @;
```

```
PUT @B EQUIP $CHAR10. @C POWER F6. @D SETUP F5. @E WEIGHT F6.;

* Subtotals ;
SP + POWER;
SS + SETUP;
SW + WEIGHT;
IF LAST.DEPT THEN DO;
   PUT @C '------' @D '-----' @E '------'
      / @C SP F6. @D SS F5. @E SW F6.;
   IF LL > 1 THEN PUT;
   END;
RUN;
```

```
Show Setup
Page 1
```

			Setup	
Section	Equipment	Power	Time	Weight
Audio	FOH	9300	8	2500
	Monitor	1800	2	500
	Fill	800	2	200
	Stage	400	9	500
		------	-----	------
		12300	21	3700
Lights	Overhead	32500	9	1400
	Stage	10000	4	500
	House	40000	0	0
		------	-----	------
		82500	13	1900
Video	Projector	5000	1	100
	Playback	100	1	100
		------	-----	------
		5100	2	200

The variables SP, SS, and SW are the subtotals. Notice that the subtotals are written in the same column positions with the same formats as the detail variables. A summary line could show any statistic; see chapter 48, "Descriptive Statistics," for more about computing statistics in a data step.

The statement

```
IF FIRST.DEPT OR LINE <= 7 THEN PUT @A DEPT $CHAR8. @;
```

writes the DEPT value only at the beginning of a BY group or on the first table row of a page. The trailing @ in this statement keeps the pointer on the same line.

The statement

```
IF LL > 1 THEN PUT;
```

writes a blank line after the summary line. The condition LL > 1 prevents the blank line if there is not sufficient room for it at the end of the page.

 If you use the TITLES and FOOTNOTES options to write title lines and footnote lines in a report, the number of lines available to the data step is less than the page size set in the PAGESIZE= system option. Lines on the page that are used for the title and footnote lines are not available to the data step. This is especially important to know if you use the LINE= variable to measure your position on the page.

Some tables can be made easier to read by leaving a blank line after every five data lines in the table. The number five is selected for this because of the human ability to instantly recognize quantities up to five. Use the LINE=LINE option in the FILE statement. Check the value of LINE for every observation, and if it is one of the lines you want to leave blank, execute a PUT statement with no terms to advance to the next line. For example, if the table rows appear on lines 5 through 51 on the page, adding a blank line after every five lines means leaving lines 10, 16, 22, 28, 34, 40, and 46 blank. Use this statement:

IF 5 <= LINE <= 51 AND MOD(LINE, 6) = 4 THEN PUT;

In some data, a single observation takes up an entire report page. This can happen, for example, if a two-dimensional array provides the variables for a table. Write all the elements of the page — a page break, the column headers, and the data — in every observation.

When a data step or proc step processes a SAS dataset, the step does not do any processing if there are no observations in the SAS dataset. For a step that produces a report, this means that no report is produced. If the lack of a report presents a problem, the solution is a data step that writes an alternate report whenever the input SAS dataset has no observations.

This can be a short, simple data step with statements to check the number of observations and a FILE and PUT statement to write the report if there are no observations. The example below writes a page with the message NO DATA TO REPORT if there are no observations in the SAS dataset WORK.T.

```
DATA _NULL_;
  DSID = OPEN('WORK.T');
  IF DSID THEN NOBS = ATTRN(DSID, 'NLOBS');
  ELSE NOBS = .;
  RC = CLOSE(DSID);
  IF NOBS <= 0;
  FILE PRINT TITLES FOOTNOTES;
  PUT #15 @21 'NO DATA TO REPORT';
  STOP;
RUN;
```

Execute this step immediately before or after the step that produces the data report. If a proc step generates the regular report, the TITLES and FOOTNOTES options give the alternate report the same title and footnote lines. If appropriate, add headers, rules, or other constant text from the data report to the PUT statement to make the alternate report appear as another version of the same report.

The ATTRN function with the NLOBS attribute code returns the number of observations in the SAS dataset. The subsetting IF statement stops processing the step if there are observations.

These are other possibilities for reporting in the data step:

- *Multiple rows.* Write each observation as multiple table rows if that makes sense. Consider leaving a blank line between observations.

- *Columns.* For some kinds of data, it makes more sense to write each observation as a column rather than a row. For example, people looking at trends usually expect to trace the passage of time from left to right in a report. If observations represent time periods, displaying them as columns allows the reader to view the data this way.

  Use the # pointer control to move from one line to the next. Use a variable to keep track of the table columns you have used on the page. Advance to the next table column for each observation, or advance to the next page after a page is filled.

- *Cells.* An observation might write just one cell in a table. In this kind of data, it takes a BY group to write a complete row. Alternatively, the BY group might form a column of the table.

- *Data-dependent footnotes.* In some reports, each footnote should appear only on pages in which observations refer to it. Use an array of temporary variables to keep track of the footnotes that are used in the page's data. Reset these variables at the beginning of each page. Keep track of the number of footnote lines needed. Save enough lines at the bottom of the page to write the footnotes, and write the footnotes after writing the last observation on the page.

- *Panels.* If a report uses less than half the width of the page, you can divide the page into panels and write a table section in each panel in turn, similar to the way this is done in a PROC REPORT step.

- *Tiling.* A data step can extend a table across multiple pages that are designed to be viewed side-by-side. This could require elaborate control flow techniques or data manipulation to get the data in the right sequence for printing.

- *Mailing labels.* Mailing labels and similar rectangular form units can be created by giving each observation multiple lines, but a fraction of the width of the page.

- *Multiple reports.* A single data step can write multiple report files. Two reports could show the same data values formatted in different ways, or valid data could be displayed in one report and exceptions in another. Write a separate FILE statement and PUT statements for each report.

- *Markup.* A data step can write markup file formats such as HTML or XML by writing the text and tags.

- *E-mail.* With the EMAIL device, a data step can write its results directly into e-mail messages.

- *Separate files for BY groups.* A single data step can create a separate report file for each BY group. Use the technique described in chapter 56, "Multiple Text Files," based on the FILEVAR= option. Reset the page number variable at the beginning of each BY group.

- *Prose.* Data steps are also very good at creating text in prose form, in which the data values are formed into phrases or sentences. A data step can mix tables and prose on the same report page. See chapter 66, "Control Reports," for examples of constructing prose. If sentences could be longer than a single line, see chapter 40, "Character Loops," for word wrap logic.

■ 60

Data Step Views

A data step view is a program and a SAS dataset. It is stored as a program, but when you are looking for data, it is a SAS dataset. The idea of a view is to create a SAS dataset from data that already exists without having to store the same data again. A data step view is the easiest kind of view to create because you write it as an ordinary data step.

Using a data step view can be more efficient because the data step view uses very little storage space and takes very little time to store. Another reason to use a view is to get the latest possible version of the data. The data step view does not read the data it works with until you read the resulting data from the data step view.

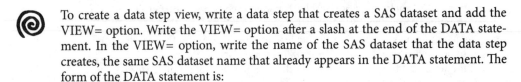

To create a data step view, write a data step that creates a SAS dataset and add the VIEW= option. Write the VIEW= option after a slash at the end of the DATA statement. In the VIEW= option, write the name of the SAS dataset that the data step creates, the same SAS dataset name that already appears in the DATA statement. The form of the DATA statement is:

DATA *SAS dataset* / VIEW=*SAS dataset*;

The step that creates a data step view does not take any action with the data values of the data step view; it only stores the data step program for later use. However, any input SAS dataset that the step uses must exist so that the data step view can incorporate the correct variable attributes.

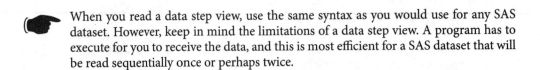

When you read a data step view, use the same syntax as you would use for any SAS dataset. However, keep in mind the limitations of a data step view. A program has to execute for you to receive the data, and this is most efficient for a SAS dataset that will be read sequentially once or perhaps twice.

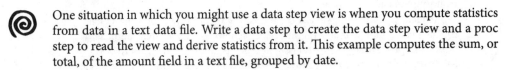

One situation in which you might use a data step view is when you compute statistics from data in a text data file. Write a data step to create the data step view and a proc step to read the view and derive statistics from it. This example computes the sum, or total, of the amount field in a text file, grouped by date.

```
DATA WORK.NEWTRANS / VIEW=WORK.NEWTRANS;
  INFILE TRANS;
```

```
   INPUT DATE : YYMMDD6. ID : $F18. AMOUNT;
   FORMAT DATE MMDDYY5.;
RUN;
PROC SUMMARY DATA=WORK.NEWTRANS PRINT SUM;
   CLASS DATE;
   VAR _NUMERIC_;
RUN;
```

A data step view cannot replace a different kind of SAS dataset. That is, if a SAS dataset of the same name already exists, and it is not a data step view, then you will not be able to store the data step view. SAS writes a series of error messages:

```
ERROR: Unable to create WORK.NOWAY.VIEW because WORK.NOWAY.DATA
       already exists.
ERROR: Unable to save DATA STEP view WORK.NOWAY.
NOTE: The SAS System stopped processing this step because of errors.
```

To avoid this error, delete the old SAS dataset before you create the data step view or use a different name for the data step view. See chapter 8, "Actions on SAS Datasets," for details of deleting SAS datasets.

It is possible to store the source code in a data step view. To do this, write the SOURCE=SAVE option in parentheses after the name in the VIEW= option:

DATA SAS *dataset* / VIEW=*SAS dataset* (SOURCE=SAVE);

Later, to retrieve the source code, use this step:

DATA VIEW=*SAS dataset*;
   DESCRIBE;
RUN;

The step writes the view's source code in the log.

Two dataset options affect details of the way a data step view is used. The OBSBUF= dataset option determines how many observations are generated at one time. For example, with OBSBUF=1000, the program generates 1000 observations each time it is accessed. This means the SAS supervisor does not have to switch back and forth between the data step view and the other programs as often as it would if the view generated only one observation at a time. Use a larger value to speed up processing; use a smaller value to conserve memory. If it is important to generate only one observation at a time, use OBSBUF=1.

The SPILL= option controls the use of a spill file, a temporary file that stores the observations of the data step view after the view program has run. The spill file is kept until the end of the step. Using a spill file will speed up some processes involving data step views, but will slow down others. Use the SPILL=YES option to write all the observations in the spill file. Use the SPILL=NO option to write a SPILL file only to the extent necessary. For example, with BY group processing, the spill file contains the entire BY group, even if you indicate SPILL=NO. If you use the SPILL=NO option, some processes may execute the data step view program twice in order to read the data twice.

■ 61

Macro Variables

Macro variables are variables that you can use to form SAS statements. A macro variable reference is written with an ampersand before the macro variable name. If the value of the macro variable ACTIVITY is Reconciliation, then this statement:

TITLE1 "Operating Budget: &ACTIVITY";

is evaluated to form this statement:

TITLE1 "Operating Budget: Reconciliation";

Macro variables and other macro objects are evaluated, or resolved, by a routine called the macro processor. The macro processor maintains many automatic macro variables, and you can create any number of macro variables to use in a program.

The word *symbol* sometimes refers to macro variables, especially in log messages and in the names of system options.

Assigning Values

You do not need to take any special action to create a macro variable. You can create the variable just by assigning a value to it. The macro statement that assigns a value to a macro variable is the %LET statement. Write the keyword %LET, the macro variable name, an equals sign, and text to assign to the macro variable. This macro variable assigns the value Seven Year Forecast to the macro variable ACTIVITY:

%LET ACTIVITY = Seven Year Forecast;

A macro variable reference can appear as part of the text in the %LET statement. This statement gives the macro variable PLACE the same value as the macro variable LOC:

%LET PLACE = &LOC;

To assign a null value to a macro variable, write a %LET statement with no text. Write the semicolon to mark the end of the statement right after the equals sign in the statement. This statement assigns a null value to the macro variable OTHER:

%LET OTHER = ;

If the text contains certain special characters, especially semicolons, it might be necessary to use macro quoting to ensure that the special characters are treated as part of the value. Usually, the macro quoting function %STR is sufficient. This statement assigns two complete SAS statements to the macro variable SUBTITLE:

%LET SUBTITLE = %STR(TITLE2 'Latest Month';
TITLE3 'Preliminary';);

The %STR function also makes it possible to assign a value that contains leading or trailing spaces. This statement assigns a value that includes two spaces to the macro variable SYMBOL:

%LET SYMBOL = %STR(+);

Without the %STR function, the %LET statement removes leading and trailing spaces before it assigns a value to the macro variable.

The %STR quoting function is especially useful when you are assigning values to macro variables. The %QUOTE function provides macro quoting for most other circumstances, and there are other macro quoting functions for specialized purposes.

To give a macro variable a value from a data step, use the SYMPUTX routine. In the first argument, provide the macro variable name as a character value. In the second argument, provide a character or numeric value to assign to the macro variable. This example creates the macro variable THISYEAR that contains the current year:

DATA _NULL_;
  YEAR = YEAR(DATE());
  CALL SYMPUTX('THISYEAR', YEAR);
RUN;

The SYMPUTX routine removes leading and trailing spaces from the value it assigns to the macro variable. To assign a value that might contain leading and trailing spaces to a macro variable, use the SYMPUT routine instead. The SYMPUT routine is similar to the SYMPUTX routine, but it requires a character value and does not remove leading and trailing spaces.

Macro variables that belong to a specific macro (see about macros in the next chapter) are local macro variables. Other macro variables are global macro variables. If you create a macro variable in a macro and want to make it a global macro variable, list it in a %GLOBAL statement. To be sure that a macro variable used in a macro is local to that macro, list it in a %LOCAL statement. This example declares two global and two local macro variables:

%GLOBAL COMPANY DEPT;
%LOCAL N X;

Usually, it is not necessary to delete macro variables. Local macro variables disappear when the macro ends, global macro variables when the SAS session ends. However, if there is a reason to delete a global macro variable, list the macro variable name in the %SYMDEL statement. This example deletes the macro variable THISYEAR:

%SYMDEL THISYEAR;

If the macro variable does not exist, the macro processor writes a warning message in the log. To delete global macro variables that might or might not exist, add the NOWARN option after a slash at the end of the statement, for example:

%SYMDEL LASTYEAR / NOWARN;

Obtaining Values

To show the value of a macro variable, write a %PUT statement that contains a reference to the macro variable. The %PUT statement writes a line in the log. This example writes the value of the macro variable SYSLIBRC.

%PUT &SYSLIBRC;

0

A %PUT statement can include a combination of macro variables and other text, as shown in this example:

%LET MIN = 1;
%LET MAX = 10;
%PUT Selected range: from &MIN to &MAX;

Selected range: from 1 to 10

It is sometimes necessary to use macro quoting in the %PUT statement. This makes it possible to write special characters such as semicolons. Usually, you can use either the %STR or %QUOTE function for macro quoting in the %PUT statement. This example uses the %QUOTE function to write a semicolon:

%PUT Range minimum: &MIN%QUOTE(;) Range maximum: &MAX;

Range minimum: 1; Range maximum: 10

To see the text that results when macro variables in a SAS statement are resolved, copy the entire statement into a %PUT statement, as shown in this example:

%PUT OPTIONS LINESIZE=&LS PAGESIZE=&PS CENTER=&CENTER PAGENO=&PAGE;

OPTIONS LINESIZE=75 PAGESIZE=60 CENTER=0 PAGENO=16

The log message shows the actual OPTIONS statement that would execute after the macro variables are resolved, except for the statement's final semicolon; the semicolon you see in the program line just marks the end of the %PUT statement.

Does a macro variable have leading or trailing spaces? Write it with punctuation immediately before and after the value to find out:

%PUT [&SYMBOL];

[+]

With the punctuation in this example, it is easy to see that the value of SYMBOL contains one leading space and one trailing space.

To see what macro variables are defined, use the special keyword _ALL_ in the %PUT statement:

%PUT _ALL_;

The statement writes the names and values of all macro variables. Other keywords, _GLOBAL_, _AUTOMATIC_, _USER_, and _LOCAL_, are available to display subsets of the available macro variables.

Does a macro variable exist? Find out with the %SYMEXIST macro function, which returns 1 if the argument is the name of a macro variable, or 0 otherwise. For example %SYMEXIST(SYMBOL) resolves to 1 if the macro variable SYMBOL exists. In a data step, use the SYMEXIST function in the same way; for example, SYMEXIST('SYMBOL'). To check specifically for a local or global macro variable, use SYMLOCAL or SYMGLOBL instead of SYMEXIST.

Use the SYMGET function to obtain the value of a macro variable in a data step. Provide the name of the macro variable as the argument of the function. The function returns a character value that contains the entire text of the macro variable. This example assigns the value of the macro variable THISYEAR to the data step variable YEARTEXT.

```
DATA _NULL_;
  LENGTH YEARTEXT $ 4;
  YEARTEXT = SYMGET('THISYEAR');
  PUT YEARTEXT=;
RUN;
```

With the SYMPUTX routine and SYMGET function, macro variables can be used to convey parameters, results, and other information items from one data step to another.

10 Automatic Macro Variables

Created automatically by the macro processor, automatic macro variables contain general information about the SAS session. These are 10 of the most valuable automatic macro variables.

★ **SYSDATE9.** The date of the SAS session.

★ **SYSTIME.** The time of day of the SAS session.

★ **SYSDAY.** The day of the week of the SAS session.

★ **SYSVER.** The SAS release number.

★ **SYSVLONG.** The long form of the SAS release number, including the technical support level.

★ **SYSSCP.** An abbreviation that identifies the operating system.

★ **SYSSCPL.** An abbreviation that supplies more details of the operating system environment.

★ **SYSSITE.** The SAS site number.

★ **SYSMAXLONG.** The maximum value of a long integer. This is the maximum value allowed for many system options.

★ **SYSUSERID.** The user ID associated with the SAS session.

To see a list of all automatic macro variables, use this statement:

%PUT _AUTOMATIC_;

Macro variable references are used mostly in SAS statements and commands. Write the macro variable reference at the point where you want to substitute the macro variable value. In this example, two of the terms in a DO statement are supplied by macro variables:

DO INT = &LOW TO &HIGH;

If LOW is 7 and HIGH is 16, the statement resolves to:

DO INT = 7 TO 16;

If a macro variable reference is followed immediately by a character that could be part of a macro variable reference, you must add a period to mark the end of the macro variable reference. The period is necessary if the character that follows the reference is a letter, underscore, digit, or period. This example shows the use of periods in macro variable references:

AMPERSAND TROUBLE

If a SAS statement contains a reference to a macro variable that does not exist, the macro processor provides a warning message in the log such as:

```
WARNING: Apparent symbolic reference
NEWS not resolved.
```

Turn the system option SERROR off to suppress this log message.

The warning message is usually accompanied by a syntax error as the ampersand and macro variable name are not the terms expected in the SAS statement.

Conversely, if you intend to write an ampersand in a program, the macro processor could interpret the ampersand as a macro variable reference. To steer clear of problems with ampersands:

- Use the word AND rather than an ampersand when writing the AND operator.
- Write a space after an ampersand in an INPUT statement.
- Enclose a character constant that contains an ampersand character in single quotes. When you use single quotes, the macro processor does not look for macro objects in the quoted string.

PROC PRINT DATA=&SERIES.X&SERIAL..OWNERS;

If SERIES is M and SERIAL is 814, the statement resolves as

PROC PRINT DATA=MX814.OWNERS;

When a SAS statement contains a macro variable, the statement appears in the log with the macro variable reference. The log does not, by default, show the value that the macro processor substitutes for the macro variable. You might need to see the value of the macro variable to know exactly what is happening when a program executes or to determine the causes of errors that occur. To show the value of each macro variable reference in a separate log note, use the SYMBOLGEN (or SGEN) system option.

■ 62

Macros

Macros are program objects that can be used to assemble the text of part of a SAS program. Macros are defined with macro statements and are stored as catalog entries.

Like macro variables, macros contain text that is used to form SAS programs, but macros are larger than macro variables. A macro variable might form part of a statement, but a macro is flexible enough to form several steps or an entire program.

To define a macro, write the text of the macro between %MACRO and %MEND statements. Write the macro name in the %MACRO statement. This is a model of the code to define a macro.

```
%MACRO name;
text
%MEND;
```

The process of defining a macro is also called compiling, but this process is different from the usual idea of compiling a program.

Write a reference to a macro with a percent sign and the macro name. This is also called calling or invoking the macro.

```
%name
```

Parameters

To add flexibility to a macro, define it with parameters. Parameters are text values that are supplied when the macro is called. They are referred to as macro variables inside the macro. The names of the macro variables are provided in the %MACRO statement when the macro is defined.

In the %MACRO statement, write the parameter names in parentheses after the macro name. If there are multiple parameters, separate them with commas. This example defines the macro IDLIST with one parameter, DATA.

```
%MACRO IDLIST(DATA);
PROC SORT DATA=&DATA (KEEP=ID) OUT=IDLIST NODUPKEY;
   BY ID;
RUN;
%MEND;
```

This is an example of calling the macro:

%IDLIST(WORK.NEW)

When the macro processor resolves the macro, it substitutes the supplied parameter value, WORK.NEW, for the macro variable reference &DATA in the macro. The macro generates this SAS step:

```
PROC SORT DATA=WORK.NEW (KEEP=ID) OUT=IDLIST NODUPKEY;
  BY ID;
RUN;
```

Do not write parentheses in a reference to a macro if the macro was not defined with parameters. This technique has been recommended in various places in macro language literature, but it results in a syntax error after the macro processor does not recognize the parentheses. If you must use parentheses in a macro reference, define the macro with at least one parameter, even if the parameter is never used for anything.

If the text of a macro parameter contains any character that could confuse the macro processor, such as a comma or equals sign, you must use a macro quoting function to enclose the parameter value. In most cases, you can use the %QUOTE macro function for quoting. This is an example:

%RRANGE(%QUOTE(10,000),%QUOTE(25,000))

This macro reference calls the macro RRANGE with the parameters 10,000 and 25,000. The parameters contain commas, but the %QUOTE function ensures that the commas are treated as part of the parameter text.

The parameters in the previous examples are positional parameters. The positions of the parameters in the macro call determine which parameter is which. Another kind of parameter is a keyword parameter. In the %MACRO statement, the name of a keyword parameter is followed an equals sign and a default value for the parameter. This code model shows a macro definition for a macro with keyword parameters:

```
%MACRO name(parameter=default, parameter=default, . . . );
text
%MEND;
```

In the macro reference, write the parameter name and the value for the parameter. You can write keyword parameters in any order in the macro reference, and you can omit any of the parameters to use their default values. This is a code model for a macro reference with keyword parameters:

%name(parameter=value, parameter=value, . . .)

Write the parentheses in the macro reference even if you omit all the parameters. That is, to use the macro with the default value for every parameter, write the macro reference this way:

%name()

The example below is a revision of the previous IDLIST example. It adds two more parameters. When you use keyword parameters, it is easy to add parameters because the macro references do not have to mention every parameter.

```
%MACRO VAL(DATA=_LAST_, OUT=_DATA_, KEY=);
PROC SORT DATA=&DATA (KEEP=&KEY) OUT=&OUT NODUPKEY;
   BY &KEY;
RUN;
%MEND;
```

This is an example of a reference to the VAL macro:

```
%VAL(DATA=WORK.NEW, OUT=WORK.LIST, KEY=ID)
```

With this reference, the VAL macro generates these statements:

```
PROC SORT DATA=WORK.NEW (KEEP=ID) OUT=WORK.LIST NODUPKEY;
   BY ID;
RUN;
```

 To make keyword parameters easier to work with, name them using keywords and option names from SAS syntax when you can. For example, use DATA for a parameter that identifies an input SAS dataset, OUT for an output SAS dataset, VAR for a list of variables to process, and so on. In some cases, you can also use the defaults that are conventional in SAS syntax, for example, DATA=_LAST_. Instances of this can be seen in the previous example.

 If you are unsure about whether to use positional parameters or keyword parameters when you define a macro, this is what I suggest. Use positional parameters for a macro that resembles a function or CALL routine. Positional parameters are similar in style to the arguments that functions and CALL routines use. Use keyword parameters for a macro that is more like a statement or step. Keyword parameters are more similar in style to the statement options that serve a similar purpose in many SAS statements and in the PROC statement of proc steps.

 Inside the macro, parameters are macro variables. They are local macro variables, existing only as long as it takes to resolve the macro. Other macro variables you create in the macro are also local macro variables unless you declare them first in a %GLOBAL statement. When the macro ends, the local macro variables no longer exist.

Macro Control Flow

In addition to text and macro variables, a macro can contain macro statements. Most macro statements fall into these two categories:

- *Actions on macro objects or the SAS environment.* For example, the %LET statement assigns a value to a macro variable; the %PUT statement writes a log message. These statements can be used in macros or outside of macros. For more information on action-type macro statements, see the next chapter, "Macro Programming."

- *Macro control flow statements that affect the way a macro generates text.* They can also be used to control the actions of other macro statements in a macro. The %IF and %DO statements are examples of macro control flow statements. These macro statements can be used only inside a macro and are described below.

Macro control flow statements use the same keywords as data step control flow statements: IF, THEN, DO, TO, BY, END, GOTO, and RETURN. It is easy to tell macro statements from data step statements, though. A percent sign always precedes a macro keyword.

Use the %IF-%THEN statement to generate text conditionally in a macro. This is an example:

PROC SORT DATA=&DATA %IF &OUT NE %THEN OUT=&OUT; NOEQUALS;

The condition in the %IF-%THEN statement, &OUT NE , tests for a nonblank value of the macro variable OUT. If OUT has a nonblank value, the condition is true. Then, the %IF-%THEN statement generates the text OUT=&OUT. Notice that the semicolon that follows this text is the end of the %IF-%THEN statement; it is not the end of the PROC SORT statement that the macro is generating. As a result of the %IF-%THEN statement, the statement could be either

PROC SORT DATA=&DATA OUT=&OUT NOEQUALS;

or

PROC SORT DATA=&DATA NOEQUALS;

In either case, the macro variables are then resolved to arrive at the actual text that the macro generates.

The %IF-%THEN statement is usually used together with the %DO and %END statements to generate statements or other blocks of text conditionally. Use the %DO and %END statements statements to delineate the block of text. This example generates a PROC SORT step if the ORDER parameter has the value SORT.

```
%IF &ORDER = SORT %THEN %DO;
PROC SORT DATA=WORK.MARK;
  BY CODE;
RUN;
%END;
```

The text inside the %DO block is either generated or not, depending on the condition in the %IF-%THEN statement.

Use a %ELSE statement to generate other text if the condition of a %IF-%THEN statement is false. This example generates a SET statement that reads WORK.BEST if it exists, or WORK.ALT otherwise.

```
%IF %SYSFUNC(EXIST(WORK.BEST, DATA)) %THEN %DO;
   SET WORK.BEST;
%END;
%ELSE %DO;
   SET WORK.ALT;
%END;
```

The macro expression %SYSFUNC(EXIST(WORK.BEST, DATA)) checks for the existence of the SAS data file WORK.BEST.

This same macro logic could be written without the %DO blocks, as shown below (although most programmers find it harder to read this way).

```
SET
   %IF %SYSFUNC(EXIST(WORK.BEST, DATA)) %THEN WORK.BEST;
   %ELSE WORK.ALT;
   ;
```

Use a %IF-%THEN statement with a %RETURN statement to stop a macro if its parameters are incorrect or if objects it needs do not exist. The example below adds simple parameter checking to the earlier VAL example. It tests each parameter to make sure it is not blank. If one of the parameters is blank, the macro does not generate any text.

```
%MACRO VAL(DATA=_LAST_, OUT=_DATA_, KEY=);
%IF (&DATA = ) OR (&OUT = ) %THEN %RETURN;
%IF &KEY = %THEN %RETURN;

PROC SORT DATA=&DATA (KEEP=&KEY) OUT=&OUT NODUPKEY;
   BY &KEY;
RUN;
%MEND;
```

The %GOTO statement can be used with a macro label in a similar way to skip over parts of a macro. Write a macro label as a percent sign, name, and colon:

%label:

In a macro, use a %DO statement with iteration controls to generate text repeatedly. This simple example generates a sequence of 25 asterisks:

```
%DO I = 1 %TO 25;*%END;
```

The index variable is a macro variable that can be used in the generated text. For example, to generate the statement

```
DATA WORK.X10 WORK.X20 WORK.X30 WORK.X40 WORK.X50 WORK.X60
WORK.X70;
```

you could use this macro code:

```
DATA %DO I = 10 %TO 70 %BY 10; WORK.X&I %END;;
```

Be sure to include the final semicolon that marks the end of the DATA statement!

Managing Macros

After you define a macro, it is available for use for the rest of the SAS session. You can use a macro any number of times.

If you define and use a macro within the same program, write the macro definition before the macro reference. If you define a macro in the autoexec file, it is available for use anywhere in the SAS session.

If you refer to a macro that is not defined, the macro processor writes a log message stating that the macro was not recognized. This is usually accompanied by a syntax error message, as the intended macro reference does not form a valid SAS statement. This is an example of log notes for an incorrect macro reference:

```
118   %A
      -
      180
WARNING: Apparent invocation of macro A not resolved.
ERROR 180-322: Statement is not valid or it is used out of proper order.
```

To avoid confusion about macro references:

- If you write a percent sign as part of the text of a quoted string, enclose the string in single quotes. The macro processor does not check the text of quoted strings enclosed in single quotes. This is a special concern in TITLE statements, variable labels, and the FORMAT procedure.
- Do not give a macro the same name as a macro keyword, a macro function, or a SAS System macro.

If you need to suppress the macro processor's warning message about a macro reference that is not recognized, turn off the MERROR system option.

A dummy macro takes no actions and generates no SAS code. You might have occasion to use a dummy macro at a stage in the development of a program when the macro calls have been written but the macro itself has not been written. Creating a dummy macro makes it possible to call the macro without generating an error message.

Use %MACRO and %MEND statements to create a dummy macro. If the macro has no parameters, use these statements:

```
%MACRO name;
%MEND;
```

If you know of parameters for the macro, add the parameters to the %MACRO statement. For a dummy macro, it is not important what names you use for positional parameters. If you do not know the exact number or the type of parameters, create the dummy macro with plenty of positional parameters. Extra parameters do not cause an error, but defining a macro with too few parameters can cause an error. These statements create a dummy macro with 10 positional parameters.

```
%MACRO name(X1, X2, X3, X4, X5, X6, X7, X8, X9, X10);
%MEND;
```

Usually, it is not necessary to delete macros; the catalog that contains macros is in the WORK library and is automatically deleted at the end of the SAS session. However, it is possible to delete a macro that you have defined. The macro is an entry of type MACRO in the catalog WORK.SASMACR.

To delete a macro in a SAS program, use the DELETE statement of the CATALOG procedure. This example deletes the macro A:

```
PROC CATALOG CAT=WORK.SASMACR;
  DELETE A.MACRO;
QUIT;
```

To delete all macros that are defined in a session, delete all of the entries in WORK.SASMACR. Use this step:

```
PROC CATALOG CAT=WORK.SASMACR FORCE KILL;
QUIT;
```

The KILL option deletes all entries from the catalog. The FORCE option is necessary because the macro processor is also using the catalog. The proc step generates log notes such as:

NOTE: Deleting entry CHOOSE.MACRO in catalog WORK.SASMACR.
NOTE: Deleting entry RPTOPT.MACRO in catalog WORK.SASMACR.

 There are several ways a macro can be used in a program without being defined earlier in the same program. If you find a macro without an accompanying macro definition, investigate these possibilities:

- The macro might be one of the macros that are included with one of the products of the SAS System. For example, the Data Step Graphics Interface of SAS/GRAPH includes a set of macros.
- Something that looks like a macro reference might instead be a macro function or a macro keyword.
- The macro might be a permanently stored macro. Check the system option MSTORED. If this option is on, check the SASMSTORE= system option. This option may point you to a library that contains a SASMACR catalog that contains previously defined macros.
- The macro might be an autocall macro, a kind of macro that is not defined until it the macro processor comes across a reference to it. Check the SASAUTOS= system option. This option may point you to one or more collections of program files that define these autocall macros.
- The macro might have been defined earlier in the SAS session in an earlier program, an autoexec program, or a secondary program file.

Errors can occur at several points in the use of a macro. First, macro syntax errors can occur in macro statements when the macro is defined. If this happens, the macro processor writes an error message and does not create the macro.

Second, the macro reference could be written with incorrect syntax. The macro processor reports a syntax error in the macro reference and does not resolve the macro.

Third, macro errors can occur when the macro is resolved or executed. The macro processor writes error messages and may stop executing the macro.

Finally, if the macro generates program text, errors can occur in those program statements. Those errors can occur either because the program text written in the macro is incorrect or because the logic of the macro generates program text that is not intended. Either way, the error messages that result point to an error in the macro.

System options can help you track down errors in macros. By default, the text generated by a macro is not reported in the log. Use the MPRINT option to write the generated text in the log. The SYMBOLGEN option, which reports the resolved values of macro variables, can also be helpful.

For more detailed information about the execution of macros and macro statements, use the MLOGIC system option when you run the program. This option generates log notes that describe such things as looping control and the evaluation of expressions in macros.

Although macros and other macro objects are usually used in SAS programs, they can be used throughout the SAS environment. Regardless of where you use a macro, it is best to define it in a SAS program. These are other possibilities for the use of macros:

- Define a macro that generates an SQL clause. Refer to the macro in an SQL statement.
- Define a macro that generates a text value as a result of processing it does with its parameters. Use the macro as a macro function.
- Define a macro that generates a display manager command string. Execute it by entering the macro reference in the command line, a function key definition, or the command associated with a menu item.
- Define a macro that generates SCL code and use it when you compile an SCL program of a SAS/AF application.

■ 63

Macro Programming

Macro language is a separate language that is implemented by the macro processor. The basics of macro programming employ macro variables and macros; see the two previous chapters for details. Macro variables and macros are just two of several kinds of macro objects you can use in a SAS program. Most of the details of macro programming are the same whether you are writing a macro or working with macro objects in "open" code, outside of any macro.

Macro Expressions

The macro processor does not deal with the SAS data types. There are no numeric or character values; all macro objects are fundamentally just text. However, the macro processor does integer arithmetic and character effects, and these can be useful at points in a SAS program, especially in connection with macro variables.

 The macro processor automatically evaluates expressions at points where it expects to find a numeric value. Anywhere else, use the %EVAL macro function to arrive at the numeric result of a macro expression. You can see this distinction in the way the %LET statement works in this example.

```
%LET THISYEAR = 2003;
%LET EXPRESSION = &THISYEAR - 1;
%LET LASTYEAR = %EVAL(&THISYEAR - 1);
%PUT THISYEAR: &THISYEAR;
%PUT EXPRESSION: &EXPRESSION;
%PUT LASTYEAR: &LASTYEAR;
```

```
THISYEAR: 2003
EXPRESSION: 2003 - 1
LASTYEAR: 2002
```

The %EVAL function calculates a value for the macro variable LASTYEAR. Without the %EVAL function, the macro variable EXPRESSION contains the resolved but unevaluated value that is assigned to it.

The %EVAL function is frequently useful when calculated values based on macro variables become parts of SAS statements. The following example demonstrates one simple way it can be used. If N is 5, this statement:

CHANGE X&N=X%EVAL(&N + 1);

resolves to:

CHANGE X5=X6;

In macro expressions, the macro processor treats arithmetic and logical operators as integer operations. The result is an integer, and an error occurs if the macro processor cannot determine the numeric value of one of the operands.

The macro processor might treat a comparison operator as a numeric comparison or a character comparison, depending on the operands. This example demonstrates a numeric comparison:

%PUT %EVAL(1 + 1 = 2);

1

This is a character comparison, comparing the letter A to the letter B:

%PUT %EVAL(A <= B);

1

You can supply fractional numbers for the macro processor's integer arithmetic, but it treats the values as integer values. The expression in the example below evaluates as 1, not 1.5, because the macro processor rounds the result of 1.5 to 1.

%PUT %EVAL(3/2);

1

To evaluate an expression that involves fractional numbers in a macro programming context, use the %SYSEVALF macro function, as shown in these examples:

%PUT %SYSEVALF(3/2);
%PUT %SYSEVALF(1.5 + 1.5);

1.5
3

Macro Functions

Macro language includes a set of functions for character effects and tests. The macro functions %UPCASE, %LOWCASE, %SUBSTR, %TRIM, %LEFT, %SCAN, %VERIFY, and %INDEX work the same way as the corresponding SAS functions. On the other hand, the %LENGTH macro function is more like the LENGTHC function; it measures the number of characters in its argument, including leading and trailing spaces.

To write a macro function with a macro variable as its argument, write an ampersand before the macro variable name, as in this example:

```
%LET N = %LENGTH(&CODE);
```

Other macro functions are used for macro quoting. The two most basic macro quoting functions, %STR and %QUOTE, are described in chapter 61, "Macro Variables." It is sometimes necessary to use macro quoting on the arguments of macro functions; usually, you can use the %QUOTE function for this purpose.

In this example, the comma in the value of the macro variable X causes the macro processor to find three arguments for the %INDEX function.

```
%LET X = 25,000;
%PUT %INDEX(&X, 000);
```

```
ERROR: Macro function %INDEX has too many arguments.  The excess arguments
       will be ignored.
0
```

This error is corrected with macro quoting, leading to the correct result:

```
%LET X = 25,000;
%PUT %INDEX(%QUOTE(&X), 000);
```

4

With the %SYSFUNC macro function, you can call almost any SAS function in a macro expression. Write the function call — translated to the style of macro language — as the first argument of the %SYSFUNC macro function. The second argument, which is optional, is a format reference for converting the return value of the function call to text.

In the macro language style that the %SYSFUNC macro function uses, character arguments to the function are not enclosed in quotes, and macro variables used in arguments must be prefixed with an ampersand. This is an example of using the %SYSFUNC macro function to call the COMB function.

```
%LET N = 8;
%LET R = 5;
%LET X = %SYSFUNC(COMB(&N, &R));
%PUT &X;
```

56

Use the %SYSFUNC macro function with the DATE function and a date format to extract parts of the current date. Similarly, use the TIME function and TIME format to extract the time of day. The example below extracts the current year, month name, day, and time of day.

```
%LET YEAR = %SYSFUNC(DATE(), YEAR4.);
%LET MONTH = %SYSFUNC(DATE(), MONNAME9.);
```

```
%LET DAY = %SYSFUNC(DATE(), DAY2.);
%LET TIME = %SYSFUNC(TIME(), TIME8.);
%PUT Year: &YEAR;
%PUT Month: &MONTH;
%PUT Day: &DAY;
%PUT Time of day: &TIME;
```

Macro Statements

Macro statements take various actions on macro objects. Macro statements can appear anywhere in a SAS program, but for clarity, it is usually best to write them between SAS steps, like global statements.

Most of the specific macro statements are discussed in other chapters.

- The %LET statement assigns a value to a macro variable. The %PUT statement writes a log message that can contain macro objects. The %SYMDEL statement deletes a macro variable. The %LOCAL and %GLOBAL statements declare macro variables in a macro. See chapter 61, "Macro Variables."
- The %MACRO and %MEND statements define a macro. The %IF-%THEN, %ELSE, %DO, %END, %RETURN, and %GOTO statements provide control flow inside a macro. See the previous chapter, "Macros."
- The %WINDOW and %DISPLAY statements display macro windows. See chapter 77, "Macro Windows."

These are a few additional macro statements:

- The %SYSEXEC statement executes an operating system command.
- The %SYSCALL statement executes a CALL routine in the macro environment, similar to the way the %SYSFUNC macro function calls a SAS function.
- The %INCLUDE statement looks like a macro statement and is implemented as one, but it is otherwise separate from macro language. It identifies a fileref or physical file name, a secondary SAS program file to execute at that point in the program.
- A macro comment statement begins with %* and continues till a semicolon is reached. Macro comment statements are especially useful in macros because, unlike other forms of comments, they cannot result in any generated program text.

Avoiding Errors in Macro Programming

Programming in macro language introduces levels of complexity that do not occur in a SAS program by itself. Keeping track of macro language actions, generated text, and the changing values of macro variables can make debugging macro programming difficult. The macro processor can provide several kinds of log messages to help locate errors. Even so, the best approach is to code in a way that avoids errors in the first place.

 These system options generate additional log messages that can be helpful in macro debugging: MPRINT, SYMBOLGEN, MLOGIC, SERROR, and MERROR.

When you write a macro to generate SAS statements, it can help to start with already-tested SAS statements. Conversely, if SAS statements in a macro are resulting in errors, the errors can often be easier to locate and correct if you take the problematic SAS statements out of the macro and run them separately.

In a mathematical expression, a macro variable can look like a single value, but the macro variable might actually contain an expression rather than a simple constant. To ensure that a macro variable is treated as a single value, enclose the macro variable reference in parentheses.

Consider this example of the way problems can occur:

```
%LET LENGTH = 5;
%LET WIDTH = &LENGTH + 1;
%LET AREA = %EVAL(&LENGTH*&WIDTH);
%PUT The calculated area is &AREA..;
```

```
The calculated area is 26.
```

In this example, the value of AREA is calculated incorrectly. It looks as if the calculation should multiply the value of &LENGTH by the value of &WIDTH, but the expression is not evaluated that way. When the macro variables are resolved in &LENGTH*&WIDTH, the resulting macro expression is 5*5 + 1, which evaluates as 26. To have this kind of expression evaluate the way it looks as if it should, write parentheses around each macro variable reference, as shown here:

```
%LET LENGTH = 5;
%LET WIDTH = &LENGTH + 1;
%LET AREA = %EVAL((&LENGTH)*(&WIDTH));
%PUT The calculated area is &AREA..;
```

```
The calculated area is 30.
```

This way, after resolving the macro variables, the expression is (5)*(5 + 1), which evaluates correctly as 30.

When you write macros that generate SAS statements, have them generate complete statements or complete steps whenever you can. If a macro generates a complete step, write a RUN statement at the end of the step. This ensures that the execution of the step is not affected by statements that follow the macro reference.

When a macro generates a part of a data step, be aware of the way data step variables inside the macro could affect the rest of the data step. If a macro creates variables for its own use, give these variables names that are unlikely to be used anywhere else, and consider writing a DROP statement in the macro so that these variables cannot be stored in any output SAS dataset that the data step creates. Likewise, if the macro uses a statement label, array, or hash object, give these objects names that are not likely to be found outside the macro.

■ 64

Program Parameters

Program parameters spell out specific areas of flexibility in the design of a program. They are values that are constant while a program is running, but that might change between one execution of a program and the next, or from time to time as changes occur in the context in which the program works. A program parameter might identify an input or output file, specify the size of an object, or provide a point of comparison that is used in selecting or validating data.

The most direct way to use program parameters in a SAS program is as macro variables. Assign a value to each one in a %LET statement at the beginning of the program file, using statements such as:

```
%LET CUTOFF = '30JUN2002'D;
%LET MARGIN = .50;
```

The macro variables might be used at various points in the program. For example, the macro variable CUTOFF might appear in this statement:

```
WHERE RECDATE <= &CUTOFF;
```

If there are several such statements in the program, writing the value as a macro variable makes the program easier to maintain. You can update the program with a different value without having to change statements throughout the program.

For many applications, it can be easier to read program parameters from a parameter file than to write them directly in the program. One easy way to set up a parameter file is with the name and value of one macro variable on each record. Consider, for example, the parameter file shown at right, which contains four parameters.

```
CUTOFF    '30JUN2002'D
TEST_SET ID =: '145970'
   LIB1    MAIN
MARGIN .50
```

To read this kind of parameter file and create the macro variables indicated, run the data step show at right near the beginning of the program.

If this step reads the parameter file shown, it creates the macro variable CUTOFF with the value '30JUN2002'D, the macro variable TEST_SET with the value ID =: '145970', and so on.

```
DATA _NULL_;
   INFILE PARM TRUNCOVER;
   LENGTH VARIABLE $ 32 VALUE $ 80;
   INPUT VARIABLE VALUE $80.;
   CALL SYMPUTX(VARIABLE, VALUE);
RUN;
```

When you create this kind of parameter file from an existing program, the %PUT statement can give you a good starting point. Use this statement to write a list of global macro variables and their values in the log:

%PUT _GLOBAL_;

The statement writes lines such as the ones shown at right. To create a parameter file, copy these lines to a separate file, select the macro variables to use as parameters, remove the word GLOBAL that begins each line, and add any additional parameters that are needed.

```
GLOBAL X X1
GLOBAL BASE 1
GLOBAL TEST_SET ID =: '145970'
GLOBAL TAB '09'X
GLOBAL LIB1 MAIN
GLOBAL WEEKDAY Thursday
GLOBAL CUTOFF '30JUN2002'D
GLOBAL MARGIN .50
```

Set default values for parameters by writing %LET statements to assign values to the macro variables before the data step that processes the parameter file. These default values apply if the parameter is not found in the parameter file. Similarly, you can check and correct the values of parameters or create additional parameters after the parameter file is processed.

You can use a data step to set parameters. This example creates the macro variable WEEKDAY, with the name of the day of the week, based on the value of the macro variable START, a SAS date.

```
DATA _NULL_;
  CALL SYMPUTX('WEEKDAY', PUT(&START, DOWNAME9.));
RUN;
```

To obtain program parameters from the operating system command line, write the parameters as the value of the SYSPARM= system option in the command line. In the data step that creates macro variables for parameters, obtain the value of the parameter string from the SYSPARM macro variable. Parse the parameter string to obtain the individual parameters; see chapter 25, "Parsing," for details.

Another way to set program parameters is to ask the user to enter values in a window — probably a macro window or data step window — at the beginning of the program. The example below uses a data step window to get values for two macro variables.

```
OPTIONS MISSING=' ';
DATA _NULL_;
  WINDOW Periods
    #1 @3 'Time Period Comparison'
    #3 @5 'Base time period:' +1 BASE $F7.
    #4 @5 'Number of time periods to compare:' +1 N 2.
    #7 @2 'Press Enter to continue.';
  DISPLAY PERIODS;
  CALL SYMPUT('BASE', BASE);
  CALL SYMPUT('N', PUT(N, F2.));
  STOP;
RUN;
```

```
Time Period Comparison

  Base time period:
  Number of time periods to compare:


Press Enter to continue.
```

If there are many program parameters and they do not tend to change every time the program runs, you can store them permanently in a SAS dataset. At the beginning of the program, read the SAS dataset and convert the parameters to macro variables.

If each parameter is stored in a separate observation, with variables for the name and value, you can convert them to macro variables with a SET statement and a CALL SYMPUTX statement, as shown in the data step at right.

```
DATA _NULL_;
   SET MAIN.PARM;
   CALL SYMPUTX(NAME, VALUE);
RUN;
```

Another way to organize a parameter dataset is with only one observation and each parameter as a separate variable. For example, the variable INIT in the parameter dataset represents the parameter INIT.

If the parameter dataset is MAIN.CONTROL, use the data step at right to convert all the variables in the parameter file to macro variables of the same names.

This program accesses all the variables of the parameter dataset

```
DATA _NULL_;
   SET MAIN.CONTROL;
   ARRAY NPARM{*} _NUMERIC_;
   ARRAY CPARM{*} _CHARACTER_;
   DO I = 1 TO DIM(NPARM);
      CALL SYMPUTX(VNAME(NPARM{I}), NPARM{I});
   END;
   DO I = 1 TO DIM(CPARM);
      CALL SYMPUTX(VNAME(CPARM{I}), CPARM{I});
   END;
   STOP;
RUN;
```

through the arrays NPARM and CPARM. The special variable lists _NUMERIC_ and _CHARACTER_ provide the elements of the arrays, so that the two arrays contain all the variables from the SAS dataset. The CALL SYMPUTX statements in the DO loops create macro variables using the names and values of all the variables. The VNAME function is a variable information function, and it returns the name of the variable provided as its argument. The name of the variable then becomes the name of the macro variable that the SYMPUT routine creates.

When this kind of SAS dataset, with one observation and many variables, is used to configure an application, it can be called a control dataset or a control file. An application that can take various forms depending on the parameters in a control file is said to be parameter-driven. An application with many control files that determine the details of various parts of its logic is a table-driven application.

Table-driven applications are more difficult to design, code, and configure than ordinary code-driven applications, but when a table-driven application is done right, it can provide a suite of related applications with better reliability and consistency than if each application were developed separately.

■ 65

Generating Program Statements

One special advantage of programming in an interpreted language is that a program can modify itself. Program logic can be used to generate program statements that become part of the program. Code that executes in the same program that generates it can be referred to as flexcode. In SAS, there are several ways to do this using data step logic to generate program statements.

A data step can generate later parts of the program, but it cannot modify its own code. A data step is compiled before it is executed, so its statements cannot be changed after it starts running. If it is necessary to generate part of the code of a data step, do so in an earlier data step.

Use any of these SAS features to generate and execute SAS statements.

- Write a SOURCE entry or other text file with PUT statements in a data step. Include the resulting code as part of the program with a %INCLUDE statement.
- Call the EXECUTE routine with individual SAS statements to execute immediately after the data step.
- Call the SYMPUTX routine to give values to macro variables that appear later in the program.

Call the EXECUTE routine anywhere in a data step to generate a statement that is executed immediately after the data step. The statement to execute is the argument to the routine. If you call the EXECUTE routine more than once, the resulting statements execute in the order they are generated in.

This example uses data values from the SAS dataset MAIN.CONTROL as part of the TITLE statements it generates.

```
DATA _NULL_;
  SET MAIN.CONTROL;
  CALL EXECUTE('TITLE1 ' || QUOTE(SNAME) || ';');
  CALL EXECUTE('TITLE2 ' || QUOTE(R23NAME) || ';');
  STOP;
RUN;
```

If the values of SNAME and R23NAME are Storage Logistics System and Capacity Utilization Report, the generated statements are:

```
TITLE1 "Storage Logistics System";
TITLE2 "Capacity Utilization Report";
```

The generated statements execute immediately after the data step. Write a RUN statement at the end of the data step to clarify the exact point in the program where the generated statements execute.

Use PUT statements to write a SOURCE entry, the same way you would write any output text file. Use program logic to write valid SAS statements.

Use the CATALOG device name in the FILENAME statement to define a SOURCE entry as an output text file. Write the full catalog name in the place where the physical file name would usually go. Usually, use an entry in the WORK library that does not already exist. It is also not necessary for the catalog that contains the entry to exist already. The example below shows a FILENAME statement for a SOURCE entry. Later in the program, use the same fileref in a %INCLUDE statement.

This example revises the previous example to use a SOURCE entry in place of the EXECUTE routine.

```
FILENAME FLEX1 CATALOG 'WORK.TEMP.FLEX1.SOURCE';
DATA _NULL_;
  SET MAIN.CONTROL;
  FILE FLEX1;
  PUT 'TITLE1';
  PUT +3 SNAME : $QUOTE80. ';';
  PUT 'TITLE1';
  PUT +3 R23NAME : $QUOTE80. ';';
RUN;
%INCLUDE FLEX1 / SOURCE2;
```

Note that it is possible to use more than one PUT statement to write a generated SAS statement. Be sure to write the semicolon at the end of each SAS statement you write. In this example, the RUN statement at the end of the data step is essential. It ensures that the SAS supervisor does not consider the %INCLUDE statement until after the data step executes.

Whenever you generate SAS statements from data values, consider the possible effects of special characters. The constructed statements should be correct regardless of what data values they are based on. Depending on how you use a value, you might have to do special processing for values that contain semicolons, quotes, delimiters, and the macro language indicators % and &. Alternatively, you might translate problematic characters to other characters or test for the presence of those characters and exclude values that contain them.

Never use values provided by unidentified or untrusted users directly in generated code (whether in SAS or any other language). Doing so would create a security hole that gives users potentially unlimited access to your computer. If you allow users to provide values used in code, it is essential to verify the values. The steps necessary to avoid this depend on the way the value is intended to be used in the program statements you are constructing.

- For a numeric value, use the F informat to convert the value to a numeric value, then use the F or BEST format to convert it to text for use in the constructed statement.
- For a character value, convert the value to a quoted string using the technique described below.
- For a name, reject the value if it contains characters other than characters that can be used in a name. The NOTNAME function can be useful in testing for invalid characters.
- For an expression, reject the value if it contains a semicolon (other than in a quoted string), a percent sign, or an ampersand (not followed by a space). If the value contains quotes, count the quotes and accept the value only if the count is an even number. Do not allow functions such as SYSTEM, DOPEN, or PEEK that would provide access to the operating system, file system, hardware, or SAS environment.

Generating program statements often involves converting character values to quoted strings so they can appear in the generated statements. To convert a value to a quoted string with double quotes, use the QUOTE function or the QUOTE format. It is possible for the quoted string to be longer than the value it is created from; remember this when you set the width of rhe QUOTE format or the length of a target variable for the QUOTE function.

Often, it is better to use single quotes to avoid the possibility of an inadvertent or unauthorized macro reference. There is no single function that does this conversion. Use the TRANWRD function to double the single quote marks in the value, and concatenate a single quote mark before and after, as shown here.

```
DATA _NULL_;
  LENGTH VALUE $ 24 QVALUE $ 50;
  VALUE = "It's ready, isn't it?";
  QVALUE = "'" || TRANWRD(TRIM(VALUE), "'", "''") || "'";
  PUT VALUE / QVALUE;
RUN;
```

```
It's ready, isn't it?
'It''s ready, isn''t it?'
```

Generated program statements can be used for some kinds of control flow that go beyond the boundaries of a single step. The most common use of this is to end a SAS session after the conclusion of a data step, based on logic contained in the data step. The ENDSAS statement ends a SAS session. Call the EXECUTE routine with this statement as the argument, as the action of an IF-THEN statement. The ENDSAS statement is executed then only if the condition of the IF-THEN statement is true.

This example is a data step that stops a SAS session if a certain date has not yet been reached. This could be used to prevent a program from being run before it would be valid.

```
DATA _NULL_;
  IF DATE() < '01JAN2007'D THEN CALL EXECUTE('ENDSAS;');
RUN;
```

If the current date, as returned by the DATE function, is before 2007, the ENDSAS statement executes after the data step executes. If the date is in or after 2007, the data step has no effect.

In some programs, a single condition determines whether various statements located throughout the program should execute or not. For example, it might be necessary to suppress all the TITLE3 statements of a program in some executions of the program. One of the cleanest ways to do this is to write a macro variable before all these statements, and assign an asterisk to this macro variable when the statements are not executed. The asterisk changes the statements into comments.

This example below uses this technique to execute a TITLE3 statement only if it is the first day of the month. If the day of the month is any number other than 1, the TITLE3 statement becomes a comment statement.

```
DATA _NULL_;
  IF DAY(DATE()) NE 1 THEN CALL SYMPUT('X', '*');
RUN;
. . .
&X TITLE3 'Beginning of Month';
```

A single macro variable, such as X in this example, can be used to control any number of statements throughout a program.

■ 66

Control Reports

For the programmer who writes a SAS program, the log is a good way to see what happens in the execution of the program. But anyone else who needs to monitor the results of the program will appreciate the benefits of a more focused presentation of the key results of the program. This kind of report is called a control report.

A control report may be a mix of counts, measurements, summary statistics, flags, and program parameters. The report serves as a document of the run, so it can include anything that is important to know about the way a program ran. It can include possible indications of trouble or totals to be compared to data from other sources.

Create the control report in a data step at the end of the program so that it can show the results of actions that take place throughout the program. Add statements and steps throughout the program, wherever they are needed, to determine the values and messages that appear in the control report. You can collect results in macro variables or small SAS data files.

 These are a few example of information that might be collected for a control report:

- the number of records read from an input text data file
- the number of records or observations rejected because of invalid data
- the number of observations created in a new SAS dataset
- in a merge, the number of observations used and rejected from each input SAS dataset and the number of resulting observations
- sums, other descriptive statistics, and frequency counts of critical variables
- performance measurements for parts of a program in which performance is critical

Include any concise information that will help show whether the program was successful and highlight anything that is questionable about the program's processing and results.

Use the END= option of the INFILE, SET, MERGE, MODIFY or UPDATE statements to know when a data step is processing its last observation. On the last observation, assemble values needed for the control report and save them in a SAS dataset or in macro variables.

The example below counts the input records read from a text data file, those rejected for invalid values, and the observations written to a SAS dataset, WORK.NEW. After processing the last input record, it writes the counts to a second SAS dataset, WORK.RLSCOUNT, that will be used in the control report. WORK.RLSCOUNT has only one observation.

```
DATA WORK.NEW (KEEP=CATALOG RELEASE TITLE)
  WORK.RLSCOUNT (KEEP=RLS_IN RLS_NOCAT RLS_NOTITLE RLS_NOT RLS_OK);
  INFILE RELEASES END=LAST TRUNCOVER;
  INPUT CATALOG $CHAR16. RELEASE ?? YYMMDD8. TITLE $CHAR24.;
  RLS_IN + 1;
  IF CATALOG = '' THEN RLS_NOCAT + 1;
  ELSE IF TITLE = '' THEN RLS_NOTITLE + 1;
  ELSE IF RELEASE = . OR RELEASE > "&SYSDATE9."D THEN RLS_NOT + 1;
  ELSE DO;
    OUTPUT WORK.NEW;
    RLS_OK + 1;
    END;
  IF LAST THEN OUTPUT WORK.RLSCOUNT;
RUN;
```

Observe these cautions when you write this kind of data step:

- Do not use subsetting IF or DELETE statements for validation logic in the same step as the END= option. Doing so could prevent the statements controlled by the END= variable from executing if the last observation is rejected. This example uses a sequence of IF-THEN and ELSE statements.
- Write KEEP= dataset options and OUTPUT statements for all output SAS datasets.

Alternatively, you can create macro variables to carry values from the data step to the control report. Replace the IF LAST THEN OUTPUT statement with a block such as:

```
IF LAST THEN DO;
  CALL SYMPUTX('RLS_IN', RLS_IN);
  CALL SYMPUTX('RLS_NOCAT', RLS_NOCAT);
  CALL SYMPUTX('RLS_NOTITLE', RLS_NOTITLE);
  CALL SYMPUTX('RLS_NOT', RLS_NOT);
  CALL SYMPUTX('RLS_OK', RLS_OK);
  END;
```

At the same time that you save information from a data step for a control report, you can also write it as a message in the log. Do this for information that would be helpful to a programmer reviewing the log. This is not necessary, of course, if the information already appears in log notes for the step.

The data step that actually writes the control report does not require any special programming logic. Often, the control report can be created in just seven statements, as shown in this code model:

```
TITLE1 'Control Report';
DATA _NULL_;
   MERGE SAS datasets;
   FILE RESULTS PRINT;
   PUT messages;
   STOP;
RUN;
```

The simplified example below writes a control report with the counts from the example above.

```
DATA _NULL_;
   SET WORK.RLSCOUNT;
   FILE RESULTS PRINT;
   PUT 'Number of new release records in input: ' RLS_IN
      / 'Number of records rejected with no catalog number: ' RLS_NOCAT
      / 'Number of records rejected with no title: ' RLS_NOTITLE
      / 'Number of records rejected with no release date or '
      / 'a future release date: ' RLS_NOT
      / 'Number of new releases recorded: ' RLS_OK;
   STOP;
RUN;
```

The resulting control report might look like this.

```
Number of new release records in input: 8
Number of records rejected with no catalog number: 2
Number of records rejected with no title: 1
Number of records rejected with no release date or
a future release date: 2
Number of new releases recorded: 3
```

Control reports often show observation counts of SAS datasets. There are many ways to determine the number of observations, but the simplest and most direct way is to open the SAS dataset and read that attribute from it. That is what the NOBS macro, shown here, does.

```
%MACRO NOBS(DATA);
%LET DSID = %SYSFUNC(OPEN(&DATA));
%IF &DSID = 0 %THEN File does not exist. ;
%ELSE %DO;
   %SYSFUNC(ATTRN(&DSID, NLOBS))
   %LET RC = %SYSFUNC(CLOSE(&DSID));
   %END;
%MEND;
```

NOBS is a function-style macro; instead of generating SAS statements, as most macros do, it generates a value for you to use. For example, you can call the NOBS macro directly in a character constant of a PUT statement, as shown here:

PUT "Number of events recorded: %NOBS(WORK.EVENT2)";

```
Number of events recorded: 25
```

Use the DATETIME function when you gather timing measurements for a control report. Use this function in a %LET statement between steps to determine the time of a specific point in the program. Subtract one value from another to get the elapsed time for a section of the program.

The simplified example below checks the time before and after a PROC SORT step, then computes and reports the elapsed time.

```
%LET TIMEBEFOREMASTERSORT = %SYSFUNC(DATETIME(), DATETIME22.3);
PROC SORT DATA=WORK.MASTER;
  BY IRR;
RUN;
%LET TIMEAFTERMASTERSORT = %SYSFUNC(DATETIME(), DATETIME22.3);

DATA _NULL_;
  TIMEBEFOREMASTERSORT = "&TIMEBEFOREMASTERSORT"DT;
  TIMEAFTERMASTERSORT = "&TIMEAFTERMASTERSORT"DT;
  TIMEELAPSEDMASTERSORT =
    TIMEAFTERMASTERSORT - TIMEBEFOREMASTERSORT;
  PUT 'Sorting the master file took ' TIMEELAPSEDMASTERSORT : F10.3
    'second(s).';
RUN;
```

```
Sorting the master file took 48.500 second(s).
```

A control report can contain results from a series of programs. Collect the results from each program in a SAS data file. Store all these SAS data files in the same library with a libref such as RESULTS. Run a separate program at the end to create the control report from the SAS data files.

It could be another computer program, rather than a person, that monitors a SAS program. In that case, the control report might take the form of a data table or an XML file. The process of collecting information for the control report is the same, and the data step that processes this information can be similar. But instead of writing a report, create a table or a file that the program can read.

■ 67
Cleaning Up a Program

On occasion you may want to revise or improve a SAS program that, however useful it may be, is in no condition to be worked on. When a program seems messy it is because its writing is obscure and indirect; instead of working directly toward its objective, the code has inexplicable twists and turns and unneeded tangents. Before you introduce changes in a messy program, start by cleaning up the program.

The purpose of the cleanup is to make the program as simple and direct as it can be and easy to read and understand without changing anything of interest in its results. As a secondary benefit, the program will tend to become more efficient. After the program is cleaned up, other changes, such as new features or bug fixes, should be easy to make.

It often takes longer to revise a program than it takes to write a new program. A program written in haste in an hour might later take a day or two to correct. If a program offers little to like and much to be suspicious of in the way it is written, and requires changes anyway, you might save time and produce a better result by writing a new program. The old program might serve as a guide you refer to as you plan its replacement. Often you will find that you can copy bits and pieces of the old program to provide about half of the code for the new program.

In a program written by someone who has a limited familiarity with SAS, you might see approaches that fail to use procedures effectively. The code might take several complicated steps to accomplish something that in SAS ought to be perfectly simple.

For example, a programmer familiar with the TABULATE procedure might use its OUT= option and a subsequent data step to create a frequency table in the form of a SAS dataset. Rewritten with the SUMMARY procedure, creating a frequency table takes a single step of just a few statements.

You might also see data step programming that duplicates the effects of procedures. Programmers who are more used to programming every detail of a process in another programming language might do the same thing in data step programming in SAS, writing dozens of data step statements when a few proc step statements would suffice. You might also see this done for the sake of efficiency, especially in programs from the 1980s and 1990s when the speed of a program was more of a concern than it is today.

When you clean up a long program, identify the parts of the program and consider them separately. If your objective is to make one change in a program, you might have to clean up only the part of the program where the change is located. Or, if one part of a program is problematic, you might rewrite just that part. The cleanup process for a long program can include breaking the program into a series of smaller programs if that makes the code easier to manage.

 Almost every SAS program contains extraneous actions and objects — statements, variables, and even SAS datasets that do not contribute in a useful way to the program's objective. To find this, start by considering the input and the required output of the program. The working parts of the program are intermediate states and stages between the input and the output. Anything else in the program can be considered a tangent, providing additional actions, distinctions, or data that are not included or not needed in the output.

These tangents are what make a program messy. They cause a problem when they distract you from the working parts of the program or the useful parts of its output. They also waste computer resources. You can improve the program by removing the unnecessary objects and actions. In a very messy program, you might find that most of the program is unnecessary and can be taken away.

These are the kinds of objects and actions you might find and remove:

- Sections of code that are commented out because they have no connection to the way the program is currently used
- Obsolete comments that describe a previous state of the program
- SAS data files that are created, but never used
- Steps that create SAS data files that are never used
- SAS data files that are replaced before they are used
- Computations to create variables that are never used
- Variables that are stored in SAS data files, but never used
- Filerefs and librefs that are defined, but never accessed
- SAS data files that are sorted for no reason
- Reports that are discarded automatically or as a matter of course
- TITLE statements for steps that do not produce any print output
- Arrays that are defined, but never referred to
- DO loops with boundary values that prevent them from executing
- IF-THEN statements with conditions that can never occur
- SAS data files that are created without any observations
- Steps that process SAS data files that never contain any observations
- WHERE conditions that logically include or exclude all observations
- A step that replaces or copies a SAS data file without making any changes
- Assignment statements meant to change the length of a character variable

 The log can help shed light on a mysterious program. Run the program, or whatever parts of it are able to be run, with these system options:

```
OPLIST VERBOSE ECHOAUTO SOURCE SOURCE2
NOTES STIMER MPRINT SYMBOLGEN MLOGIC
```

With these options, the log shows the actual SAS code that is executed along with notes that explain some of the program's actions. Just seeing how statements and steps execute can give you an idea of how much cleanup work may be required.

A SAS program is easier to follow if you know what variables are in each SAS dataset. Use the KEEP= dataset option when the SAS dataset is created to specifically indicate what variables it contains.

Include only the variables that are actually needed in the SAS dataset. If you are not sure whether some of the variables are needed or not, include them at first, and take them away later if you learn they are not needed.

The legitimate actions of a program can still contribute to a sense of messiness if they are done in an unnecessarily complicated or indirect way. The most common culprit is extra data steps. A program might take two or three data steps to accomplish a task that can more easily be done in a single data step. The more steps there are in a program, the harder it is to follow the flow of the program when you read it, so consolidate data steps whenever you can. Combining data steps also dramatically improves the performance of a program. Look for these signs of data steps you can combine:

- *SET statements.* If a SET statement reads a single SAS dataset created in a data step earlier in the same program, you can combine the two data steps. Place the logic of the second data step at the point of the OUTPUT statement in the first data step.
- *Repeated BY statement.* If the same BY statement appears with more than one MERGE statement, see if you can combine the merges into a single merge.
- *Copies, variations, and subsets.* If you must make several variations, copies, or subsets of the same data, make them all at the same time.
- *_NULL_.* It can become a habit to start data step report writing with a DATA _NULL_ statement, but doing so is not a requirement, and it is often simpler to create the report at the same place that the data is created (provided, of course, that that is a data step).
- *Sorting and eliminating duplicates.* Use the SORT procedure to sort a SAS dataset and eliminate duplicate observations in a single step. No data step is needed.
- *Subsetting.* Use dataset options to select variables and observations. Usually this is faster than having a separate data step.
- *Assignment statements that assign one variable to another.* If the objective is to rename a variable, use the RENAME= dataset option — or give the variable the appropriate name in the first place.

It comes up less often, but sometimes it is possible to combine proc steps.

- Instead of sorting a dataset one way, then another, then the first way again, use the OUT= option in the PROC SORT statement to create a sorted copy of the data.
- A PROC TABULATE step can have any number of TABLE statements. A PROC FREQ step can create any number of frequency tables. Use one step to create all the output you need from one SAS dataset.

- Some procedures do not require input data to be sorted. Do away with unnecessary sort steps before procedures such as SUMMARY and REPORT.

 Combining data steps is one of the easiest ways to simplify a program and make it more efficient. Often a program has one data step to read an input text file and another for data cleaning and other processing. Combining the two steps can be as easy as removing the DATA and SET statements of the intermediate SAS dataset, as shown below. The result is not only easier to read; it is twice as efficient, using only half as much time and storage space when it runs.

Before (messy, inefficient)	After (simplified, efficient)

DATA RAW;
  INFILE RAWDATA TRUNCOVER;
  INPUT ID : $F21. VALUE;
RUN;
DATA REAL;
  SET RAW;
  IF VALUE < 0 THEN VALUE = 0;
RUN;
	DATA REAL;
	  INFILE RAWDATA TRUNCOVER;
	  INPUT ID : $F21. VALUE;
	  IF VALUE < 0 THEN VALUE = 0;
	RUN;

 Within a data step, look for processes expressed as a series of actions that could be more clearly expressed as a single action. Look for other ways in which something long and complicated can be replaced with something shorter and simpler.

- *Initial values.* If a variable has the same value throughout a data step, provide the value in a RETAIN statement rather than an assignment statement.
- *Assign results to variables.* If a data step uses the same calculated value several times, assign the result of the calculation to a variable and use the variable.
- *Use expressions in place of variables.* If a data step uses a calculated value only one time, write it as an expression rather than creating a variable. It is perfectly okay to use expressions as array subscripts, arguments to functions, DO loop boundaries, etc.
- *Calculate group values.* If you create a variable that has the same value throughout a BY group, calculate its value once at the beginning of the group.
- *Subset early.* If a data step discards an observation, do this before any subsequent processing intended for the other observations.
- *Blocks.* If several actions result from the same condition, form them into a DO block. Tame multiple ELSE IF-THEN statements by replacing them with SELECT blocks.
- *Simplify logical expressions.* Write a logical expression in its simplest form. Truth tables, described in chapter 34, "Boolean Values," can help you identify the simple form of a logical expression.
- *Common control flow path.* Write control flow statements so that the common or expected case is the easiest to follow and the unusual or exceptional cases appear as exceptions. Do not use GOTO or LINK statements in the common control flow path, but use them if they are needed for error conditions and other exceptional cases.

■ 68

Macro Cleanup

If you need to correct errors, make changes, or improve the efficiency of a very poorly written program, the first thing to do is to clean up the program, to get it under control, as described in the previous chapter. This is all the more important and more difficult when the program is built on impenetrable layers of macro programming.

You should understand at the outset that macro cleanup can be a demanding and unrewarding task, not necessarily preferable to writing an entirely new program. Macro cleanup is difficult because you must find or create clarity and certainty out of the indirectness and ambiguity that macro logic introduces. It is unrewarding because in the most optimistic case, the likely result of your efforts is a body of SAS code that is just as deficient as the macro code was. There can be no guarantee of success. If the program depends on macros that cannot be located — a disturbingly common occurrence — it is like having a few pieces of a jigsaw puzzle and trying to guess at the completed picture.

 Do not try to guess whether a program is a candidate for macro cleanup based on the length of the program file. A macro cleanup project can be much less or much more than it appears on the surface because it depends on what macros and parameters are actually used when the program runs. A program might come with a library of 100 macros, but actually use only seven of them. Likewise, a macro might be defined with 20 parameters, but only use two in practice. On the other hand, a macro-based program might rely on a macro library that you do not see at first. A single call to an unknown macro can have potentially unlimited consequences.

To evaluate a program that uses macros, start at the beginning and make a list of all the macros that are called when the program runs, and all the parameters used with these macros. Then locate the definition of every macro that is called. After you take away all the macros that are defined but not used and add in all the macros that are called from an external source, how big is the program? How much smaller is it after you take away the parts of macros designed to deal with parameters and values that do not actually occur?

If you have searched for and cannot locate a macro that is used in a program, you do not have a complete working program and you cannot use it or clean it up.

Macro language permits fiendish degrees of indirectness, including techniques that make it impossible to tell what happens in a program. If you see any of the following, you cannot say what macros the program uses, and you will probably want to abandon the program.

- *A macro variable reference in a macro name.* When this happens, you cannot know the name of the macro until you know every possible value of the macro variable. If you see the sequence %& or these characters with letters between them, you have a problem on your hands.
- *Multiple definitions of the same macro.* When the same macro name is used in multiple macro definitions, you have to consider the execution sequence of the program to determine which macro is being referred to when there is a reference to a macro with that name.
- *Nested macro definitions,* that is, a %MACRO and %MEND statement between another %MACRO and %MEND statement. This means that the resolution of one macro causes another macro to be defined.
- *A macro that calls itself, either directly or indirectly.* This technique, called *recursion*, flirts with disaster.

Start macro cleanup by eliminating macros and macro variables that are defined but not used. Next eliminate sections of macros that handle parameters that are not used.

Then, you can make the program easier to read by eliminating some macros, replacing them with directly coded SAS statements. These are the kinds of macros you should look to remove:

- A macro that is called only once
- A macro that does something different every time you call it
- A macro with a large number of parameters compared to the number of lines of generated code
- A macro that uses multiple steps to simulate BY group processing

But keep these kinds of macros:

- A macro that is called repeatedly and repeats nearly the same actions every time it is called
- A macro that depends on macro control flow statements to generate the right SAS statements (unless the logic could be coded more easily with data step control flow statements)

A macro might do more than just generate SAS statements. If a macro takes actions of its own in macro statements, you can usually replace the macro statements with global statements and data step statements. An advantage of data step programming over macro programming is that the equivalent data step statements tend to be much easier to read.

If you can run the program, the MPRINT system option can show you exactly what macros are called and what SAS statements are generated. With the MPRINT system option, the macro processor writes all generated SAS statements in the log for you to read.

If you want to obtain the generated code from a macro, you can do so with the MFILE system option. This option writes the generated SAS statements in a separate text file. Use the MPRINT and MFILE system options, associate the fileref MFILE with a text file. Then, when the macro processor resolves a macro reference, it writes the generated SAS statements in the MFILE file. Execute the macro references with actual or representative parameter values, and the resulting text file contains the actual resulting SAS code with the macro programming removed. You might have to execute a macro reference several times with a range of parameter values to see the variations of the resulting SAS code. Perhaps the SAS code that you find in the MFILE file can be cleaned up and used.

If the MFILE code leaves a few questions to be answered, you might be able to answer the questions with two other system options. The MLOGIC and SYMBOLGEN system options provide additional log notes about macro logic and macro variables.

It is a common result of macro cleanup that you replace all function calls with directly coded SAS statements. If you reach this point, the SAS statements will likely also need the same degree of cleanup. See the previous chapter for a discussion of this process.

It is also a common result of macro cleanup that you end up with a program that includes several macros. In this case, you can clean up both the SAS code and the macro logic that you find in each macro. Simplify macro logic in much the same way you might simplify data step logic.

Also consider the macro logic together with the SAS code it generates. If you decide to change the SAS code, that may lead you to change the macro code along with it.

■ 69

Efficiency

Efficiency means doing more with less; an efficient computer program is usually one that completes its objectives with relatively light use of time, storage space, and other computer resources. Usually, the most important resource is time, and when people talk about improving the efficiency of a program, the primary objective is making it run faster.

Efficiency was once a vital measure of any program, but with computers running faster and computer resources costing less, efficiency becomes an issue only for a few critical applications, mainly interactive applications and programs that handle exceptionally large volumes of data. Even so, it is good to be aware of efficiency and write every program with an efficient approach. A programmer cannot predict how a program might eventually be used, so the efficiency could become an advantage, and efficient programs tend also to be reliable, simple, and easy to read.

 If it seems that an existing program is not efficient enough and you are thinking of improving it, consider the effort to improve the program's efficiency in business terms, as an investement. The cost of the improvements is the programming effort required to create and test the revised program. The payback you expect is measured in the benefits that result from the reduced use of computer resources.

If the benefits you expect are strictly a matter of the computer resources themselves, the revisions are probably not a good business investment. The use of a computer is not a large expense compared to the cost of a computer programmer's services. As a rule of thumb, you need to save 2,000 hours of computer time to pay back the investment of one hour of programmer time — not usually a likely result. These days, few programs even log a total of 2,000 hours of computer time within their useful lifetimes. However, the use of a program is not strictly a matter of machines. What are the human benefits of getting results that much sooner, or that much faster? How often are people sitting around waiting for the program? If one hour of programmer time can save two hours of user time, most businesses would consider that a good investment in efficiency.

Before you start working on the efficiency of an existing program, consider these points:

- Accuracy is always more important than efficiency. Do not look for ways to make a badly written, disorganized, or confused program more efficient. It can be done, but only with difficulty, and the chances of introducing new errors in the process are high enough that any gains in efficiency will likely be negated by the new errors. Instead, start by cleaning up the program so that it is organized, clear, and readable. See chapter 67, "Cleaning Up a Program," for details. In the process of cleaning up the program, you will also improve its efficiency, but focus on clarity and accuracy first.

- When you revise a program to improve its efficiency, do not give up clarity or good writing in the process. No matter how important efficiency is, it is not a reason to have a poorly written program. Fortunately, most of the opportunities to make major improvements in efficiency also improve the clarity of a program at the same time.

- If a program is slow because it works with a large volume of data, the greatest potential for improving its speed comes from using storage space efficiently, so start with that first. See the next chapter for more details.

 When you look at the efficiency of a program, identify the most important or constrained resource in the execution of a program. It could be one of the following:

- Elapsed time, also called real time, clock time, or wall time.
- CPU time, the time during which the program occupies the central processor on a busy multiuser computer.
- Permanent storage space, the amount of space occupied by programs and data when the programs are not running.
- Working storage space, used by a program while it is running.
- Memory used by a program while it is running.
- Volume of data delivered over a network.

 Read the performance messages in the log to find measures of the system resources used by each step. The STIMER and FULLSTIMER options determine the content of these performance statistics.

5 Good Reasons to Make a Program More Efficient

Most existing programs are efficient enough if they work correctly. Consider revising an existing program to make it more efficient only if there is a special reason to do so. For the most part, it is the human impact of a program that should prompt you to find ways to improve the program's efficiency. These kinds of programs are likely candidates to be made more efficient.

★ **Response time.** Whenever interactive applications take more than a second to respond to a user request, look for ways to make them faster. If people are using a program all day long, every second of response time is critical.

★ **Timely information.** Regularly scheduled programs that provide business information under strict deadlines provide information that needs to be timely. Compare the cost of the programming effort to the added value of more timely information.

★ **Out of resources.** If a program uses so much memory, storage space, or another resource that it crashes, you need to revise it. First consider whether it would be less expensive to replace the computer than to revise the program.

★ **Heavy use.** The computer resources add up for programs that are installed on a large numbers of computers or that run millions of times. Programs that run regularly during busy times on a network or server use computer resources that are especially expensive.

★ **Other revisions.** When a program requires revisions for other reasons, make the revised parts of the program as efficient as they should be.

If your concern is run time, let the performance statistics guide you to the parts of the program that use the greatest amounts of time. If the first step uses 1 second and the second step uses 1,000 seconds, then it is the second step you must revise to make the program go faster. On a busy mainframe computer, look at each step's CPU time. On other computers, the elapsed time is usually a more reliable indicator.

For an interactive application, run time statistics are meaningless. Look exclusively at elapsed time. At which points does the program take more than one second to respond to a user request? Work to make those parts of the program faster.

Reducing the size of stored data is the easiest way to speed up a program. Another is to reduce the number of times that the program accesses the data. There are many ways to do this, and these are some of the most important:

- Eliminate unnecessary steps. Combine steps when it can be done easily.
- Use dataset options in place of steps. It does not take a separate step to extract or select a part of a SAS dataset. Instead, use the KEEP= or DROP= option to select variables. Use any combination of the WHERE=, FIRSTOBS=, and OBS= options to select observations. To rename variables, use the RENAME= option.
- Use data step views for SAS datasets that are used only once. See chapter 60.
- Save SAS datasets that you can use again later. Store a SAS dataset in a library other than the WORK library to make the same data available for a later program that uses it.
- Save summary data if you use it in more than one step. Calculating summary data is a large amount of work; storing the summary data is a small amount of work by comparison.
- Use original data so you do not have to make a copy. Unless you are working with tape or a slow storage medium, it is not necessary to copy SAS datasets to the WORK library before you start to work with them. Likewise, it is not necessary to create SAS datasets in the WORK library and then copy them to another library.
- Change SAS datasets in place when you can. To change attributes or header information of a SAS dataset, use the DATASETS procedure. Use dataset options in the MODIFY statement to change the dataset label or dataset type of a SAS dataset. Use secondary statements of the MODIFY statement to change attributes of variables. To add data to the end of a SAS data file, use the APPEND procedure. To change a few data values in a SAS dataset, use the MODIFY statement of the data step.
- Read only the data you actually use.

Check the run time statistics in the log to see how the change affected the speed of the program.

When you evaluate SQL performance, think of each CREATE TABLE, SELECT, INSERT, and DELETE FROM statement as a separate step. Use the STIMER option in the PROC SQL statement to get time reports for each statement separately. SQL is not a procedural language. An SQL statement describes a result, and the actions and the time it takes to carry them out can be hard to predict.

Certain kinds of SQL queries tend to take a long time to run. Be especially alert to queries with two tables with no WHERE clause or a WHERE clause that is something other than simply testing whether columns match. Also be alert to any query that joins more than two tables.

An ORDER BY clause requires sorting the data, and its performance may be no different from a PROC SORT step.

The performance of WHERE clauses, whether in SQL or in any SAS step, can often be substantially improved with the use of indexes. The most decisive improvements can be seen when a WHERE clause involves just one variable and selects a small fraction of the observations from a SAS dataset. In cases like this, the index can point the WHERE clause to the needed observations. It avoids the need to read all the other observations.

If you never use all the observations of a large SAS dataset together, split it into the parts that you do use. Accessing a small SAS dataset is much faster than accessing a small part of a large SAS dataset.

If a data step does not need to create a SAS dataset, write the special name _NULL_ in the DATA statement. This prevents the data step from writing an output SAS dataset.

Techniques that reduce the amount of computation and logic in a data step are well known, but the differences may be measured in microseconds. Still, you will see experienced programmers using these techniques consistently. They are easy to do and make the program that much smaller and simpler.

- In place of array references, use direct references to the variables.
- Define an array with temporary variables rather than named variables.
- Stop processing a loop as soon as it is done with what it is doing. Use the LEAVE statement to exit the loop.
- Use informats to create the values of variables from input fields. Use formats to create the text of output fields. When you can process fields directly with informats and formats, it is simpler than using programming logic with IF-THEN and assignment statements, for example.
- To change part of the value of a character variable, use the SUBSTR pseudo-variable rather than an expression involving concatenation operators.
- Use a RETAIN statement rather than an assignment statement to initialize a variable.
- Stop processing an observation as soon as you know you will not be using it. Write a subsetting IF or DELETE statement immediately after the INPUT statement or other statement that creates the variable that tells you the observation is not wanted.
- When you can, use constants and variables in place of function calls.
- Simplify expressions. Expressions that use a smaller number of functions, variables, and operators execute faster.
- Avoid actions and conditions that might result in log messages. For example,

if you know the automatic variable _ERROR_ might be 1, use an assignment statement to reset it to 0. Before dividing, make sure you are not dividing by 0. Use the PUT and INPUT functions for type conversion to avoid automatic type conversion. If you can, avoid using missing values in a way that generates more missing values. Use error controls if an informat might read invalid data. All this makes a difference because generating log messages takes more time than the actual actions of the statements the messages describe.

 If your concern is memory, find the step that uses the largest amount of memory and work exclusively on it.

SAS memory problems usually fall into these categories:

- interactive applications that have many windows open at once
- steps with enormous numbers of variables or very large arrays
- proc steps with CLASS statements, when there are a very large number of class levels
- procedures that use large amounts of memory in order to run faster

If the problem is located in a proc step that summarizes data, change the way it uses memory by changing the value of the SUMSIZE= system option, options or the use of variables in the proc step, or the structure of the data. Sometimes it helps to change one or all of the class variables to BY variables. If a summary report is the problem, create the summary data first, in a separate step, before you create the report.

If a data step uses too much memory, it is because there are too many objects in the data step program. To reduce the use of memory in a data step, do one or more of the following:

- Reduce the number or size of arrays.
- Use the keyword _TEMPORARY_ in an array definition to use temporary variables instead of named variables as elements of the array.
- Reduce the number of variables.
- Reduce the number of statements or expressions.

 Sorting is a special efficiency problem. It is one of the most demanding things that a SAS program can do, and almost every SAS program does it. Sorting is demanding because, unlike other processes that consider one observation at a time, sorting has to work with all the observations in the SAS dataset. When programs involve large volumes of data, sorting often takes up most of the programs' time.

The reason sorting is such a big deal with large amounts of data is that the work involved in sorting is not simply proportional to the size of the data. When the volume of data increases, the time it takes to sort increases even faster. Sorting twice the amount of data takes about three times as long. When the number of observations is large, it takes a long time to get the observations in order. When the length of the observation is especially large, that slows down the sort process because the sort routine can compare only a few observations at a time.

The sorting process is found throughout SAS programming. It is what the SORT procedure does, of course, but it is also found in:

- SQL statements that use ORDER BY clauses, grouping, distinct values, and some kinds of WHERE clauses.
- creating indexes, or integrity constraints that use indexes.
- PROC REPORT steps that use order, group, or across variables.
- interactive applications that allow a user to change the sort order of data.
- other processes that connect data or make lists of distinct values.

Sorting is expensive enough that sometimes it is better not to sort after all. Depending on the objective and on the nature of the data, it is sometimes possible to create a sorted result without sorting a SAS dataset.

- Use a procedure with class variables to create summary data from unsorted detail data. In the REPORT procedure, use group variables.
- To read a SAS data file in sorted order without actually sorting it, read it using an index. This is not necessarily faster than sorting, but it works well if you are already using a WHERE clause to read only a small part of the data or if the SAS data file is one that you need to read in several different sort orders.
- If data is already in a suitable order for forming groups, but not in a sorted order, form groups using the NOTSORTED option in the BY statement.
- If the data is assembled from sorted data, maintain the sort order as you assemble the data. With the SET statement, for example, use the BY statement to interleave data rather than concatenate it.

Consider whether you need to sort the entire SAS dataset. The most powerful way to speed up sorting is to reduce the volume of data. If there are observations or variables you will not be using in the sorted data, eliminate them before sorting to make the sort go faster. Similarly, if you have a large SAS dataset that you will use only in parts after it is sorted, split it into parts before sorting. This is faster if the SAS dataset is large. If you need to sort and split a SAS dataset that is small to begin with, it is faster to sort first, then split the data.

On some computers, SAS can use either its own sort routine or the operating system's. If you determine that one or the other is better or faster in a specific case, use the SORTPGM= system option to select the sort routine. SORTPGM=SAS selects the SAS sort routine; SORTPGM=HOST selects the host sort routine, or the routine that the operating system uses.

For some kinds of data on some kinds of computers, a tag sort is faster than the default sort algorithm. In a tag sort, the sort key is sorted first. The rest of the variables are sorted only after the key has been sorted. This is an advantage if the sort key is a small part of the total length of the observation. If it is, the tag sort uses much less memory and temporary storage space than the standard sort. Depending on the nature of the data and the disk it is stored on, a tag sort can be much faster or much slower than a standard sort. On a mainframe computer, it is generally much slower; on a typical business computer, it is often faster. Write the TAGSORT option in the PROC SORT statement to do a tag sort.

If no other way of sorting works, you may be able to sort a SAS dataset by creating an index and reading the SAS dataset with the index using a SET statement with a BY statement. This usually takes much longer to run, but it can sort SAS datasets that cannot be sorted with the SORT procedure.

■ 70

Saving Storage Space

 The need to conserve storage space becomes obvious when a SAS program fails because it uses up all the disk space on the computer and still needs more. However, there are good reasons to be careful and selective in the way you use storage space in your SAS programs long before a program fails from lack of space.

- The way you store data affects the speed of your SAS programs. SAS programs spend most of their time reading and writing data files. If you keep extra data in SAS datasets, the SAS programs take longer to run.
- Extra variables that you store in a SAS dataset can conflict with other variables in a SAS program, and this can create mysterious errors.
- A program is easier to read and understand when its files contain only the data that the program actually uses.

 The size of the data in a SAS data file is the product of the observation length and the number of observations. To reduce the size of a specific SAS data file, you can:

- Reduce the length of the observation.
- Reduce the total number of observations.

To reduce the total storage size of a project, you can also:

- Eliminate some SAS data files entirely.
- Save some SAS data files for a shorter period of time.

Compression is another option that can affect the storage size of SAS data files. See the next chapter, "Compression," for more information.

Observation Length

It is the variables of a SAS data file that determine the length of the observation. You can only change the length of the observation by changing the variables. The length of the observation is not affected by the data values. Each observation in the SAS dataset has the same length regardless of the values of the variables in that observation. You can reduce the observation length — and reduce the size of the SAS data file — by eliminating variables or shortening variables.

The length of the observation is approximately the total length of variables, that is, the sum of the lengths of all the variables. The actual observation length is a few bytes longer than the total length of variables, but for most purposes, it is sufficient to consider the total length of variables.

The reason you store data in a SAS dataset is so you can use it later. If you will not be reading the SAS dataset, then do not create it. The same logic applies to the individual variables. If you do not use a variable when you read the SAS dataset, then do not store the variable when you create the SAS dataset.

The default action of a data step is to create a SAS dataset that contains all the variables of the data step, with a few exceptions for things such as automatic variables and I/O statement options. When you create a SAS dataset, you should include only the variables that are needed. This means you need to specifically indicate what variables to include. Use the KEEP= dataset option in the DATA statement to list the variables to keep in the SAS dataset. Alternatively, use the DROP= dataset option to exclude specific variables from the output SAS dataset.

Exclude from the output SAS dataset any variables that are strictly part of the data step logic. If a data step contains DO loops that execute the same way for every observation, do not store the index variables of the DO loops. Similarly, do not store counter variables or any other variables that are only meaningful in the context of the specific data step.

This example shows the use of the DROP= dataset option to exclude an index variable from the output SAS dataset.

```
DATA NEW (DROP=I);
  . . .
  DO I = 1 TO 15;
    . . .
    END;
  . . .
```

Include variables in an output SAS dataset only if there is a reason for them to be there. When a data step creates multiple SAS datasets, decide on the variables separately for each of the SAS datasets.

Similarly, when a proc step creates a SAS dataset, do not store any variables that the procedure creates that will not be used for anything. Use the KEEP= or DROP= option with the name of the output SAS dataset in the proc step. The SUMMARY procedure creates the variables _TYPE_ and _FREQ_, which may or may not be useful. The example below uses the DROP= dataset option to exclude these two variables from the output SAS dataset.

```
PROC SUMMARY DATA=VISIT NWAY;
  CLASS LOC;
  VAR ANGLE;
  OUTPUT OUT=EXT (DROP=_TYPE_ _FREQ_) MIN=MIN MEAN=MEAN;
RUN;
```

These are other ways to reduce the lengths of observations:

- If a character variable contains names or text values, set its length so that it is long enough to hold the values it contains, but not any longer.

- Consider shortening a variable that contains names or phrases so that it is long enough for about 99 percent of the values it contains. You might use as few as 14 characters for place names. This works because the longer values are still recognizable in their truncated forms. For example, `Truth or Conse` can be recognized as a shortened form of *Truth or Consequences*.

- If a code variable or character variable has only a few distinct values, save storage space by encoding it as a one-byte binary code. See chapter 30, "Discrete Binary Encoding," for details. This technique allows a variable of any length to be shortened to the minimum length of 1 byte, provided that the variable has fewer than 256 distinct values.

- Ordinarily, numeric variables are stored with a length of 8, but some numeric variables can be stored with shorter lengths. For example, variables with integer values can usually be shortened to a length of 4. See chapter 9, "Data Type and Length," for details.

- If a SAS dataset contains multiple kinds of observations that use different sets of variables, save storage space by storing them in separate SAS datasets.

- If two variables contain the same information, keep only one of the variables. For example, if START is a SAS date value and YEAR is the year of that date, you can omit YEAR without losing any information.

- Use special missing values to indicate the reason why a value is not available for a numeric variable. This is more efficient than having a separate variable to indicate the reason why there is no value.

Number of Observations

Store observations that are part of the data you are working with, but do not store other observations that a program happens to generate. For example, if you are studying customers, and an input text data file contains records for both customer accounts and internal accounts, create observations only for the customer accounts.

 The default action of a data step is to create an output observation for every repetition of the automatic data step loop. In a data step that reads a text data file, this can mean creating one observation from each input record. If not all these observations are relevant, use data step logic to store only the observations you need.

There are several ways to select observations in a data step, including these:

- one or more statements of the form IF *condition* THEN OUTPUT;
- subsetting IF statements
- conditional DELETE statements
- a STOP statement that executes when the end of the relevant data has been reached
- the WHERE= dataset option in the DATA statement

 When you create multiple SAS datasets in a data step, use OUTPUT statements with the SAS dataset names to write observations to specific output SAS datasets. Include in each SAS dataset only those observations that are needed in that output SAS dataset.

If you use the SUMMARY procedure with class variables, the procedure creates summaries for every possible combination of the class variables. However, you can limit the procedure to the class combinations that you are actually interested in. Especially when you create an output SAS dataset, use the features of the procedure to store only the class combinations that matter. Use one or more of these features:

- the NWAY option
- the TYPES statement
- the WAYS statement
- the CLASSDATA= and EXCLUSIVE options

When you create a SAS dataset in a proc step or data step, you can use the WHERE= dataset option to select the observations to store based on a condition of the data. The example below shows an OUTPUT statement from the SUMMARY procedure that stores the summary observations in which the value for REVENUE is at least 1.

```
OUTPUT OUT=FX (WHERE=(REVENUE >= 1)) SUM=;
```

Saving and Deleting Data

An important part of managing storage space is deciding what data to save and what to discard. Any file you create takes up storage space for as long as you keep it, but after you delete the file, then you can reuse that space for something else.

The default action of a data step is to create an output SAS dataset. It does this even if you do not provide a SAS dataset name in the DATA statement. When an output SAS dataset is not needed, use the special name _NULL_ in the DATA statement. The statement then reads:

```
DATA _NULL_;
```

To save storage space when you create a SAS dataset in a data step, create a view instead of a SAS data file. See chapter 60.

Save storage space by keeping only the most important versions of data. If a body of data goes through several stages of processing, it is usually sufficient to save only the original data, before any processing is done, and the final data, after all processing is completed. Sometimes, saving the original data is all that is needed. Of course, you should also save the programs you used. If you have the original data and the programs, you can run the programs again if it becomes necessary to take a new look at the processed data.

If you need to use the same SAS dataset in two or more different sort orders, one alternative is to create indexes for each set of key variables. This allows you to read the SAS dataset in each sort order without actually having to sort it or save several versions of it in different sort orders.

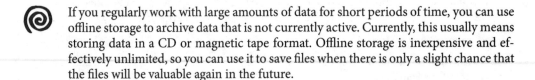

If you regularly work with large amounts of data for short periods of time, you can use offline storage to archive data that is not currently active. Currently, this usually means storing data in a CD or magnetic tape format. Offline storage is inexpensive and effectively unlimited, so you can use it to save files when there is only a slight chance that the files will be valuable again in the future.

The WORK library is automatically deleted at the conclusion of the SAS session. Use the WORK library to store SAS files that will not be needed any longer than that. Use other libraries (sometimes called permanent libraries because they are not automatically deleted) for SAS files that should be saved for a longer period of time. In any library, use the DATASETS procedure to delete files that are no longer needed.

In most operating systems, if a SAS session ends abnormally, the WORK library is not deleted. These stranded WORK libraries can occupy any amount of storage space, so it is important to find and delete them. Check for stranded WORK libraries after a system crash. Also check for them as part of the regular maintenance of the computer.

Use operating system commands to locate the stranded WORK library. If it contains any files you want to recover from it, move them to another directory that you use as a SAS data library. Then delete the stranded WORK library to recover that storage space.

Use this statement in a SAS session to find out the path of the WORK library:

LIBNAME WORK LIST;

The path is either the same for every SAS session or slightly different in each SAS session. If it is the same, then any stranded WORK library is automatically deleted when the next SAS sessions starts up. If it is different, then you need to look for directories in the same place with names that follow the same pattern. Any such directories that you find are WORK libraries. Make sure you do not delete the WORK library of any currently running SAS session.

■ 71

Compression

The term *compression* includes any technique for storing any kind of data in less space than the data naturally occupies. In the SAS environment, compression refers specifically to the effects of the COMPRESS= dataset option, which reduces the length of observations in a SAS data file.

The main purpose of compression is to save storage space; compression can reduce the size of SAS data files containing some kinds of data by more than half. When compression is most effective, it can also speed up SAS programs by reducing the size of the data that the programs read and write.

Compression has its costs, though; the compression and decompression processes use CPU time. Also, direct access techniques on a compressed SAS data file are much slower than for an uncompressed SAS data file. Use compression only when it makes a significant difference in the size of a SAS data file.

 When you create a compressed SAS dataset, a log note tell how much space was saved. This is an example of what the log says:

```
NOTE: Compressing data set WORK.OPENB decreased size by 11.11 percent.
      Compressed is 8 pages; un-compressed would require 9 pages.
```

If the compression process could not save any space, SAS ignores the request to compress the data and writes it in uncompressed form.

 SAS lets you choose between two compression algorithms.

- Character compression uses a run length encoding (RLE) algorithm. It compresses data when consecutive bytes have the same value or when there is a repeating pattern in the byte values. Run length encoding is very effective for long character values that are mostly or entirely blank and for numeric values that are exactly 0 — both common occurrences in actual data. For character compression, use either of these options:

  ```
  COMPRESS=CHAR
  COMPRESS=YES
  ```

- Binary compression uses a very different algorithm that works with bits rather than bytes. It is quite effective when consecutive numeric variables have similar values and when character data mainly uses the same few characters. For binary compression use the option:

  COMPRESS=BINARY

To create a SAS data file without compression, use the option:

  COMPRESS=NO

Usually, compression is applied to a single SAS dataset with the COMPRESS= dataset option. Use this option when a new SAS data file is created. However, you can set a default compression algorithm for all new SAS data files with the COMPRESS= system option. For example, after this statement, new SAS data files are created with character compression:

OPTIONS COMPRESS=CHAR;

You can override the system option by using the COMPRESS= dataset option for a specific new SAS data file.

Most of the time, compression should not be the default. Use this statement to reset the system option so that SAS data files are not compressed by default:

OPTIONS COMPRESS=NO;

Compression has no effect on very small SAS data files. SAS reads and writes SAS data files in blocks of data that it calls pages. If a SAS data file already fits in 1 page before it is compressed, then it cannot be made any smaller. If it occupies 2 or 3 pages, then it would be very difficult to make it smaller by compressing it. Use compression only for SAS data files that are larger than this.

Some kinds of data are easier to compress than other kinds of data. Therefore, when you test the effectiveness of compression, it is important to test with actual or representative data. Even then, if the nature of the data changes, the amount of compression will also change.

Each observation is compressed separately. This means that compression cannot work well on very short observations, because if an observation is already short, it is hard to make it shorter. Do not attempt compression unless the total length of variables is at least 17. Compression is much more likely to be effective when the total length of variables is at least 50.

The order of variables can have a major effect on compression, especially on character compression. Make compression more effective by putting variables with similar values next to each other.

- If there are several character variables that are blank in many observations, position these variables together at the end of the observation.

- Among the numeric variables, if several variables tend to have the same or similar values, make those variables consecutive.
- Short character variables that contain codes or binary values are the hardest variables to compress. Keep these variables separate from the other variables.

When you create a SAS dataset in a data step, use a LENGTH statement at the beginning of the data step to set the order of the variables. While you are at it, choose efficient lengths for the variables. For many kinds of data, choosing the right lengths for variables can make a SAS dataset even smaller than compression can. See chapter 9, "Data Type and Length" and the previous chapter, "Saving Storage Space," for more on this.

Compressing a SAS data file saves storage space, and it can also save time, depending on the nature of the data, the way you use it, and the performance of the specific computer hardware you use.

The process of creating the compressed observation is an extra task that uses additional CPU time. In comparing the two compression algorithms, binary compression uses more CPU time than character compression. However, if compression is effective, it creates a smaller file that takes less time to write. Usually, the reduction in I/O time is greater than the increase in CPU time and the program runs faster.

Reading the compressed SAS data file can be much faster than reading an uncompressed SAS data file. Decompression is a simpler process than compression and uses only a slight amount of CPU time, so the reduced I/O time is more noticeable.

The increased speed in reading a compressed SAS data file applies only for sequential reading. For the best performance in direct access of a SAS dataset (such as reading with the POINT= option of the SET statement or with an index), use an uncompressed SAS data file.

If compression is not effective and the SAS data file is not significantly smaller, then compressing slows down a program. Use compression only when it is likely to be effective.

When a compressed SAS data file is created, these other dataset options are available:

- The REUSE= option can have a value of YES or NO to indicate whether the space of observations that are deleted from the SAS data file can be reused. Use REUSE=NO unless the SAS dataset has observations added and removed on a continuous basis.
- With the REUSE=NO option, you can use the POINTOBS=YES option to make it possible to use direct access techniques, such as the POINT= option in the SET statement, with the compressed SAS data file. The REUSE=YES option overrides the POINTOBS= option and prevents direct access techniques.

COMPRESSION MANAGEMENT REPORT

The following program generates a report that can help you manage the data storage space of a project using compression. The report lists the SAS data files of a library (MAIN in this case, but you could substitute any libref) and their data size in megabytes before and after compression. The program uses an SQL query to extract this information from one of the DICTIONARY tables of SAS SQL, DICTIONARY.TABLES, then formats it in a PROC REPORT step.

```
PROC SQL;
CREATE TABLE WORK.DATASIZE AS SELECT
   TRIM(LIBNAME) || '.' || MEMNAME
     AS DATASET LABEL='SAS Dataset Name' LENGTH=20,
   LIBNAME AS LIBREF LABEL='Libref',
   MEMNAME AS MEMBER LABEL='Member',
   NVAR LABEL='N Vars', NOBS LABEL='N Obs',
   OBSLEN LABEL='Obs Len',
   NOBS*OBSLEN/1048576 AS MBDATA LABEL='MB Data' FORMAT=S7.3,
   COMPRESS LABEL='Compress',
   PCOMPRESS LABEL='Comp%' FORMAT=F5.,
   (1 - PCOMPRESS/100)*(CALCULATED MBDATA)
     AS MBCOMP LABEL='MB Comp' FORMAT=S7.3
   FROM DICTIONARY.TABLES;
QUIT;
PROC REPORT DATA=WORK.DATASIZE (WHERE=(LIBREF='MAIN'))
   NOWD HEADSKIP COLWIDTH=7;
   COLUMN DATASET NVAR NOBS MBDATA MBCOMP COMPRESS SAVE PERCENT;
   DEFINE NVAR / DISPLAY SPACING=0;
   DEFINE NOBS / DISPLAY SPACING=1;
   DEFINE DATASET / ORDER SPACING=0;
   DEFINE SAVE /' Saved' COMPUTED SPACING=0 FORMAT=S7.3;
   DEFINE PERCENT /'  %' COMPUTED SPACING=0 FORMAT=F4.;
   RBREAK AFTER / OL SUMMARIZE;
   COMPUTE SAVE;
     SAVE = MBDATA.SUM - MBCOMP.SUM;
     ENDCOMP;
   COMPUTE PERCENT;
     IF MBDATA.SUM THEN PERCENT = SAVE/MBDATA.SUM*100;
     ENDCOMP;
RUN;
```

SAS Dataset Name	N Vars	N Obs	MB Data	MB Comp	Compress	Saved	%
MAIN.JOURNAL	13	35308	11.853	2.608	CHAR	9.245	78
MAIN.NEW	8	8145	1.018	0.397	CHAR	0.621	61
MAIN.SUM	26	68	0.030	0.030	NO	0.000	0
MAIN.TRANS	6	201971	14.831	8.454	CHAR	6.377	43
			-------	-------		-----------	
			27.732	11.488		16.243	59

■■72

Porting Files and Data

Moving a project from one kind of computer to another can require some adjustments in the SAS programs and in the files that contain the programs and their associated data. The need to translate data files from one form to another can become a routine part of a system that involves multiple computers, with data delivered from one computer to another.

The issues of rewriting a SAS program to run on a different kind of computer are discussed in the next chapter, "Porting SAS Programs." This chapter covers the process of moving files and data values between computers.

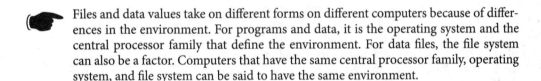 Files and data values take on different forms on different computers because of differences in the environment. For programs and data, it is the operating system and the central processor family that define the environment. For data files, the file system can also be a factor. Computers that have the same central processor family, operating system, and file system can be said to have the same environment.

When you move the files of a project between environments, you need to adjust for differences between the computers. For data, these are the essential properties of an environment:

- *Character set.* Most computers use the ASCII character set with additional characters; however, a SAS project typically only uses the ASCII characters. IBM mainframe computers use the EBCDIC character set.
- *Floating-point form.* Most computers follow the IEEE standard for floating-point representation. IBM mainframes and some other kinds of computers use other floating-point forms.
- *Byte sequence for numeric values.* The design of a central processor determines the byte sequence of numeric values. The Intel-standard central processors used in most desktop computers arrange numeric values with the least significant byte first, in the reverse of the mathematical meaning of the bytes (a style called little-endian). Most other kinds of central processors arrange the bytes in mathematical order, with the most significant byte first (a style called big-endian).

If two environments have the same character set, floating-point form, and byte sequence, then you can copy SAS data files from one computer to another without making any changes.

The file system affects the form of SAS libraries. Most file systems organize files into directories, allowing each SAS file to be stored as a separate file. In a few file systems, notably the z/OS file system, there are no directories, and an entire SAS data library is stored as one file. This kind of library, called a bound library, is not compatible with any other environment.

In environments that use directories, you can exchange SAS data files between environments with relatively few restrictions, a feature called Cross-Environment Data Access (CEDA). You can create a SAS data file in one environment and read it in another environment. CEDA also allows access to SQL views. There are limitations on the ways in which you can read and write CEDA files; if you encounter these limitations, use the COPY procedure to copy the file to a library that uses the base library engine. CEDA was introduced in SAS release 8.2.

To read files using CEDA, use an ordinary LIBNAME statement for the CEDA library, then read the members of the library.

If you create a library for use in another environment, create it as a CEDA library. Write the OUTREP= option in the LIBNAME statement that creates the library. The value of the option identifies the target environment. Values include WINDOWS, OS2, HP_UX, INTEL_ABI, MAC, MIPS_ABI, RS_6000_AIX, and SOLARIS.

If a CEDA file contains more than about 2 billion observations, an error condition can occur. For these files, if errors occur, do not use CEDA to access the files. You can still transfer the data through CEDA by breaking the SAS data file into multiple files, each one containing fewer than 2 billion observations.

If none of the special cases mentioned above apply, convert SAS data files and catalogs to transport format, and move the transport file between computers. A transport file is an ASCII text file that contains a SAS data library. There are two kinds of transport files, one created by the XPORT library engine and another creaed by the CPORT procedure. An XPORT engine transport file can contain one or more SAS data files, but with limited features. A CPORT procedure transport file can contain one or more SAS data files and catalogs or selected entries of a catalog, but it cannot transfer files to an older SAS version.

To create a transport file using the XPORT library engine, write:

- a LIBNAME statement with the XPORT engine and the physical file name for a file.
- a PROC COPY step to copy members to the library. Copy all or selected members of another library.

The example below creates a transport library and copies all SAS data files from the WORK library to the transport library.

```
LIBNAME MOVE XPORT 'transport1.txt';
PROC COPY IN=WORK OUT=MOVE MTYPE=DATA;
RUN;
```

Move the transport file to the destination computer and, again, use a LIBNAME statement and PROC COPY step to copy the members to a library on the destination computer.

The XPORT engine limits the files it copies to a subset of SAS version 6 features. The names of SAS files and variables are limited to a maximum length of 8 characters. Indexes and similar features are omitted.

To create a transport file with the CPORT procedure, define a fileref for the transport file. In the PROC CPORT statement, use the FILE= option with this fileref. Use one or more of these PROC CPORT options to identify the files to copy:

Proc CPORT

- LIBRARY= to identify the source library
- MTYPE=CATALOG or MTYPE=DATA to copy a specific member type
- CATALOG= to identify the source catalog
- ET= to copy specific entry types
- DATA= to identify a SAS dataset to copy

Write a SELECT or EXCLUDE statement to select specific members or entries to copy. Move the transport file to the destination computer and use the CIMPORT procedure to copy files from the transport file. In the PROC CIMPORT statement, use the INFILE= option to identify the transport file and the LIBRARY=, CATALOG=, or DATA= option to select the destination for the copy.

The XML library engine provides another way to move SAS data between computers. XML is a kind of text markup that you can read as text or display in a web browser. A small example of a SAS table in XML is shown at right.

In the XML markup, it is easy to pick out the member name, HOLIDAY, and the variables, DATE and NAME. The character entity &apos in this example stands for the apostrophe character.

The XML engine does not support variable attributes such as format, label, and length. If a SAS dataset contains these attributes, the engine writes this log message:

```
<TABLE>
   <HOLIDAY>
      <NAME> New Year&apos;s Day </NAME>
      <DATE> 2001-01-01 </DATE>
   </HOLIDAY>
   <HOLIDAY>
      <NAME> Memorial Day </NAME>
      <DATE> 2001-05-28 </DATE>
   </HOLIDAY>
   <HOLIDAY>
      <NAME> Independence Day </NAME>
      <DATE> 2001-07-04 </DATE>
   </HOLIDAY>
   <HOLIDAY>
      <NAME> Labor Day </NAME>
      <DATE> 2001-09-03 </DATE>
   </HOLIDAY>
   <HOLIDAY>
      <NAME> Thanksgiving </NAME>
      <DATE> 2001-11-22 </DATE>
   </HOLIDAY>
   <HOLIDAY>
      <NAME> Christmas </NAME>
      <DATE> 2001-12-25 </DATE>
   </HOLIDAY>
</TABLE>
```

```
NOTE: SAS variable labels, formats, and lengths are not written to
      DBMS tables.
```

Even though the XML engine does not support formats, it looks for format attributes to determine the kind of data a numeric variable contains. Associate a SAS date format with a SAS date variable to tell the XML engine to format the values of the variable as dates. Use SAS time formats and SAS datetime formats in a similar way. If you associate a date or time format with a numeric variable, the engine formats it as an XML date or time value in the XML file.

With the sequential format of a transport or XML file, you can write to it only once. Copy all the members to it in a single PROC COPY or PROC CPORT step. If you write to a transport or XML library in two steps, the files written in the second step replace the ones that were there before. If you are moving files from multiple libraries to another computer, it might be necessary to create multiple files to move.

Transfer a view or a compiled data step by transfering its source code as a SAS program.

SAS versions and releases have different library engines, and using a different engine changes the way SAS files are stored. To move SAS files to an older SAS version in the same environment, use the newer SAS version to convert the files to the older version. Copy the files to a library that uses the library engine of the older SAS version.

When you move a SAS project from one computer to another, take along all the files that are needed to make the project work. You might need to move any combination of these kinds of files:

- SAS data files
- SAS catalogs
- Transport files (SAS libraries in transport format)
- XML libraries (SAS data files encoded as XML)
- Program files
- Secondary program files
- Autoexec files
- Configuration files
- Parameter files
- Macro catalogs or libraries
- Formats and informats, and their source code
- Views, and their source code
- Text data files
- Binary data files

The communications software that connects computers, such as FTP software or a network file server, gives you two main choices of protocol when you transfer a file: text or binary. When you transfer a binary file, the contents of the file are not changed at all. When you transfer a text file, the communications software converts the file to the way text files are conventionally written on the destination computer.

When you transfer files between environments, it is very important to select the correct protocol for transfering the files.

- Transfer all SAS files, including transport files, as binary files.
- Transfer program files, parameter files, configuration files, and text data files as text files.
- Transfer data files that contain binary fields as binary files, even if the files also contain some text fields.

 Even though transport files are ASCII text files, you must transfer them as binary files. The most common reason a transport file is unreadable is that it was transferred as a text file.

 If character variables in a SAS data file contain binary values, you cannot transport them successfully between EBCDIC and ASCII environments. Instead, convert the binary values to binhex encoding before creating the transport files. Binhex encodes binary values using text characters, so it can survive the transfer when binary data cannot. See chapter 14, "Binary Files," for a description of binhex.

Whenever you create character variables containing binary values, protect them from being converted among variations of the ASCII character set by using the transcode variable attribute. Set this attribute in the ATTRIB statement, writing TRANSCODE=NO to tell SAS to maintain the binary value of the variable.

 If a file contains binary fields or a combination of text and binary fields, you must transfer it as a binary file. This can create special issues in reading the file.

- If you move an EBCDIC file to an ASCII environment, use the $EBCDIC informat to read the text fields in the file.
- If you move an ASCII file to an EBCDIC environment, use the $ASCII informat to read the text fields.
- To read binary numeric fields, use compatible binary informats. In particular, if you move an IBM mainframe file to any other environment, use the informats whose names begin with the S370F prefix for compatibility, such as the S370FPD informat for packed decimal fields.

■73
Porting SAS Programs

SAS is designed to be portable. That is, a SAS program that you write for one kind of computer can run on another kind of computer with relatively few changes. Often, no changes are necessary; the code examples throughout this book do not depend on the features of a specific environment.

If a program is intended to run on two or more different kinds of computers, you can design the program to be completely portable, so that the same program can run on the various computers. When changes are necessary to move a program to another kind of computer, the process of making the changes is called porting.

Revise a program in its original environment. If it is badly written, start by cleaning it up; see chapter 67, "Cleaning Up a Program," for details. Next, rewrite parts of the program to remove or isolate any operating system dependencies, as described in this chapter, verifying that the program still produces the same results. Copy the revised program and its associated data to the new environment; see the previous chapter, "Porting Files and Data" for details of this. Then make any additional changes that are necessary and verify that the program works correctly in its new environment.

Dependencies

Most SAS features are portable; they are essentially the same regardless of the environment they run in. When you port a SAS program, most of it will be unchanged. You only need to make changes in the statements, routines, and options that depend on the specific environment.

To find dependencies in a SAS program, look for anything it contains that is not completely portable. This includes any direct references to objects outside of the SAS environment in the operating system environment. It also includes program logic that depends on specific properties of the operating system, properties that are not shared by other operating systems.

These are the most important dependencies to look for:

- *Operating system commands.* Every operating system has a different set of commands, so any use of operating system commands in a SAS program is an operating system dependency. Look for operating system commands in the

Portability Checklist

When you write new programs, write them in a way that lets you move them to another environment with a minimum of effort. This coding approach does not require any special effort. There are just a few areas to watch out for when you program for portability.

✓ **Use portable SAS features.** Do not rely on SAS features that work only in a specific environment. Do not use operating system commands. Minimize and isolate references to the operating system or file system.

✓ **Isolate file references.** When you refer to a physical file name or any other property of the file system or operating system, isolate those references so they are not part of the main body of code.

✓ **Write with portable characters.** Write the program using only the standard ASCII character set, but do not use the caret character, which is not included in the EBCDIC character set.

✓ **Do not rely on a specific sort order for character values.** Character values in general do not necessarily sort in a particular order. However, you can rely on the sort order of a variable if all the characters are uppercase letters (with spaces). The same is true for lowercase letters and for digits.

✓ **In character comparisons, test for matching values only.** Do not use the comparison operators <, <=, >, and >= with character values. Use functions such as ANYUPPER and ANYDIGIT to check for character classes.

✓ **Do not rely on character hexadecimal constants for character values.** If you must use character hexadecimal constants, as for the tab character, isolate them as macro variables so that you can change them for another platform.

✓ **Use sufficient lengths for numeric variables.** If you set lengths for numeric variables, base the lengths on the IEEE double precision format. For example, a length of 3 allows accurate integer values up to 256.

✓ **Stay well within the limits of numeric precision.** In scientific applications, do not use numeric values that are close to the maximum or minimum values of double precision. The precision of these numbers could be very different in different computers, and this could lead to differing results or the possibility of overflow or underflow errors.

✓ **Use portable binary formats or informats.** Do not use the native versions of binary formats and informats. If you use binary formats, use portable formats such as S370FPIB for unsigned integers.

X statement, SYSTEM function, %SYSEXEC macro statement, and other SAS features that pass commands to the operating system.

- *Physical file names.* Different file systems form physical file names in different ways. To make a program portable, use SAS names such as filerefs and librefs rather than physical file names. Look for references to files in FILENAME, LIBNAME, FILE, INFILE, and PROC PRINTTO statements. Also look for physical file names in the FILENAME and LIBNAME functions.
- *Special qualities of files.* Different file systems construct and access files in different ways. A portable SAS program cannot rely on any of the special properties of files that are supported in a specific environment. Look for dataset options, system options, engines and engine options, and devices and device options that depend on the special features of the file system.
- *Character set.* Most computers use their own variations of the ASCII character set. IBM mainframe computers use the EBCDIC character set. The differences in character sets can produce different results in comparisons and sorting.
- *Numeric data.* SAS numeric values use the native double-precision format, which follows the IEEE standard on most computers, but is different on IBM mainframe computers and some other computers.
- *Compiled program units.* Compiled programs such as data step views, compiled data steps, and stored compiled macros may have to be recompiled for the new operating system.
- *Operating system features expressed in SAS features.* In every environment, SAS includes routines, statements, options, and other features that provide access to specific features of the operating system. These SAS features are implemented in that specific environment and cannot be ported to another environment.

These factors in particular must be considered before you decide whether a project can be moved from one computer to another:

- *SAS products installed.* If programs depend on specific SAS products, they will not run on another computer where those SAS products are not installed.
- *Operating system.* If programs depend on operating system features, they may not be able to run in a different operating system.
- *Operating system version.* If programs depend on newer features of an operating system, they may not be able to run in an older version of the operating system.

Character set differences can cause a few kinds of problems when a program is moved to a new environment.

The EBCDIC character set does not include the ^ character. The ASCII character set does not include the ¢ and ¬ characters found in the EBCDIC character set.

The sort order of character values is different when the data is moved to a different character set. Data that is in sorted order in one environment might not be in sorted order in a different environment. For example, this comparison is true with ASCII characters, but false with EBCDIC characters:

'A' < 'a'

Some very old printers and terminals do not support lowercase letters.

If you use comparisons to extract specific sets of characters, the comparisons might not be valid in a different character set. For example, this condition might be used to identify ASCII capital letters:

'A' <= CHAR <= 'Z'

In EBCDIC, the set of characters identified by this condition includes capital letters, but it also includes a few special characters. The ANYUPPER function provides a more reliable way to test for capital letters, and similar functions test for other character classes.

When necessary, use the $ASCII and $EBCDIC informats and formats to translate character data between the two character sets. See the preceding chapter, "Porting Files and Data," for details.

If a program contains hexadecimal character constants, the constants will represent different characters if you move them to a different operating system. This is especially a concern with tab characters. In ASCII, a tab character is '09'X; in EBCDIC, it is '05'X.

Numeric data formats are different on some computers, including IBM mainframe computers. This can affect the precision of numeric values when they are moved from one environment to another, especially when numeric variables have a length shorter than 8. If necessary, increase the length of a numeric variable by one byte.

The 2-byte length allowed for numeric variables on IBM mainframe computers is not supported on most computers; use a length of 3 for these variables.

Differences in numeric data formats also affect the behavior of some informats and formats, such as PIB. These informats and formats work with native numerics, so their behavior is different in different environments. For portability, use portable informats and formats such as S370FPIB.

If a program will be running in different environments, find out what SAS releases are running in each environment. If a program must run in different SAS releases, you might have to rewrite parts of the program so that they use only the common features of the SAS releases.

Identifying the specific ways in which a SAS program depends on its environment is the first step in making it portable. Then, as much as possible, rewrite the program so that it does not use the specific features that are tied to the environment. These are some examples of specific situations you might find and changes you might make:

- The PIB format is not portable. Use the S370FPIB format instead.
- A numeric variable has a length of 2. Increase the length to 3.
- A FILE statement refers to a physical file name. Change the statement so that it uses a fileref.
- The program uses an operating system command to generate a list of files. Use directory functions instead to generate the list.

Isolating Nonportable Code

It is rarely practical to write an entire program using only portable code. When a portable program must contain nonportable code, you can make the nonportable code easier to work with by isolating it in one part of the program, separating it from the main program file, or using macro logic to execute it only in the environment where it is used.

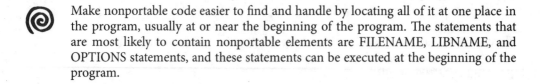

Make nonportable code easier to find and handle by locating all of it at one place in the program, usually at or near the beginning of the program. The statements that are most likely to contain nonportable elements are FILENAME, LIBNAME, and OPTIONS statements, and these statements can be executed at the beginning of the program.

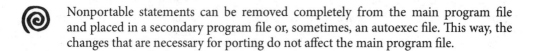

Nonportable statements can be removed completely from the main program file and placed in a secondary program file or, sometimes, an autoexec file. This way, the changes that are necessary for porting do not affect the main program file.

Another approach is to implement nonportable code items such as physical file names as program parameters. They can be placed in a parameter file, for example. See chapter 64, "Program Parameters," for details.

Inside macros, use conditional macro programming to execute different statements in different environments. The automatic macro variables SYSSCP and SYSSCPL let you identify the operating system you are executing in.

To find out the values of these macro variables in a particular environment, use these statements:

```
%PUT &SYSSCP;
%PUT &SYSSCPL;
```

This example creates the macro variable TAB, with the constant value of a tab character.

```
%GLOBAL TAB;
%IF &SYSSCP = OS %THEN %LET TAB = '05'X;
%ELSE %LET TAB = '09'X;
```

The macro %IF-%THEN statement can execute only inside a macro. The %GLOBAL statement makes TAB a global macro variable, which exists outside of the macro.

If you are also dealing with issues of SAS releases, use similar macro logic with the automatic macro variable SYSVER, which identifies the SAS release number. The macro variable SYSVLONG, which also includes the technical support level, can be useful if you are checking for a specific bug fix.

■74
Translating Programs

There are various reasons why a set of programs developed in SAS might then be translated to another programming language. Most often, the idea is to translate the program to a compiled language such as C so it can be distributed as a standalone application. Such projects can come about when there is a need to run on a large number of computers. A standalone application has these potential advantages:

- Being easy to install.
- Occupying a small area of storage space.
- Using less memory while running.
- Running in any combination of operating systems.

As the numbers of users and installations increase, advantages such as these eventually provide reason enough to take on the substantial programming effort that a translation requires.

In addition, there are advantages in the programming languages themselves. A language such as C offers structured programming, more data types, and easier access to operating system routines.

 To translate a SAS program to another language, you need to understand the actions hidden in the many automatic features of SAS. These features must be coded specifically in the translated program. In addition, if the program uses SAS routines such as functions, procedures, informats, and formats, you will have to find or create equivalents in the other language. If a SAS program makes heavy use of automatic features and SAS routines, the translation of it will be a much longer program.

Much of the SAS language can be translated rather directly to other languages: for the most part, blocks are still blocks, operators are still operators, constants are still constants, and so on. But other features have no direct translation:

- *Observation loop.* Code an observation loop as an infinite loop with an index variable to count observations and a mechanism for ending at the end of data. Add actions for any automatic features such as resetting values with every repetition of the loop.
- *Missing values.* If necessary, use a separate variable to indicate missing values.

- *I/O statements.* Single statements in SAS such as INPUT, OUTPUT, and MERGE become separate routines in a structured programming language.
- *System options and title lines.* Global settings, if you use them, might be implemented as global variables. In object-oriented programming, you will probably have some kind of global environment object.
- *Log and standard print file.* If you create print files, you might need separate routines to keep track of their formatting, pagination, etc.

If you are translating to C, these C features can help to replace some SAS features:

- The pow function replaces the exponentiation operator.
- The strcmp function replaces comparison operators for strings.
- The ++, +=, and -= operators replace sum statements.
- for loops replace DO loops with index variables.
- while loops replace DO WHILE loops.
- do while loops replace DO UNTIL loops.
- case statements replace SELECT blocks.
- Preprocessor symbols might replace macro language objects.
- Global variables can replace some uses of macro variables.

The main reason to translate a program written in another language to SAS is to add some of the special features of the SAS environment. These could be features of SAS procedures or just the unparalleled I/O flexibility that SAS provides.

In this kind of translation, the biggest challenge is making the program structure fit into the restrictions of the SAS language. A short, simple program can be translated to a single data step. To translate more elaborate programs, you need to find ways to break the program into SAS steps. This can require extensive changes to the program structure, especially if you are translating a structured program.

Look for processes in the program that could be replaced with proc steps. Find tables of data and make them SAS datasets. Replace translation routines with informats and formats when you can. With luck, you can translate enough of the program in this way that you will be able to see how to translate whatever remains.

If you have elaborate processing written in C that you want to use in combination with SAS processing, it might be easier to place the existing logic into a procedure, engine, or other routine for use in the SAS environment. To do this, you have to add logic that connects to the SAS data model and the SAS/TOOLKIT APIs, but you might be able to use most of the processing routines of an existing C project intact.

■ 75

Style

An effective programming style uses the flexibility of the programming language to emphasize the purpose of a program. Style makes the program easier to read and understand. Every program has its own purpose and shape, its own points of emphasis, so there cannot be any blanket rules about good and bad style points. For every mechanically defined rule of style, there will sooner or later be an exception.

In fact, exceptions are the key to effective style. An effective style is based on a continual tension between uniformity and distinctiveness. That is, you make everything the same so that when you eventually make something different, it says something.

You can see this in indentation, which is the style point that seems to get the most mention. Indentation simply means that the programmer decides how many spaces to write at the beginning of a line of code. As a rule, secondary statements are indented, and continuations of statements, when a statement continues beyond a single line, are indented still more. In proc steps in this book, I treat PROC and RUN statements as primary statements, and I indent most other statements — but I do not indent statements in the SQL procedure. What makes SQL different? The SQL procedure is an interpretive procedure, executing each statement as an independent action. The unindented statements in a PROC SQL step may remind you to read each statement separately. The distinction I show in the treatment of the PROC SQL step points to a real difference I want you to notice. This is the kind of meaning a programming style can convey.

These are some of the distinctions in the SAS language that you might want to add to programs you write as a matter of style:

- *The various meanings of the equals sign (=) and slash (/).* Write these symbols with or without spaces around them to show differences of meaning.
- *The effects of control flow statements on other statements.* You can show this by indenting statements inside blocks or by writing blank lines at appropriate places.
- *Unary and binary uses of the - and + operators.* Many programmers write spaces around the binary operators, but no spaces after the unary operators. This practice follows the notation conventions of mathematics.
- *Executable and nonexecutable statements in a data step.* Most nonexecutable statements can be written anywhere in the step, but you can make them easier to see by grouping them together.
- *Names of routines, as distinguished from other names.* You can highlight this

distinction by writing the left parenthesis immediately after the name of a function, CALL routine, or macro, but writing a space between other words and left parentheses that follow them.

- *Functions and arrays.* Use braces for array subscripts. When you name arrays, do not use names of functions or names that look like function names.

Some style points provide benefits beyond mere appearance. I recommmend:

- Use the words AND, OR, NOT, and NE for these operators, rather than the symbols. For OR, NOT, and NE, this is because the vertical bar, logical not, and caret characters used in the symbols for these operators can sometimes present problems if you move program files from one computer to another and translate the programs from one character set to another. For AND, it is because the ampersand character could look like a macro variable reference.
- Write RUN statements to mark the ends of steps (or QUIT statements, if appropriate). Write global statements between steps. This makes it easier to find the steps of a program. It also makes it easier to run, debug, or test the program in the interactive environment.
- Write the LENGTH and ARRAY statements among the first statements in a DATA step. These statements work only if they come before any reference to a character variable or an array element.
- Use single quotes to enclose a quoted string when you want to emphasize that the macro processor does not process the text of the quoted string.

Use spacing, punctuation, and comments to clarify code that might confuse other programmers.

- *Null statements.* A null statement is just a semicolon, so when you write a null statement as the action of a control flow statement, the null statement can seem to disappear. Make the null statement easier to see by writing a space before it.
- *Sum statements.* If it helps, write parentheses around the expression of the sum statement.
- *MERGE statement with no BY statement.* This usually occurs by mistake, so if it is what you intend, add a comment statement to clarify it.
- *Assignment statement with character truncation.* You can truncate a character value by assigning it to a character variable that has a shorter length. However, this is far from the first thing most programmers think of when they see an assignment statement, so clarify the action by writing a comment.

The statements below demonstrate the points mentioned above.

```
OTHERWISE ;

SUM + (-A*B + C*D);

* Unmatched merge. ;
MERGE WORK.MAIN WORK.OTHER;

LENGTH INITIAL $ 1;
INITIAL = LASTNAME; * Extract first letter of name;
```

■ 76

Data Step Windows

Data step windows are not widely used because other windows that can be created in the SAS System offer more capabilities. However, data step windows are easy to program and provide a quick way to add a text-mode windowing user interface to a SAS program within the context of a data step. Data step windows are actually the easiest SAS windows to develop because all of the programming that is required is contained in just a few data step statements.

Creating data step windows requires two statements. The WINDOW statement defines the layout of a window. The DISPLAY statement displays the window.

 The WINDOW statement defines a data step window using these terms:

```
WINDOW window name
  window options
  fields
  groups
  ;
```

These are the parts of the WINDOW statement:

- The window name is a SAS name that identifies the window. You will use the name in the DISPLAY statement that displays the window. The name is displayed in the window, so use a name that will be meaningful to the user and write it in upper- and lowercase letters.
- Window options apply to the window as a whole. These options can set the size and location of the window. The IROW= and ICOLUMN= options position the upper left corner of the window using numeric values that represent character positions or relative positions. To control the size of the window, use the ROWS= and COLUMNS= options with numeric size values.
- A field designates an area of the window that displays a text value or the value of a variable or in which the user can enter a value for a variable. The syntax for fields includes numerous terms and options and is discussed in detail below. The window must contain at least one field or group.
- A group is a set of fields that are displayed together. To indicate a group, write GROUP= followed by the name of the group, then the fields in the group. A window can be defined with groups to display different fields at different times. A window defined without groups always displays the same fields.

This statement defines the Greeting window with one field that displays a message.

WINDOW Greeting "You are looking at a data step window.";

Use the DISPLAY statement to display a data step window. Write the window name in the DISPLAY statement. If the window is defined with groups, follow the window name with a period and the group name. There are several options that can appear in the DISPLAY statement. One useful option is the DELETE option, which closes the window when the user responds.

    This is an example of a data step that displays the Greeting window.

```
DATA _NULL_;
  WINDOW Greeting "You are looking at a data step window.";
  DISPLAY Greeting DELETE;
  STOP;
RUN;
```

Greeting
You are looking at a data step window.

These other options can be used in the DISPLAY statement: BLANK, to erase previously displayed fields; BELL, to beep; and NOINPUT, to not wait for a user response.

    A STOP statement is usually a necessary part of a data step that displays a window. A data step automatically repeats if it contains a DISPLAY statement. The STOP statement keeps it from repeating indefinitely.

A data step window can display three kinds of fields.

- A *constant field* displays a text message or label.
- A *protected variable field* displays the value of a variable.
- A *user entry field*, or *unprotected variable field*, displays the value of a variable and allows the user to enter a different value for the variable.

All three kinds of fields use pointer controls to indicate their location in the window. The pointer controls #, /, @, and + have the same meaning as in the PUT statement.

    Use the # and @ pointer controls before a field to indicate the line number and column number where the field is located. This example positions a field at line 2, column 6.

#2 @6 "You are looking at a data step window."

    The line pointer control is not necessary if the field is on the same line as the previous field. Use a line pointer control without a column pointer control to start a field at the beginning of a line.

    Write a constant field as a character constant, as shown in the previous example.

    Write a protected variable field with the variable, a format, and the option PROTECT=YES. This is an example of a protected variable field that displays the variable START using the format TIME8.

#4 @6 START TIME8. PROTECT=YES

Write a user entry field with the variable and a format/informat. The format/informat must be a valid indication of both a format for displaying a value and an informat for interpreting a value that the user enters. This is an example of a field that allows the user to enter a value for the variable START.

#5 @6 START TIME8.

Several field options can be useful for some kinds of user entry fields. Use the REQUIRED=YES option to prevent a user from leaving the window with a field left blank; the AUTOSKIP=YES option to automatically move the cursor to the beginning of the next user entry field when the user types a character in the last position of the field; and the DISPLAY=NO option for passwords, to allow the user to enter a value without the value being shown in the field.

Use the $CHAR format/informat for user entry fields of character variables. To left-align values that the user enters, use the $F format/informat. For most numeric fields, use the BEST format/informat. The BEST informat is an alias for the F informat.

Before displaying a window that contains user entry fields, set the values of the variables appropriately. Give the variables missing values if you expect the user to enter new values in the fields. Use the system option MISSING=' ' so that missing values are displayed as blank fields in the window. This makes it easier for the user to enter new values in numeric fields. With the default, MISSING='.', a missing value is displayed as a period, and the user must erase the period when entering a new value.

 When the window is displayed to the user, the user can take various actions, such as:

- Typing values in user entry fields.
- Pressing the Tab key to advance from one user entry field to the next.
- Typing commands.
- Selecting items from menus.
- Pressing function keys.
- Changing the size of the window.
- Closing the window with the END command or window controls.

However, there is no interaction if the window is displayed with the NOINPUT option. Then, the user must wait until the data step reaches a point where it displays a window without the NOINPUT option, or until the data step ends.

In a window that has user entry fields, the window expects the user to enter a value in every user entry field. The window does not accept the user input and return control to the data step program until the user has entered a new value in each user entry field or has pressed the enter key in each field that does not have a new value.

If the user closes the window, it immediately ends the data step that displays the window. Write the data step in such a way that it can end correctly at the execution of any DISPLAY statement.

There are two automatic variables associated with data step windows. The variable _MSG_ contains a message from the program to the user. The value of this variable is displayed in the message line when the window is displayed. Displaying the window automatically resets the value of the variable to blank.

To display a message to the user, assign a value to _MSG_ before the DISPLAY statement, as shown in this example.

```
_MSG_ = 'Press Enter to continue.';
DISPLAY Alert DELETE;
```

The automatic variable _CMD_ lets you receive commands from the user, but you must be certain that the commands are not valid display manager commands. Any command that appears to be a display manager command is intercepted by display manager before it can reach the data step program. To be safe, do not use commands that begin with letters or with a semicolon (;) or colon (:). Begin the commands with other special characters or with digits.

After the DISPLAY statement, check the value of _CMD_, and if it is not blank, parse the command and respond accordingly.

The following example demonstrates elements of the programming logic of user interaction with a data step window. It also demonstrates a window with multiple groups. This program adds and multiplies numbers as requested by the user.

```
OPTIONS MISSING=' ';
DATA _NULL_;
  WINDOW Math
    ROWS=10 COLUMNS=40 IROW=7 ICOLUMN=16
    GROUP=MENU
    #1 @2 '1   Add two numbers'
    #2 @2 '2   Multiply two numbers'
    #4 @2 '.Q  Quit'
    GROUP=ADD
    #1 @2 'Enter two numbers to add.'
    #3 @2 TERM1 BEST15. ATTR=REV_VIDEO
    +1 '+'
    +1 TERM2 BEST15. ATTR=REV_VIDEO
    GROUP=SUM
    #1 @2 'The sum is ' SUM BEST16. PROTECT=YES
    #3 @2 'Press ENTER to continue.'
    GROUP=MULTIPLY
    #1 @2 'Enter two numbers to multiply.'
    #3 @2 FACTOR1 BEST15. ATTR=REV_VIDEO
    +1 'x'
    +1 FACTOR2 BEST15. ATTR=REV_VIDEO
    GROUP=PRODUCT
    #1 @2 'The product is ' PRODUCT BEST18. PROTECT=YES
    #3 @2 'Press ENTER to continue.'
  ;

DISPLAY MATH.MENU BLANK; * Menu;
SELECT(SCAN(COMPRESS(UPCASE(_CMD_)), 1, ';'));
  WHEN('1') DO;
    DISPLAY MATH.ADD BLANK; * Addition dialog box;
    SUM = SUM(0, TERM1, TERM2);
    DISPLAY MATH.SUM BLANK; * Sum dialog box;
    END;
  WHEN('2') DO;
    DISPLAY MATH.MULTIPLY BLANK; * Multiply dialog box;
    IF FACTOR1 AND FACTOR2 THEN
      PRODUCT = FACTOR1*FACTOR2;
    ELSE PRODUCT = 0;
    DISPLAY MATH.PRODUCT BLANK; * Product dialog box;
    END;
```

```
Command ===> 1_____

1    Add two numbers
2    Multiply two numbers

.Q   Quit
```

```
Command ===> _____

Enter two numbers to add.

2_____   + 25_____
```

```
Command ===> _____

The sum is              27

Press ENTER to continue.
```

```
Command ===> 2_____

1    Add two numbers
2    Multiply two numbers

.Q   Quit
```

```
Command ===> _____

Enter two numbers to multiply.

.125_____   + 128_____
```

```
WHEN('.Q') STOP;
OTHERWISE DO;
   IF _CMD_ = ' ' THEN
      _MSG_ = 'Enter option on command line.';
   ELSE _MSG_ = 'Option not recognized.';
   END;
END;
RUN;
```

```
Command ===> _____

The product is                    16

Press ENTER to continue.
```

In practical interactive applications, it is often easier to have a user select menu items from the menu bar than to enter commands in a command line. See chapter 79, "Menu Bars," for the details of creating a PMENU entry to define a menu bar. Have the menu bar return commands that begin with a period or other special character. After you define the PMENU entry, add it to the data step window by naming it in the MENU= window option in the WINDOW statement.

```
Command ===> .q_____

1   Add two numbers
2   Multiply two numbers

.Q  Quit
```

When the window is displayed and the user selects a menu item, it results in a command, the same as if the user pressed a function key or entered the command text on the command line. The resulting command text, as defined in the menu bar definition, is assigned to the automatic variable _CMD_, and you can examine this variable to determine the action to take in response.

To enter data directly into a data step, use a data step window with a separate field for each variable. To make the window easier to use, assign missing values to variables before you display the window, if necessary, and use the MISSING=' ' system option so that the missing values display as blank fields. Display an appropriate text label before each variable field so that the user knows which variable to enter where. If there are just a few variables, it is usually easiest to align the fields vertically, that is, start them all at the same column.

This example below displays a window for the user to enter four variables and stores the entered values in a SAS dataset. The automatic variable _N_ is displayed in a protected variable field in case it might be useful to the user. In this example, it is not necessary to reset variables to missing because this is done in the automatic processing of the data step.

```
OPTIONS MISSING=' ';
DATA NEW.ENTRY;
   WINDOW Entries
      #1 @4 'Entry submitted by:'
      @24 CONTACT $F24.
      #2 @6 'Recording artist:'
      @24 ARTIST $F24.
      #3 @17 'Title:'
      @24 TITLE $F32.
      #4 @7 'Number of songs:'
      @24 SONGS F1.
      #6 @2 'Observation' +1 _N_ F8. PROTECT=YES
      ;
   DISPLAY Entries;
RUN;
```

```
Entries

   Entry submitted by: _____
     Recording artist: _____
                Title: _____
      Number of songs: _

Observation        1
```

The user types a value for each variable, then presses the enter key to complete an observation and proceed to the next one. After entering all the observations, the user closes the window or enters the END command to complete processing.

The same kind of window is used to edit a SAS dataset. It is not a particularly convenient way for a user to edit a SAS dataset that has multiple variables and many observations because it requires the user to go through every variable for every observationk but it can be very easy to program and it can be combined with other data step logic. This example lets a user edit a SAS dataset that contains a list of names.

```
DATA NEW.NAMES;
   WINDOW Names
      #1 _N_ F8. PROTECT=YES
      #3 @12 NAME $F24.
      ;
   MODIFY NEW.NAMES;
   DISPLAY Names;
RUN;
```

```
 Names

         1

              Kim Li_____
```

Any changes the user makes are stored in the SAS dataset. If the user closes the window before going through the complete list, the remaining names are not affected.

A status dialog is a small window that a noninteractive part of an interactive application uses to tell the user the actions that are taking place or that an unexpected event has occurred. A data step that is part of an interactive application can display a status dialog as a data step window.

Use the NOINPUT option in the DISPLAY statement when you display a status dialog. With this option, the program does not stop to wait for a user response.

Use options in the WINDOW statement to make a status dialog window small and locate it near the center of the screen. This makes it easier for the user to recognize the window as a status dialog.

The simplest status dialog just describes what the data step is doing. Define the message as a data step window. Display it at the beginning of the data step. The window automatically closes when the data step ends. Use messages of this sort to reassure the user during processes that can take more than a few seconds to run.

```
DATA _NULL_;
   WINDOW Status
      IROW=9 ICOLUMN=14
      ROWS=9 COLUMNS=54
      #2 @8 'Exporting list of CR events.';
   IF _N_ = 1 THEN DISPLAY Status NOINPUT;
   SET WORK.CREV;
   . . .
```

```
 Status


              Exporting list of CR events.
```

In this example, the condition _N_ = 1 is used to display the window only at the beginning of the data step. The text in the window does not change, so it is not necessary or efficient to display it more than once.

If you have status dialogs in several data steps in the same application, give them the same name, size, and position to make them easier for the user to follow.

An animated progress bar gives the user a picture of the progress a program is making. This familiar user interface device is like a simple bar chart that changes to show the relative degree of completion of a process.

You can display an animated progress bar only if you have a way to calculate the relative progress. If a data step contains a sequential SET statement, calculate progress as the ratio of the current observation number to the total number of observations (determined using the NOBS= option).

To create the animated progress bar, display a constant field at a moving position. Calculate the position of this field based on the relative progress you calculate. Use the PERSIST=YES field option so that the previously displayed characters continue to be displayed.

For efficiency, update an animated progress bar — or any window — only when it changes. The example below displays a progress bar with 39 character positions. It redisplays the window 39 times — once for each character it displays in the progress bar.

The program uses several variables to manage the progress bar. PROGRESS_N is the number of observations represented in each character of the progress bar. NEXT_N is the observation of the next observation at which the progress bar is incremented. PROGRESS is the relative progress measured in character positions, from 0 to 39. An expression in the WINDOW statement uses PROGRESS to calculate the character position where it displays each character of the progress bar.

```
DATA _NULL_;
  RETAIN PROGRESS_N NEXT_N PROGRESS 0;
  WINDOW Status
    IROW=9 ICOLUMN=14 ROWS=11 COLUMNS=54
    GROUP=STATIC
    #2 @8 'Exporting list of CR events.' PERSIST=YES
    #4 @6 '|' PERSIST=YES @46 '|'  PERSIST=YES
    #5 @6 "|   '   '   '   |   '   '   '    |" PERSIST=YES
    GROUP=PROGRESS
    #4 @(6 + PROGRESS) '*' PERSIST=YES
  ;
  IF _N_ = 1 THEN DO;
    DISPLAY Status.STATIC NOINPUT;
    PROGRESS_N = ROUND((NOBS/39) MAX 1);
    NEXT_N = PROGRESS_N/2;
  END;
  SET WORK.CREV NOBS=NOBS;
  IF _N_ > NEXT_N THEN DO;
    PROGRESS + 1;
    NEXT_N + PROGRESS_N;
    DISPLAY Status.PROGRESS NOINPUT;
  END;
  . . .
```

```
Status

        Exporting list of CR events.

  |***                                        |
  |    '    '    '    |    '    '    '    |
```

```
Status

        Exporting list of CR events.

  |**********                                 |
  |    '    '    '    |'   '    '    '    |
```

```
Status

        Exporting list of CR events.

  |*********************************          |
  |    '    '    '    |    '    '    '    |
```

■ 77
Macro Windows

 Macro windows are windows in which a SAS program can display values of macro variables or a user can enter new values for macro variables. Macro windows are much like data step windows (described in the previous chapter), but they are not limited to the environment of the data step.

The syntax of macro windows is almost the same as that of data step windows. Some differences are necessary to adjust for the ways in which macro variables are different from the data step variables that data step windows display. This is a list of the main differences.

- A macro window is defined and displayed in macro statements. Use the %WINDOW statement to define the window and the %DISPLAY statement to display it.
- Use macro variables in place of data step variables.
- Macro variables do not use informats and formats, so do not write informat/format terms for fields in the %WINDOW statement. Instead, write an integer term to indicate the width of the field.
- The same pointer controls are used. However, you cannot use a data step expression with a pointer control. Instead, use a macro expression.
- In place of the automatic variables _CMD_ and _MSG_, use the automatic macro variables SYSCMD and SYSMSG.
- In a macro window, it is never acceptable for fields to overlap.
- The PERSIST= field option is not available.

If a macro window is displayed inside a macro, the window is closed when the macro ends. If a macro window is displayed outside a macro, the window closes as soon as the user responds.

The simplest macro window just displays information without giving the user a way to make any changes or choices. The displayed information can be any combination of constant fields and protected variable fields. Use the PROTECT=YES field option to protect the variable fields.

This example displays a window that shows several macro variables with information about the SAS environment.

```
%WINDOW Env
    #2 @5 'SAS release' +1 SYSVER 32 PROTECT=YES
```

```
#4 @5 'Operating system' +1 SYSSCP 8 PROTECT=YES
+1 SYSSCPL 8 PROTECT=YES
#6 @5 'Site' +1 SYSSITE 32 PROTECT=YES
#8 @5 'User' +1 SYSUSERID 32 PROTECT=YES
;
%DISPLAY ENV;
```

A macro window can allow the user to enter program parameters, as shown in the example below. In this example, default values are assigned to the macro variables before the window is displayed.

```
%WINDOW Data
    #2 @5 'Input data' @21 DATA 41
    #4 @5 'Year' @21 YEAR 4
    #5 @5 'Month' @21 MONTH 2
;
%LET DATA = _LAST_;
%LET YEAR = %SYSFUNC(DATE(), YEAR4.);
%LET MONTH = %SYSFUNC(DATE(), MMDDYY2.);
%DISPLAY DATA;
```

```
+----------------------------------------------+
| Data                                         |
|                                              |
|    Input data       work.recon               |
|                     _____              |
|    Year             2002                     |
|    Month            02                       |
|                                              |
+----------------------------------------------+
```

Text values that the user enters in the fields become the new values of the macro variables.

Another example of a use for a macro window is to allow the user to set selected system options. The example below defines the macro RPTOPT, which allows the user to view and change four system options related to print output.

```
%MACRO RPTOPT;
%LET LS = %SYSFUNC(GETOPTION(LINESIZE));
%LET PS = %SYSFUNC(GETOPTION(PAGESIZE));
%LET PAGE = %SYSFUNC(GETOPTION(PAGENO));
%LET CENTER = %EVAL(%SYSFUNC(GETOPTION(CENTER)) = CENTER);
%WINDOW Options
    #2 @5 'Line size' @19 LS 3
    #3 @5 'Page size' @19 PS 5
    #4 @5 'Center' @19 CENTER 1
    #5 @5 'Page number' @19 PAGE 6
;
%DISPLAY OPTIONS;
OPTIONS LINESIZE=&LS PAGESIZE=&PS
    CENTER=&CENTER PAGENO=&PAGE;
%MEND;
```

```
+----------------------------------------------+
| Options                                      |
|                                              |
|    Line size        75                       |
|    Page size        56                       |
|    Center           0                        |
|    Page number      47                        |
|                                              |
|                                              |
+----------------------------------------------+
```

When the RPTOPT macro executes, it displays a window such as the one shown above, with the current values of the system options. The user can enter other values. The OPTIONS statement in the macro then sets the system options to whatever values the user enters.

You can incorporate a macro window into the control flow of a macro to allow a user to select from one of several actions. A simplified code model for this follows.

```
%MACRO CHOOSE;
%WINDOW SELECT
    #2 @5 'Select option' +1 OPTION 1
    #4 @5 'Write more text to describe the options here.'
    ;
%DISPLAY SELECT;
%IF &OPTION = 1 %THEN %DO;
actions for selected option 1
%END;
%ELSE %IF &OPTION = 2 %THEN %DO;
actions for selected option 2
%END;
%ELSE %IF &OPTION = 3 %THEN %DO;
actions for selected option 3
%END;
%MEND;
```

 For a status window, display a macro window inside a macro with the NOINPUT option. Assign a status message to a macro variable and display this variable in the window. Change the status message after every step to let the user know what the program is doing. The user cannot interact with the window, and the window closes as soon as the macro ends.

The macro below generates two SAS steps and shows four status messages in its macro window. The window displays two macro variables, ACTION and STEP. To update the window, the macro uses %LET statements to assign new values to these variables, then a %DISPLAY statement to redisplay the window.

```
%MACRO STATUS;
%WINDOW STATUS ROWS=12 COLUMNS=50
    #3 @5 ACTION
    #4 @5 'Step' +1 STEP +1 'of 4';
%LET STEP = 1;
%LET ACTION = Initializing;
%DISPLAY STATUS NOINPUT;
%LET STEP = 2;
%LET ACTION = Sorting;
%DISPLAY STATUS NOINPUT;
PROC SORT DATA=WORK.X OUT=WORK.X2;
    BY LOCATION GROUP TRANS;
RUN;
%LET STEP = 3;
%LET ACTION = Formatting report;
%DISPLAY STATUS NOINPUT;
PROC PRINT DATA=WORK.X2 HEADING=H NOOBS;
    BY LOCATION;
RUN;
%LET STEP = 4;
%LET ACTION = Finishing;
%DISPLAY STATUS NOINPUT;
%MEND;
```

```
STATUS


        Initializing
        Step 1 of 4
```

```
STATUS


        Sorting
        Step 2 of 4
```

```
STATUS


        Formatting report
        Step 3 of 4
```

```
STATUS


        Finishing
        Step 4 of 4
```

78

Interactive Line Mode

Interactive line mode is a user interface style designed for the teletype terminals that provided an early form of interactivity between computer programs and users. The interaction is displayed as a text sequence, with each line of text displayed below the line that preceded it. An interactive line mode interface style is supported in some SAS environments. Usually, it appears in a separate terminal-style window, sometimes called a console.

SAS includes a TERMINAL device to support interactive line mode I/O. Use FILENAME statements to associate filerefs with the TERMINAL device, as shown in this example.

```
FILENAME IN TERMINAL;
FILENAME OUT TERMINAL;
```

If these statements result in error messages, it is probably because the environment you are running in does not support the TERMINAL device.

After the filerefs are defined, you can use them in data steps with ordinary INPUT and PUT statements. PUT statements display messages and responses from the program to the user. INPUT statements read values, selections, and commands supplied by the user.

The programming logic of the line mode user interface is essentially the same as that of a windowing interface in a data step. The example below is a variation on an example presented in chapter 76, "Data Step Windows."

```
DATA _NULL_;
  INFILE IN UNBUFFERED TRUNCOVER;
  FILE OUT;

  PUT 'MATH  Select option:'
    / @5 '1  Add two numbers'
    / @5 '2  Multiply two numbers'
    / @5 'Q  Quit';
  INPUT LINE $80.;
  SELECT(SCAN(UPCASE(LINE), 1, ' ;'));
    WHEN('1') DO;
      PUT 'Enter the two numbers to add.';
      INPUT LINE $80.;
```

```
          TERM1 = SCAN(LINE, 1, ' ,;+*&');
          TERM2 = SCAN(LINE, 2, ' ,;+*&');
          SUM = SUM(0, TERM1, TERM2);
          PUT 'The sum is ' SUM :BEST16.;
          END;
       WHEN('2') DO;
          PUT 'Enter the two numbers to multiply.';
          INPUT LINE $80.;
          FACTOR1 = SCAN(LINE, 1, ' ,;+*&');
          FACTOR2 = SCAN(LINE, 2, ' ,;+*&');
          IF FACTOR1 AND FACTOR2 THEN PRODUCT = FACTOR1*FACTOR2;
          ELSE PRODUCT = 0;
          PUT 'The product is ' PRODUCT :BEST18.;
          END;
       WHEN('Q') STOP;
       OTHERWISE ;
       END;
RUN;
```

```
MATH   Select option:
    1   Add two numbers
    2   Multiply two numbers
    Q   Quit
1
Enter the two numbers to add.
2, 25
The sum is 27
MATH   Select option:
    1   Add two numbers
    2   Multiply two numbers
    Q   Quit
2
Enter the two numbers to multiply.
  .125*128
The product is 16
MATH   Select option:
    1   Add two numbers
    2   Multiply two numbers
    Q   Quit
q
```

In the Microsoft Windows environment, the TERMINAL device is not associated with a line mode style, although it can display output in a similar way. It does not support input, and its support for output is unofficial.

Instead of displaying a terminal window, it displays each line of output as a separate alert box. You can use a fileref associated with the TERMINAL device to display alert messages. As with any alert message, if a message is too long to display in one line in the alert box, it wraps to display on multiple lines. Run this example to see the effect:

```
FILENAME OUT TERMINAL;
DATA _NULL_;
   FILE OUT;
   PUT 'This is an example of a message displayed in an alert box.'
      / 'This line is displayed as another message.';
RUN;
```

■ 79
Menu Bars

Windowing user interfaces developed in the SAS System can use menu bar definitions, which are catalog entries of type PMENU. A menu bar can replace the window's menu bar or be combined with the existing menus and menu items.

A menu bar definition is more than just menus and menu items. It includes selection (command) strings and dialog boxes that go with the menu items.

 Use a PROC PMENU step to define and store a menu bar. Each statement in the step defines a separate item, or object. In the PROC PMENU statement, write the CAT= option to identify the catalog where you will store the PMENU entry. This is an example:

PROC PMENU CAT=WINDOW.MENUBARS;

The order of statements in the step is critical. The statements should follow the hierarchical structure that links the objects. For example, the statement that defines a menu must come before any of the statements that define the menu items in that menu.

Start with statements to define the menu bar — a MENU statement and several ITEM statements. In the MENU statement, write the entry name of the menu bar. Write an ITEM statement for each pull-down menu with the menu text as a quoted string and the option MENU= with a name for the menu. The name appears only in the PROC PMENU step itself; it is not displayed to the user.

These statements begin to define a menu bar with three pull-down menus.

```
MENU TEXTR;
ITEM 'Text color' MENU=TC;
ITEM 'Background color' MENU=BC;
ITEM 'Commands' MENU=C;
```

Subsequent statements define each menu in turn. Start with a MENU statement with the name that you previously assigned to the menu. Follow this with ITEM statements for each menu item and other statements that define the actions of the menu items.

There are several possibilities for a menu item, with corresponding options in the ITEM statement. Use the SELECTION= option for a menu item that executes a command. Use the MENU= option for a menu item that displays a submenu. Use the DIALOG= option for a menu item that displays a dialog box. For any of these options, simply provide a name for the object.

```
PROC PMENU CAT=WINDOW.MENUBARS;
   * Menu bar;
   MENU TEXTR;
   ITEM 'Text color' MENU=TC;
   ITEM 'Background color' MENU=BC;
   ITEM 'Commands' MENU=C;

   * Text color menu;
   MENU TC;
   ITEM 'Black' SELECTION=TCK;
   ITEM 'Blue' SELECTION=TCB;
   ITEM 'Red' SELECTION=TCR;
   ITEM 'Green' SELECTION=TCG;
   ITEM 'Gray' SELECTION=TCA;
   SELECTION TCK 'COLOR TEXT BLACK';
   SELECTION TCB 'COLOR TEXT BLUE';
   SELECTION TCR 'COLOR TEXT RED';
   SELECTION TCG 'COLOR TEXT GREEN';
   SELECTION TCA 'COLOR TEXT GRAY';

   * Background color menu;
   MENU BC;
   ITEM 'White' SELECTION=BCW;
   ITEM 'Yellow' SELECTION=BCY;
   ITEM 'Cyan' SELECTION=BCC;
   ITEM 'Magenta' SELECTION=BCM;
   ITEM 'Gray' SELECTION=BCA;
   SELECTION BCW 'COLOR BACKGROUND WHITE';
   SELECTION BCY 'COLOR BACKGROUND YELLOW';
   SELECTION BCC 'COLOR BACKGROUND CYAN';
   SELECTION BCM 'COLOR BACKGROUND MAGENTA';
   SELECTION BCA 'COLOR BACKGROUND GRAY';

   * Commands menu;
   MENU C;
   ITEM 'Command line' SELECTION=CL;
   ITEM END;
   ITEM CANCEL;
   SELECTION CL 'COMMAND';
RUN;
```

After you define the items of a menu, write SELECTION, MENU, and DIALOG statements to define the objects associated with the menu items. In a SELECTION statement, write the selection name and the text of the command. For a submenu, the MENU statement and the associated statements are the same as for a pull-down menu. The DIALOG statement and its associated statements are discussed in the remainder of this chapter.

The complete example defining the TEXTR menu bar is shown at left.

The END and CANCEL items at the end of this example show another possibility for the ITEM statement. The menu item can be the actual text of a display manager command.

The menu bar appears approximately like this:

```
Text color  Background color   Commands
```

It displays these menus:

```
Black        White          Command line
Blue         Yellow         END
Red          Cyan           CANCEL
Green        Magenta
Gray         Gray
```

 To define a dialog box, write a DIALOG statement and statements to define any combination of text labels, text boxes, radio boxes, and check boxes.

In the DIALOG statement, write the dialog box name and a command string. The command string is the result of the dialog box. It is the command that the dialog box returns to the command processor when the user clicks the dialog box's OK button. The command string includes symbols that represent the information provided by the user in check boxes, radio boxes, and text boxes in the window. The user's selections and text are substituted for the symbols in the command string, and the string with the substituted values is returned to the command processor.

The symbols &1, &2, &3, and so on, in the command string represent the state of check boxes in the dialog box. The symbol &1 corresponds to the first CHECKBOX statement defining a check box, &2 to the second CHECKBOX statement defining a check box, and so on. The label of the check box is substituted for the symbol in the command string if the check box is on (checked). No text is substituted if the check box is off (unchecked).

The symbols %1, %2, and so on, represent radio boxes in the command string. The first RADIOBOX statement is associated with the symbol %1, the second one with %2, and so on. The label of the selected radio button in the radio box is substituted for the symbol in the command string.

The symbols @1, @2, @3, and so on, in the command string represent data entered in user entry fields. The text entered in the first user entry field defined is substituted for the symbol @1, the text entered in the second user entry field defined is substituted for the symbol @2, and so on. The order in which the TEXT statements defining the user entry fields determines which symbol a user entry field is associated with. The position of the fields in the dialog box does not affect the use of the symbols. Not all TEXT statements define text fields. Those with the LEN= option do, but other TEXT statements define text labels. Only the TEXT statements that define text boxes, not those that define text labels, are counted in assigning the symbols @1, @2, @3, and so on.

For example, if the command string is '.=&1 &2 %1 =@1 =@2' and the user checks the check box defined by the first CHECKBOX statement, labeled "24-hour", does not check the check box defined by the second CHECKBOX statement, selects the radio button labeled "Hours" in the one radio box, types "Eastern" in the first user entry field defined, and types "Pacific" in the second user entry field defined, the user actions produce the string:

> '.=24-hour Hours =Eastern =Pacific'

This is the value returned to the command processor by the dialog box.

This string, of course, is not a valid display manager command. Dialog boxes usually do not produce display manager commands. The command string, however, can be passed to the window's program — a data step, macro, or SCL program — as an unrecognized command. The program parses the command string to determine what values the user entered in the dialog box, and take the appropriate actions.

The dialog box also has a Cancel button. No command is returned if the user clicks the Cancel button.

To define a text label, use a statement of this form:

TEXT #line @column 'text ';

To define a text box in which the user can enter a value, use a statement of this form:

TEXT #line @column LEN=length;

The text that the user types in the text box is substituted for a symbol in the command string.

A check box lets the user select an on or off condition. To define a check box that is off by default, use a statement of this form:

CHECKBOX #line @column 'label ';

To define a check box that is on by default, add the ON option:

CHECKBOX ON #line @column 'label ';

If the check box is on, its label is substituted for the check box's symbol in the dialog box's command string.

A radio box allows the user to select from a list of options. The button for each option is called a radio button. To define a radio box, use statements of this form:

```
RADIOBOX DEFAULT=n;
RBUTTON #line @column 'label ';
RBUTTON #line @column 'label ';
. . .
```

The DEFAULT= option specifies the number of the radio button that is selected by default. The label of the selected radio button is substituted for a symbol in the command string.

There is an alternate form of the RBUTTON statement that allows no text to be substituted in the command string. Write the option NONE immediately after the keyword RBUTTON.

The example that follows defines a menu bar with dialog boxes. The PMENU entry displays the menu bar, pull-down menus, and dialog boxes shown.

```
Window  Command  Find
```

```
Activate...
Command line
All command lines
Color...
Close
```

```
Activate window:
_____

 OK    Cancel
```

```
Change color:

Area:            Change to:
• Text           • Red
o Background     o Green
o Data           o Blue
o Source         o Cyan
o Notes          o Magenta
o Warning        o Yellow
o Error          o Black
o Title          o Gray
o Header         o White
o Byline
o Numbers        Video
o Scrollbar      attribute:
o Banner         • None
o Command        o Reverse
o Border         o Blink
o Menu           o Highlight
o Menuborder     o Underline

         OK    Cancel
```

```
PROC PMENU CAT=WINDOW.MENUBARS;
MENU DMR;
ITEM 'Window' MENU=W;
ITEM 'Command' MENU=C;
ITEM 'Find' MENU=S;

* Window menu;
MENU W;
ITEM 'Activate' DIALOG=W1;
ITEM 'Command line' SELECTION=W2;
ITEM 'All command lines' SELECTION=W3;
ITEM 'Color' DIALOG=W4;
ITEM 'Close' SELECTION=W5;
SELECTION W2 'COMMAND';
SELECTION W3 'PMENU';
SELECTION W5 'END';

* Activate dialog box;
DIALOG W1 'NEXT @1';
   TEXT #1 @1 'Activate window:';
   TEXT #2 @1 LEN=17;

* Color dialog box;
DIALOG W4 'COLOR %1 %2 %3';
   TEXT #1 @1 'Change color';
   TEXT #3 @1 'Area:';
   RADIOBOX DEFAULT=1;
   RBUTTON #4 @1 'Text';
   RBUTTON #5 @1 'Background';
   RBUTTON #6 @1 'Data';
   RBUTTON #7 @1 'Source';
   RBUTTON #8 @1 'Notes';
   RBUTTON #9 @1 'Warning';
   RBUTTON #10 @1 'Error';
   RBUTTON #11 @1 'Title';
   RBUTTON #12 @1 'Header';
   RBUTTON #13 @1 'Byline';
   RBUTTON #14 @1 'Numbers';
   RBUTTON #15 @1 'Scrollbar';
   RBUTTON #16 @1 'Banner';
   RBUTTON #17 @1 'Command';
   RBUTTON #18 @1 'Border';
   RBUTTON #19 @1 'Menu';
   RBUTTON #20 @1 'Menuborder';
   TEXT #3 @15 'Change to:';
   RADIOBOX DEFAULT=1;
   RBUTTON #4 @15 'Red';
   RBUTTON #5 @15 'Green';
   RBUTTON #6 @15 'Blue';
   RBUTTON #7 @15 'Cyan';
   RBUTTON #8 @15 'Magenta';
   RBUTTON #9 @15 'Yellow';
   RBUTTON #10 @15 'Black';
   RBUTTON #11 @15 'Gray';
   RBUTTON #12 @15 'White';
```

```
       TEXT #14 @15 'Video';
       TEXT #15 @15 'attribute:';
       RADIOBOX DEFAULT=1;
         RBUTTON NONE #16 @15 'None';
         RBUTTON #17 @15 'Reverse';
         RBUTTON #18 @15 'Blinking';
         RBUTTON #19 @15 'Highlight';
         RBUTTON #20 @15 'Underline';


   * Command menu;
   MENU C;
   ITEM 'SAS command' DIALOG=C1;
   ITEM 'Operating system' DIALOG=C2;

   * SAS command dialog box;
   DIALOG C1 '@1';
      TEXT #1 @1 'Execute SAS command:';
      TEXT #2 @1 LEN=32;

   * Operating system dialog box;
   DIALOG C2 "X '@1'";
      TEXT #1 @1
       'Execute operating system command:';
      TEXT #2 @1 LEN=32;


   * Find menu;
   MENU S;
   ITEM 'Find' DIALOG=S1;
   ITEM 'Find again' SELECTION=S2;
   ITEM 'Change' DIALOG=S3;
   ITEM 'Change again' SELECTION=S4;
   SELECTION S2 'RFIND';
   SELECTION S4 'RCHANGE';

   * Find dialog box;
   DIALOG S1 'FIND "@1"  &2 &1';
      TEXT #1 @1 'Find what:';
      TEXT #1 @12 LEN=24;
      CHECKBOX #3 @12 'Word';
      CHECKBOX #3 @21 'All';

   * Change dialog box;
   DIALOG S3 'CHANGE "@1" "@2" &2 &1';
      TEXT #1 @1 'Find what:';
      TEXT #1 @12 LEN=24;
      TEXT #2 @1 'Change to:';
      TEXT #2 @12 LEN=24;
      CHECKBOX #4 @12 'Word';
      CHECKBOX #4 @21 'All';
RUN;
```

■ 80

Command Processing

An interactive application that displays a window in the SAS environment can receive user commands from that window. These can be commands entered on the command line, but they can also be the result of menu selections and function keys. An application cannot intercept display manager commands, but it can process commands that SAS does not recognize. These unrecognized commands are passed to the program, and the program can retrieve them and process them. A data step can obtain a command string from a data step window in the automatic variable _CMD_. A macro window returns a command string in the automatic macro variable SYSCMD.

Two fundamental programming ideas, parsing and switching, form the heart of command processing. Parsing extracts the meaningful parts from the text of the command; it is described in chapter 45, "Parsing." Switching executes different actions or blocks of code based on different values of a variable; it can be done with the SELECT statement in the data step or with %IF-%THEN/%ELSE statements in a macro.

The first word of a command identifies the basic action of the command. This first word is often called the keyword of the command. Subsequent words are terms or options that provide additional details. In simple cases, it is sufficient to separate the keyword from the rest of the command. If the command text is the automatic variable _CMD_, you could extract the keyword this way:

```
LENGTH KEYWORD $ 32;
KEYWORD = UPCASE(SCAN(_CMD_, 1, ' '));
```

Most users expect computer programs to ignore the case of letters in commands — to treat uppercase and lowercase letters as interchangeable. The UPCASE function in the expression above ensures that case is disregarded by converting all letters in the command keyword to uppercase.

There is no reason that command strings from a menu bar or function key must resemble commands that a user might type on a command line. You could start the keyword of the command string with a period because SAS does not recognize any command that begins with a period.

After you extract the keyword, use it in a comparison SELECT block. In the first WHEN statement, check for a blank value. If the keyword is blank, then there is no command to process, and no action is required. In subsequent WHEN statements, check for each keyword that the program recognizes. Include statements to check for other terms in the command, if necessary, and statements to carry out the actions implied by the command.

A command keyword that the program does not recognize will fall through to the OTHERWISE statement. In the OTHERWISE statement, write statements to take actions in response to the incorrect command keyword.

The following code model summarizes the logic of command processing in the data step.

```
LENGTH KEYWORD $ 32;
KEYWORD = UPCASE(SCAN(_CMD_, 1, ' '));
SELECT (KEYWORD);
  WHEN (' ') ;
  WHEN ('command 1') DO;
    actions for command 1
    END;
  WHEN ('command 2') DO;
    actions for command 2
    END;
  . . .
  OTHERWISE DO;
    actions for incorrect command
    END;
  END;
```

■ 81

Text Processing

You can use data step programming to create and process text values such as sentences, phrases, and names. The simplest text processing can be performed with the functions described in chapter 24, "Strings." If you work with text as data, however, you will shortly need to combine functions with data step logic to process the text, using techniques such as the ones described here.

Names and Alphabetic Keys

In order to sort a text variable in alphabetical order, you may need to create a separate alphabetic sort key variable. This variable includes alphabetic information from the text variable, but omits all other information.

These are the non-alphabetic things you need to remove from text before you can sort it alphabetically:

- *Spaces.* To alphabetize by letter, remove all spaces. To alphabetize by word, leave single spaces between words and remove all other spaces. As always in SAS character data, trailing spaces do not affect the way values compare and sort.
- *Punctuation.* Ordinarily, no punctuation characters are considered in alphabetizing. However, when you alphabetize by word, you have to distinguish between symbols that can be part of words and those that occur only between words.
- *Case.* Convert all letters to uppercase. It also works to convert letters to lowercase.

The text values below generate the alphabetic keys shown for sorting by letter and by word.

Text	Alphabetic key (by letter)	Alphabetic key (by word)
blue-tongued lizard	BLUETONGUEDLIZARD	BLUETONGUED LIZARD
butterfly	BUTTERFLY	BUTTERFLY
Siberian Husky	SIBERIANHUSKY	SIBERIAN HUSKY

These are other issues in alphabetization that are important in some applications:

- *Little words.* When titles and other names of inanimate objects are alphabetized, words such as *the* and *a* at the beginning of the name are usually disregarded.
- *Numerals.* Numerals are often sorted by substituting words. For example, *100* might be sorted as ONE HUNDRED. Similarly, words might be substituted for some symbols, such as AND for &.
- *Accented letters.* Accented letters such as *å* and *è* are found in names from most European languages. Convert these characters to the unaccented form of the letter for strict alphabetical sorting.

In the code examples that follow, the text variable is TEXT, and the alphabetic variable for sorting is ALPHA. If the values are single words with no punctuation, left-align and convert to uppercase to create the alphabetic key:

```
ALPHA = LEFT(UPCASE(WORD));
```

To create a key for sorting alphabetically by letter, use the COMPRESS function to remove spaces and all punctuation symbols that might occur. This example removes the 10 most common punctuation characters.

```
ALPHA = COMPRESS(UPCASE(TEXT), " !'(),-./:?");
```

Creating a key for sorting alphabetically by word is more complicated because you have to treat punctuation characters that are parts of words differently from characters that would come between words. The apostrophe, hyphen, and period can be part of a word, so use the COMPRESS function to remove these characters. Use the TRANSLATE function to convert other punctuation symbols to spaces. Finally, use the COMPBL and LEFT functions to remove any extra spaces. Use an expression such as the one shown here:

```
ALPHA = LEFT(COMPBL(
    TRANSLATE(COMPRESS(UPCASE(TEXT), "-'."), ' ', "!(),/:?")
    ));
```

If you prefer, write this process as several statements:

```
ALPHA = COMPRESS(UPCASE(TEXT), "-'.");
ALPHA = TRANSLATE(ALPHA, ' ', "!(),/:?");
ALPHA = LEFT(COMPBL(ALPHA));
```

To remove little words from the beginning of titles or names, use statements such as these:

```
IF SUBSTR(ALPHA, 1, 2) = 'A ' THEN ALPHA = SUBSTR(ALPHA, 3);
IF SUBSTR(ALPHA, 1, 3) = 'AN ' THEN ALPHA = SUBSTR(ALPHA, 4);
IF SUBSTR(ALPHA, 1, 4) = 'THE ' THEN ALPHA = SUBSTR(ALPHA, 5);
```

Write these statements after creating the variable ALPHA for sorting alphabetically by word. If you will be sorting alphabetically by letter, add this statement afterward to remove the spaces between words:

```
ALPHA = COMPRESS(ALPHA);
```

People's names are usually sorted by word, with the last name first. Form a single sort key for a name by writing the last name, a comma, and the first name. Add a space after the comma to give the reversed name a conventional appearance. For example, for the names `Elton John` and `Bernie Taupin`, the sort keys are:

```
JOHN, ELTON
TAUPIN, BERNIE
```

The statement below creates the sort key variable NAMESORT from the variables LASTNAME and FIRSTNAME, assuming that these variables are already correctly left-aligned:

NAMESORT = UPCASE(TRIM(LASTNAME) || ', ' || FIRSTNAME);

A person with no last name is alphabetized by first name. If this might occur, add this statement:

IF LASTNAME = '' THEN NAMESORT = UPCASE(FIRSTNAME);

In some databases, names are recorded with a special character written before the last name or the alphabetical beginning of the name. If the symbol is >, this value for a name

```
Jon >Bon Jovi
```

indicates that the last name is *Bon Jovi* and the value is alphabetized as `BON JOVI, JON`.

A character might also mark the end of the last name. For example, in this name

```
Cal >Ripken< Jr.
```

the last name is *Ripken*, and the name is alphabetized as `RIPKEN, CAL JR`.

Use the SCAN function to obtain the parts of the name:

FIRSTNAME = SCAN(NAME, 1, '><');
LASTNAME = SCAN(NAME, 2, '><');
NAMESUFFIX = SCAN(NAME, 3, '><');

Form an alphabetic key from the parts like this:

NAMESORT = UPCASE(TRIM(LASTNAME)
  || ', ' || TRIM(FIRSTNAME) || ' ' || NAMESUFFIX);
IF LASTNAME = '' THEN NAMESORT =
  UPCASE(TRIM(FIRSTNAME) || ' ' || NAMESUFFIX));

To display the name correctly you must remove the special characters. Use the COMPRESS function and assign the result to another variable, as shown here:

PERSONAL NAMES

When you work with the text of personal names, do not assume that a name consists of a first name and a last name. Some databases force names to conform to this format, but names found in the outside world can be incomplete, and these other occurrences are not uncommon:

- a first name that consists of multiple words, such as Dee Dee
- a middle name or initial
- two or three initials written in place of a first name
- a last name that consists of multiple words, such as Bon Jovi
- a name preceded or followed by other words (often abbreviated) that are not strictly part of the name, such as Princess, Sr., or IV
- a name in which the first name is the family name and is considered first for alphabetical order, as is customary in China, Japan, and other countries

If names are recorded only as whole text values, the name values do not provide enough information to accurately identify their parts.

```
VISUALNAME = COMPRESS(NAME, '><');
```

Use the new variable, VISUALNAME, to display the name.

Similarly, titles may be written with a special character before the alphabetic starting point. A title written as `The >Two Towers` is alphabetized as `TWO  TOWERS`, disregarding the initial word *The*.

Extract the alphabetical part using the SCAN function or as shown here:

```
ALPHA = SUBSTR(TITLE, INDEXC(TITLE, '>') + 1);
```

Then proceed to form the alphabetic key as described previously.

Words

An array or other list of character values may be converted to a list in text form for display or for further processing. For example, if the array ING contains a list of ingredients, you can create a text list INGLIST, as shown in the example below. The DO loop concatenates each array element to the end of the list, with a comma before it, until a blank array element is found.

```
ARRAY ING{10} $ 48 ('water', 'high fructose corn syrup', 'tea',
   'citric acid', 'natural lemon flavor', ' ', ' ', ' ', ' ', ' ');
LENGTH INGLIST $ 200;
INGLIST = ING{1};
DO I = 2 TO DIM(ING);
  IF ING{I} = '' THEN LEAVE; * Blank value, end of list. ;
  INGLIST = TRIM(INGLIST) || ', ' || ING{I};
  IF LENGTH(INGLIST) >= VLENGTH(INGLIST) - 1 THEN LEAVE;
  END;
PUT INGLIST;
```

```
water, high fructose corn syrup, tea, citric acid, natural lemon flavor
```

Use the SCAN function in a loop to convert a comma-separated text list to an array, as shown here:

```
ARRAY ING{10} $ 48;
DO I = 1 TO DIM(ING);
  ING{I} = LEFT(SCAN(INGLIST, I, ','));
  END;
```

Similarly, use the SCAN function to extract the individual words of a text value. First use the UPCASE and TRANSLATE functions to convert the letters to uppercase and remove the punctuation between words. Then use a DO loop with the SCAN function to create an array of the words.

```
ARRAY WORD{50} $ 20 _TEMPORARY_;
WORDTEXT = TRANSLATE(UPCASE(TEXT), ' ', '!(),/:?');
DO I = 1 TO DIM(WORD);
  WORD{I} = SCAN(WORDTEXT, I, ' ');
  END;
```

The action of a thesaurus application is to replace one word with another. Usually, the idea is to replace a recognized form of a word with its preferred form or an abbreviation or to replace a word with a preferred synonym. This kind of substitution might be done for several of the words in a text value. By reducing the amount of variation in a set of text values, a thesaurus can make the data easier to work with.

The nature of a thesaurus application can be seen in something as common as mail. Most pieces of postal mail sent in the United States are addressed with standardized addresses, in which, for example, *Street* is always abbreviated as *ST*.

An address thesaurus uses two variables. The first variable contains a form of a word that you might find in a text value. This form of the word might be described as original, colloquial, or loose. The second variable contains the preferred form of the word, sometimes described as standard, canonical, or strict. The program uses the thesaurus as lookup table. It attempts to match the original form, which is the key value in the table, in order to find the standardized form. See chapter 52, "Table Lookup," for a description of this process. The address thesaurus would contain observations such as those shown at right.

FROM	TO
AV	AVE
AVENUE	AVE
BOULEVARD	BLVD
COURT	CT
CENTER	CTR
DRIVE	DR
DRV	DR
EAST	E
. . .	

The variables shown here are called FROM and TO to emphasize the process of changing a word from its original form to the standard form.

The example below shows how the thesaurus can be used. Starting with an address selected to demonstrate the process, it extracts the individual words and looks for each word in the thesaurus MAIN.ADTHES. If it finds the word in the thesaurus, it substitutes the standard form of the word, the variable TO. It assembles the standardized address by concatenating each word.

```
DATA _NULL_;
  LENGTH ADDRESSTEXT WORDTEXT ADDRESSSTD $ 48;
  ADDRESSTEXT = '1448 East Mill Avenue';
  ARRAY WORD{9} $ 20;
  WORDTEXT = TRANSLATE(UPCASE(ADDRESSTEXT), ' ', "!(),/:?");
  DO I = 1 TO DIM(WORD);
    WORD{I} = SCAN(WORDTEXT, I, ' ');
    FROM = WORD{I};
    IF FROM = '' THEN LEAVE;
    * Substitute word from thesaurus. ;
    SET MAIN.ADTHES KEY=FROM/UNIQUE;
    IF _IORC_ THEN DO; * Not found. ;
      _IORC_ = 0;
      _ERROR_ = 0;
      END;
    ELSE WORD{I} = TO;
    IF I = 1 THEN ADDRESSSTD = WORD{I};
    ELSE ADDRESSSTD = TRIM(ADDRESSSTD) || ' ' || WORD{I};
    END;
  PUT ADDRESSSTD;
STOP;
RUN;
```

```
1448 E MILL AVE
```

In a thesaurus application, words that are not found in the thesaurus are not changed. If you want to use a thesaurus to remove words, list them in the thesaurus with a blank value as the standard form.

Name Matching

Text values such as names are rarely used as key values or for any kind of matching because any slight change in the text can prevent values from matching. As an example, the following values represent the same name, but they are not equal values:

```
Bjorn's Pizza
Bjorns Pizza
BJORNS PIZZA
```

In a comparison, sorting, match merge, or any other process that matches values, these values are treated as distinct values that have no connection to each other. To avoid the difficulties of matching text values, most databases are designed with ID codes that identify each distinct object or entity in the database. The ID codes can be created by the database itself, or they can come from an independent source. As an example of this, in employment databases in the United States, employees are usually identified by their Social Security numbers. These are ID codes that are generated not by the employer, but by the Social Security Administration, a government agency.

As long as ID codes are available, matching names is probably not necessary. However, if you are collecting data that does not come from an organized database with ID codes, it may be necessary to attempt to match names. Name matching may also be necessary when you combine data from multiple databases, if the databases do not use the same ID codes. This is a challenge you are likely to face if you design a data warehouse that combines data from various departments of a company or if you integrate the data of two companies after a merger.

Usually, name matching is done with company names. Most personal names are not unique — it is common to find two people using the same name — so a name can be used to match up personal information only if it is combined with other information, such as an address or phone number. By contrast, most company names are distinctive enough that you can do name matching with some degree of confidence, and many companies have multiple addresses, making matching on addresses more difficult. Still, name matching cannot be an entirely automated process; a person familiar with the data should check the results and change them as needed. For the most accurate results, all available data, not just the name text, should be considered in deciding whether two names match.

You can find most matching names by applying these conversions:

- Convert letters to uppercase and normalize spacing, as described earlier for creating an alphabetic key.
- Remove most punctuation. Change & and + to *and*.
- Remove numbers, but keep numbers that you find at the beginning of a name. For example, *Furniture Place #2* and *Furniture Place #5* are probably two separate locations of the same company.
- Remove words that are not distinctive, especially *the*. Remove business-form suffix words, such as *Inc.*, *LP*, and *LLC*.
- Use a thesaurus to convert words to their most common spelling. This is especially important for words that are commonly abbreviated. For example, change *Corporation* to *Corp*, *Fdn* to *Foundation*.

If two names match after you apply these conversions, you can consider them a likely match. The code below looks for matching names in two SAS datasets, EAST.LIST and WEST.LIST.

```
*
  Normalize East names.
*;
DATA WORK.EASTTEXT;
  SET EAST.LIST;
  LENGTH NAMEEQV ALPHA $ 32;
  ARRAY WORD{10} $ 16;
  ALPHA = COMPRESS(UPCASE(NAME), "'.");
  ALPHA = TRANWRD(ALPHA, '&', ' AND ');
  ALPHA = TRANWRD(ALPHA, '+', ' AND ');
  ALPHA = TRANSLATE(ALPHA, ' ', "!(),/:?-");
  ALPHA = LEFT(COMPBL(ALPHA));

  DO I = 1 TO DIM(WORD);
    WORD{I} = SCAN(ALPHA, I, ' ');
    END;
  NAMEEQV = '';
  DO I = 1 TO DIM(WORD);
    FROM = WORD{I};
    IF FROM = '' THEN LEAVE;
    * Remove numbers. ;
    IF I > 1 THEN
       IF NOT VERIFY(FROM, '0123456789. ')
       THEN FROM = '';
    * Substitute word from thesaurus. ;
    SET MAIN.NAMETHES KEY=FROM/UNIQUE;
    IF _IORC_ THEN DO; * Not found. ;
      _IORC_ = 0;
      _ERROR_ = 0;
      END;
    ELSE WORD{I} = TO;
    IF NAMEEQV = '' THEN NAMEEQV = WORD{I};
    ELSE NAMEEQV =
       TRIM(NAMEEQV) || ' ' || WORD{I};
    END;
RUN;
PROC SORT DATA=WORK.EASTTEXT;
  BY NAMEEQV ALPHA NAME;
RUN;


*
  Normalize West names.
*;
DATA WORK.WESTTEXT;
  SET WEST.LIST;
  LENGTH NAMEEQV ALPHA $ 32;
  ARRAY WORD{10} $ 16;
  ALPHA = COMPRESS(UPCASE(NAME), "'.");
  ALPHA = TRANWRD(ALPHA, '&', ' AND ');
  ALPHA = TRANWRD(ALPHA, '+', ' AND ');
```

```
  ALPHA = TRANSLATE(ALPHA, ' ', "!(),/:?-");
  ALPHA = LEFT(COMPBL(ALPHA));

  DO I = 1 TO DIM(WORD);
    WORD{I} = SCAN(ALPHA, I, ' ');
    END;
  NAMEEQV = '';
  DO I = 1 TO DIM(WORD);
    FROM = WORD{I};
    IF FROM = '' THEN LEAVE;
    * Remove numbers. ;
    IF I > 1 THEN
       IF NOT VERIFY(FROM, '0123456789. ')
       THEN FROM = '';
    * Substitute word from thesaurus. ;
    SET MAIN.NAMETHES KEY=FROM/UNIQUE;
    IF _IORC_ THEN DO; * Not found. ;
      _IORC_ = 0;
      _ERROR_ = 0;
      END;
    ELSE WORD{I} = TO;
    IF NAMEEQV = '' THEN NAMEEQV = WORD{I};
    ELSE NAMEEQV =
       TRIM(NAMEEQV) || ' ' || WORD{I};
    END;
RUN;
PROC SORT DATA=WORK.WESTTEXT;
  BY NAMEEQV ALPHA NAME;
RUN;


*
  Merge and print matches.
*;
DATA WORK.MATCH;
  MERGE
    WORK.EASTTEXT (IN=IN1 RENAME=
    (ID=ID1 NAME=NAME1 ALPHA=ALPHA1))
    WORK.WESTTEXT (IN=IN2 RENAME=
    (ID=ID2 NAME=NAME2 ALPHA=ALPHA2))
    ;
  BY NAMEEQV;
  IF IN1 AND IN2;
RUN;
TITLE1 'Equivalent Names';
PROC PRINT DATA=WORK.MATCH
    HEADING=HORIZONTAL;
  ID ID1 ID2;
  VAR NAMEEQV NAME1 NAME2;
RUN;
```

The program applies the same name normalization logic to both sets of names. It removes punctuation, converts letters to uppercase, removes numbers, substitutes synonyms, then normalizes spacing. The SAS datasets WORK.EASTTEXT and WORK.WESTTEXT contain the normalized text values, the variable NAMEEQV, along with the original text values, the variable NAME. The new SAS datasets are merged, and when there is a match, the values are printed in the report.

The thesaurus MAIN.NAMETHES contains observations such as these:

```
FROM              TO

COMPANY           CO
CORPORATION       CORP
INC
INTERNATIONAL     INTL
LLC
LP
THE
UNIVERSITY        UNIV
```

The thesaurus logic looks for the FROM values and changes them to the corresponding TO values. If the TO value is blank, the thesaurus removes the word from the text. Words that are not considered a significant or distinctive part of a name can be removed in this way.

If the program is used to match these two sets of names:

```
East Names                              West Names

ID        NAME                          ID        NAME

0001      A-B Test Equipment            0001      A B TEST EQUIPMENT
0002      Kodiak Corp                   0002      KARMA INTERNATIONAL
0003      Parker & Locker, Inc          0003      THE KODIAK CORP.
0004      Parrot Business Systems       0004      PARKER AND LOCKER
0005      The Karma Company             0005      UNIVERSE UNIVERSITY
```

these are the resulting matches:

```
Equivalent Names

ID1    ID2    NAMEEQV             NAME1                   NAME2

0001   0001   A B TEST EQUIPMENT  A-B Test Equipment      A B TEST EQUIPMENT
0002   0003   KODIAK CORP         Kodiak Corp.            THE KODIAK CORP.
0003   0004   PARKER AND LOCKER   Parker & Locker, Inc.   PARKER AND LOCKER
```

Practical applications of name matching involve thousands of names. This example is limited to just a few names so that you can trace the program's logic more easily. A report such as this could be reviewed, along with other information, to make the final decisions about which names actually are different versions of the same name. Notice the following points:

- The original sets of names include ID numbers. The two sets of ID numbers come from different sources and are not related to each other. Name matching might be part of a larger process that includes ID code conversions to produce a single set of ID codes, but that would be a separate task.

- The name matching process matches the two forms of the name *A-B Text Equipment* despite the different punctuation. Other details are involved in the other two matches.

- The names *The Karma Company* and *Karma International* do not match because the thesaurus considers *company* and *international* to be significant words. By contrast, the *Inc.* at the end of one form of the *Parker and Locker* name is considered an insignificant word; the thesaurus removes it so the names can match even though Inc. is present in one value and absent in the other.

You can use the same logic to match names among three or more sets of names. In place of the IF statement

IF IN1 AND IN2;

use one of this form:

IF SUM(OF IN1-IN3) > 1;

For a more thorough name matching process, you can go on to these additional steps to find other names that might match:

1. Look for partial matches. Names might match if the first several words are the same.

2. Match individual words. Make a list of all the words in each name, and count the number of names in which each word appears. For each word that appears infrequently, in less than about 1 percent of the names, look at all the names in which the word appears to see if there are any likely matches among them.

3. Look for near-matches among words. Consider the possibility that two words are the same if they differ only in a final *s*, if they have the same phonetic encoding in the SOUNDEX function, if they have a low spelling distance as measured by the SPEDIS function, if the first four letters are the same, or if the only difference is a *.com* suffix.

4. Combine consecutive words to see if the result matches another word. For example, *The Tea Box* might be the same name as *The Teabox*.

5. Combine consecutive words to look for near-matches.

6. If a name contains initials or a sequence of letters, see if they match a pattern of initial letters of words in another name. For example, *CNN* might match *Cable News Network*.

■ 82

Text Analysis

In SAS, a text file is usually a text data file, a file of records divided into fields, each containing a separate data element. However, it is also possible for a SAS program to make something of the other kind of text file, a file that contains the text of a document. These are some of the objectives of text analysis:

- to score a document for reading difficulty, or how easy or hard it is to read
- to look for overused expressions or other patterns in the writing
- to identify the possible author of a written message

Do not make the mistake of trying to use a word processing file as a text file. Word processing files are document files that only word processing programs and a few other programs can read. To analyze the text of a word proceessing file, use the word processing application to create a text file (use the "text only" file format) containing only the text of the document. Use this text file as the input to a SAS program.

Text is usually organized as one record for each paragraph. This creates some very long records. Use a large record length, such as 8192, when you read a text document.

The text analyzed in the examples in this chapter is the first paragraph of the Henry David Thoreau essay "Civil Disobedience":

> I heartily accept the motto, -- "That government is best which governs least";
> and I should like to see it acted up to more rapidly and systematically. Carried
> out, it finally amounts to this, which also I believe -- "That government is
> best which governs not at all"; and when men are prepared for it, that will
> be the kind of government which they will have. Government is at best but
> an expedient; but most governments are usually, and all governments are
> sometimes, inexpedient. The objections which have been brought against a
> standing army, and they are many and weighty, and deserve to prevail, may also
> at last be brought against a standing government. The standing army is only
> an arm of the standing government. The government itself, which is only the
> mode which the people have chosen to execute their will, is equally liable to be
> abused and perverted before the people can act through it. Witness the present
> Mexican war, the work of comparatively a few individuals using the standing
> government as their tool; for in the outset, the people would not have consented
> to this measure.

Start by creating a SAS dataset of the words in the text file. In this SAS dataset, each word is an observation. With several variables and as many observations as there are words, storing the data as a SAS data file would take several times the size of the text itself; it is usually more efficient to avoid this use of storage entirely by creating the SAS dataset as a data step view.

These features of SAS text input make it easy to read the words of the text file:

- The trailing @@, which keeps the INPUT statement on the same record.
- List input, which selects each word in turn from the input file.
- The FLOWOVER option in the INFILE statement, which tells the INPUT statement to advance to the next record when it is done reading a record.

Create variables that contain all the information you might use about each word. This chapter uses these variable names:

- WORDTEXT. The original text of the word, including punctuation.
- WORD. The word converted to uppercase, with punctuation removed.
- N. A word index, counting the words of the document.
- LENGTH. The number of letters in the word.
- SENTENCE. A sentence index, counting the sentences of the document.
- SN. An index of the words in the sentence, counting the words of the sentence.

For sentence statistics, a second SAS dataset is necessary, with these variables:

- SENTENCE. The sentence index.
- SLENGTH. The number of words in the sentence.

The data step below reads the input text file TEXT and creates the SAS dataset WORK.WORD.

```
DATA WORK.WORD (KEEP=WORD WORDTEXT LENGTH SENTENCE SN)
  / VIEW=WORK.WORD;
  LENGTH WORDTEXT WORD $ 24 ENDCHAR $ 1;
  RETAIN SENTENCEEND 0 SENTENCE 1;
  INFILE TEXT FLOWOVER;
  INPUT WORDTEXT @@;

*
  Word: convert word text to uppercase
  and remove most punctuation.
*;
  WORD = UPCASE(COMPRESS(WORDTEXT,
    '!"#$%&()*+,-./:;<=>?@[\]^`{|}~'));
  LENGTH = LENGTH(COMPRESS(WORD, "'-"));

IF WORD NE '' THEN DO;
  * Check for sentence break. ;
  IF SENTENCEEND THEN DO;
    * If first letter is uppercase, start new sentence. ;
    LI = ANYALPHA(WORD);
    IF LI THEN LETTER = SUBSTR(WORD, LI);
    ELSE LETTER = ' ';
```

```
      IF ANYALPHA(LETTER) THEN DO;
         SENTENCE + 1;
         SN = 0;
         END;
      ELSE SENTENCEEND = 0;
      END;
   N + 1;
   SN + 1;
   OUTPUT;
   END;


*

   Possible end of sentence: word text ends in period,
   exclamation point, or question mark, possibly followed
   by quotation marks.
*;
   IF SN > 0 THEN DO;
      ENDCHARI = LENGTH(TRANSLATE(WORDTEXT, ' ', '"'));
      ENDCHAR = SUBSTR(WORDTEXT, ENDCHARI, 1);
      SENTENCEEND = ENDCHAR IN ('.', '!', '?');
      END;
RUN;
```

In this program, the INPUT statement reads the text one word at a time. However, the word text might include punctuation. The subsequent assignment statements remove punctuation to extract the word itself, then count the letters of the word to arrive at the word length. The most complicated logic in the data step is the processing that attempts to identify sentence breaks. It identifies a new sentence whenever one word ends in a period, question mark, or exclamation point and the first letter of the next word is a capital letter.

This next data step uses WORK.WORD to create WORK.SENTENCE with the word count of each sentence.

```
DATA WORK.SENTENCE (KEEP=SENTENCE SN RENAME=(SN=SLENGTH));
   SET WORK.WORD;
   BY SENTENCE;
   IF LAST.SENTENCE;
RUN;
```

 Use WORK.WORD and WORK.SENTENCE, created above, to compute statistics. The three most common statistics for a text document are the word count, or the total number of words, the average word length, and the average number of words in a sentence. The program below reports these three statistics along with the sentence count.

```
PROC SUMMARY DATA=WORK.WORD;
   VAR LENGTH;
   OUTPUT MEAN= OUT=WORK.WSUM (RENAME=(_FREQ_=WCOUNT));
RUN;
PROC SUMMARY DATA=WORK.SENTENCE;
   VAR SLENGTH;
   OUTPUT MEAN= OUT=WORK.SSUM (RENAME=(_FREQ_=SCOUNT));
RUN;
```

```
TITLE1 'Thoreau Paragraph';
DATA _NULL_;
  SET WORK.WSUM;
  SET WORK.SSUM;
  FILE PRINT;
  PUT / 'Word count: ' WCOUNT : COMMA9.
    / 'Average word length: ' LENGTH : 5.2
    / 'Sentence count: ' SCOUNT : COMMA7.
    / 'Words per sentence: ' SLENGTH : 6.2;
RUN;
```

```
Thoreau Paragraph

Word count: 187
Average word length: 4.68
Sentence count: 7
Words per sentence: 26.71
```

Sentence length, the number of words per sentence, is commonly used as an indicator of reading level, or the reading skill that a document requires. If the average sentence length is larger than is appropriate for the intended audience, that might tell you to rewrite the document to make it easier to read. Specifically, look for the longest and most complicated sentences in the document; rewrite each of these sentences as a series of shorter sentences.

 To find out what words are used in a document, use the SUMMARY procedure to create a frequency table from the word dataset. Arrange the words in order of frequency, with the words that are used most often at the beginning of the list.

The program shown here counts words and also computes the frequency of each word as a percent. It is the second step that computes the percent. See chapter 49, "Summary Statistics in Computations," for a description of the process of computing percents.

The PROC PRINT step shown here uses a WHERE condition to limit the report to words that have a relative frequency of at least 1 percent. This makes the report much shorter.

```
PROC SUMMARY DATA=WORK.WORD ORDER=FREQ;
  CLASS WORD;
  OUTPUT OUT=WORK.WORDLIST1 (RENAME=(_FREQ_=N));
RUN;
DATA WORDLIST (KEEP=WORD N PERCENT);
  IF _N_ = 1 THEN SET WORK.WORDLIST1 (WHERE=(_TYPE_ = 0)
    RENAME=(N=WORDCOUNT));
  SET WORK.WORDLIST1 (WHERE=(_TYPE_ > 0));
  PERCENT = N/WORDCOUNT*100;
RUN;
PROC PRINT DATA=WORDLIST (WHERE=(PERCENT >= 1))
  HEADING=HORIZONTAL NOOBS;
  VAR WORD N PERCENT;
  FORMAT N COMMA6. PERCENT F7.3;
RUN;
```

Thoreau Paragraph

WORD	N	PERCENT
THE	14	7.487
GOVERNMENT	8	4.278
AND	8	4.278
WHICH	7	3.743
TO	7	3.743
IS	6	3.209
STANDING	5	2.674
IT	4	2.139
ARE	4	2.139
HAVE	4	2.139
I	3	1.604
THAT	3	1.604
BEST	3	1.604
AT	3	1.604
WILL	3	1.604
BE	3	1.604
OF	3	1.604
A	3	1.604
PEOPLE	3	1.604
GOVERNS	2	1.070
THIS	2	1.070
ALSO	2	1.070
NOT	2	1.070
ALL	2	1.070
FOR	2	1.070
THEY	2	1.070
BUT	2	1.070
AN	2	1.070
GOVERNMENTS	2	1.070
BROUGHT	2	1.070
AGAINST	2	1.070
ARMY	2	1.070
ONLY	2	1.070
THEIR	2	1.070

One possible use of a word list is to check spelling. Merge the word list with a spelling dictionary, and create a list of words in the word list that are not in the spelling dictionary. Examine this list for words that might be misspelled.

The word frequency table of a document is a surprisingly potent measure of writing style. Reading the word list tells you the mood of a document: upbeat or downcast, emotional or technical, any sense of action or place, and similar qualities. Around the middle of the list, you can look for overused words and clichés; if it is your own writing you are analyzing, you are likely to be surprised at how often you use some words.

Word frequencies show a writer's distinctive habits in the use of specific words and specific kinds of words. These habits are consistent enough in most writers' work that literary analysts can often identify the author of an unattributed work just by comparing word frequencies between documents.

■ 83

Random Numbers

Probability distributions and random numbers from probability distributions are used to describe and simulate random events. A set of random numbers behaves in ways like those of a set of measurements of random events belonging to the same probability distribution.

In the SAS environment, functions and CALL routines generate random numbers for several distributions. Expressions that use these functions (or the numbers provided by the CALL routines) can produce random numbers of other distributions.

Random Number Streams

The process of generating random numbers starts with a mathematical routine called a random number generator, which produces a stream of whole numbers. The stream arranges all the whole numbers of the interval from 0 to a large positive integer (2^{31} – 1) in a set sequence. This means that computer-generated random numbers are not truly random; the sequence in which they occur is predetermined. For most purposes, they are indistinguishable from true random numbers. However, they have these properties that true random numbers do not have:

- The exact same number is never repeated, unless you generate the entire stream (more than 2^{31} random numbers). In that case, the sequence of numbers repeats itself.
- If you use arrangements of multiple random numbers, they may show some predictable tendencies.

The random integers are divided by a large positive integer (2^{31}) in order to produce values between 0 and 1. These random numbers represent the uniform distribution on the interval from 0 to 1. In the uniform distribution, all values within the interval are equally likely to occur.

The starting point in the stream is controlled by a positive number argument called a seed. The seed value does not correspond in any obvious way to the first random number that is generated or any of the subsequent random numbers; however, by using the same seed value, you can obtain the same sequence of random numbers.

Use a negative seed argument to have the seed initialized based on the system clock. This way, you can get a different sequence of random numbers every time the program runs.

Random Number Functions and CALL Routines

You can use either a function or a CALL routine to generate random numbers. The random number CALL routines make the seed a variable. Use CALL routines if you need to alter the seed value. Random number CALL routines have the same names and most of the same arguments as random number functions.

 To call a random number function, write a seed value as the first argument and any required parameters of the probability distribution as subsequent arguments. The parameters for each function are described in the function's documentation. The statement below uses the RANUNI function to generate a random number from the uniform distribution, with a seed value of 5. The resulting random number is assigned to the variable X.

```
X = RANUNI(5);
```

 To generate random numbers from a CALL routine, start by initializing the seed variable once. The arguments are the same as for a random number function, except that the seed argument must be a variable, and an additional final argument is a variable where the routine places the random number it generates. The statements below demonstrate this.

```
RETAIN SEED 5;
CALL RANUNI(SEED, X);
```

The seed variable is initialized in the RETAIN statement. The CALL statement generates the random number and assigns it to the variable X.

 When you generate a sequence of random numbers, use a single function call so that all the random numbers are drawn from the same stream. If for some reason it is necessary to use more than one random number function call, use a different seed argument for each.

If you use a CALL routine to generate a sequence of random numbers, use the same CALL statement or at least the same seed variable so that all the random numbers are drawn from the same stream.

 It is incorrect to initialize a seed variable every time you generate a random number. Doing so would generate the same number every time.

Distributions for Random Numbers

 Use the RANUNI function to generate random numbers from a uniform distribution. By itself, as shown in the example below, the RANUNI function generates random numbers from the uniform distribution on the interval from 0 to 1.

```
X = RANUNI(5);
```

To generate random numbers from a uniform distribution on a different interval, use multiplication and division to transform the results of the RANUNI function. Multiply by the range of the interval, then add the low endpoint of the interval.

For example, this statement generates random numbers on the interval from 0 to 100.

X = 100*RANUNI(5);

This statement generates random numbers on the interval from 100 to 123.

X = 23*RANUNI(5) + 100;

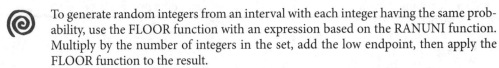

To generate random integers from an interval with each integer having the same probability, use the FLOOR function with an expression based on the RANUNI function. Multiply by the number of integers in the set, add the low endpoint, then apply the FLOOR function to the result.

This example generates random integers from 1 to 12.

X = FLOOR(12*RANUNI(5) + 1);

To make a random selection from a set, use index values assigned to each element of the set. For example, define an array with each element of the set being an element of the array. Generate a random integer, and use it as an index value to select an item.

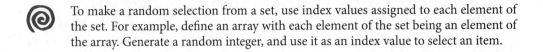

Use the RANNOR function to generate random numbers from the normal distribution. By itself, as in this example, the RANNOR function generates random numbers from the normal distribution with a mean of 0 and a standard deviation of 1.

X = RANNOR(5);

To generate random numbers from the normal distribution with a different mean and standard deviation, multiply by the standard deviation and add the mean, as shown here.

X = MEAN + STD*RANNOR(5);

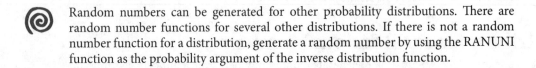

Random numbers can be generated for other probability distributions. There are random number functions for several other distributions. If there is not a random number function for a distribution, generate a random number by using the RANUNI function as the probability argument of the inverse distribution function.

■ 84

Simulations

A simulation uses mathematically defined objects and events to represent the elements of real-life or hypothetical occurrences. The results of the mathematical events in a simulation can be used to predict the results of real-life or hypothetical events.

There are two main kinds of simulations. A stochastic simulation is based on random events, which are represented by random numbers. An exhaustive simulation considers all possible events; this can be done only if the model is defined with a finite set of possibilities. It is possible for a simulation to be built from a combination of stochastic and exhaustive elements, or from either or both of these combined with actual data measurements.

Stochastic simulations are based on random numbers. See the previous chapter for details on generating and using random numbers.

 The science of probability had its origins in games of chance. In a game of chance, a random physical event results in one of a specifically defined set of outcomes, each having an equal probability. These are a few examples:

- The flip of a coin results in one of two outcomes, called heads or tails. Either outcome is equally likely.
- The roll of a die results in a number from 1 to 6. The probability of any one number occurring is 1/6.
- The draw of a card from a full deck selects any one of 52 cards. The probability of any one card being drawn is 1/52.

Simulate these or any similar events with random integers. This example simulates the flip of a coin.

```
X = FLOOR(1 + 2*RANUNI(5));
IF X = 1 THEN FLIP = 'Heads';
ELSE FLIP = 'Tails';
```

This example generates a random number from 1 to 6 to simulate the roll of a die.

```
ROLL = FLOOR(1 + 6*RANUNI(5));
```

Simulations such as these are usually repeated many times so that a statistical measurement can be made of the results. This next example uses a stochastic simulation to estimate the average value that results from the roll of a die.

```
DO I = 1 TO 1000;
   ROLL = FLOOR(1 + 6*RANUNI(5));
   SUM + ROLL;
   END;
MEAN = SUM/1000;
PUT MEAN;
```

3.48

The answer that this simulation finds is close to the true answer of 3.5. The answer is relatively precise because of the large number of repetitions of the simulation. It would tend to be more accurate with more repetitions or less accurate if there are fewer repetitions.

A better way to simulate a phenomenon as simple as this is with an exhaustive simulation. An exhaustive simulation uses a DO loop, or several nested DO loops, to generate all possible results. In the simple example of the roll of a die, a single DO loop is sufficient.

```
DO ROLL = 1 TO 6;
   SUM + ROLL;
   END;
MEAN = SUM/6;
PUT MEAN;
```

3.5

Instead of being generated as a random number, the variable ROLL is generated as the index variable of a DO loop for this exhaustive simulation. This is the only major change that is necessary to change a stochastic simulation to an exhaustive simulation.

 To simulate the result of two random physical events, use two random numbers or two nested DO loops. This stochastic simulation estimates the average maximum value found in the roll of two dice.

```
DO I = 1 TO 1000;
   MAX = 0;
   DO J = 1 TO 2; * The roll of two dice. ;
      ROLL = FLOOR(1 + 6*RANUNI(5));
      IF ROLL > MAX THEN MAX = ROLL;
      END;
   SUM + MAX;
   END;
MEAN = SUM/1000;
PUT MEAN;
```

4.563

This exhaustive simulation measures the same thing and produces a perfectly accurate result.

```
DO ROLL1 = 1 TO 6;
  DO ROLL2 = 1 TO 6;
    MAX = ROLL1 MAX ROLL2;
    SUM + MAX;
    N + 1;
    END;
  END;
MEAN = SUM/N;
PUT MEAN;
```

4.4722222222

Most practical uses of simulations are much more complicated than the simple examples described so far. The more realistically complex example below is based on the game of Risk. This game is played on a board styled as a world map divided into continents and territories. Each territory is occupied by the armies of one player.

A Risk game consists of a sequence of battles in which one territory attacks a neighboring territory. The roll of dice determines the result of a battle. The attacking player may roll one, two, or three dice; the defending player may roll one or two. The highest dice are compared. The attacker wins and the defender loses one army if the attacker's die is higher than the defender's die, but if the two dice are equal or the defender's die is higher, the defender wins, and the attacker loses one army. The highest attacking die is compared to the highest defending die. If both players roll at least two dice, the second highest attacking die is compared to the second highest defending die.

The programs below measure the probabilities of the outcomes for every combination of the number of attacker and defender dice. This first program estimates the probabilities using a stochastic simulation. It counts the occurrences of each outcome and displays the results in a table.

```
DATA WORK.RISK1 (KEEP=D_DICE A_DICE OUTCOME COMPRESS=NO);
  LENGTH D_DICE A_DICE 3 OUTCOME $ 2;
  RETAIN N 10000;
  DO D_DICE = 1 TO 2; * Number of defending dice;
  DO A_DICE = 1 TO 3; * Number of attacking dice;
    ARMIES = A_DICE MIN D_DICE; * Number of armies decided;
    DO I = 1 TO N;
      ROLL_D1 = CEIL(6*RANUNI(7)); * Defending dice roll;
      IF D_DICE >= 2 THEN ROLL_D2 = CEIL(6*RANUNI(7));
      ELSE ROLL_D2 = 0;
      DEFEND1 = LARGEST(1, OF ROLL_D1-ROLL_D2); *Defending dice, sorted;
      DEFEND2 = LARGEST(2, OF ROLL_D1-ROLL_D2);
      ROLL_A1 = CEIL(6*RANUNI(7));   * Attacking dice;
      IF A_DICE >= 2 THEN ROLL_A2 = CEIL(6*RANUNI(7));
      ELSE ROLL_A2 = 0;
      IF A_DICE >= 3 THEN ROLL_A3 = CEIL(6*RANUNI(7));
      ELSE ROLL_A3 = 0;
      ATTACK1 = LARGEST(1, OF ROLL_A1-ROLL_A3);
      ATTACK2 = LARGEST(2, OF ROLL_A1-ROLL_A3);
      * Count results;
      IF ARMIES = 1 THEN SELECT (ATTACK1 > DEFEND1);
```

```
          WHEN (1) OUTCOME = ' A';
          OTHERWISE OUTCOME = ' D';
          END;
      ELSE SELECT ((ATTACK1 > DEFEND1) + (ATTACK2 > DEFEND2));
          WHEN (2) OUTCOME = 'AA';
          WHEN (1) OUTCOME = 'AD';
          OTHERWISE OUTCOME = 'DD';
          END;
        OUTPUT;
        END;
      END;
    END;
  STOP;
RUN;

PROC TABULATE DATA=WORK.RISK1 FORMCHAR='        ';
   CLASS D_DICE A_DICE OUTCOME;
   TABLE D_DICE*A_DICE, OUTCOME*ROWPCTN*F=7.3
     / RTSPACE=15 BOX='A=Attacker D=Defender';
   KEYLABEL ROWPCTN=' ';
RUN;
```

A=Attacker D=Defender		OUTCOME				
		A	D	AA	AD	DD
D_DICE	**A_DICE**					
1	1	42.170	57.830	.	.	.
	2	57.350	42.650	.	.	.
	3	66.030	33.970	.	.	.
2	1	25.600	74.400	.	.	.
	2	.	.	23.110	32.400	44.490
	3	.	.	36.970	33.310	29.720

The second program, below, computes the same probabilities in an exhaustive simulation.

```
DATA WORK.RISK2 (KEEP=D_DICE A_DICE OUTCOME COMPRESS=NO);
   LENGTH D_DICE A_DICE 3 OUTCOME $ 2;
   DO D_DICE = 1 TO 2; * Number of defending dice;
   DO A_DICE = 1 TO 3; * Number of attacking dice;
     RES_A = 0; RES_AA = 0; RES_DD = 0;
     ARMIES = A_DICE MIN D_DICE; * Number of armies decided;
     DO ROLL_D1 = 1 TO 6; * Defending dice roll;
     DO ROLL_D2 = (D_DICE = 2) TO 6*(D_DICE = 2); * 1-6 or 0-0;
       DEFEND1 = LARGEST(1, OF ROLL_D1-ROLL_D2); *Defending dice, sorted;
       DEFEND2 = LARGEST(2, OF ROLL_D1-ROLL_D2);
       DO ROLL_A1 = 1 TO 6; * Attacking dice;
       DO ROLL_A2 = (A_DICE >= 2) TO 6*(A_DICE >= 2);
       DO ROLL_A3 = (A_DICE >= 3) TO 6*(A_DICE >= 3);
         ATTACK1 = LARGEST(1, OF ROLL_A1-ROLL_A3);
```

```
        ATTACK2 = LARGEST(2, OF ROLL_A1-ROLL_A3);
        * Count results;
        IF ARMIES = 1 THEN SELECT (ATTACK1 > DEFEND1);
          WHEN (1) OUTCOME = ' A';
          OTHERWISE OUTCOME = ' D';
          END;
        ELSE SELECT ((ATTACK1 > DEFEND1) + (ATTACK2 > DEFEND2));
          WHEN (2) OUTCOME = 'AA';
          WHEN (1) OUTCOME = 'AD';
          OTHERWISE OUTCOME = 'DD';
          END;
        OUTPUT;
        END;
        END;
        END;
      END;
      END;
    END;
    END;
  STOP;
RUN;
```

Notice that the exhaustive simulation uses most of the same logic as the stochastic simulation. Its results, summarized in the same way, are:

```
A=Attacker                        OUTCOME
D=Defender
                       A        D        AA       AD       DD

D_DICE A_DICE

1      1         41.667   58.333        .        .        .

       2         57.870   42.130        .        .        .

       3         65.972   34.028        .        .        .

2      1         25.463   74.537        .        .        .

       2              .        .   22.762   32.407   44.830

       3              .        .   37.166   33.578   29.257
```

More elaborate simulations may combine actual data, hypothetical values, exhaustive elements, and stochastic elements. They may have many interrelated variables and use complicated formulas for measuring their results.

■85
Legacy Systems

The flexibility of SAS makes it easy for a SAS program to make the connection to older technology.

Data Center Files

Traditional data center programming is built around a special kind of data file. SAS programs can easily read and write these data center files. Files of this kind may also be referred to as mainframe files, as they are used almost exclusively on mainframe computers; Cobol files, because they are designed to the particular I/O limitations of the Cobol programming language; or flat files, although this is a vague term that might imply various qualities of a file. They are binary files or, sometimes, text files. They contain fixed-field records; fields are located at predetermined positions in the record.

See chapter 10, "Text Data Files," for information about fixed-field records. Most data center files have a fixed record length, often 80, the length of the common punch card. However, a file can contain more than one record type, and the different types of records might have different lengths, so some files are defined with variable-length records, especially in IBM mainframe environments.

 Some data center files contain header and trailer records, extra records whose purpose is to mark the beginning and end of the file. Be careful not to read these records as ordinary data records.

 Most of the field types found in data center files are designed to work with Cobol and are rarely found in any other kind of file. Look for these types of fields:

- *Packed decimal.* In a packed decimal field, each byte contains two decimal digits, except for the last byte, which contains one decimal digit and a code that indicates a positive or negative sign. The field contains an odd number of digits, one less than twice the length of the field. Use the S370FPD informat to read packed decimal fields. Use the decimal argument to indicate the number of decimal places in the field.
- *Unsigned packed decimal.* An unsigned packed decimal field is organized exactly the same way as a regular packed decimal field. The only difference is that the field should not contain negative values. Use the same informat to read it. If necessary, use data step logic to validate the resulting value; treat negative values as errors.

- *Packed decimal code.* If a numeric code is stored in a packed decimal field, use the $PHEX informat to get the digits from the field. The $PHEX informat reads only the digits and ignores the sign.
- *Zoned decimal.* In a zoned decimal field, each character is a decimal digit, except for the last character, which is a code character that indicates both a digit and a positive or negative sign. Use the S370FZD informat to read a zoned decimal field. Several variations of the zoned decimal format have their own SAS informats.
- *Packed decimal Julian date.* In this field, the five or seven digits of a year and day of year are stored in a three- or four-byte packed decimal field. Use the $PHEX informat to get the digits of the packed decimal field, then use the JULIAN informat on the result to obtain the date.
- *Julian date* (the year and the day of the year). Use the JULIAN informat. If you are reading an EBCDIC file in an ASCII environment, use the $EBCDIC informat, then use the JULIAN informat on the result.
- *Binary integer fields.* A binary field in a data center file usually contains an unsigned integer. Use the S370FPIB informat to read these fields.

Data center files also contain ordinary text fields, usually in the EBCDIC character set of IBM mainframe computers. Use the $EBCDIC informat to read a character field. Use the S370FF informat to read a numeric field. Use the corresponding formats S370FPD, S370FZD, JULIAN, S370FPIB, $EBCDIC, and S370FF when you write a data center file. There is no format to correspond to the $PHEX informat.

PACKED LEADING ZEROS

A packed decimal field holds an odd number of digits. When numeric codes have an even number of digits, a leading zero is added before the code. If you use the $PHEX informat to read the digits of the field, apply the SUBSTR function to extract the code digits.

In the example below, the 10-byte, 19-digit ACCOUNTFIELD yields an 18-digit code ACCOUNT. It is important to declare the length of ACCOUNT, as shown, to make the variable the correct length. The ACCOUNTFIELD variable is used only in the process of reading the field. Do not include this variable in an output SAS dataset.

```
INPUT ACCOUNTFIELD $PHEX10.;
LENGTH ACCOUNT $ 18;
ACCOUNT = SUBSTR(FIELDDIGITS, 2);
```

There is a leading zero when a date or time of day with an even number of digits is in a packed decimal field. A 5-byte packed decimal field that contains a date is usually a leading zero, year, month, and day. This example reads packed decimal date and time fields to create the variables DATE and TIME.

```
INPUT DATEDIGITS $PHEX5. TIMEDIGITS $PHEX3.;
DATE = INPUT(SUBSTR(DATEDIGITS, 2), YYMMDD8.);
TIME = HMS(INPUT(SUBSTR(TIMEDIGITS, 1, 3), F3.),
   INPUT(SUBSTR(TIMEDIGITS, 4, 2), F2.), 0);
```

The SUBSTR and INPUT function calls extract the hour and minute numbers from the time field's digits. The HMS function converts the hours and minutes to a SAS time value. The DATEDIGITS and TIMEDIGITS variables are used only to extract the digits of the fields. Do not include them in an output SAS dataset.

The PDTIME informat is specifically for reading a 4-byte packed decimal field that contains the digits of the time of day or a time in hours, minutes, and seconds.

You can run a SAS program to read or write a mainframe file on any kind of computer. However, because the files are binary files, you must transfer them between computers with a binary file transfer.

To read a mainframe file that has a fixed record format, use options in the INFILE statement to indicate the record format and record length. If the record length is 80, use these options:

RECFM=F LRECL=80

Use the same options in the FILE statement to create a fixed-length mainframe file on another kind of computer.

There are two mainframe record formats for variable-length records: V (variable-length) and VB (variable-length blocked). To read these files on another computer, use the corresponding record format option, one of these:

RECFM=S370V
RECFM=S370VB

You might have to trick a file transfer program to get it to transfer a variable-length file as a binary file. Use a mainframe file utility to make a copy of the file, creating the copy with file attributes that indicate a binary file. Then the file transfer program will accept the copy as a binary file.

Use the reverse process if you create a variable-length mainframe file on another computer and transfer it to a mainframe computer.

Year 2000 Checklist

SAS itself never had a Year 2000 (Y2K) problem, but SAS programs might. Old programs written with incorrect date logic have to be revised to work with dates later than 1999. If you are reviving a long-dormant program and want to check for Year 2000 compliance, these are the main things to check for.

 Two-digit years. Look for them in character variables that indicate years or dates (such as "90", "900525", or "90179"), numeric variables that contain year numbers or numeric conversions of dates (such as 90, 900525, or 90179), and SAS date and datetime constants (such as '17OCT61'D). Instead, use SAS date values for dates, use four-digit numeric values for years, and write constants using four-digit years.

 The automatic macro variable SYSDATE. The value of this macro variable is the current date written with the DATE7. format, such as 17OCT04. If this value is used in conditional logic, it could lead to incorrect results. Use the SYSDATE9 automatic macro variable instead.

 The YEARCUTOFF= system option. This system option controls the interpretation of two-digit years. Two-digit years that are present in input data or in the program may be interpreted incorrectly if this system option is set incorrectly.

 Date fields in input and output text files. If the SAS program reads or writes a date field with two-digit years, find out whether the date field was expanded in a Year 2000 conversion. Increase the width of the informat or format if necessary.

Older SAS Versions

Every SAS version has its own engines and file formats, its own features and rules of syntax. This can require changes in programs when you move between versions.

Changes are usually not required when you move a program from an older SAS version to a newer one. A good approach is to test the program in the new version and look for indications of problems in the log.

The implicitly subscripted array is a major feature from SAS version 5, also supported in version 6, that you should remove from any current SAS program. An implicitly subscripted array reference is not written with a subscript; instead, it uses a subscript variable.

- Add the subscript range, written in braces, to the ARRAY statement.
- Add the subscript, in braces, to each array reference, such as *array*{_I_}.
- Replace DO OVER statements with statements of this form:

    DO _I_ = LBOUND(*array*) TO HBOUND(*array*);

The meaning of the data step BY statement has changed between versions. In any version, a data step BY statement is correct if it is located immediately after the statement that it refers to (such as a SET or MERGE statement).

Moving a program from a newer SAS version to an older version is more likely to be problematic. Older versions do not have all the features of newer versions, so you might need to find a way to rewrite the program without using a specific function, format, statement, or option. It depends on the features a program uses. These are example of features that were introduced in recent versions:

- Character processing functions and CALL routines: version 9.
- The SASFILE statement: version 8.
- Process control: version 8.
- Library and catalog concatenation: version 7.
- ODS: version 7.
- Picture formats for time: version 7.
- The WHERE= dataset option for output SAS datasets: version 7.
- Variable information functions: version 7.
- I/O functions and CALL routines: release 6.12.
- International date formats: release 6.10.

Length limitations are likely to force changes if you move a program from a newer SAS version to version 6. In version 6, all names are limited to 8 characters, labels are limited to 40 characters, and character values can be no more than 200 characters. Until version 8, informat and format names were limited to 7 or 8 characters. Try to stay within the version 6 length limitations if you are writing a program that might be moved to version 6.

■ 86
Database Applications

A database is more than just a collection of data. It is organized data; it is a structure to which data is added. The structure of a database should be designed to make it easy to manage the data and to retrieve any part of the data.

SAS is well suited for database applications, not just because of its own ability to organize data, but also because of the SAS/ACCESS products that can connect to many of the major database management systems.

Database Design

 Database design is based on much more than just the abstract idea of being organized and systematic. These are the essential ideas to consider when you design a database:

- *Tables.* A database table is simply data organized in the manner of a SAS data file. A table has several data elements, which in the SAS environment are usually called variables. These occur in each row, or record, of the table. In a SAS data file, a row is usually called an observation.

  When you can, put closely related data in the same table. However, in a database, all the data is connected, and that does not mean that the database has only one table. When two data elements are connected only indirectly, regardless of how important the connection is, they must usually be put in separate tables.

- *Keys.* Keys are what connect tables to each other. Every table in a database has a primary key, consisting of one or a few data elements that are sufficient to identify each record in the table. These same data elements can appear in another table as a foreign key. You can link one table to another by matching the primary key to the foreign key.

  Database design starts by identifying all the keys — all the identifying values needed in the data. In some cases, a key must be created as a new data element to make the database work. After the keys are identified, all the other data elements are associated with the appropriate primary keys, and to the extent possible, the keys are connected to each other.

- *Indexes.* Indexes serve the same purpose in database design as in SAS data. They help you find the rows of a table. Indexes are an essential part of most database designs. If you are not sure what indexes a SAS database requires, a good rule of thumb is to create an index for every key of every table.

- *Attributes.* In designing a database, pay careful attention to questions of data type and length of variables. See chapter 9, "Data Type and Length," for a discussion of the issues involved. The other attributes of variables are also important. Select an informat and a format for every variable. Depending on how a database will be used, you might also need to create a label for every variable. In some databases, it is also helpful to create labels for the SAS data files.

Database Programming

Part of the purpose of the database approach is to make most programming tasks routine. Most database programming fits into one of these categories of actions:

- Adding data
- Changing data
- Deleting data
- Reorganizing data
- Using data
- Measuring and managing data

If you create a database in the SAS environment, most of these tasks are familiar.

- To add data to a database table, create a new SAS dataset that contains the new observations. Use the APPEND procedure, concatenation, or interleaving to add the data to the database table.
- To change data, use the MODIFY and REPLACE statements of the data step. To change data interactively, use the Viewtable window or any of the interactive editing features of the SAS System.
- To delete data, use the MODIFY and REMOVE statements of the data step.
- To reorganize data, use a data step to create a new table, with a SET statement to copy the data into it from the old table.
- Use any of the available procedures and data step features to work with data. Use WHERE clauses to extract the data of interest. Use indexes, described in chapter 7, "Indexes," and table lookup techniques, described in chapter 52, "Table Lookup," to combine data from multiple tables. Use the SUMMARY procedure and other procedures to summarize data.
- Use procedures such as DATASETS, CONTENTS, FREQ, and SUMMARY to measure and manage data.

Details of some of these processes can be found in chapter 8, "Actions on SAS Datasets."

There are many SAS features that are designed for database applications. These are some of the features that are available:

- *SQL* is a language designed for database applications. It includes features for all the actions described above. See chapter 42, "SQL."

- *Integrity constraints* prevent users from entering erroneous data. For example, you can create an integrity contraint to prevent users from adding an observation that would duplicate an existing key value. Use the MODIFY and IC statements in the DATASETS procedure to create and manage integrity contraints. See chapter 23, "Validation."
- *Passwords* can be used to limit access to SAS files. Use dataset options such as PW= to implement passwords for SAS datasets.
- *Encryption*, the dataset option ENCRYPT=, makes it very difficult to determine the contents of a SAS data file without the password.
- *SAS/ACCESS interfaces* connect to database management systems to retrieve data from databases.
- *Generation datasets* keep multiple versions of a SAS data file so that you can look into the file's history when necessary. Use dataset options to create and access generation datasets.
- A *SAS/SHARE server* makes it possible for multiple users to work in the same libraries simultaneously.
- An *audit trail* automatically logs selected changes in a SAS data file. Create and manage an audit trail with the AUDIT statement of the DATASETS procedure.
- *Compatibility and interface engines* make it possible to exchange data with other software and other SAS versions.

Metadata

A common part of databases and one of the fundamental values of data warehousing is metadata. Metadata means data about data, and it starts with detailed information about the data elements of a database. The SAS System includes some features specifically for metadata, and support for the essentials of metadata is built into the SAS data model.

 Every SAS dataset includes the names and other attributes of its variables. The CONTENTS procedure prints a table of these attributes, and you can also save them as a SAS dataset with the OUT= option of the PROC CONTENTS statement. The output dataset contains one observation for each variable and these variables:

- LIBNAME, MEMNAME, MEMTYPE, MEMLABEL: identifying information for the SAS dataset
- NAME, TYPE, LENGTH, INFORMAT, INFORMATD, INFORMATL, FORMAT, FORMATD, FORMATL, LABEL, NPOS, VARNUM: the attributes of the variables
- many more variables with information about the SAS dataset's engine, indexes, sorting, and compression

You can start with some of these variables and add others to create a table that contains metadata for the database.

Another source for metadata information is the DICTIONARY tables of SAS SQL. In particular, query the DICTIONARY.COLUMNS table for the essential information about every variable. First execute LIBNAME statements to define all the libraries. Then execute a query such as the one below to extract information from the table.

```
PROC SQL;
CREATE TABLE WORK.COLUMNS AS SELECT * FROM DICTIONARY.COLUMNS
   WHERE LIBNAME IN ('MAIN', 'CORP', 'WORK');
```

The DESCRIBE TABLE statement of SQL provides column and table information in the form of an SQL statement that might create the table. The example below demonstrates the DESCRIBE TABLE statement and lists the columns of the DICTIONARY.COLUMNS table.

```
DESCRIBE TABLE DICTIONARY.COLUMNS;
```

```
NOTE: SQL table DICTIONARY.COLUMNS was created like:

create table DICTIONARY.COLUMNS
   (
    libname char(8) label='Library Name',
    memname char(32) label='Member Name',
    memtype char(8) label='Member Type',
    name char(32) label='Column Name',
    type char(4) label='Column Type',
    length num label='Column Length',
    npos num label='Column Position',
    varnum num label='Column Number in Table',
    label char(256) label='Column Label',
    format char(49) label='Column Format',
    informat char(49) label='Column Informat',
    idxusage char(9) label='Column Index Type',
    sortedby num label='Order in Key Sequence',
    xtype char(12) label='Extended Type',
    notnull char(3) label='Not NULL?',
    precision num label='Precision',
    scale num label='Scale',
    transcode char(3) label='Transcoded?'
   );
```

Data warehouse design typically requires much more metadata than this. A data warehouse can include metadata that describes the source of each data element and any available information about how current or accurate it might be. Metadata can also include statistics about the use of the tables, columns, and rows of the database — giving a general idea of how much each part of the data is used, and by whom.

■ 87
Client-Server Design

The client-server model of computing is based on the idea that more is better — that several computers working together can complete tasks more easily than a single computer working in isolation. Client-server designs use the idea of specialization. One computer, the client, takes care of the processes that are connected most directly to the user. Other computers specialize in specific computing resources. A network connects the computers, and messages between computers take the form of requests and responses. Most requests originate at the client, but in the process of responding to client requests, all the computers on the network request things from each other and respond to each other's requests.

With a client-server design, a database can be located and managed on just one database server, but connected to users anywhere on the network. A larger database could occupy several database servers, and the change in scale can be made without making any changes in the user experience.

Effective client-server design divides work between computers in a way that steers parts of the work toward the computers that can do those parts best without creating too much of a work load for any one computer during any time period.

 A programmer making the move from a mainframe environment to a client-server environment has to take on new ideas about what efficiency means. The bottleneck on a mainframe computer is the central processor — so much so that mainframe programmers can use CPU time as their only measure of the performance of a program. The client-server environment is the opposite of this. With processing divided among several computers, processing power is abundant. Processing is rarely the factor that limits the performance of a client-server application; instead, the processors are idle most of the time, waiting for other things to happen. Almost any computing resource can become the limiting factor in a client-server application, and the limiting factor can change from one second to the next. In large-scale applications, though, the most common limiting factor is the movement of data from one computer to another. To make a client-server application run faster, look for ways to move smaller amounts of data between computers. This could mean creating a subset or summary of a dataset on the server where the data is located instead of copying the entire dataset to the client system. It could also mean moving data during the weekend at a time when the network is relatively quiet.

A client-server environment can use SAS on servers, clients, or both. If SAS is on both client and server platforms, SAS processing can be divided between client and server. Often SAS client-server processing follows this sequence:

1. An initial batch process on the server, which creates SAS datasets as its output
2. Moving the output SAS datasets from the server to the client
3. Additional processing on the client, creating more SAS datasets
4. Browsing or additional analysis of the resulting SAS datasets in an interactive SAS session on the client

Other than the need to write separate server and client programs, there is nothing fundamentally different about SAS programming for client-server applications. The combination of a server program and a client program should work together in the same way as any sequence of SAS programs.

 For efficiency, locate data files where they are needed. If a client program makes extensive use of server data, it is usually most efficient to copy the data to the client computer. Of course, delete these files from the client system as soon as they are no longer needed.

SAS/CONNECT

SAS/CONNECT, if it is installed on the client and server, can allow a client SAS session to start and control a SAS session on the server. This permits the server and client processes to be written into the same program and provides many other capabilities. SAS/CONNECT can also allow a SAS session on a server to start a SAS session on another server.

In SAS/CONNECT:

- The other computer, usually a server, where SAS/CONNECT creates a SAS session, is the *remote system*.
- The SAS session on the remote system is the *remote session*.
- The original SAS session is the *local session*.

 Before you can use SAS/CONNECT, you have to install it and configure it with the information necessary to find and connect to the remote system and start a SAS session there. Details of the connection process are written in a SAS/CONNECT script, and several system options are also necessary to set up SAS/CONNECT.

After SAS/CONNECT is configured correctly, use four global statements to start and operate a remote session. Start the remote session with a SIGNON statement. To execute statements in the remote session, write them between RSUBMIT and ENDRSUBMIT statements. Use a SIGNOFF statement to end the remote session. This code model summarizes the effects of the SAS/CONNECT statements:

local session statements
SIGNON;

local session statements
RSUBMIT;
remote session statements
ENDRSUBMIT;
local session statements
SIGNOFF;
local session statements

When statements executing in the remote session generate log messages or print output, the output is returned to the local session. You see the results of a remote session the same way you see the results of statements that execute in the local session.

You can use macro logic to react to events in the remote session. Two macro statements, %SYSLPUT and %SYSRPUT, make this possible by exchanging information between the local and remote sessions.

The %SYSLPUT statement is similar to the %LET statement, but you execute it in the local session to assign a value to a macro variable of the remote session. For example, this statement assigns the value of the local macro variable N to the remote macro variable M:

%SYSLPUT M = &N;

The %SYSRPUT statement has the opposite effect. It executes in the remote session to assign a value to a local macro variable. The example below assigns the value of the remote macro variable SYSVER to the local macro variable REMOTEVER.

%SYSRPUT REMOTEVER = &SYSVER;

Starting a remote session makes it possible for the local session to access SAS libraries on the remote system, a feature called remote library services. This is accomplished with a LIBNAME statement in the local session. In the LIBNAME statement, the SERVER= option identifies the remote session. You can provide the physical file name in the LIBNAME statement or use the SLIBREF= option to provide the libref used in the remote session.

SAS/CONNECT also provides two procedures, UPLOAD and DOWNLOAD, for data transfer with the remote system.

Remote library and data transfer services are usually not necessary if the local session can access the server files directly through network file services.

Control Level

The idea of control level is important if a SAS dataset or catalog might be used in two places at the same time. With control level, a program can prevent conflicts by preventing another program or another user from getting access the same file or record at the same time. When a SAS program accesses a SAS data file, it can set the control level with the CNTLLEV= option, which has three possible values, RECORD, MEMBER, and LIBRARY.

- With *record control*, a program prevents any other program from accessing the same record at the same time. A record is an observation of a SAS data file or an entry of a catalog. With record control, multiple programs can update different observations of a SAS data file at the same time. Each program or user locks only the one observation it is working on. Locking the observation prevents data conflicts with other users or programs. If you attempt to access an observation that another program is already using, the SAS supervisor returns an error message telling you that the observation is in use at the moment.
- With *member control*, a program locks the entire file — the entire SAS dataset or catalog. Member control is necessary for processes such as sorting that would not work correctly if the data were changing in the middle of the process. SAS automatically uses member control for processes that require it. Use the CNTLLEV=MEMBER dataset option for member control in other situations.
- With *library control*, a program locks an entire library. This option is available for unusual situations in which a program needs to keep all the data in a library unchanged during a process.

A SAS/SHARE server is necessary for multiple users or jobs to access the same libraries at the same time without conflicts, and the correct use of control level allows the jobs and users to work at the same time. But the concept of control level is not limited to situations with multiple users. It is also applicable with just a single user. In an interactive session, more than one program (such as a window or interactive application) can be running at the same time. The control level used by each program protects it from data conflicts that might be caused by the other programs.

The LOCK statement can control a SAS file or library for a process that takes longer than a single step. Write a LOCK statement before the first step with the libref of the library or the name of the SAS file or catalog entry. This statement locks the SAS file CORP.CALENDAR:

LOCK CORP.CALENDAR;

Later, use the CLEAR option to unlock the library or file, for example:

LOCK CORP.CALENDAR CLEAR;

■ 88

Classic Problems

This chapter presents a set of SAS programs as solutions to a few old, well-known problems. These programs demonstrate the range and flexibility of the SAS language and may serve as examples of ways to approach programming problems.

Prime Number Sieve

A prime number is a positive integer that cannot be obtained by multiplying any two other positive integers. By contrast, a composite number is a positive integer that can be obtained as the product of other positive numbers. The number 1 is usually considered a special case, neither prime nor composite.

A prime number sieve identifies prime numbers by tagging composite numbers. Values that are not tagged as composite numbers at the end of the process are identified as prime numbers. The prime number sieve shown below writes a list of prime numbers in the log. A prime number sieve can run for a long time and use a large amount of memory, so the program parameters TOTAL, DIM, and TIME are used to limit the extent of the program's processing. If you wish, you can increase these values to generate a larger number of prime numbers.

The program also checks the maximum exact integer value that the computer supports (this is different on different kinds of computers). This value is returned by the function call CONSTANT('EXACTINT'). The program stops processing if it reaches this number.

```
%LET TOTAL = 2000; * Limits the number of prime numbers generated ;
%LET DIM = 1000; * The size of the sieve arrays used ;
%LET TIME = 30; * Time limit in seconds ;

DATA _NULL_;
  ARRAY P{&DIM} _TEMPORARY_; * Prime numbers;
  ARRAY M{&DIM} _TEMPORARY_; * Multiples of prime numbers;
  TIMEOUT = DATETIME() + &TIME; * Time limit;
  FILE PRINT NOTITLES;
  SQUARE = 4;

  DO X = 2 TO CONSTANT('EXACTINT'); * Is X prime? ;
    IF DATETIME() >= TIMEOUT THEN STOP; * Time limit reached ;
    IF X = SQUARE THEN DO; * Extend sieve;
      IMAX + 1;
      IF IMAX >= &DIM THEN STOP; * Sieve size limit reached. ;
```

```
      SQUARE = M{IMAX + 1};
      CONTINUE;
      END;
   * Find least prime factor (LPF). ;
   LPF = 0;
   DO I = 1 TO IMAX UNTIL (LPF);
      DO WHILE (M{I} < X); * Update sieve with new multiple. ;
         M{I} + P{I};
         END;
      IF M{I} = X THEN LPF = P{I};
      END;
   IF LPF THEN CONTINUE; * Composite number found. ;
   PUT X @; * Write prime number in output. ;
   N + 1;
   IF N >= &TOTAL THEN STOP; * Output maximum reached. ;
   ELSE IF N <= &DIM THEN DO; * Add prime number to sieve. ;
      P{N} = X;
      M{N} = X*X;
      END;
   END;
 STOP;
RUN;
```

```
2    3    5    7    11   13   17   19   23   29   31   37   41   43   47   53   59   61   67   71   73   79   83   89   97
101  103  107  109  113  127  131  137  139  149  151  157  163  167  173  179  181  191
193  197  199  211  223  227  229  233  239  241  251  257  263  269  271  277  281  283
293  307  311  313  317  331  337  347  349  353  359  367  373  379  383  389  397  401
409  419  421  431  433  439  443  449  457  461  463  467  479  487  491  499  503  509
521  523  541  547  557  563  569  571  577  587  593  599  601  607  613  617  619  631
641  643  647  653  659  661  673  677  683  691  701  709  719  727  733  739  743  751
757  761  769  773  787  797  809  811  821  823  827  829  839  853  857  859  863  877
881  883  887  907  911  919  929  937  941  947  953  967  971  977  983  991  997  1009
1013 1019 1021 1031 1033 1039 1049 1051 1061 1063 1069 1087 1091 1093
1097 1103 1109 1117 1123 1129 1151 1153 1163 1171 1181 1187 1193 1201
1213 1217 1223 1229 1231 1237 1249 1259 1277 1279 1283 1289 1291 1297
1301 1303 1307 1319 1321 1327 1361 1367 1373 1381 1399 1409 1423 1427
1429 1433 1439 1447 1451 1453 1459 1471 1481 1483 1487 1489 1493 1499
1511 1523 1531 1543 1549 1553 1559 1567 1571 1579 1583 1597 1601 1607
1609 1613 1619 1621 1627 1637 1657 1663 1667 1669 1693 1697 1699 1709
1721 1723 1733 1741 1747 1753 1759 1777 1783 1787 1789 1801 1811 1823
1831 1847 1861 1867 1871 1873 1877 1879 1889 1901 1907 1913 1931 1933
1949 1951 1973 1979 1987 1993 1997 1999 2003 2011 2017 2027 2029 2039
2053 2063 2069 2081 2083 2087 2089 2099 2111 2113 2129 2131 2137 2141
2143 2153 2161 2179 2203 2207 2213 2221 2237 2239 2243 2251 2267 2269
2273 2281 2287 2293 2297 2309 2311 2333 2339 2341 2347 2351 2357 2371
2377 2381 2383 2389 2393 2399 2411 2417 2423 2437 2441 2447 2459 2467
2473 2477 2503 2521 2531 2539 2543 2549 2551 2557 2579 2591 2593 2609
2617 2621 2633 2647 2657 2659 2663 2671 2677 2683 2687 2689 2693 2699
2707 2711 2713 2719 2729 2731 2741 2749 2753 2767 2777 2789 2791 2797
2801 2803 2819 2833 2837 2843 2851 2857 2861 2879 2887 2897 2903 2909
2917 2927 2939 2953 2957 2963 2969 2971 2999 3001 3011 3019 3023 3037
3041 3049 3061 3067 3079 3083 3089 3109 3119 3121 3137 3163 3167 3169
3181 3187 3191 3203 3209 3217 3221 3229 3251 3253 3257 3259 3271 3299
3301 3307 3313 3319 3323 3329 3331 3343 3347 3359 3361 3371 3373 3389
3391 3407 3413 3433 3449 3457 3461 3463 3467 3469 3491 3499 3511 3517
3527 3529 3533 3539 3541 3547 3557 3559 3571 3581 3583 3593 3607 3613
3617 3623 3631 3637 3643 3659 3671 3673 3677 3691 3697 3701 3709 3719
3727 3733 3739 3761 3767 3769 3779 3793 3797 3803 3821 3823 3833 3847
```

```
3851 3853 3863 3877 3881 3889 3907 3911 3917 3919 3923 3929 3931 3943
3947 3967 3989 4001 4003 4007 4013 4019 4021 4027 4049 4051 4057 4073
4079 4091 4093 4099 4111 4127 4129 4133 4139 4153 4157 4159 4177 4201
4211 4217 4219 4229 4231 4241 4243 4253 4259 4261 4271 4273 4283 4289
4297 4327 4337 4339 4349 4357 4363 4373 4391 4397 4409 4421 4423 4441
4447 4451 4457 4463 4481 4483 4493 4507 4513 4517 4519 4523 4547 4549
4561 4567 4583 4591 4597 4603 4621 4637 4639 4643 4649 4651 4657 4663
4673 4679 4691 4703 4721 4723 4729 4733 4751 4759 4783 4787 4789 4793
4799 4801 4813 4817 4831 4861 4871 4877 4889 4903 4909 4919 4931 4933
4937 4943 4951 4957 4967 4969 4973 4987 4993 4999 5003 5009 5011 5021
5023 5039 5051 5059 5077 5081 5087 5099 5101 5107 5113 5119 5147 5153
5167 5171 5179 5189 5197 5209 5227 5231 5233 5237 5261 5273 5279 5281
5297 5303 5309 5323 5333 5347 5351 5381 5387 5393 5399 5407 5413 5417
5419 5431 5437 5441 5443 5449 5471 5477 5479 5483 5501 5503 5507 5519
5521 5527 5531 5557 5563 5569 5573 5581 5591 5623 5639 5641 5647 5651
5653 5657 5659 5669 5683 5689 5693 5701 5711 5717 5737 5741 5743 5749
5779 5783 5791 5801 5807 5813 5821 5827 5839 5843 5849 5851 5857 5861
5867 5869 5879 5881 5897 5903 5923 5927 5939 5953 5981 5987 6007 6011
6029 6037 6043 6047 6053 6067 6073 6079 6089 6091 6101 6113 6121 6131
6133 6143 6151 6163 6173 6197 6199 6203 6211 6217 6221 6229 6247 6257
6263 6269 6271 6277 6287 6299 6301 6311 6317 6323 6329 6337 6343 6353
6359 6361 6367 6373 6379 6389 6397 6421 6427 6449 6451 6469 6473 6481
6491 6521 6529 6547 6551 6553 6563 6569 6571 6577 6581 6599 6607 6619
6637 6653 6659 6661 6673 6679 6689 6691 6701 6703 6709 6719 6733 6737
6761 6763 6779 6781 6791 6793 6803 6823 6827 6829 6833 6841 6857 6863
6869 6871 6883 6899 6907 6911 6917 6947 6949 6959 6961 6967 6971 6977
6983 6991 6997 7001 7013 7019 7027 7039 7043 7057 7069 7079 7103 7109
7121 7127 7129 7151 7159 7177 7187 7193 7207 7211 7213 7219 7229 7237
 . . .
```

Life

Life is the name of a mathematical model that is intended to mimic the tenuous balance that is required for life to propagate. Life belongs to a class of mathematical games called cellular automatons. A cellular automaton depicts mathematically determined actions on a grid. Each grid location, or cell, takes on one of a set of possible values, or states. For each move, or clock tick, the state of each cell is determined based on the states of cells in the previous clock tick. The challenge for the player of a cellular automaton is to initialize the grid in a way that produces interesting results.

In Life, a cell can have either of two possible states, identified as live and dead. In each clock tick, a dead cell becomes alive if exactly three of the eight cells that border it are alive. A live cell stays alive if two or three of the surrounding cells are alive; otherwise, it becomes dead.

The version of Life implemented in this example is based on a grid of 16 rows and 32 columns. The grid is purposefully kept small so that it can be displayed in a text-mode data step window. The program implements the grid as an array of 16 character variables that have a length of 32 characters. Live cells are shown as the letter X; dead cells are blank.

The program reads the initial state of the grid from text data stored in the catalog entry WORK.LIFE.INIT.SOURCE. When the program reads the input data, it treats any nonblank character as a live cell. A data step window displays the results, which include a count of the clock ticks and the number of live cells.

```
FILENAME LIFEINIT CATALOG 'WORK.LIFE.INIT.SOURCE';
```

```
DATA _NULL_;
   ARRAY L{1:16} $ 32;
   ARRAY NEW{1:16} $ 32 _TEMPORARY_;

   WINDOW Life ROWS=22 COLUMNS=35 IROW=2 ICOLUMN=10
      #1 L1 $CHAR32. PROTECT=YES
      #2 L2 $CHAR32. PROTECT=YES
      #3 L3 $CHAR32. PROTECT=YES
      #4 L4 $CHAR32. PROTECT=YES
      #5 L5 $CHAR32. PROTECT=YES
      #6 L6 $CHAR32. PROTECT=YES
      #7 L7 $CHAR32. PROTECT=YES
      #8 L8 $CHAR32. PROTECT=YES
      #9 L9 $CHAR32. PROTECT=YES
      #10 L10 $CHAR32. PROTECT=YES
      #11 L11 $CHAR32. PROTECT=YES
      #12 L12 $CHAR32. PROTECT=YES
      #13 L13 $CHAR32. PROTECT=YES
      #14 L14 $CHAR32. PROTECT=YES
      #15 L15 $CHAR32. PROTECT=YES
      #16 L16 $CHAR32. PROTECT=YES
      #17 'Life' COLOR=BLUE
      +5 'Time' COLOR=CYAN +1 TIME F4. COLOR=GREEN PROTECT=YES
      +5 'Live' COLOR=CYAN +1 LIVE F4. COLOR=GREEN PROTECT=YES
      ;

   * Read initial grid from file, converting any nonblank character to X;
   INFILE LIFEINIT TRUNCOVER;
   INPUT (L1-L16) ($CHAR32. /);
   DO Y = 1 TO 16;
      DO X = 1 TO 32;
         IF SUBSTR(L{Y}, X, 1) NE ' ' THEN SUBSTR(L{Y}, X, 1) = 'X';
         END;
      END;

   DO TIME = 0 TO 1000;
      * Count live cells.;
      LIVE = 0;
      DO Y = 1 TO 16;
         DO X = 1 TO 32;
            LIVE + SUBSTR(L{Y}, X, 1) = 'X';
            END;
         END;
      * Display grid and check for end of game. ;
      _MSG_ = 'Press Enter to continue.';
      IF STSTATE THEN _MSG_ = 'Steady state. Press Enter to finish.';
      IF LIVE = 0 THEN _MSG_ = 'Game over. Press Enter to finish.';
      DISPLAY LIFE;
      IF STSTATE OR LIVE = 0 THEN STOP;
      * Recalculate grid. ;
      DO Y = 1 TO 16;
         NEW{Y} = L{Y};
         DO X = 1 TO 32;
            LIVECELL = SUBSTR(L{Y}, X, 1) = 'X';
            * Count surrounding cells. ;
            COUNT = 0;
            DO DX = -1 TO 1;
               DO DY = -1 TO 1;
                  IF DX = 0 AND DY = 0 THEN CONTINUE;
```

```
                IF 1 <= X + DX <= 32 AND 1 <= Y + DY <= 16 THEN
                    COUNT = COUNT + (SUBSTR(L{Y + DY}, X + DX, 1) = 'X');
                END;
              END;
          * Change state of cell. ;
          IF NOT LIVECELL AND COUNT = 3 THEN
              SUBSTR(NEW{Y}, X, 1) = 'X'; * New live cell;
          ELSE IF LIVECELL AND COUNT NOTIN (2, 3) THEN
              SUBSTR(NEW{Y}, X, 1) = ' '; * New dead cell;
          END;
        END;
      * Activate new grid and check for steady state.;
      STSTATE = 1;
      DO Y = 1 TO 16;
        IF NEW{Y} NE L{Y} THEN STSTATE = 0;
        L{Y} = NEW{Y};
        END;
      END;
    STOP;
  RUN;
```

```
      XX  XX
     X XX  X
     X    X  X
     X  X X  X
      XX    XX




Life        Time     0      Live    19
```

```
      XXXXXX
     XX XXX X
     XX X   XXX
     X XXXXX X
      XX    XX




Life      Time     1      Live    29
```

```
        XXXX
      XX     X
     X         X
     X         X
     X   XX    X
      XX X XX




Life      Time     2      Live    20
```

```
        XX
       XXXXX
       XXXXXX
     X       X
     XXX       XXX
      X  XXXX X
       X XX X




Life      Time     3      Live    31
```

```
          X
      X
      X    XX
     X   XXX XX
     X X  XX  X
     X   X X X
       XX   XX




Life      Time     4      Live    24
```

```
          XX
      X X XXXXX
          XX    X
     XX   X     XX
      X  X X X
       XX   XX




Life      Time     5      Live    25
```

```
                ...
```

```
       X X
        X      X
      XX    X X  X
     X  X        X
     X   X   X   X
     X X XX  X  X
       XX    X X
          X
          XX

Life      Time    15      Live    29
```

```
          X
         XX
        XXX       X
       X X    X  XX
      XXX XX       X
       X  XX   XX XX
        X    XXX
             XX
             XX
Life      Time    16      Live    33
```

```
         XX
          X
       X          X
     X              XX
     X X X X   X
       X  X X XXXX
          X   X X


       XXX
Life      Time    17      Live    26
```

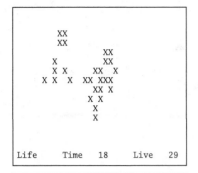

Life   Time   18   Live   29

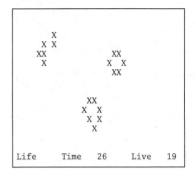

Life   Time   26   Live   19

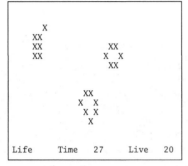

Life   Time   27   Live   20

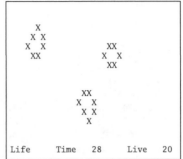

Life   Time   28   Live   20

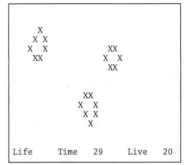

Life   Time   29   Live   20

Global Distances

The surface distances between places on Earth have practical implications in radio communications and transportation. A relatively simple SAS program can compute these distances. The program presented below makes the simplifying assumption that Earth is a perfect sphere. It ignores issues of planetary oblateness and asymmetry and the altitude of specific points, but it still produces useful results.

The program reads a set of places from the input text data file shown at right, with location indicated by latitude and longitude.

Bombay	19°00'N	73°00'E
Cairo	30°00'N	31°15'E
Calcutta	22°30'N	88°15'E
Jakarta	6°15'S	106°30'E
Johannesburg	26°00'S	27°45'E
London	51°30'N	0°00'W
Los Angeles	34°00'N	118°15'W
Mexico City	19°30'N	99°15'W
New York	40°45'N	74°00'W
Sao Paulo	23°30'S	46°45'W
Seoul	37°30'N	126°45'E
Sydney	34°00'S	151°15'E
Tokyo	35°45'N	139°45'E

The first step in the program produces the SAS dataset CITIES of this set of locations. The next step crosses this SAS dataset with itself to produce the city pairs that appear in the output.

```
* Convert coordinates to degrees N and degrees E;
DATA CITIES (KEEP=CITY LATI LONG);
   INFILE CITIES;
   INPUT CITY $CHAR20. LATI_D 2. +1 LATI_M 2. +1 LATI_NS $CHAR1.
      +1 LONG_D 3. +1 LONG_M 2. +1 LONG_EW $CHAR1.;
   LATI = LATI_D + LATI_M/60;
   IF LATI_NS = 'S' THEN LATI = -LATI;
   LONG = LONG_D + LONG_M/60;
   IF LONG_EW = 'W' THEN LONG = -LONG;
RUN;
```

```
TITLE 'Distances Between Cities';
DATA _NULL_;
  RETAIN DIAMETER 12741; * Approximate Earth diameter (km);
  RETAIN R .017453292; * Factor to convert degrees to radians;
  FILE PRINT COLUMN=COLUMN;
  IF _N_ = NOBS THEN STOP;
  SET CITIES (RENAME=(CITY=CITY1 LATI=LATI1 LONG=LONG1));
  PUT / 'FROM ' CITY1 'TO:' +3 @;
  DO POINT = _N_ + 1 TO NOBS;
    SET CITIES (RENAME=(CITY=CITY2 LATI=LATI2 LONG=LONG2))
      POINT=POINT NOBS=NOBS;
    DISTANCE = DIAMETER*ARSIN(SQRT(
      (1 - COS(LATI1*R)*COS(LATI2*R)*COS((LONG1 - LONG2)*R)
       - SIN(LATI1*R)*SIN(LATI2*R))*.5));
    IF COLUMN > 60 - LENGTH(CITY2) THEN PUT / @2 @;
    PUT CITY2 DISTANCE : COMMA7. +2 @;
    END;
RUN;
```

```
Distances Between Cities

FROM Bombay TO:    Cairo 4,371    Calcutta 1,632    Jakarta 4,620
 Johannesburg 6,993    London 7,197    Los Angeles 14,001
 Mexico City 15,650    New York 12,547    Sao Paulo 13,794
 Seoul 5,568    Sydney 10,150    Tokyo 6,722
FROM Cairo TO:    Calcutta 5,689    Jakarta 8,952
 Johannesburg 6,238    London 3,508    Los Angeles 12,210
 Mexico City 12,375    New York 9,023    Sao Paulo 10,225
 Seoul 8,472    Sydney 14,419    Tokyo 9,566
FROM Calcutta TO:    Jakarta 3,763    Johannesburg 8,455
 London 7,951    Los Angeles 13,134    Mexico City 15,273
 New York 12,745    Sao Paulo 15,426    Seoul 4,029    Sydney 9,152
 Tokyo 5,153
FROM Jakarta TO:    Johannesburg 8,580    London 11,689
 Los Angeles 14,482    Mexico City 16,865    New York 16,177
 Sao Paulo 15,612    Seoul 5,298    Sydney 5,531    Tokyo 5,819
FROM Johannesburg TO:    London 9,034    Los Angeles 16,638
 Mexico City 14,567    New York 12,802    Sao Paulo 7,419
 Seoul 12,479    Sydney 11,070    Tokyo 13,561
FROM London TO:    Los Angeles 8,767    Mexico City 8,938
 New York 5,575    Sao Paulo 9,502    Seoul 8,848    Sydney 16,999
 Tokyo 9,550
FROM Los Angeles TO:    Mexico City 2,473    New York 3,939
 Sao Paulo 9,890    Seoul 9,609    Sydney 12,073    Tokyo 8,810
FROM Mexico City TO:    New York 3,364    Sao Paulo 7,433
 Seoul 12,057    Sydney 12,963    Tokyo 11,283
FROM New York TO:    Sao Paulo 7,679    Seoul 11,061    Sydney 15,991
 Tokyo 10,836
FROM Sao Paulo TO:    Seoul 18,338    Sydney 13,343    Tokyo 18,515
FROM Seoul TO:    Sydney 8,344    Tokyo 1,175
FROM Sydney TO:    Tokyo 7,847
```

This program could be modified to calculate distances in miles by substituting the appropriate diameter measurement in the RETAIN statement. To compute surface distances of another planet, use that planet's diameter and provide an appropriate set of locations in the input data file.

Afterword

Return to the Real World

Show your friends snapshots from your vacation, and they will see the interesting places you visited, but they won't see what the vacation was like. In a similar way, the examples in books such as this one are snapshots that can't give you the whole picture of the world of professional SAS programming. If you are trying to get a picture of real-world SAS programming from the examples in this book, it may help to know what kind of lens you have been looking through.

In a word, the difference between a book and the real world is that the real world is bigger. Examples are small and simple in order to demonstrate a principle or technique with a minimum of distraction. The smaller a program is, the easier it is to see how the parts of the program go together. That is not the only reason why the programs and data you see in books are small. The small examples save paper and make it possible to cover more in one book.

The most dramatic change you may see in going from the book to the real world is in the size of the data. It is simply not possible to show the scale of real-world data in a book. A SAS dataset with 30 variables and 5,000 observations would completely fill a book of this size, but in the real world, data is that big and 1,000 times bigger. The number of observations in a SAS dataset does not affect the logic of a SAS program, so some examples in this book show as few as four observations. The programs work the same way no matter how many observations are in the data.

For the same reasons, the examples of reporting in this book are artificially small. Real-world reports are printed on larger paper and may contain many pages.

Real-world SAS programs tend to be longer and more complicated than the examples you see in books. Indeed, few of the examples in this book would be complete programs in the real world; they would be fragments of longer programs.

And that brings me to another point. Many of the steps in those longer programs are more mundane and repetitive in approach than what you see in a book like this. In a book, every program demonstrates something different. In the real world, you find the same techniques used repeatedly, and there is much that is the same from one program to the next.

The simple far outweighs the complex in real-world programs. The simplest proc steps, such as PROC SORT and PROC PRINT steps, account for a disproportionate share of all the steps in SAS programs. Take descriptive statistics as another case in point. Every now and then I compute a KURTOSIS or a CV, but nine out of ten statistics in the programs I write are the two most basic, SUM and N.

Individually, the programs in this book represent real-life SAS programming. And collectively, as long as you consider the qualities of a book that make it different from the world it represents, the programs in this book can give you some idea of the world of SAS programming.

Index